LAKE ONTARIO

Brockport

ROCHESTER

ERIE CANAL

GENESEE R.

Geneva

CANANDAIGUA LAKE

CAYUGA LAKE

SENECA LAKE

KEUKA LAKE

N E W   Y O R K

N

W · E

S

Hornell

Corning

ELMIRA

P E N N S Y L V A N I A

Miles

0   5   10   20

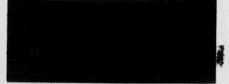

The Light
of Other Days

Books by Rexford G. Tugwell

THE LIGHT OF OTHER DAYS

THE ENLARGEMENT OF THE PRESIDENCY

EARLY AMERICAN POLICY: SIX COLUMBIA CONTRIBUTORS
  (Co-author)

THE ART OF POLITICS

THE DEMOCRATIC ROOSEVELT

A CHRONICLE OF JEOPARDY

GREAT CITIES OF THE WORLD (with others)

THE PLACE OF PLANNING IN SOCIETY

THE STRICKEN LAND

PUERTO RICAN PUBLIC PAPERS

BOOKS THAT CHANGED OUR MINDS (with others)

ROADS TO KNOWLEDGE (with others)

THE BATTLE FOR DEMOCRACY

THE INDUSTRIAL DISCIPLINE AND THE GOVERNMENTAL
  ARTS

INDUSTRY'S COMING OF AGE

SOVIET RUSSIA IN THE SECOND DECADE (with others)

REDIRECTING EDUCATION (with others)

AMERICAN ECONOMIC LIFE AND THE MEANS OF ITS
  IMPROVEMENT (with others)

THE TREND OF ECONOMICS (with others)

THE ECONOMIC BASIS OF PUBLIC INTEREST

The Light
of Other Days

REXFORD G. TUGWELL

DOUBLEDAY & COMPANY, INC.
GARDEN CITY, NEW YORK
1962

In memory of my father

CHARLES HENRY TUGWELL

who defended my
liberty
and gave me
support

TUGWELL, REXFORD G. The light of other
days. 404p $5.95 Doubleday
   B or 92   62-7690
     An "account of [the author's] own boyhood
and youth in rural New York.... Mr Tugwell
was born in Chautauqua in 1891 and this autobiography covers the period from then to 1911,
during which time the family moved to Niagara
and the author went to school in Buffalo....
A boy growing up then was subjected to good
influences as well as new and exciting
ideas.... From this good formative period
of his youth [Mr. Tugwell] advanced to a...
career as an educator, author and government
administrator." (Springf'd Republican)

Reviewed by Gerald Carson
   + Chicago Sunday Tribune p2 F 4 '62
    480w
    "Autobiographical material, however lively
or evocative of nostalgia, is prone to interest
author more than reader. And however typical

"Former Roosevelt brain-trustee Tugwell's
recollective purpose is to explain how the small
town Protestant culture which spawned him
led to two world wars, one major depression
and the current complex of international military and industrial dissension known as the
nuclear age. In doing so, propulsion as the
gressivism, public commented upon and more or less
cles are all found wanting. He describes glowingly
his poetic mother, his youthful ardor, idealistic
schooling and firm friendships; he seems just-
ing opting for a socialist statesman's idyll.
a little like an elder warmth is apparent. Nevertheless,
the wisdom of his questioning, as well as
the gravity of a socialist meet-
— Kirkus 29:1072 D 1 '61 220w

"[Tugwell] translates the images in his
memory into accurate and moving words.
Particularly in his depiction of the lake-shore
town of Wilson does he bring alive the quiet
dignity, beauty and innocence of a pre-World
War I, upstate New York community. World
Artistically Mr. Tugwell is guilty of destroying
the mood of his best passages; He continually
moves out of his realistic experiences a half-
to discuss later. The light of other days is
century consistently focused to rest on modern
medicine."
— N Y Times BK R p6 F 4 '62 800w

"An absorbing self-portrait of the New Dealer
as a young man. In his book Professor
Tugwell knits two strands together, sometimes
as if by force. The first is a mellow and
straightforward account of the author's
recollection is here laced with upbringing. But
a somber meditation on what Mr. Tugwell views
his lifetime. This was the decision to drop the
first atomic bomb on Hiroshima in 1945.
At bottom, if we separate the strand of Mr. Tug-
tion from the to be concerned with education,
well is seen in the training of Americans
of his generation that permitted the lapse of
1945... fit to the serious questions of
raises, much to be pondered by all of us, there
is much to fancy the unorthodox. And this is not at
refreshing and selective; to drop the
all soured by a peculiarly view of media-
capricious, view of recent history." E. M.
Yoder
   + Sat R 45:22 F 3 '62 1100w
   + Springf'd Republican p4D F 18 '62
    150w

Da...
this...
with...
clusion...
his pictu...
villages a...
But reader...
many boyish a...
a nuclear age...
one must ques...
is objective. Mos...
about the heedles...
ruption, and the ast...
trolled industrialism...
a more humane an...
problems, would have m...
But it is less evident tha...
planning Mr. Tugwell su...
averted the ills that trouble...
van Richardson
   + 700w   Christian Science Monitor p9 F 7 '62

Explanation

The title for this book is taken from Thomas Moore's *Oft in the Stilly Night*. This was one of his National Airs, written to fit a Scottish tune along about 1818.

No one represents better than Moore the romantic literature of the nineteenth century; and no one has surpassed the charming unreality of his verse. A diffused light seems to soften the outlines of his objects and to illumine his characters. Landscapes take on a Turner-like beauty and people exist in a perpetual melancholy, but one transfused with a persistent saving resignation. Nothing comes to a happy end, but it always happens in a mist of admirable sentiment.

My mother found Moore to her liking. He was mellifluous in a way she had a weakness for; it was the way of Longfellow and Tennyson, other favorites, and, in her regard, of the New England poets, of Will Carleton and, I am afraid, even of Jean Ingelow. She found their verses easy to read aloud or to say over, half to herself and half to me, in the intervals of her busy days when she could stop to rest. And when I was being put to bed or when I lay half sick, perhaps with a cold, and begged her to read—I much preferred adventure stories myself —she would sit beside me and recite the well-known lines of a hundred such lyrics. She went on reluctantly to the pages of racing narrative if I insisted. But she will still repeat those lyrics if anyone will listen.

Words, even meanings, were not important. It was the effect they had, as they fell lightly on the ear, that she found irresistible. They were half lullaby and half persuasion, because she obviously hoped that I would grow up to be the kind of irreproachable figure the poets praised—or, at the very least, would come to appreciate their singing as she did.

Oft in the Stilly Night was one of her favorites. I heard it over and over until I was old enough to resist with determination. Its lines recall for me my earliest days. They take me back to many an hour in the airy rooms of our village home—bright wallpaper lit by the glow of a kerosene lamp with a flowered globe, quilted coverings on the bed—my mother and I secluded, and she trying her best to invoke for me, even if I resisted, a faraway landscape where pleasant figures moved, where no one was ever ill or tired—languid, perhaps, but not exhausted by naughty intrusions—or if he was not too happy, still able to bear his ill fortune, whatever it might be, bravely.

Often she could not bear to let the melody go, as Moore himself could not, and said the lines she had fixed on over and over. This fascination with stately rhythm made the poem. I put it down here as it appears in the *Collection* printed (by Crowell in this country) in 1895 when I was four years old:

> Oft in the stilly night,
>   Ere slumber's chain has bound me,
> Fond memory brings the light
>   Of other days around me;
>   The smiles, the tears,
>   Of boyhood's years,
> The words of love then spoken;
>   The eyes that shone,
>   Now dimmed and gone,
>   The cheerful hearts now broken!
>
> Thus in the stilly night,
>   Ere slumber's chain has bound me,
> Sad memory brings the light
>   Of other days around me.

When I remember all
  The friends so linked together,
I've seen around me fall,
  Like leaves in wintry weather,
    I feel like one,
    Who treads alone
  Some banquet-hall deserted,
    Whose lights are fled,
    Whose garlands dead,
  And all but he departed!

Thus in the stilly night,
  Ere slumber's chain has bound me,
Sad memory brings the light
  Of other days around me.

                          R.G.T.

Introductory Note

The elation that followed the dropping of the bomb on Hiroshima, followed closely by the second one dropped on Nagasaki, tailed off into decades of guilty rationalization by all those who had been involved in the decision to use them. Americans have not absolved themselves of the guilt they assumed on those days. So long as any of that generation are alive, they never will.

What had to be admitted when the euphoria of victory had passed was that an ultimate crime had been committed, and that there was no possible expiation. It had been preceded, it was true, by saturation bombings of German and Japanese cities—not military targets—for years before; but entry into this final sin, even if gradual, could not be excused by similar preceding sins. Hiroshima may have seemed no more than a logical extension of something by then accepted; it proved to be an apocalypse.[1]

What had happened to a nation whose leaders could make such a decision in the name of its people? When this was considered, it could be understood that this was not the first moral crisis Americans, by their own standards, had failed to come through with honor.

They had, for instance, consented to the growth of a business system founded on the cruel rules of competition whose consequences were, in human terms, frightful. They had failed as

[1] My own apology was published ten years after Hiroshima in *A Chronicle of Jeopardy* (University of Chicago Press).

neighbors; all around them other nations less fortunate were in perennial distress. They had never implemented the Fourteenth Amendment or the Fifteenth. The discriminations forbidden in those declarations were still alive everywhere, even in the churches.

A considerable catalogue of such derelictions could be made.

On the other hand, there had been remarkable victories for justice and liberty and some quite wonderful exhibitions of faithfulness to the democratic tradition. Technically, progress had been more rapid here than anywhere else in the world, although it had begun to lag as the century passed its midpoint—we had been too reluctant to support impractical researchers.

There had been a convulsion of conscience after the depression of the 'thirties, and this had resulted in a certain effort to catch up on welfare measures. The Social Security Acts had corrected many old injustices. Also, free education, conservation, and economic equality, seemed to be making gains.

I felt the need to account both for the failures and the successes. They were those of my generation; I had lived through them; and yet it was not at all clear to me why more had not been accomplished, why conscience had not had a firmer hold, why our deepest convictions—of neighborliness, of fairness, of respect for others' rights—had been systematically violated.

There must be explanations, and these must be entangled in the history of my generation. But considering what kind of exploration would be of any use, I realized that to be adequate it ought to begin a long way back, even farther than my own recollections went. I do not mean merely that every event in the past has in its own degree helped to shape the present; I mean something more particular—that the institutions we now possess were hammered out and struggled over by our predecessors as well as ourselves; that the customs and loyalties we still honor and try to preserve, and the rights we enjoy, were won for us in efforts and battles now almost forgotten; that all these were created for us as much as by us. True, we reshaped them and added to them; but they were not ours to begin with, and our responsibility has been in considerable part one of stewardship.

Still, we ourselves have made many things, and the world is not at all what it was when we began to grow up in it. If no one person's recollections go back to the beginning of customs and things, he still can remember enough of what was contributed to have a certain significance. The changes of his generation do show what the mistakes may have been.

When I reached seventy, the boys who had been the fathers of still living men could recall when there had been no electricity, no automobiles or hard-surfaced roads, no airplanes, no telephones, no typewriters, no bathrooms—and no genocidal weapons. Those who had helped to make these changes, or who had lived while they were permeating our culture, ought to have some conception of their significance, some idea why they had been thus and not otherwise.

At any rate, I thought some search on my part might turn up some causes of the effects that now seemed so formidable and might even be leading on to disasters of vast magnitude. The uncovering would require persistence, and it would have to be discursive and enveloping as well as patient, for the transitions had often been tortured and sometimes convulsive, not an easy merging of one era into the next. Also, it was obvious that our representatives had often been confused, ignorant, or unwilling to honor our moral traditions. Almost fatal mistakes had brought punishment on us even far in the past, not ones it was impossible to recover from, but still terrible to think of. Wars were the worst; but depressions had hardly been less destructive; and there had been others.

But there had been successes, too, rewarded by immense gains in well-being. And it was often difficult to distinguish what would prove in the long run to have been right and what would show itself to have been wrong. But there had been gross departures from our standards and they stood plainly against our record.

The boy who had been my father had grown up in all of it,

taking part, and in the end had survived what he had once hoped was the worst of it. He now knew better. The worst ordeals were yet to come. Still, seven decades he could look back on had been a time of changes more significant than any between, say, the fall of Rome and the nineteenth-century revolutions. And, if he forgot his fears for the moment, he could see for his descendants even more astonishing prospects. They would look inward to the infinitely small and outward to the unimaginably immense; space would be foreshortened and time syncopated.

With such glittering interests, they might have none to spare for the commonplace events of pre-nuclear, pre-space times. And indeed these might have only a limited relevance. Yet, as Hiroshima had shown so glaringly, mistakes were becoming more and more consequential. Soon it might be that only one more would be allowable. In that case, how we had made our mistakes might be something they would do well to study. This was the more true because the men who had to make the decisions of the future did not seem in any way different from us, nor did our way of selecting our leaders seem to be changing. It was the penalty for making mistakes that had enlarged.

So I would try to explain what had happened, keeping to my writ as well as I was able, telling only of what I knew or could rightly infer. In spite of this resolve, I knew well enough that I should find some of my recollections faulty—it is amazing how the memory fails when it is most wanted—and that I should strain the legitimacy of inference, venturing into hearsay and speculation. Nostalgia, too, would very likely tempt me to explore byways that had little real bearing on the question at issue.

I had had a good life—work I believed in, repeatedly enlivened with controversy, set among pleasant scenes, and rich with the affection of family and friends. I would hardly be able to resist recounting adventures and incidents along the way of interest only to myself. For these departures I can only ask indulgence, hoping, of course, that they may at least prove entertaining. But I do ask a certain leeway, because only comprehensiveness can be at all sufficient for my purpose. It may well be that explanations really lie in marginalia or below the outer layers of common experience. If I am to explain at all, I must have some latitude; and an explanation, I do insist, is in order.

R.G.T.

Chautauqua

1   *1891–1904*

One

Chautauqua was a name known more widely in 1891, when I was born, than in later years. This was because of the Institution, that semi-religious, semi-intellectual gathering of good people which took place every summer in a kind of compound—the Assembly Grounds—on the shore of Chautauqua Lake. It must have seemed, to skeptical observers, smug, pretentious, even hypocritical. Many of them, in fact, said so. But I cannot wholly agree. Its old maples, elms, and beeches and its cottage boardinghouses sheltered two generations of particularly influential citizens. Its visitors were decent, serious, middle-income people who would set American standards for a long time to come. They were deacons of the churches, Sunday-school teachers, leading citizens, ladies who taught school or who organized other ladies for self-improvement. Even as late as 1940 Franklin D. Roosevelt would find them worth appealing to in support of his policies. But actually it would have become another sort of place by then, less serious, less educational.

Magnificent rolling hills surrounded it, and the long gray lake gave it charm. Its people gave it character. The nice spinsters, the correct clergymen, the eager teachers, the small-town laymen and laywomen in search of culture—all joined there in the proper exercise of learning, superficial perhaps, but not by any means useless. It was the direct ancestor of the summer session at the universities, which, when it began to grow, would strangle its parent. But that would be a good deal later. As the nineteenth century entered its last decade, the

Institution was in full being and would continue to flourish
for a quarter century more. It was known throughout the land,
a gathering ground for the semi-learned, a place, too, for the
enjoyment of the tempered pleasures allowed by Protestant
rules—prayer meetings, concerts, readings, edifying lectures,
social teas, and guided reading.

My mother had been a teacher and so had a sort of professional interest in gentle culture. To be sure, she herself had
had no more than a high school education and had been
entrusted only with one-room schools in the country. But at
that time most Americans began their schooling in such places
and were taught by young women who, devoted as they were,
nevertheless were always conscious, too, of being potential wives
and mothers. Their probable future did not make them less
effective teachers. On the contrary, the expectation that sometime she might make a contribution to similar rows of small
faces confronting other teachers may well have lent a certain
earnest satisfaction to what must have been for the schoolma'am
an exacting service. The terms were long—forty weeks, my
mother says, although farmer boys were wanted when harvesting and planting had to be done, and their attendance was
irregular in fall and spring—and the hours were not easy, beginning at eight-thirty or nine and going on until three-thirty
or four. There was anything up to seven grades, and among
them there might be distributed thirty or forty children, although
this would be large; there were more usually twenty or fewer.
The teacher had somehow to keep not only the pupils but also
the premises in order; she had to sweep and dust, tend fires in
winter (perhaps persuading the larger boys to help); and, in
whatever season, she might have to walk a mile or two each way
—going in early morning and returning in late afternoon, through
dust, mud, or snow. She boarded with a family not her own,
and the accommodation was sometimes difficult. Caring for a
farm or village home and raising a family cannot have seemed
too hard a life after a few years of such employment.

My mother had not had an easy life even before she became a teacher. I recall how surprised I was when I discovered that she had been born in Michigan. Even if that state had been part of the Union since 1837, it still seemed remote to a village boy in New York; and the idea of anyone having gone West—which was a familiar occurrence—and having come back again—which was not—was enough to arouse my curiosity. But the forest areas of that land, when the trees had been cut, were as hard to bring into agriculture as similar areas in New York State had been. Her father had died in the struggle, and my grandmother had come back to Ellington (a village not far from Sinclairville, but over a formidable ridge unless a roundabout way was taken through No God Hollow). She had married again, which accounted for my mother's two half sisters, a relationship I had found somewhat puzzling. It also accounted for my mother and her brother Will living with her father's uncle and his wife—the Tylers I shall speak of—for most of their childhood. This was on a hard-scrabble farm in No God Hollow, where pioneer conditions still prevailed and where life was poor in goods if rich in experience. She went to a little school there; but, getting to her teens, she looked longingly out at a more civilized world. She was a bright girl, and for bright girls there was a ready occupation in teaching. There were never enough teachers, because they continued for so short a time. My mother, at any rate, perceived the opportunity and somehow made the transition to the high school in Sinclairville, working for her board and room—as in the future many other girls would live and work with us in the same way. She had been completely without income. Hill farms in Chautauqua County did not produce many cash crops, but somehow she not only got through her high school course but became a popular member of the younger set in the village community.

My father was not long on education and he had no literary interests, but he was an enterprising young man who knew a pretty face and a fine figure when he saw them—from her pictures, and from what my father has told me, I gather that Mother was a genuine beauty. He had some competition,

naturally; but if he had no intellectual offerings, he had other
ones. His father was, in the village sense, prosperous; he was
handsome in the English way; he could dress well; and he had
equipages of the latest and best design, always a good resource
in courtship, and his horses—his father's, really—were spirited.
Altogether my mother made up her mind that Charlie's attractions, even if he did have certain philistine tendencies—concealed, no doubt, but still perfectly apparent to my mother—
were sufficient. Probably she thought she could educate him,
a form of self-deception women have practiced immemorially.
My father's ardent suit was given in to, but not until he had
been made to suffer for a year or two. What it came to I
recently discovered to have been recorded in the columns of the
Sinclairville *Star* for June 30, 1889. Between the leaves of an
old book of my mother's, the following clipping had lain for
seventy years:

A Sinclairville Wedding

A notable society event was the wedding which came off at the
residence of Dr. G. F. Smith, in this village on Wednesday evening
of this week. It was that of Charles H. Tugwell and Miss Dessie
M. Rexford. Rev. J. E. Tinker performed the ceremony. Some fifty
of the elite of the vicinity, including friends, erstwhile school mates
and the relatives of the happy couple being present. Mr. Tugwell is
the junior partner in the firm of William Tugwell & Son, and is a
popular, energetic, wide-awake young business man. Miss Rexford
is a most estimable young woman, has troops of friends, and has
for some time been a teacher in two or more of the schools in the
immediate neighborhood. The wedding supper, a sumptuous affair,
was much enjoyed at tables in the dining room and on the lawn, the
latter being carpeted, brilliantly illuminated, by Chinese lanterns,
and furnished with several hammocks, in which the "happy hours
were whiled away" by members of the party, and the night air
"made resonant with tuneful melody." Accompanied by several
other couples, the contracting parties, amidst showers of rice and
old shoes, left by the "overland" route the next morning for a trip to
Lake Chautauqua, where Dr. Smith, Albert Phillips, and others
have erected cottages near Bemus Point and Jack Pickard's, the

typical boniface of that region. Mr. T. and his bride have the con-
gratulations of many friends all of whom wish them all the happiness in this life.

So my mother's case had been a usual one. Her last school had
been in one corner of a pleasant but rather lonely meadow on
Tackley's farm, about halfway between Sinclairville, where we
lived, and Gerry, a four-corner village some five miles below
us on the Jamestown road. I recall having had the schoolhouse
pointed out to me; yet it must have been quite an early victim
of the consolidation movement, being so close to town; before
we moved away, anyhow, it had disappeared into a crumble,
buried throughout the summer under old lilac and elderberry
bushes and overrun with clambering wild-rose vines, and in
winter visible only as a rocky outcropping above the snow. It
had a sentimental meaning for my mother—even after it was
no longer visible—I suspect, perhaps because associated with
what must have been a memorable courtship.[1]

My own earliest recollections of school attach to a larger
building at the end of the village common. It was conspicuous
without being distinguished, square, many-windowed, red brick,
with a worn and weedy yard. A range of wooden toilet facilities
convenient to a back door hid at the rear; and a loud, if

[1] If what I cannot myself recall about my mother seems vague, it is because of her unwillingness to discuss the past. She could never be pinned
down to any orderly recollections, and her responses to leading questions
were always sketchy and unsatisfactory. There are several interesting passages in her history—at least I suspect them to have been interesting—
that she would never talk about at all, such, for instance, as her long feud
with Minnie Smith, the wife of the doctor at whose home the wedding
was held. Burt Smith, the son, was my best friend, and I was frequently at
his house, but my mother and Minnie did not speak for many years—as
long as we lived in Sinclairville. My mother's reticence cannot have been
because of unhappy associations. On the whole, she must have had a wonderfully satisfying life, aside from the griefs which come to all. And she
was always outgoing, a participant in every activity, and something of an
organizer of many. She simply has had so much interest in the present and
the future that dwelling on the past has seemed unrewarding. My attempts to
convince her that recollections have their uses, too, have always been treated
with a humorous digressiveness, at once exasperating and final. But then no
one has ever been able to "do anything with her" if she does not want it
done. She has always been the despair and delight of all her descendants.

decidedly untuneful, bell swung in a belfry at the top. As we played games during recess, the sound of hammers on iron, as tires for wagons or shoes for horses were shaped on the anvils of a busy shop across the street, was a constant undertone; and the smell of burning hoofs, as shoes were fitted, was often pungent in the air. Besides a dozen houses, three churches also faced the common, the houses with well-proportioned doors and the churches in the classical white of the New England tradition, with graceful steeples and sensitively placed windows.

The rambling and shabby premises of the Prentice blacksmith shop, which was one of two in our village—my relatives, the Truslers, ran the other—where the old man worked with his two sons, all developed as only blacksmiths could be, with rippling muscles, deep chests, and slender waists, were an accepted part of the scene. The indeterminate yard with its litter of wagon wheels, discarded tires, and the other miscellaneous paraphernalia of the trade does not seem, as I look back, at all incongruous, facing the common, across the way from a church and several restrained white houses as well as the school. Nothing about it was offensive in the way the pretentious schoolhouse was, standing uncompromising and monstrous in the midst of so modestly executed a village.

But I suppose the attainment of such a building was the end of the usual long campaign, something planned for and wanted for a generation and finally managed after innumerable disappointments. It was in such a way that Americans got their better schools. And if, when it was built, it was ugly, I presume no one objected if it served the purpose. It did have, at any rate, four lower rooms for grades and two large upper ones for high school; these were separated by a partition which slid back to make of the whole floor an auditorium.[2] There was a

[2] This school had been built in 1881 and so must have been about fifteen years old when I went to first grade. But it seemed ancient to me, perhaps because it actually was shabby from the first. The construction was cheap and it probably went to pieces fast. It was replaced about 1920, but until I was thirteen and we moved away I progressed one by one through its grades.

stage at one end, and this was something of a center for the intellectual improvement of the valley. On it graduates were presented with diplomas, of course, and from it we heard our principal's—or perhaps a distinguished visitor's—words of wisdom or caution several times a week and were practiced in the rituals of song and recitation, which would thus become forever familiar to all of us; but also it was used for lyceum lectures and entertainments. On winter nights, sleighs converged on the school, horses were blanketed, and families found places where they could listen to a lecture, a demonstration of popular science, or a group of singers or Swiss bell ringers. The lyceum course was supported by the sale of season tickets, so much the same audience appeared for each occasion. I recall that my father and some of his friends thought the entertainment label doubtfully deserved, and there were other occupations they would have preferred; but the ladies were firm and the men generally good-natured. I recall the familiar demonstration of steam rising from dry ice, one that was a sure hit for lecturers on popular science, and, in quite another cultural vein, a quartet of females who sang loudly and then produced a rack of tumblers on which they proceeded to play familiar tunes. I suppose there were addresses on public affairs and social problems—in fact, I know there were—but those I do not at all recall. Perhaps I was taken only to the entertainments and judged too young to appreciate the heavier fare. I suppose Sinclairville was too remote and too small to have had the important touring lecturers of the early century. But it will be recalled that this was a second occupation for Emerson, Alcott, and other popular philosophers as well as Dickens, Mark Twain, and other literary figures. Some of the important ones of the 'nineties may have come to Sinclairville, but I could hardly be expected to recall them.

My mother's small schoolhouse and my larger one were both in the same valley near the center of Chautauqua County, at about the same distance from Fredonia to the north and Jamestown to the south. It was back over the hills from Lake Erie, which was west of us, and Chautauqua Lake, which was southwest. The valley was spacious enough to contain a life of its own, but not so large that any part was uncomfortably far from any other.

The distance from Sinclairville to the lake at Bemus Point was about twelve miles by a road which ran past the McAllister and Tichnor stands, through the swamp at the valley's lower end, through the four-corner settlement at Red Bird, and up over the Ellery hills. It came down to the Point rather rapidly after furnishing several tantalizing views of the distant lake. It was not far down those hills, but it seemed a long way after the glimpses from the road.

Bemus Point was about halfway down the lake (and on the opposite side from the Assembly Grounds) toward Jamestown. It was the closest of any place on the lake to Sinclairville, which was why my father and mother, following other townspeople, had established a summer community there, first on their honeymoon and later for every summer's use. It is almost as large as Sinclairville in my recollections, though we cannot have spent more than a few weeks there in any season. This is probably to be accounted for by the pleasures of the waterside for a growing boy in vacation time. My father's visits were short, mostly weekends. On the whole, it was a place where mothers and children enjoyed the freedom of cottage life.

Perhaps this may have been part of the reason why my mother's was much the stronger influence on my development, although this cannot have been attributable so much to mere propinquity as to the obvious fact that I was more my mother's than my father's boy, winter as well as summer. She had a literary bent. For instance, she was always writing papers to read at women's meetings; and her output of what I am afraid was very bad verse was immense. She was—and still is, at more than ninety—a lively talker. Books to her were as necessary as food, and they were always about her. Her regard for them sometimes seemed almost independent of what was in them, so wide was the range of her interests. But I have since thought it was not the books so much as what they represented that she felt the need of. They were her way of keeping in touch with the world in spite of living in a small village among the hills. But there were preferences, as I learned; apart from politics and current affairs, she preferred her literature to touch on emotions of the gentler sort and not to be brutally realistic. But she had a certain weakness, too, for nature lore and she introduced me to John Burroughs, Ernest Thompson Seton, and John Muir. These naturalists were inclined to underscore the beauties and triumphs of nature and not to attend too much to the savagery which is a chief mechanism of natural selection. She knew far more than any of our familiars about the wildlife of the region and about the meadows and woods most people saw every day without understanding anything about them but their economic importance to themselves. She knew all the names and many of the habits of the birds and beasts and flowers—and passed on a good deal of this to me. We were often together on long drives, and this gave her an opportunity for education disguised as storytelling.

These long trips behind a pair of horses—or when it was my mother and myself just old Dolly—come back to me with a special sort of recall. The ones I took with my father are similarly vivid. But his orientation was different. He told me all about the deals he was making, about how to judge cattle and how to handle horses. Driving twenty miles with a team was very different from journeys in later automobiles. Toiling up the slopes was a slow business, and there was no point in being impatient. Most of the time was so relaxed and lazy that impressions could take hold without much resistance and conversations could be leisurely, drawn out until the last small lesson had been explored. The roads were dusty in summer, piled with snow in winter, and deep in mud in spring and fall. But my father traveled in all weathers. I suppose he could not have taken me with him very often—after I was five I was in school on weekdays, and before I was ten he had changed occupations —but I certainly have the memory of numbers of such trips.

They might be in autumn when the trees were in full color (but the half-frozen roads deep in mud) or in winter when the hills were looming ghosts of their summer selves. Only when it was seriously stormy or very cold were we protected by more than the usual buffalo robes, but at such times, with the top up and a bib reaching nearly to our chins and fitting over the dash, we were alone in a kind of special traveler's domain with snow scenes passing slowly outside.

I was very close to my father during these early years, even if my mother's interests soon became more obviously my own. There were qualities I could admire in him—very important to a boy—and I had no doubt that we were altogether superior people. His business was with farmers, and to drive into a yard, pull up in the driveway, and be made welcome in a warm house was an adventure of sorts. There was always something to eat and drink, pressed on us by prideful housewives; and sometimes we happened by at mealtime and shared a country meal. It was always ample and, to my appetite, good; but then I always liked baked beans, boiled dinners, crisp salt pork with gravy, and baked potatoes, or sausage from the fall hog-killing taken from the crocks stored in the cellar. And there was, inevitably, apple or mince pie to follow. Replete, and with perhaps a deal completed, we resumed our journeys after such stops, in a kind of somnolent companionship. My father's affection was almost as much felt as the footwarmer the farmer's wife had reheated for me; and we went on through the winter world and into its early twilight content to be together, a small boy and a man considering the future and scheming to make it more prosperous.

One particular incident out of many stands out sharply in my recollection. It concerns a long day's drive over the Ellery hills in cold and rainy weather. My father had stopped at a number of places—he was buying calves or arranging to buy them from the spring crop, intending to put them to grass in some pastures he had rented—and I was desperately cold and tired and hungry. Somewhat after noon we came to the farm of some friends—the Batchelors—where, if we were in time, he was confident that we might share the family dinner (country dinners were at midday). Lynn Batchelor was a school friend of my mother's who had been a teacher, too, but had characteristically married and come to live on what was really a remote and lonely farm. But no one was at home. My father guessed that they had gone to town. It was a terrible disappointment; for hours, it seemed, I had been anticipating the noon break. We were a long way from home and it was late to try another family's hospitality. My father, however, was at no loss at all. Soon the horses were steaming in the barn, content with borrowed measures of oats, and I was warming myself at the kitchen range, where he had built a fire with kindling from the woodshed. Working together, we soon had ham and eggs from the buttery, where we also found the usual range of pies on the shelves. Meals have seldom been so welcome in my life, and food has hardly ever tasted so good. After we had done some cleaning up, we left a note of acknowledgment and went quite cheerfully on our way.

It turned out that Lynn had been in Sinclairville that same day and had visited my mother. The coincidence was cause for conversation in later years. Our going into the house—it was not locked, as I suppose farmhouses never were—and helping ourselves was not regarded as anything remarkable. It was the coincidence of mutual visits that was discussed. Perhaps this tells something of the kind of life we had.

Two

Ours was an authentic upland country; our winters, in consequence, were long and our summers brief. One of my half cousins used to say that the only trouble with the climate was that it never snowed in August. The considerably older cousin, George, who used to say this was a good-natured, easygoing fellow who was one of my favorites—the sort who always has time for a word with small boys and always thinks their dogs remarkable. He was, at the time I recall him best, the proprietor of a barbershop, and he used to make the observation about snow in August for its provocative effect on the old-timers who habitually sat chewing tobacco and gossiping in the row of armchairs against the wall of his establishment. Reacting, they would swear to recollections of times when it *had* snowed in August. Their citings of such antic occurrences he would then belittle as mere summer hailstorms on the Arkwright or Gerry hills—backcountry to us.[1] This belittling would, naturally, induce

[1] On the subject of winter, prolonged in that country, I can do no better than to quote one of my favorite authorities, Obed Edson, to whom I shall defer about other matters as well. Writing in the *History of Chautauqua County and Its People* (American Historical Society, 1921; quotations by permission), after confessing winter's hardships in the high country, Edson went on defiantly to say, "Here among the uplands the snow comes earliest in Autumn, falls deepest in Winter and lies latest in Spring. Sometimes in Spring when the grass is green and the fruit trees are blossoming along the shores of Lake Erie, the hills of Arkwright and Charlotte are white with snow. But what cares the tenant of those snowy hills? There he has passed his early years and breasted the storms of many a winter! He would not change his bleak highland farm for the pleasantest fields along the Lake. Love of home is strong indeed! . . . In winter the drifts lie deeply around the farmhouses and bury the fields and fences from view.

protestations, corroborations, and elaborations. The matter would be come back to again and again, and a distinct air of grievance would surround the later argument. It might go on for days.

The weather was certainly a favorite topic, but scarcely more so than such others as the sicknesses of neighbors, the farmers' crops, local improvements, the behavior or misbehavior of officials, the degenerate condition into which the younger generation was falling, and, in season, national politics. I can have been no more interested in oldsters' talk than most small boys would have been, but as I look back it seems to me that I witnessed a way of declining into age which was in most ways tolerable. The old men had lived to see their families disperse and perhaps lived on now with their wives in comfortable familiarity. The old house might be too big, but part of it could be closed off; there was no central heating. If the wife was gone too, they might live with children, contributing what they could from a small income of some sort. They were at least not alone, and life was easy and relaxed. These little daily gatherings in shops, along the sidewalks, on the hotel porch, or in the saloon were their last stretch of life. To pass it with familiars was a blessed thing. It cannot have been so agreeable to be dependent, but the households of those days were more elastic than they have since become.

Recollections were precious enough to be refined over and over and long drawn out, possibly even improved. They were exchanged in old and well-worn clothes, in equally well-worn chairs or on benches polished by long occupancy, and there were such sitting places everywhere.

This was the age, too, of the front porch. Every house had one, and some were broad and capacious, furnished with

Travel is blocked upon the highway and the farmer is for a while imprisoned by the storm. Propitiously as the Spring season opens, it is subject to chilly relapses. . . . The ice which gathers in Lake Erie during the colder months, loosened by the warmth of the advancing season, drifts to the foot of the lake, and sometimes remains unmelted until almost June, bringing raw and inclement weather to its adjacent shores. Nipping frosts often visit the farmer during the last days of May, and even in the month of June, cutting his corn and destroying his fruit. . . ."

hammocks, rockers, and blooming plants. These, however, were
the women's domain, except that in the evening the courting
couples took them over. The men, old and getting old, preferred
drifting together into little groups away from home, in a
tolerant proprietor's store or shop where there was a big stove,
inside the gristmill, where they liked the floury smells and could
sit in a circle outside the center of activity, or, in summer, on
the streets.

It was not only Cousin George who pleasantly thus elicited
for his own amusement, and for the edification of small boys,
tales of what life had been like in more heroic days and what
it was like then in heroic imaginations; there were others who
had a gift for baiting the local wiseacres in a bitterish vein—Alf
Hinchliffe and Carl Rood, for instance, especially Alf, who was
nothing like so well disposed as Cousin George or even his own
younger brother, Allen, who, since the Hinchliffes lived next
door, was something like an older brother to me. Alf had a
streak of malice, and some of his practical jokes and his practiced
baitings of the old men really wounded simpler folk than he.
Allen, however, was kinder and more tolerant. Even though he
was older than I, he was not above helping me with all the elaborate contrivances of play invented among my circle of friends. But
that was perhaps partly because he so much envied our family
the stalls full of horses in the old barn between our houses. He
haunted that barn, and when my father allowed him to assist
in the handling of the horses, he was obviously exalted. At
any rate, he was a bulwark for me against the world and helped
me immensely in my induction to the society of more advanced
males.

In this same connection I should speak of Jake Evans, who
was a kind of belated Daniel Boone. Nominally he ran a general
store, but it was frequently closed at hours peculiar in the
shopkeeping trade. When his door was locked we knew that he
had gone fishing, or perhaps hunting, if the season was appropriate. It was he who took me on my first brook-fishing,
coon-hunting, and squirrel-shooting expeditions, as he took

every boy who wanted to go and was able to get away from his chores, or from school, or simply from his mother. Mothers disparaged association with him on principle, not only because he inducted us into blood sports and taught us irregular ways, but because he got along very well without a wife. He and his son, who was Allen's age, carried on a sketchy, carefree existence in a clean little house, and this seemed to challenge the central position of women in that village and farm economy. It was they who tamed men to thrift and plodding husbandry—"kept their noses to the grindstone," Jake said—and the variety of faults they could find with Jake's behavior was remarkable.

But our mothers' disapproval did not prevent us from utilizing his ready talents as a teacher and leader. I have often thought what a tame and uninspired program the Boy Scouts have in comparison with the swinging tramps we had with Jake and the secrets of nature he disclosed to our receptive minds. He taught us how to handle gun, knife, and hatchet in pursuit of such wildlife as came under the heading of game. He knew their habits, their weaknesses (curiosity, for instance), and when they might be dangerous. He taught us patience and canniness and guile. When we had success he showed us how to make fires and prepare fish or animals for cooking. And sitting on logs around such fires, we heard much about the freer life and the more abundant game in the Tennessee mountains, whence, for reasons never made clear, he had come to our hill country. He asked no thanks but our company, and it never occurred to us that he was being extraordinarily kind. He was just one of the better arrangements of our environment, uncomplicated by any attempt to moralize or teach us anything we were not eager to learn. He must have been something like sixty when I was ten, but he covered an incredible mileage with his peculiar slouching stride. He saw animal trails where they were invisible to the uninitiated, and many a day he led us home at dark, exhausted and limp but happily certain of having put in a thoroughly valuable day.

The coon hunts by night were a more highly organized affair

and usually involved our fathers, since otherwise we would not have been allowed to go. I recall only a few. But they were high spots of boyhood. Starting out with Jake's three hounds (but there might be more; he always seemed to have litters of puppies in his storeroom between a vinegar barrel and a pile of soap-boxes) and with a few other men, we made straight for the swamp where the coons were at home. I presume Jake did not always find one, but I do not recall any failures. The dogs ranged widely for a while until their distant baying changed to yelps. This meant that they had treed an animal and we had only to catch up with them. The poor coon, peering down from his branch, was shot and, if time permitted, the dogs were started on another chase. There can be few such romantic memories for men to recall of their boyhood. The autumn forest, lit by flaring torches, the belling of the hounds, far away, then near, the suspense of wondering what animal had been treed—once it turned out to be a bobcat which snarled viciously; but such really wild creatures were very scarce by then. The coons merely looked bewildered, and if we had had a modicum of decency we should never have had the heart to shoot one. But the privilege of bringing down the victim was usually allowed the smallest boy, thus accustoming him to slaughter. He was never, I think, overcome with sympathy, but he often missed his shot because of excitement. I am afraid the hunting of helpless coons was stuff for a boys' paradise.

Sometimes there was meat enough from one of these hunts for a coon pie, made in a great dish, rich with sauce, and with thick biscuits on top. Otherwise they were roasted whole. The meat tasted to me much like the more usual squirrel and, if the truth has to be told, was too gamy for my youthful palate—boys seldom care much for flavorful food—but I always bravely ate my portion. I would not think of holding back merely because I was revolted. It was the end of, and the excuse for, a precious adventure.

Burt Smith, Earl Roberts, and I were inseparable—a curious trio, perhaps, but one that seemed natural to us. That I should

have had for my earliest comrades a doctor's son and the son
of a teamster seems now to illustrate a characteristic of that
society which made it so inevitably a democracy. Probably my
parents had little in common with those of Earl Roberts and
they seldom associated, but I was never told that I ought not run
around with Earl. I was fascinated by the Robertses' living arrangements. I realized later they were different from ours because
the family was poor, but I never thought of it then. They were
just different. I do recall thinking it was peculiar that they should
eat bacon drippings on their bread instead of butter and that they
should have no sheets on their beds. Their carpets had holes,
their furniture was patched, and the house had that peculiar
musty, sourish smell that so many farm homes had—the result,
I suppose, of a scarcity of soap and hot water and of consequently
flourishing molds. Earl was apt to brag that his father wore his
long underwear all winter and plowed it under in their garden
patch when spring came; and we were impressed—we must
have been if I recall his saying so all those years ago. But we
were not less good friends because of these peculiarities. We
had the freedom of each other's houses, and our joint enterprises
did not suffer.

There were a few others of our age who were almost, but not
quite, so familiar: Floyd Parsons, Burley Reed, Jim Dalrymple,
the Wesley boys, and Burt's brother Charlie, who fitted in between us and Allen Hinchliffe's set. We grew into a first awareness
of the world in such intimacy as could have bound us together
only in a tiny village isolated in the hills before the days of
motors, good roads, or even of telephones. We played ball
endlessly, when the weather was propitious, on the common or,
when the grass there was too long or when the older boys pre-
empted the playing space, in the wide road beside the Congregational church. We had a cramped but favored diamond
there, irregular, dusty, and with the protruding roots of two
old maples on either side of the street for first and third bases.
It was, anyway, claimed by no other gang, and knowing all its
peculiarities, we made allowances for them. Our balls more often

than not were ones we had made ourselves by winding string around a rubber core (or a paper one if we were reduced to that), but we usually had a bat or two, treasured from year to year and put away carefully over the winter. This was the sandlot baseball which developed many professional players. None of us became so skilled, but the hours we spent at one-old-cat or in chosen sides, when we had enough for two teams of five or more, ought to have made professionals of us all.

But winter was the long season, and winter games were our most familiar ones. They were simple too. We did not skate often, because the snow was usually too deep on the ponds; but we did everything else that can be done in or with snow. Especially we skied and slid down the long hills on sleds that were almost part of us for months. We even dragged them to school and stacked them outside; I could slide much of the way home on mine, since there were two passable slopes on the way. On Saturdays we divided our time between sledding down the hills and catching tows, for that was the day when farmers came to town and traffic was heavy. It must have been customary to tolerate this minor nuisance; at any rate, we hitched rides in this way for hours on end, especially ones drawing us back up the hills so that we could escape that toilsome penalty for sliding down. We envied the older set who made evening parties of this sport. Allen and some of his friends made elaborate bobsleds, some of them ten or twelve feet long, and when the snow was deep and closely packed they borrowed horses to tow them to the top of Cobb Hill, and then, several couples packed closely, they slid all the way down through Main Street and sometimes even beyond the old stone house.[2]

Our skis were homemade. We selected carefully the proper pieces of elmwood, steamed and bent them in a retort used by a local furniture maker, and rigged the leather foot ties. They

[2] A landmark mentioned in all the local histories. Set beside Mill Creek and overhung by willows, it had simple lines that were reminiscent of Old World craftsmanship. It had been there longer than the oldest resident could say. One of our poor families always lived in it.

were a good deal below the manufactured standard, no doubt, but they got us over the snowy ground and gave us many an hour of sport. The nights came early and there was not much time left when school was over, but we skied or sledded into the twilight and got home tired, cold, and often wet, something our mothers viewed with displeasure, and mine, at least, with good reason—I was frequently ill.

Of the fancier sports, we knew nothing. Even at the lake resorts there were no golf courses, so far as I can recall, and tennis was regarded as hopelessly exotic. But we played ball, swam, fished, and hunted. And often at night, mothers permitting, or simple exhaustion not having overcome us, we ran and ran for miles among the hills, playing blank-o-li-lo, run sheep run, pom-pom pullaway, or prisoner's base. Run sheep run could be adapted to skiing, too, but it was a risky game at night and I was not often allowed to play. It was best in autumn, when it was chilly but not frigid, when the leaves were falling and we ran through drifts of them. In the village there was a smell of smoke, sharp on the evening air, from the many bonfires along the streets.[3]

Nostalgia is probably bound to overcome any aged person with such a boyhood in his past, lived so securely in a somewhat

[3] The history's description of autumn in the upland is vivid, as only the writing of a native could be; and if a little flamboyant, no more so than the subject makes appropriate:

"The glory of the American forest in autumn has often been told, but nowhere does the woodland appear in greater splendor than among our Chautauqua hills. There nature seems to have spilled her choicest pigments upon the woods. At length, frosts and falling leaves point to the return of winter, yet . . . the season lingers for a while; the year ripens into mildness and Indian summer comes. The sharp contrasts of the clear air of Spring disappear in Autumn. In the hazy atmosphere the line between earth and sky is dimly drawn and only the filmy outline of the hills in seen . . . While yet the air is soft and the heavens serene, wild geese begin their southward flight in long converging lines, as if moving runic letters were written in the sky foretelling the approach of storm. Distant sounds seem near in the hollow air . . . Responsive to these warning signs, freezing winds and pinching frosts, and at last the keen blasts of December, howl winter to a fierce welcome to his ancient and favorite domain among the whitening hills of old Chautauqua."

isolated environment, and so intimately with a few satisfactory companions. It is a characteristic of this sentiment that it tends to stifle or obscure the unpleasant experiences, the unhappinesses, and the terrors of successive ages. Of these there were certainly many, and when I stop to recall them consciously they too come back with a like vividness.

Boys are always savages among themselves, and the processes of establishing leadership are seldom nicely peaceable. I was one of those who must assert his claim to give directions. Sometimes I had to fight for it, and I was not of heroic size. Then too, I was often unhappy—without reason—because of indefinite fears. I recall the fears now much more vividly than the reasons for them. But they were depressingly frequent, that I do recall. These terrors and unhappinesses now, of course, tend to merge in a whole which cannot have been, on balance, dominated by them. In my life there were too many happier experiences, I was surrounded with too much affection, and I was sufficiently successful in my various endeavors, so that I must be said to have had a singularly fortunate childhood. If there are deductions, they are only that; they do not dominate the account.

Three

On those evenings when I could not run with the other boys there was a compensation. It was the same one that made illness less tedious than it might have been. My mother left her work and read aloud to me. It happened often, because I was subject to colds and especially to what was then called croup, the beginning of a lifelong allergy problem. And since I was spared none of the other diseases of children, I was laid up pretty regularly. The reading aloud went on long after I had learned to read myself, and the commentary that went with it, even though I was not too patient about interruptions of narrative, must have counted for education.

I learned to read early, partly, I suppose, because I was so often confined; my mother says it was between four and five, which must be an exaggeration; but, at any rate, from young boyhood on I never lacked amusement. My later pleasure in having books about me, in haunting libraries, and in cultivating bookish friends surely goes back to those early associations. The security of my home and my room, with my parents near and with a busy household making itself known by sounds I could always expect, and I sitting in my bed surrounded by books and magazines yet to be enjoyed—this was a richness I could not then, and cannot now, regard as having any limit.

There was some shortage of reading matter if I was not sufficiently foresighted. Our home was far from being an austere one and we never had to consider expense overmuch, but still the resources were not unlimited. Sinclairville was,

after all, a village of a few hundred people,[1] and no one bought
or possessed many books. But there *was* the library. There was
reason for pride in this community institution, which had been
founded as long ago as 1870 and had an accepted status. It
occupied premises intended for a store, as could be told from
the show windows at the front which had nothing to show and
had to be curtained, and it was open only a few afternoons
and an evening or two during the week; but it was administered
by ladies who made much of me as a steady borrower. I
presumed on their consideration and rifled their shelves, at first
for the works of Henty, Mayne Reid, Castlemon, Jules Verne,
Oliver Optic, Horatio Alger, Kipling, and other romantic authors; and later I arrived at *Robinson Crusoe, Swiss Family
Robinson,* and the tales of Marryat and Hawthorne. I made
the acquaintance there of Mark Twain's immortal boys; and
Dana's *Two Years Before the Mast* was, I discovered, the kind
of adventure I could imagine myself undertaking. I find it
quite impossible to fix these in sequence; I am afraid, indeed,
that taken altogether my reading was badly jumbled; and it
certainly was wholly undirected, but it was amazingly and
continuously fascinating. I never doubted that there would be
more to come, either, and that was a wonderful comfort.

The books I have mentioned, together with certain boys'
magazines, were regarded as suitable. Anything I got from the
library was approved. This was in contrast with what were
called "dime novels" (why, I do not know, because the price
was always a nickel). The Frank Merriwell, Nick Carter, and
Buffalo Bill series I found by chance in my Uncle Will Tugwell's
house (he was my father's much older half brother and the father
of my cousins George and Lawrence), where, as in Jake Evans'
establishment, there was no woman, my aunt having died before
my recollection runs. The house was empty during the day, even
on Saturdays (the five-day week was as yet unheard of), and the
doors were never locked; so I devoured dime novels many and

[1] The census reports it to have been 507 in 1900, and in 1920 it would be
514. By the 1950s it would be so decimated as to consider deincorporation.

many an hour when I was supposed to be doing something else. There were years of accumulation, piles of the tales in their gaudy covers set away on shelves in the parlor. And there was always a barrel of apples in the adjacent woodshed. The musty smell of a closed and neglected house and of withering apples (russets), together with the sight of the sun coming through dusty small-paned windows and illuminating the figures of a faded carpet—these are associated in my memory with the literature of lurid adventure and of life lived in the fantastic world of the imagination. This world was one of wonderfully simplified motives without moral problems, its characters impossibly good or fiercely vicious, and its climaxes reached in intense moments when virtue always prevailed over vice. For boys, and for men who were still boys in heart and mind, it had unfailing interest. My Uncle Will had apparently never outgrown these tales; or perhaps it was my cousins, with no mother to deny them such indulgences, who had accumulated the hoard. My intrusions were never discovered, and, for all I know, those shelves may still hold the same piles of yellowing paperbacks.[2]

School days were passed in a routine of recitations, study hours, and all too brief recesses. The study hours were passed in the same room where other classes were reciting, so there cannot have been very much concentration or very strict supervision. Some teachers were kind and patient, but there were others who were not. For some I had an affection which has continued through the years; for others I developed an almost uncontrollable antipathy. These last were the punishers. One in particular, who was free with the heavy ruler she used on our

[2] The dime novel, it seems, began to be published in 1860, just as the Civil War was about to begin. They were first issued, according to Edmund Pearson's study, in June of that year by Erastus F. Beadle in William Street, New York City. Through the next forty years various other publishers issued them. They were a favorite resort of soldiers during the war, as comic books and other paperbacks were in later and greater wars. They had no competition from the *littérateurs* of the time—Holmes, Longfellow, Hawthorne, Thackeray, George Eliot, Collins, Dickens, etc.; they were read by another audience. If there was ever an escape literature, this was it. Toward the end of the century they had begun to die out, and in a few more years they were almost gone.

hands and knuckles with what seemed unnecessary enthusiasm, succeeded only in provoking such a flood of ingenious mischief that she was in the end defeated. She had to send so many of us to the principal for further discipline that her methods came into question and she was dismissed. But on the whole the teachers in my life, like the librarians, are stored among my pleasantest recollections. That so many of them succeeded in helping their pupils to start effective educations still seems to me miraculous. Their handicaps were formidable.

Much of the work was necessarily carried on by rote. We had books to memorize—and this was true of all subjects, English as well as arithmetic. Our Readers, containing a few pages each from chosen authors, may well have been the only actual contact many of my fellow students would ever have with literature. And teachers were inclined to discourage explorations—not all of them, but some—because, I suppose, they were concerned about what young minds might encounter in the wide reaches of undirected reading. In this way the system of grading pretty strictly by age and of passing almost automatically from one grade to another (except for a few utter imcompetents) was unsuitable for me. But in other ways I think I should defend it. I doubt that it did me harm, and I can see how it may have been very useful to have had companions whose outlook was so very different from mine. We still had a range of common interests. We lived in the same sorts of homes, we came in contact with the same elders, we played the same games. I learned to be tolerant, as I suppose others learned to be tolerant of me.

And I am not so sure that the mixture, so hopelessly miscellaneous, of preferences, aptitudes, standards of living, and so on, encountered by American children as they progress through the public schools, can be written off summarily. Well-to-do parents usually, or often at least, come to a time when they feel that their children ought to be taken out of the ruck and inducted into the elite where they belong, and if the children are of sufficient ability they do go to private schools and are separated out as potential members of the upper class. I would come to such a time too but find myself frustrated and soon back in high school. Perhaps it was just as well. Public schools cannot serve their mission in the creation of the democracy to which we are committed unless they keep all sorts within their group. Grade and high school children are part of the democracy too and always will be. To drain off their leadership and then try to return it at a later stage may make for better education; in high school, particularly, the slower students may hold up the quicker ones. But this too can be exaggerated. The slower ones will plod along behind and the quicker ones venture out ahead, but the association between the two may make both of them realize that they must jointly inhabit the world, each contributing what his abilities allow. I will just say that my childhood associations with friends who would "never get anywhere" seem to me now to have been just as fond and perhaps as valuable as associations with those who got farther than I was able to do.

But there was one deficiency in that schooling, perhaps caused by the overworking of teachers or by the insufficient training or education they had had, and contributed to by the crowded classrooms, which was for me, as it must have been for others, a serious handicap. I was allowed to fall into slovenly habits even in my best subjects, tending to spread out in a kind of sprawl through history and literature without any order or discipline. Worse than that, I fell into the habit of shirking what I did not like. I did only what was exacted in arithmetic, for instance, and later in mathematics of the higher sorts, getting farther and farther behind where I should have been. And to this day I am essentially uneducated, however interested I may be, in the physical sciences. I find, by inquiring, that this was true—and it may be significant—of my whole generation. We divided early into those who manipulated numbers with pleasure and those who, like myself, preferred to read. Even later, when aptitudes came to be studied and their indications respected, this dichotomy persisted and went uncorrected.

In my time and place those of us who seemed to take naturally to one or the other kind of study were still supposed to be taught the other disciplines. Some of us resisted, and when we did, nothing much was done about it. Most of my companions left school for more practical training on parental farms or in small businesses; but others went on, dragging one educational foot as I was to do.

In Sinclairville, school fringed out into other interests. Our teachers were our mothers' friends, and our fathers were intimates of the principal. We saw them at our table or at many social occasions. There were not so many children that everyone did not know a good deal about most of them. Which ones did well or badly, which were mischievous, which were trustworthy— all this was gossiped over and advice given or withheld as a community concern. There were other activities, too, which blended with those of the school. I can hardly separate in my recollection the occasions when we performed in school for our parents and when we performed in church. Those were the days—before movies, television, or automobiles—of "performances." The child who could play the organ or the piano had ample opportunity to display the proficiency; some could sing, others just recited. I was among the latter. Many a time I was drilled by my mother in a "piece." At first they were short lyrics, but they tended to become narrative or dramatic as I grew up. They were said before an audience. These occasions were dreaded by the performers, but protests were useless. The parents were obliged to display the talents of their offspring, and they were resistant to argument. Only illness excused a dereliction.

My mother was as insistent as any. She had a brisk way about it. She was convinced of my superior looks, talents, and behavior, and she had no intention of keeping the conviction to herself. In later years she could laugh at her determination, but as a young mother she took the display very seriously. She has one story she still repeats with mixed amusement and a still-lingering chagrin. The recitation I was to make was at a church occasion. It was my first. I was three years old and terrified at the prospect. It had been no trouble to see that I was letter-perfect. But the extra trouble was taken to stage a rehearsal in the church, where the minister, to make things more realistic and to allay my apprehension, took the place he would have as he presided next evening. I spoke my piece to him successfully. But when the occasion arrived and my name was called to go up to the platform in front of all those people, I marched like an automaton up the steps and stood facing the minister, back to the audience, and went perfectly through my lines. My mother's embarrassment was terrible, according to my father; but it taught some other lesson than humility, which was something she never learned.

I cannot, of course, recall this small incident. But as my mother tells it, there are re-created for me the reluctances and embarrassments, as well as the triumphs over my fears, that I experienced on many other occasions when I was somewhat older. And I can see with peculiar intensity the scene at school or in church as I waited my turn to face the audience. The anxiety was somewhat more intense in church, perhaps because it was a less familiar venue. Like most Congregational meeting houses, ours was a severely austere edifice, consisting of a vestibule and one large room. The steeple above had one bell, which, with the bells of the Methodists and Baptists, rang through the valley on Sunday mornings. As the bell stopped ringing, the service within began and the congregation faced an hour and a half of preaching and hymn singing. It was a light-laced room, painted white, inclined to be cold in the areas away from the two large stoves at the rear, but never gloomy or portentous. The pews were uncomfortable for a small boy over so long a stretch, but he could always doze against his father's side or ponder the eccentricities he could see displayed in the faces about him. But when the reciting took place, the occasion was not religious but social. The same light room held the same audience. But the minister was inclined to joviality, and there were adult performers as well as immolated children. It

passed for entertainment. And it did have the value of all
associations in village life. We lived together in a sense not known
anywhere in the later world.

Even if it had not been entertaining, I still feel that the
time I spent on much of my miscellaneous reading was well
used. If it did not emerge as a patterned accumulation, it at
least gave me an accustomedness to the tradition of our literature and, through that, a sense of historical depth. Lamb's *Tales
from Shakespeare,* Plutarch's *Lives,* collections of Greek and
Roman myths and fables (whose editors, except for Bulfinch,
I cannot recall) were all on the library shelves, their covers
made alike by uniform brown paper jackets. I did not take
them down because of attractive appearance or even because
someone suggested it. I opened them at random, was caught
by a passage, and went on and on, often forgetful of time. But
Lamb and Plutarch must have been special, for not long afterward I was given them for Christmas, probably because I made
the request. I still had them as late as my collegiate years. But
perhaps the purest pleasure would be represented by my premature, perhaps clandestine, plunge into the novel by way of
Scott, Dickens, Thackeray, Balzac, Dumas, George Eliot, and
the Brontës. I acquired a copy of *Pickwick Papers*—the first
book I ever bought for myself—and it stood close to my bed
from then on. But I recall, too, that I read a good deal of
history—Bancroft, I suppose—Prescott and Parkman; at any
rate, there was a thorough indoctrination going on all during my
youth which had progress as its central idea—progress with a
distinct righteous cast.

One of the major manifestations of national morality during
my boyhood was the conquest of the West, but another was the
victory of right and justice in the Civil War. I cannot now
recall in what reading I followed the boys in blue through their
tribulations to victory, but I recall the emotions well enough. The
war might still have been going on, to judge from my partisan
excitement. The tales of battle, of camps and marchings through

the countryside, of charges and sieges, were an endless interest. And it had the value of having ended as it should, just as the winning of the West from the savages had.

I had no company in these several adventures. The fact was, I now understand, that not one of my boyhood friends was a reader as I mean it here; and not another one, therefore, developed the same sense of tradition. If we sometimes wonder why it is that we have to live through interludes when the whole nation seems to forget its reason for being and behaves as though the Bill of Rights and the other amendments to the Constitution had never been heard of, it is because there are so many, now adults, who as children did not learn of the struggles out of which our institutions came. Even when I had lived long enough not to be surprised, I never got used to such manifestations of intolerance as the red hunts directed by an Attorney General of the United States after World War I and the later attempt of a United States Senator to impose thought control in the wake of World War II. It seemed incredible that such things should happen; yet they did and have to be accounted for. They must occur because we have large numbers of citizens who are not horrified—as I learned to be—by the determination of some to force on others the acceptance of their beliefs. Yet I recall my own feelings and realize that as I was stirred by the adventure of western expansion and the crusade to free the slaves, I had no very kindly regard for the Indians—even Cooper did not persuade me—who were deprived of their inheritance, nor for the Southerners who fought because they believed themselves oppressed. And I end by merely being glad that we have always survived with our democracy intact, however narrow the victories might be over our worse selves. Perhaps the severe struggles have taught us how to be better democrats; certainly they have been severe enough.

The wild thoughts of my early teen-age mind were hardly to be contained by it; they had often to find release in attempts to act, or at least to imagine myself acting, as my heroes had. I identified myself with the pioneers moving out across the plains to Oregon and California, fighting hardships and Indians all the way; with the soldiers of the Civil War; with those who hid escaping slaves along the "underground railway," and even with the characters from imported fiction come down to us in storied glamor—Jason questing for the Golden Fleece, for instance, and the Crusaders seeking to win back the Holy Land from the infidel. When years later I studied more formally the history of literatures, I realized that I had been exposed without willing it to hopelessly diverse and doubtful adventurers, many of them pursuing aims I found objectionable. There had converged upon me lines of influence—for just the wonderful liveness and unconquerability of my heroes was enough to hold my admiration, no matter in what service the energy was expended—from our own Far and Middle West, from New England, and from lands across the sea, especially our own mother England. Sinclairville might be a tiny village in the Chautauqua hills, hardly touched by the main currents of civilization, but here were the books from all those other places, written by those who had lived in them. Some were their own biographers, some created the figures they portrayed. Ivanhoe, Robin Hood, Sir Lancelot, Cap'n Ahab, Long John Silver, Crusoe, Sam Weller, the Mississippi pilots, the miners in Roaring Camp, Andy Jackson, General Phil Sheridan, Frank Merriwell—they made an infinitely various set of companions.[3]

[3] That others of my generation had something of the same experience I was made aware, as I was writing, by one of Mr. Ralph McGill's columns (Washington *Post,* April 15, 1960):

"It startles me to recall it, but I am one who actually hid in a barn loft to read the Merriwell stories. And that fact now seems almost as fictional as Merriwell himself. But it is true. I read the Buffalo Bill stories and the Wild West paper novels in the same study—the barn loft.

"They weren't bad books. If Britain thought her first world war was won on the playing fields of Eton, because there her leadership obtained a set of values and ideals which stiffened its back in time of adversity and danger, I think perhaps the average American in our AEF obtained theirs in barn lofts reading the Merriwell stories. I know we smoked cigarettes

The most impressive literary figure of my youth and the one who did most to create the atmosphere I lived in was, I now know, William Dean Howells, who first functioned as an editor in Boston and then moved to New York. He was born a Midwesterner, of course, but his residence in Italy and his dominance among contemporary *littérateurs* made him a cosmopolitan figure. Luckily he was a welcoming and sympathetic editor and, as critic, had the most catholic tastes. But this was the mark, too, of the Chautauquans. They were hospitable to almost every sort of creative writer. Over there by the lake they walked among the trees, made lectures, and could be talked to—my mother often did just that. And I can see now that, apart from my own explorations, I was raised in a remarkably varied and tolerant tradition; Protestant, Congregational, and self-important, but not narrowly so. It reached out to all America, at least, with welcoming interest, and occasionally entertained a foreigner who might be exotic but yet was listened to with a certain curiosity.

From the region of Howells' origin, there were other writers—Eggleston of *The Hoosier Schoolmaster,* for instance; but much more important in a folk sense were the midwestern poets; these homely versifiers had some rather more respectable brothers in Longfellow and Tennyson, for instance. Even these are recognized now as prissy, popular fare. But Longfellow had

---

of rabbit tobacco and corn silk and not marijuana, and I am convinced the propaganda of those stories and books had an effect. Right always triumphed. Honesty emerged as the best policy. Integrity and fair play were strong assets. The villain, while he flourished for a while even as the green bay tree, had his comeuppance.

"In the Wild West stories courage was rewarded. A man faced the odds, whatever they were. . . ."

Mr. McGill was raised in another part of the country, and I have no idea what rabbit tobacco was; but I know about corn silk and, above all, I read the Buffalo Bill and the Merriwell stories. And he is quite justified in saying that they had a lasting influence, and that it inculcated virtues. Moreover, it uplifted hearts and convinced boys that the struggles they were to enter on as they became adults were worthwhile. Their triumphs would gain them honor among honorable men.

been a Harvard professor, and Tennyson a lord.[4] To my
generation, as can be seen by looking at contemporary criticism
these were accepted for what they were, having qualities not of
greatness but of merit. And they were almost as ubiquitous as
Riley and Carleton. My mother, crooning to me as I was readied
for bed, might well launch suddenly into *Evangeline* or
Hiawatha, run through some lines of *The Lady of Shalott,* or
repeat with obvious emotion the lovely measures beginning
"Come into the garden, Maud, . . . the black bat, night, has
flown . . ." She knew long passages from both these poets with
amazing certainty. They were agreeable to her, in sentiment, in
moral implication, in rhythmic impression. They were the poets of
her world, and they became the poets of mine, at least for many
years. They were Emerson made more melodious than he
could ever be himself. They were transcendentalism set to music.

[4] Fred Lewis Pattee, for instance, was a very respectable historian of
literature, one of the first to treat American literature separately. His
History, first published in 1896, said rather reluctantly, after noting that
Longfellow had had the unusual honor of commemoration in Westminster
Abbey, that "he was not the singer of fierce and violent passions, nor of
the profounder depths of tragedy . . . he was not profound like Emerson,
nor intensely individual like Poe; he was not strikingly original like Whittier, nor grand and elemental like Bryant . . . So, while Longfellow can
never be ranked among the great poets who have brought burning messages
to men, he will ever remain the most popular of poets, the one whose sweet
sympathy has dried the tears of thousands . . ." *A History of American
Literature* (Boston and New York: Silver, Burdett Co.), 1896, 272–73.
When this was written, Longfellow had been dead only fourteen years and
was at the height of his influence in a popular sense. The appraisal seems
to me to have been remarkably accurate. My elders are not to be thought
of as drowned in sentiment. They were as shrewd as their successors.

Four

Boys and girls who were born to be Americans in 1891 opened their eyes on an upward surge of national power and influence, but this was not thought to be at all remarkable. It was taken for granted that such was the nation's destiny and that it would go on and on. Changes were not actually to be seen in Sinclairville, however; we were still marking time. Workmen and shopkeepers still kept pretty much to their accustomed ways. The cracker barrel was not too far from the potbellied stove in Crofoot's store, and in the lean-to out back molasses, vinegar, and kerosene were still run from barrels into pails or jugs brought by customers, and plug tobacco lay on the counter alongside an array of penny candies. It was a store our grandparents would have recognized.

The elder Crofoot, proprietor of the store, took turns with other merchants on Main Street in watering down the dust of summer and shoveling away the snow of winter—the between-seasons mud was simply endured. But Crofoot's store was like others and, in relation to time and place, symbolic of Sinclairville—lingering in a state fast becoming obsolete. But it was an interesting state for a boy to grow up in. It was a slack family that did not tend a quarter-acre kitchen garden and lay away root crops in cellars for the winter. Some villagers still kept a cow, a few chickens, and a pig or two, and others bought milk from Burt Smith's grandfather, who came down from his hill-top farm every day with five-gallon cans from which the fluid was dipped and poured into housewives' own tins. There were laborers to be hired for whatever jobs there were to do at seven or eight cents an hour, and they worked a ten- or twelve-hour day as a matter of course. What I mean to say is that we were more like the past than the future.

Farmers, and others with businesses like my father's, kept hired men, and these were in the Yankee line—hard-working, loyal, eccentric, almost part of the family. I recall them at our table from my earliest years, sometimes smelling richly of the stable but belonging among us just the same. Most farmers still cradled their grain and scythed their grass, but some were beginning to use horse-drawn tools. Corn was planted and hoed, and manure was forked, by hand; work was done in the wood lots with ax, maul, wedge and cross-cut saw. It was stacked in great piles near the woodshed or drawn to town and sold to villagers who still cooked on ranges of the old-fashioned sort. Fires in the stoves had to be tended all day; moreover, they had to be built every morning. It was a boy's chore to keep the wood basket filled.

But more changes than occasional mowing machines were coming. About the time I began to run around the village the first telephones were installed and it became possible to talk with Jamestown or Fredonia—if there was anything to talk about. Bathrooms were unheard of before this decade, but they soon became something more than curiosities. And even Crofoot's store began to carry packaged merchandise of certain kinds. The cobbler no longer made shoes; he merely repaired them. And when Allen Hinchliffe's father, who had been the village tailor, died, his shop was closed. For years it was merely vacant, as though waiting for a new tenant; but one never came. My father and his friends began to patronize a haberdasher in Jamestown. In their photographs they look very smart, too, and as though they knew exactly what they were dressing for. This was, of course, to impress young ladies and to get ahead in the world. The photographs now have an antique air, but the young men they show seem alert and energetic, mustaches trimmed, heavy gold chains across their high-cut vests, jackets tight, and collars starched. It was they who were to change things radically. It can be seen in their pictures.

There were some million babies, born to these fathers in 1891, who began to be aware of their environments a few years later.[1] There can have been only a few times in history when a generation awoke to a similar destiny. Roman youths during a few hundred years, English children in the century of Empire— these might have had a consciousness from their first days such as we had of unlimited opportunity, of belonging to a people destined to fortune and favor. But even they can hardly have had more anticipation than we of sharing in remarkable events about to happen. Children are not conscious of status, and youths grow into a sense of their futures only gradually; but it must have made a tremendous difference to us, all the same, that ours was a growing nation, a fast-growing one, with endless possibilities. We probably never heard of the Manifest Destiny which had been adduced to justify territorial expansions during the generations just past and which would excuse the excursion into imperialism after the impending Spanish war; but intimations of it must have helped to form our attitudes and to hold out incentives from our earliest years. We might be small boys in an obscure village back in the hills, but we belonged to a nation that was reaching out and growing richer, with a suggestion of infinitude. We were among those who would inherit what our lively fathers would make.

These were some of the circumstances of our early lives, but there were others of equal importance—not known to us as children but, all the same, fixing the nature of our environment. The prospect of vast expansion meant that any child of the 1890s might expect to become wealthy or famous—perhaps both—and this gave him a confidence in his future that he might not otherwise have had. I know it was true of me. There

[1] The population in 1890 was 62,622,250; the number of children 5 to 7 years old was 18,543,201; of these, 12,722,581 were in school, so I must be about right in estimating that a million entered the first grade at the same time I did.

never was a time when I did not anticipate, however generally, some remarkable good fortune. I never in my life thought it possible that I might be merely a worker and earner of wages. I anticipated venturesome exploits and glorious achievements. There was a tinge of missionary feeling about this too. I would always champion worthy causes and win victories for the right. There would, naturally, be approbation, even plaudits.

Still another of these influences was important; like the others, it was never mentioned and may never have been thought of explicitly even by statesmen and scholars at the time. This was the complete security of the nation. Besides having a whole continent to exploit, we were to be, during my genera-tion—until the 1940s—inviolate, unreachable. There was no conceivable way, before the long-range bomber was perfected, that our territory could be menaced. To be sure, there were Canada and Mexico to north and south, and their proximity aroused the xenophobe in such statesmen as Theodore Roosevelt and Henry Cabot Lodge; but any danger from them was too remote to arouse much interest in others. It was getting on for a century since Napoleon had briefly entertained designs on the Mississippi basin; and the relationship with Canada had been stable since the War of 1812. It was already clear that the English-speaking peoples were, however reluctantly, joined in that unspoken union which would survive so many vicissitudes. This, in effect, admitted us to the protective custody of the British navy as well as Canadian guardianship of our longest border.

So the good fortune of our position not only gave us the security within which the generations could follow one another with careers uninterrupted by conscription or the fear of it, but also gave us this blessing almost without cost. It was not necessary to have military forces of any considerable size, and we were excused that expense. We accepted the British pro-tection without acknowledgment and without making any re-turn. Consequently we had no income taxes, and what others there were bore lightly on everyone but property owners. With small obligations of this sort for public purposes, enterprisers could develop their many projects without check and without causing any serious general inflation. Speculations did sometimes end in disasters and there were recurrent depressions and panics (such as the one in 1893), but, however disastrous, they were regarded as inevitable, something natural, which would pass. Prosperity would presently return. It always had.

Almost without feeling it, because the expense was borne locally, a nationwide school system was being built. It was calculated to educate every child to the extent of his abilities. This was regarded as the guarantee of democracy. But also roads were being built by towns and counties, and cities were paving their streets, installing water and sewer systems, and building monumental courthouses and city halls. The age of electricity was arriving, and factories and office buildings were multiplying with amazing speed. All was movement, change, progress.

Grover Cleveland, who was the big man of my infancy, was, in a way, one of our own. He had been a minister's son, left early to fend for himself. He had migrated from the village to the city—Buffalo—and had got his education and risen in his profession in the way Americans were supposed to do.[2] He had asserted the power of the Presidency in national and international affairs and was a credit to our tradition. To hear about him was like following the career of one of the Alger heroes. But most of all he represented solidity and integrity. He stood between the people and any dangers they might imagine.

That confident sense of security would not be shaken in any serious way for half a century. During all that time we would remain optimistic, unafraid, and concerned with expansion. In 1940, when, in immediate prospect of war with the aggressive dictators of Europe, and with Britain prostrate, President Roosevelt would say in a loud voice that we were at last in danger—

[2] *The Honorable Peter Sterling,* the story of an honest man in the jungle of politics, is supposed to have been at least inspired by Cleveland's experience.

actual physical danger—the shock would be profound. Everyone knew that what he said was true. They had been aware of it for some time. But they had not taken it in. And even when he spoke, there was a tendency to deny, even to ridicule, his facts. But there were actually bombing fleets in the air, and the British navy no longer stood between us and the enemy. The age of safety ended in that year.

I would by then have grown up and lived for many years in a nation exempt from the commonest danger of most men in most times and places. True, security or danger was beyond our area of concern, even if there had been those among our elders who had understood our position and its implications. Yet it must have had its influence on us. The subtle pressures on children who sense the fears of their elders, the consciousness somehow communicated to them that something may happen to destroy their homes, injure their parents, and disrupt their communities, must have been a torment from the earliest history of mankind. We were free of such fears to a degree that even left us ignorant of the privileges of safety.

Then too, there was the prospect of probable prosperity. The rich lands of our prairie states were just emerging from the pioneer phase. Sod houses were giving way to proper farmsteads, and city centers were growing. Even the short-grass country, so inhospitable to farming, was being occupied in a kind of recoil from West Coast disappointments. Everybody could consider whether he ought to go West and join those others who were creating farms and businesses where none had existed before. There need be no preliminaries, no permission—hardly, even, any capital. Anyone could go and, if he had energy and a little luck, could succeed.

None of my friends' families actually joined the pioneer migrants; but we knew of others, a little older, whose parents decided that such a move was best. All of them, however, were farmers, none villagers. The recollection I have of this is that there was a general awareness of the possibility. For anyone who found that circumstances were pinching—the farm running down, too many boys growing up, the winters too long—there was always a way to escape. That way now was West; later it would be cityward. But the city lure was already beginning to operate. My friend Earl Roberts was soon abstracted from us, his father having chosen a job in the steel mills of Lorain out on Lake Erie rather than the hazards of casual teamstering in our village. And even our own Dr. Smith, Burt's father, would move to the environs of Jamestown; country doctoring, he said, was just too strenuous for an aging man. By the time our decision to go was made, the signs were clear. The village, like thousands of old communities in the eastern states, was no longer a place of promise. It was a backwater, and only the lethargic and ambitionless would stay to see its withering.

It was about this time that Frederick Jackson Turner was pointing out to his fellow historians what a difference the open frontier of the past century had made—and was making—in American life.[3] Theodore Roosevelt had already gone West and come back to write engagingly about his experiences. At this moment he was rising through various government posts— after having been an unsuccessful candidate for Mayor of New York in 1886. But he was best known to us for his *Winning of the West,* a book calculated to stir the latent adventurousness of almost any youth. We heard of him in this way, and of course would presently hear much of him as a Rough Rider and then as a more successful politician; he would, in fact, be much heard of throughout my growing up, more and more disapproved of in my family as he became more notedly Republican, and by me as I realized my inheritance of Democracy. Then too, my mother, for some reason, conceived an intense dislike for him— he was a showoff and a hypocrite, she said, and said frequently, in her argumentative style (calculated to arouse her solidly Republican neighbors; she loved the ensuing ruckus and was quite willing to take the risks involved of offending those she otherwise depended on for friendship).

[3] In a paper called "The Significance of the Frontier in American History" read at a meeting of the American Historical Association in 1893.

We heard of Roosevelt all right; but not, naturally, of Turner. The proceedings of learned societies were slow in filtering down to the Sinclairvilles of the land (although Chautauqua literature did bring some of them to us at second hand and rather late); and, anyway, boys absorb such large generalizations by a kind of osmosis rather than by direct communication. Turner did not instruct me, but I knew from an early age about the West; no one had to explain its significance: too many dime novels had to do with pioneer settlers, with cowboys and the wars between cattlemen and sheep owners, to say nothing of Californian adventures. The knowledge I had was romanticized and unreliable; but there *were* those acquaintances of ours who had been drawn westward. They wrote home and we heard of their vicissitudes. They seemed to be forever in trouble, and some even came back defeated.

This did not comport very well with the glamorized plains and mountains of my stories; but, like most others, I refused to accept any dimming of the glow by mere sordid reality. The West remained a land of excitement.

What I want most to emphasize is that, in spite of Sinclairville's lack of specific promise, ours was a world of opportunity. We entered on it, my friends and I, with a certain expectancy. We had no real knowledge of other times and places for comparison, and, since we were constricted in our valley, our luck was not appreciated in any conscious way; but we were sure that we would make good, and maybe even better than good.

I would even say that we escaped many of the influences responsible for the intolerance and suspiciousness that would infuse the society of our later lives. The need to acquire possessions and to guard them has been a trait of many people I have observed, and not I alone; a distinguished theorist would characterize the society of my maturity as an acquisitive one and trace many of its ills to this habit.[4] But this was an observa-

---

[4] This, of course, was R. H. Tawney, and his book *The Acquisitive Society* (New York: Harcourt, Brace, 1946).

tion about the larger capitalist economy. It sprang from an environment quite different from ours.

Yet it has to be said that the boys and girls who were growing up in rural America at the beginning of the century would not turn out to be the kinds of citizens needed for their times. Even the civic virtues and the more general ideals, so faithfully held, would be dangerously anachronistic. But the children of my time could hardly have emerged into adulthood with any other attitudes. Their fathers, after all, had set the pattern. They were farmers or shopkeepers, or, if they were laborers, they worked so intimately with an employer that no class distinction existed between themselves and him. Many became independent; any of them might easily enough become a blacksmith, wheelwright, carpenter, or tinsmith; a harness- or shoemaker; a baker or miller.

In the course of our lives these trades would practically disappear, but we would have been bred to them and to the attitudes they implied. To me and to my generation, no other arrangement for working and living would seem quite natural. Many of us would graduate into other occupations and be swept into factories or offices; we would be convinced that the old trades were inoperable and the old views obsolete; but our accommodation to the change would be made with reluctance and strain and with many a backward look.

The small-scale arrangements worked so well in our relatively self-contained community that adjustment to them tended to become fixed and rigid. They seemed right. A man could work for himself and at the same time be serving others. When at a later time I came to the study of Adam Smith's economic theory, I understood, with intimations of previous familiarity, the dictum that each individual, in working for his own interests, was led, as by a hidden hand, to the service of others. That is how it was in Sinclairville. When the butcher, the baker, the dressmaker, the druggist, the grocer, the undertaker—and all the others— had premises up and down one street and were each other's customers, there was little danger that any one of them would exploit the others; there was a presumption of fairness in exchange.

I did not understand—and probably none of my elders did —that the disastrous depression of '93 might be a consequence of—an integral part of—our national system of enterprise. When village economics was projected into the big-business system, its inappropriateness resulted in chaos. Something incomprehensible occurred in this transition. Mechanisms changed, but ideas did not. And the machinery ran wild. When it did, many people were hurt.

Further west, Populism had appeared in the wake of depression. Ignatius Donnelly, Mary Ellen Lease, Sockless Jerry Simpson, and other colorful demagogues had preached revolt; but the echoes of their strident voices were faint in our hills. And actually, of course, the Populists were reactionary. They wanted to go back. They wanted no progress except on their own terms—larger profits for the small farmer and businessman.[5]

If afterward I sometimes tried to make something among my friends of having been born simultaneously with Populism, they had no difficulty in locating the betraying fact that my

[5] It was in 1891 that 1400 delegates from 32 states met in Cincinnati to organize the People's Party of the United States. Present were Donnelly, Simpson, Mary Lease, Thomas E. Watson, W. A. Peffer, and James Kyle. All these were strident advocates of "reform." They nominated J. B. Weaver for President. And actually Weaver got more than a million popular votes and 22 electoral votes. He at least frightened eastern conservatives, a fright which was intensified when, after the events of 1893, Bryan was nominated by the Democrats. Coxey's Army had marched on Washington in 1894, and the Democrats were appealing to all those who were in economic straits. McKinley defeated Bryan in 1896, but by only 601,854 votes (in a total of fourteen million). So I was born at a time of turmoil, when social dissidents were angry and violent, and the defenders of the status quo uncertain and wavering. I am probably wrong in saying that all the excitement passed us by; certainly the campaign of 1896—the first I think I can recall, and that only because of its torchlight parades—roused the whole country. But I am certain that I am right in saying that the hysteria did not reach us. The issues that divided the world were still subordinate, in our village, to local concerns. This was partly, I suppose, because we were so safely Republican; but it must have been mostly because we were diverted only reluctantly from the demanding business of everyday life in our accustomed round.

part of the country not only did not contribute to the challengers but consistently voted to suppress them. I do not pretend to know at what age I became aware of such issues. Perhaps not at all, in any understanding way, while we still lived in Sinclairville. But I seem to recall commentaries, communicated to the men by the women who were introduced to such things in the Chautauqua reading matter they regularly discussed in their Circle meetings. Probably the campaigns of 1896 and 1900 did cause some heated exchanges. All the animosity cannot have been worn off in organizing the parades and meetings I associate with chill evenings in October, with flaring torches set about the common, with orators on the bandstand, and with slogans which we boys slung at each other like so many snowballs in 1900.

The Chautauqua influence spread through the society of those decades in such a moderating way! The strangely strict, yet tolerant, temper of the Chautauquans was more consistent, I sometimes think, with the professions of Christianity than the excited evangelism of more popular movements. Even a mild sort of socialism was given a hearing in the literature going out to the Reading Circles. But I was not so precocious that I knew anything about such matters when I was nine or ten; my inquisitiveness about social and economic arrangements began rather early, but not so early as that.

What I did listen to and recall was the slow, considered, and conservative talk of men who knew how to run their small businesses and who usually did well enough to suit their ambitions. I doubt whether the hard times of '93 and the years following actually had such devastating effects in our village as it had in larger centers of trade; but the farmers must have had troubles. Their cash crops could hardly have brought in enough support money for the long winter, and they must have been forced to be almost as self-sufficient as their grandfathers had been.

I know that my father decided to get out of the cattle business because of the depression. Raising stock on the hill pastures was no longer profitable. He may have feared for this reason that his business had been permanently injured, but he had been restless anyway. He wanted more scope. His ambitions nagged at him. He would have looked at anyone uncomfortably who said to him that an old order was breaking up and that he was escaping from the ruins. But subconsciously he knew it. He was well enough aware that something deep and permanent was happening. But he made a drastic change not because he had a theory about it or any long view of the situation, but because he was a lively young fellow who knew enough to abandon something unprofitable when he got the chance and go to something with promise for the future. He would become a big businessman in a small way (if I may be allowed the paradox); and, watching with him and working with him through the years as I grew older, I would witness the dying of one economy and the growing of another. He would go through this experience, I am afraid, without ever drawing any conclusions as to its significance; and in the end he would be a victim of the forces he helped to strengthen. There would be many like him, still living at mid-century and a little later; mostly, however, they would be broken old men, puzzled and sad, as he then would be broken and puzzled and sad. But that was still a long way ahead.

As the Spanish war came and went, after the years of depression and slow recovery, and as the overwhelming completeness of the victory enlarged their self-importance, Americans became even more assured and prideful than they had been before. The pioneer swagger spread; complacence became a national fault. Sufficient power had been generated among us to defeat a historic European empire, to make an American lake of the Caribbean, and to begin the civilizing of the Far East from a nucleus in the Philippines. The belief was confirmed that, in spite of occasional and temporary setbacks, expansion and progress were inherent in the American way of life. That this dream of greatness comported badly with individualism, with a persistent nostalgia for country scenes, with a belief in competition and across-the-street familiarity, occurred to no one.

I ought to note here that even before I was born the railroads had earned disapprobation and that several other kinds of businesses had coalesced into trusts and were showing the monopolistic traits which the Sherman Act of 1890 was intended to suppress.[6] To have resulted in disciplinary legislation sponsored by Republicans, this enlargement of business must have frightened small businessmen and farmers pretty thoroughly. But it would not for a long time be suspected that what was being dealt with was the logical consequence of that progress everyone believed in so thoroughly. The trusts, it was thought, were merely being bad; they must be punished. The business pattern still to be seen in our valley—or something not very unlike it—must be restored where it had been destroyed by unfair competition. Such was the program of the radicals of that day; it was what the Populists wanted;[7] it would remain the progressive program down through the New Deal of the second Roosevelt, thus exhibiting a power of survival which seems most remarkable now—most remarkable and hard to explain, especially since the conservatives adopted the anti-trust program and, as we have seen, passed the original disciplinary legislation. Progressives merely wanted to go a little farther.

Public policy required, in general, very little government; even the anti-trust laws were no more than police measures and would not advance to regulatory ones until Wilson's Presidency. And if this was the policy in the nation, it was even more notably the policy locally. In our community there was so little regulation, and what there was bore so easily on our

[6] Signed by President Harrison, July 2, 1890. It was the joint product of Senators Sherman of Ohio, Edmunds of Vermont, Hoar of Massachusetts, and George of Mississippi. The wide spread of its sponsorship shows how general a protest it represented, and the conservatism of the Senators shows how deep the resentment ran.

[7] Anticipated by Wendell Phillips and Peter Cooper in the East, but more prominently by the forerunners of Bryan and Debs in the West. Henry George, Edward Bellamy, and Henry Demarest Lloyd reached very wide audiences and were enormously effective in influencing the opinion which culminated in the Sherman Act.

citizens, that I was never conscious of any organization for it. I have said on occasion that I was grown up before I ever saw a policeman. This cannot have been quite accurate; there must have been police in Jamestown, where we sometimes went, and in Celeron, that center of all delights, where we went on rare holidays. On such excursions I was occasionally allowed to wander alone, but usually I preferred to anchor myself firmly to my father with one hand while the other clutched a toy balloon, a box of Crackerjack, and an all-day sucker. Crowds were a little unsettling, especially when the spielers were in full throat and the brassy instruments of the merry-go-round were blasting away at capacity, and although I do not recall any policemen to keep order, there must have been some.

As a matter of fact, I do not recall much of anything about government. Everything in Sinclairville and in Bemus Point seemed to happen spontaneously and to be self-managing, even the simple public works of which we were the possessors. There were drunken men occasionally, especially on days when some sort of celebration brought crowds in from the country. Most such errant individuals were disposed of by dragging them out to the barn behind the hotel or into the alley behind Anderson's saloon, where they slept it off in peace. Or, if they had been fighting, which also happened, bystanders saw that they got to Dr. Smith's or Dr. Cleland's office to be patched up. All this happened without intervention by anyone with official standing. There were lawsuits, which I heard about at second hand. They concerned mostly small matters, but some of these could become wildly controversial and cause acrimonious takings of sides. We had a justice of the peace and a constable, but at this distance I could not name them. They cannot have loomed very large in village life.

There was very little overhead direction. There were separate civic arrangements for special functions; everyone was proud of the village water system; not many communities of our size had so good a one (it used the water from springs several miles from town, reservoirs and piping had been expensive); of Evergreen

Cemetery, where our dead were buried on a carefully tended hill; of the volunteer fire company, which, if it did not really put out many fires, gave spectacular exhibitions on the Fourth of July; and, as I have suggested, of the Free Library. They were, all of them, organized by interested citizens and run autonomously. But this did not seem like government; the positions were unpaid, but no one refused them; being on their Boards was both duty and honor. We were an incorporated village, of course, and so there *was* a government. The Village Board, however, was much like the others. It arranged for a few services in an economical way, but these were not of a sort to be known to a boy. There were contests and arguments: I even remember some of them. But their scope was narrow. They involved our own affairs.

As with the Cemetery Association, so with the brass band. The cemetery and the band are somehow linked in my memory, perhaps because they came together in the celebration of Memorial Day. Then too, my father was the owner and operator of the alto horn. How he managed this I cannot imagine, for anyone less musical than he never lived. But, at any rate, there have been few prouder moments in my life than when, as a schoolboy, I marched in the processions which went to decorate the graves of soldiers with my gaudily uniformed father up ahead among the bandsmen sounding out the marches practiced so faithfully for many evenings in the firehouse. The roads were dusty and the marchers were still hot and disheveled as they moved from grave to grave between the hedges and among the sculptured trees; but there was a bandstand from which martial music coursed over the allotment for the dead as we moved about. Sweet bottled drinks were still unheard of, at least in our parts, but ladies served lemonade—large cool pitchers of it dipped from washtubs in which chunks of ice bobbed and floated. We straggled back to the village, refreshed, or our elders did; we boys were likely to slip down the high bank to the north and into the millpond; the water would still be chill, but such deterrents were scorned. To this day I can recall

the sharp, resinous, sun-distilled smells of the clipped evergreens
and picture the well-frilled matrons presiding at the lemonade
table, the band banging and blowing its best in the stand above
their heads. The preachers finished with their short dedicatory
prayers as the flowers were placed on the heroes' graves, children
were released from their compliant but not very orderly companies, and the elders prepared to retreat to shaded porches
for the rest of the day. Summer was beginning. Memorial Day
was much less a salute to the past than an opening of the
season that freed us from heated houses and heavy clothes and
would presently free us from the disciplines of school.

Speaking of the band, our community rather improbably
supported "Professor" Billy Scott, the music master who trained
that devoted organization and gave private lessons on all its
instruments. It must have been from him, by sheer grit and
with endless repetition, that my father learned to play a certain
number of selections. Scott was a jolly round man with an
incongruous goatee (goatees seeming more naturally to be associated with long, lugubrious faces), and he was as fixed in our
society as the high school principal, the postmaster, the station
agent, or any of its other functionaries. But he was a benign
member and was universally liked, even by small boys who,
without any natural facility at all, were put to the trumpet or
the clarinet by ambitious fathers. It was Scott's theory that
anyone could learn to play, and fathers were evidently of the
same belief. I escaped. I do not know why, because later I was
required to suffer the tortures of piano lessons. The initiative
for this came from my mother, who, I suppose, was following
a pattern of seeing that children had some genteel accomplishment. I would have liked to play the piano, but not if I had to
learn; a reluctance my father supported as well as he could—
in fact, he always supported my resistance to what must have
seemed to him unnecessary harassments.

So Scott gave my father lessons and was a friend of the
family. My recollection of him is a pleasanter one than I have
of some of the others in authority, especially those, as I now

realize, who represented government. The postmaster must have been a political appointee; but he was a local man named Kelly, who sorted mail himself with the aid of one of the Anderson girls, putting it in the little boxes through whose tiny glass apertures those who gathered for the twice-daily distribution could see him puzzling over letters as he peered through the spectacles that persisted in slipping far down his nose. When the last piece of mail was pigeonholed, he would throw up the window and peer dourly out at the demanders. He always seemed about to tell those who did not have lock boxes, and who therefore had to come to his window to ask for their correspondence, that there were receptacles for rent, and if they would rent them he would not need to be bothered. My father had a box, one of the large ones, but I always cringed when I caught Kelly's glance through the delivery window. He seemed to want to know what an irresponsible youngster was doing in his post office. I got out as quickly as I could, clutching the family bundle.

Neither the postmaster nor the music teacher was important to a small boy. But the high school principal was. He disposed of very real power. So, in quite another way, was the proprietor of Bargar's pharmacy. In the cool, herby depths of his cellar there were produced the incredible delights of the soda fountain; and he was, therefore, an individual to be propitiated. It did not detract from his charm that a large Newfoundland dog on a treadmill turned the freezer and that there was no objection, when a boy was careful not to be a nuisance, to his viewing the performance. To go back through the prescription room, down the back stairs, and to watch, perhaps even to help a little, in the manufacture of the ambrosial mixture—and then to be allowed to catch and consume the mellow gobs that melted from the dasher! Of such recompenses for life's harsher moments there are not many! The process was undoubtedly so unsanitary that later regulations would forbid it altogether. But by then the concoctions of the factories would have supplanted all the small home-contrived mixtures. They would be sold in drugstores under the same name and accepted by small boys who, alas, would never know anything better. So far as I am concerned, however, I long ago despaired of finding anything remotely like Jay Bargar's chocolate ice cream and, in season, strawberry. And that would be *wild* strawberry!

The gains and losses chargeable to the changes of which we who were then young lingered on the verge of are not easy to assess. We who were young in those years would know both; and the balance is not easy to strike. Anyway, the commitment to change had been made and there was no chance of reversal. We recall the familiar items of a life that, in retrospect, seems rich and satisfying; and we find that many of them have been exchanged for ones that are meretricious and disappointing. But when we are pressed we admit the gains in comfort, in mobility, and in security. People no longer starve or freeze even if their neighbors are not kindly; they no longer go to the poorhouse after lives spent in hard work; they live longer, have more amusements, and are more nearly citizens of the world. Our list of losses, however, is not entirely made up of nostalgic fancies. The neighborliness of village life gave us a sense of belonging to one another, and this satisfied a need now often unfilled. We developed ingenuity about the exploitation of our environment which modern gadgets have stifled. We were active in matters now become passive. We had less personal security, but we did not go in daily fear of vast uncontrollable dangers.

But lingering as we were in the last stages of a disappearing rural economy, and clinging to its customs, we still undertook —or enough of us did—the adventures which would change, reorganize, transform everything—work, ways of living, attitudes toward each other, kinds of ambitions and satisfactions. We believed in progress even more than in our customs; we abandoned them, even if sometimes slowly and reluctantly. The change was inexorable, however, and even those who were most recalcitrant made some sort of adaptation, or most of them did. Just the other day I met a lady who said she still made an apple pie every morning of her life, just as my mother did in 1895. This lady said, moreover, that she made her pies on a wood-burning cookstove—as, again, my mother had—and that it was nonsense to say that decent food could be prepared on an electric range. What floods of reminiscence this conversation loosed can only be imagined by my contemporaries. And they, sitting before their television sets and consuming frozen foods warmed up at a few moments' notice, minds at peace because of steadily arriving social security checks, will probably not care to be so disturbed. The balance of gains and losses will never be struck.

Five

My father and mother were about as exemplary a couple as any boy could have had for parents. They had married because of an attraction that was to last a lifetime. It was strong enough to resist erosion, competition, familiarity, and the radical difference in their interests. And I had the tremendous advantage —never thought of, but nevertheless real—of being part of a family so united that nothing but death could be imagined to affect its relations. It is true that my mother showed very little interest in my father's business affairs and that he had none in her literary bent, but this had no effect on our home. After all, my mother was a country girl, a wide-awake one, and she knew what was involved in my father's work. And although he must have been puzzled by her involvement with books and her gradual increase of interest in public issues, he never said so. If at first she may have tried to draw him into her enthusiasms, she soon gave up. So far as my recollection runs, there was an almost absolute separation of interests. Yet my father, even if he did not understand her preoccupation, was never critical. He withdrew when the conversation concerned such matters.

My mother, for all her romantic leanings, was an earnest housewife—not a very efficient one, perhaps, but energetic and well intentioned. The house was well kept in spite of being hardly used; and, in a day of generous provisioning, ours was a notably rich table. My father had nothing to complain of in that area, but he probably would not have complained anyway;

his tastes were so simple that they were hardly tastes at all. He had accepted things as his father and mother had had them; he accepted things as my mother preferred them. Yet he took the initiative in many innovations, and we were always the first family in town to have anything new.

It was somewhat the same way with our church affiliation. My father's mother had been a Baptist; yet we were affiliated with the Congregationalists. It was my father's—as it had been his father's—idea that religion was women's affair. Ours was certainly not the harsh Congregationalism to be read about in New England annals; it seems to me now to have been more the Unitarianism of the dissidents who left the church to be free of dogma. At any rate, it was a tolerant faith and made no strict theological demands. My parents conformed to the Protestant prohibitions in some respects. But in others they did not. There was no cardplaying in our home; but they seem to have liked to dance and to have gone often to parties where dancing was the main attraction. We were quite gay, take it altogether, and life was enjoyed without puritanical restraint.

My young father was very proud to have a son who, even though his health seemed precarious, was normal in every other way, fond of the activities other boys found fascinating and recalled by his father from his own youth. What my mother has never known, I think, is how close the bond between us was in those years. It was close because I found out very early how helpful it was to go to him for advice. It was always given carefully and seriously. My boyish sins were not very awful, but they seemed awful if they were carried as a secret burden. And the puzzles of developing sex carried overtones of guilt. Without making much of the matter, he explained that mine were the usual troubles and transgressions. The best way to meet them, he told me, was to share them with someone else, someone who had been through the same ordeal. The immense relief this was on many occasions, I am thankful for to this day.

These confessions must have been something like the Catholic ones made to priests. I was not exactly given absolution, but a burden was lifted that I may have been carrying for days or weeks. Since he knew all about me from these intimacies, in a way my mother did not—I never thought of consulting her in any moral crisis, and I have the impression that my father never told her of my delinquencies—I had a special relationship with him that lasted all through my boyhood and into my youth. Then too, there was my pride in him; he was young, good-looking, energetic, admired; I could feel that it was a good thing to be a Tugwell. It was a respected name, and now it was mine. Even though we lived very much together in our village and were so intermingled in everything we did that there were no class distinctions, there were some names that did not quite rank with Tugwell. The several professional men, I suppose, outranked us—the doctors and lawyers—but I do not recall that I ever heard of it. There were two of the lawyers who were hardly professionals at all because they were alcoholics and quite unreliable. But then there was Obed Edson, of whom I shall say more, who would have adorned the Bar in any community. The doctors, aside from their skills, were country folk and made no pretension to be otherwise. No, ours was a family of good standing.

I do not recall that my father ever told me that I ought not associate with boys who were chronic misbehavers. It would have been impractical. I was in school with them all day and I could hardly avoid them in our games. What he did tell me was that they were foolish and that he expected me to behave differently. It was effective advice. When, however, I did get into trouble, I went to my father. He told me, in effect, not to be so foolish again and proceeded to straighten out my involve-ment. He must have had some embarrassing interviews with offended old people and with parents of other boys, but he seldom even let me know what happened. I was to go and sin no more. It was strange for the time, but clearly he had no faith in punishment; in all my boyhood, I was disciplined seri-ously by him only twice, once when I told an outright lie, and once when I shirked outrageously some chores my mother had given me to do. Much more serious offenses were the occasion of consultation and repair of whatever damage there had been; but there was no punishment.

His love for me must have been intensified by the loss of his other sons, who died in infancy—Donald and Kenneth. They came along in succession to me; but one died at seven months and the other at two years, both of diseases not exactly diagnosed, but obviously infections that later would have been cured. I was often ill with infections, too, and I must have been the cause of fright whenever this occurred. Perhaps as a consequence I was spoiled—whatever that means. I got a good deal of attention and was rather more closely looked after than other boys; but a village was practically an extension of home, and I was free in it in a way no city boy could ever be. If my mother did not always know exactly where I was, she was not apt to become hysterical if I did not appear at an expected time. This became more the fact as I grew older, of course; by the time I was ten I was quite satisfactorily emancipated.

It was when I was obviously very ill that terror overcame her and I could see how frightened she was. I too recalled how my baby brothers had died. I had seen one die in her arms. And I had ridden in the carriage beside my father as he had carried the small coffin on his lap to the cemetery and helped to lower it into the ground. Such recollections are imperishable, but neither I nor my parents gave way to morbid anticipations. My father had his business to attend to, and my mother had her household. She was a courageous opponent of disease. Nothing done in those days could have been effective for my worst weaknesses, but it was a comfort to have her doing so briskly what was indicated by the doctor.

One bad fright, which might have made a scar, was almost entirely obliterated by my father's handling of it. He made it an adventure, something, almost, to brag about. One day in fall when I was about eight, Allen Hinchliffe and I were allowed to go with him on a short journey. He was visiting one of his leased pastures, he explained to us, where he had a herd of fattening steers—not that he needed to explain to me; I kept eagerly current in all such matters—which he had to dispose of for the winter. They were not yet right for market, or the price was too low. At any rate, he had to decide what he would do with them as winter came on. Allen and I took turns driving, a privilege we competed for. The horse was Ned, a big black gelding, a favorite of my father's because he could show exciting bursts of speed and yet was a tractable harness animal. The more usual turnout for country trips was a team of bays whose pace was slower but whose stamina was more suitable for all-day trips. But for this short run up into the hills and back, Ned was the choice; and once or twice we let him out. The rubber-tired runabout raised a cloud of dust, and we crossed the flats in what seemed like no time at all, soon coming to the haul uphill through the woods, now turning color. It was Saturday—no school—and we were on the road. My father was in good humor.

We arrived at the hilltop. My father climbed the rail fence and began poking among the steers and looking over the pasture, all a familiar process, but an absorbing one in which he lost himself completely. While he was gone, Allen got out too and climbed the fence. I sat for a while, then restlessly gathered up the lines and undertook to turn around in the narrow road so that we should be ready to start for home. I forgot that this would face Ned down a steep grade and bring the runabout close to his heels. There were high banks on either side, and I misjudged the distance for turning. One side of the rig canted; the wheels cramped, then came off the slope in a rush; Ned jumped in fright, then pulled ahead to escape. I dropped the reins so that I could cling to the seat, and they slithered over the dash and out of reach. Feeling no control from the lines, Ned jumped into the collar and started down the hill toward home on a dead run. The clatter was loud, and I roared. My father heard and emerged instantaneously from his preoccupation with the steers. He flew out from among them, leaped the fence, and met Ned at an angle just as he got fairly into his gallop. He launched himself from the road bank, caught the bridle, was carried and dragged for some distance, but soon brought the snorting and trembling horse to a stop. I was practically paralyzed but still holding on and quite unhurt. Allen was standing in the field still, like a statue. My father soothed and scolded Ned in low tones for a moment, then climbed in beside me. Allen, subdued and feeling that he should not have left me alone, hoisted himself to the seat. My father looked at Ned's still-quivering hindquarters for a moment and then said, "Say, did you see me clear that fence?"

For a man who was unlearned in the academic sense and who held himself to be severely practical in all his dealings, this, I have thought, was a remarkable exhibition of sensitivity and understanding. He had just made a tremendous effort, and he had an excited horse and two frightened boys within his responsibility. He would also have to deal with a perturbed and accusing mother when the incident became known at home. He got immediate control of himself, calmed the horse, reassured his charges—and took precautions for the future; he suggested that it might be better not to worry my mother. But, leading up to that, he deflated the incident by telling several stories of similar occurrences; runaways were common; he had seen many of them; ours was only another, and not a serious one at that. I am not sure that my mother ever heard of the adventure; if she did, it was not until long afterward. My father made sure of that by suggesting gently that if she did hear of it she might not want us to go on such trips any more. That made mutes of us; we even hesitated to brag about it to our friends.

I do, however, carry with me to this day the recollection of my father leaping that fence and diving at Ned's bridle, being dragged for many yards, and finally bringing him to a trembling halt. If his action had not been instantaneous he would have been too late; we would have passed the point from which he could leap, and Ned would surely have wrecked the runabout as he careened wildly down the road, more and more frightened by the swaying and clattering vehicle behind him. I would have been thrown out, and although I might not necessarily have been hurt, there was a good chance that I would have been.

Everything was normal within a few minutes, and on the way home we gave Ned another chance to see how fast he could trot—this time with the reins tight and his behavior strictly controlled. How quickly the springs of love surged up to set my father's whole being in action! I was more than ever, after that, his admiring slave.

This boyhood relationship with my father, I now realize, was extraordinarily easy. There was very little of the tension that sometimes makes communion difficult for both fathers and sons. There were several reasons for this, I suppose, besides his gift of understanding. Ours was a busy household, and my father's was a busy occupation. He was an enterpriser of the old-fashioned sort, always considering new ventures, turning his energies to whatever promised to yield a profit, and always, I may say, making money—not so much in these Sinclairville years as in the later ones I shall tell of; Sinclairville offered narrow scope for profitable deals. At any rate, he was always busy, and this, I think, made him easier in the family, and especially with me; he always had something to instruct me in, and I was always eager to learn. My bookishness did not interfere with these interests; rather, it enlarged them, gave them setting. They were part—as my books were—of a continuously fascinating series of events unrolling endlessly into the future.

But then too, my father and I shared a fascination with my mother's moods and vagaries that never failed, and this was a bond between us. She could be at one moment all smiles and favors and the next a stormy and offended victim of our neglect. We were seldom able to discover the causes of these rapid changes and were never really immune to the surprises they furnished; but we learned to suffer them with a certain stolid tolerance which was reinforced by our sharing of the experience. She realized this and often tried to gain the sympathy of one or the other in order to drive a wedge between us, but this we usually avoided, which added to her indignation. An enraged beauty is still a beauty, even if her diatribes seem utterly un-principled and unfounded. My father was often exasperated, and in forgetful moments he talked back. But this he was always sorry for; there was no way of winning a battle of words with my mother. The subject under review had a way of melting and being transformed into something entirely irrelevant; and the more unaccountable the transition, the greater the increase of indignation, so the only thing to do was to suffer in silence, although this was regarded as offensive also and was apt to be separately denounced. When I was involved in these outbreaks, I was more apt to react with counter-arguments; but I soon learned that these, if well based, would be ignored, and, if specious, would be denounced. However I might smart with injustice, I learned to dissemble and even to offer apologies. I might not mean them, but they offered the quickest way out.

I was not very old before the constant wonder furnished by my mother made us males feel more stable; and faced with the insoluble mystery of woman, we drew together. But there were compensations. When she was compliant, she was the source of such an outpouring of affection that it washed away all traces of resentment. None of her tantrums ever went uncompensated for long. On the whole, it made life interesting. In fact, I came to think that my father rather liked these manifestations of spirit. I suspect he knew all about them long before they were married. Somehow this suspicion rather deepens my admiration for him.

My mother's concentration on me might have been a smother-ing one if she had not had so many other interests and duties. Besides the household, she maintained a busy social schedule. The Reading Circle was one of her preoccupations; the church was another; she had a proprietary interest in the school; and she had many relatives and friends with whom she kept in touch. The result was that I was no more than normally supervised. She was, nevertheless, almost fiercely possessive, and this involved a certain unrealism about my abilities and

virtues that embarrassed both me and my father. She was
certain, for instance, that I was extremely talented in practically
every kind of endeavor, and she was just as insistent that
I had been born truthful, honest, generous, and kind. My
behavior, I need not say, often belied these attributions; but
by cultivating a certain blindness and by manipulating the facts
a little she managed to maintain her faith.

She had one weakness, however, which operated to break
up these patterns of prejudice, even her dogmatic belief in
my virtue. This was her sense of humor. It was always showing
her the comic element in others' behavior and revealing the
twists in events that made them ridiculous. She especially
enjoyed the discomfiture of the pompous and the staid. When
preachers, for instance, showed some human failing, it tickled
her risibilities. And she had robustious fun with spinsters and
bachelors in the community who were trying to entrap mates
or nimbly avoiding capture. She allowed politicians very little
leeway for falsity, and she even permitted my father to draw
on his small store of faintly scatological jokes in mixed company.
It was noticeable that her sense of humor tended to weaken,
however, when she herself was involved in something ridiculous
or when I, so much a part of herself, became entangled. My
father had some difficulty in distinguishing what was acceptably
funny from what was not. This was the more true because on
occasion she would be convulsed by some situation or some
story that he—and I—would have sworn would be inadmissible.
This capacity of hers was illustrated by an incident I cannot
actually recall but which I must have heard her recount a hundred times to circles of friends with every evidence of the keenest
enjoyment. Whether she ever quite realized how it contradicted
her fixed view of my virtues, we never knew. Such explorations
were blandly blocked.

It seems that one year when I cannot have been more than
four or five the spring broke early, the snow melted, and the
sun was strong. On a deceptively summerish day our small gang
was seized with a desire to go swimming—we called it swimming

—in one of the smaller branches of Mill Creek. The ice was hardly gone and the water was frigid, but we undressed and splashed around for an hour in the sunshine. Earl Roberts and I were helped in our dressing afterward by Earl's older sister Nina—what a girl was doing on a boys' expedition of this sort, I cannot imagine—a fact that came out when my mother was putting me to bed that night and discovered that my pants were on backward. This was so devastatingly funny because the front was obviously marked by a small hole with a flap and should have been noticed even by an older sister. It was this detail that overcame my mother's chagrin. I had concealed the excursion; I had exposed my susceptible system to the danger of a cold; worst of all, when I was asked how my pants happened to be on backward, I had pretended not to have the faintest idea how it could have occurred. Of course it all came out. But the obvious mistake made by a girl old enough to know better was so funny that whenever she thought of it my mother dissolved into helpless laughter. I escaped punishment. But I did not escape the embarrassment of hearing the incident recounted before company innumerable times. And my mother did not allow the obvious mendacity and deceit involved to influence her belief in my instinctive truthfulness. If mothers do not believe in boys, it is to be supposed that no one will. I could at least depend on one person who would always be rock-certain of my good conduct, whatever the facts might seem to indicate. But even I could be ridiculous, something I was never quite allowed to forget; it was probably quite good for me.

In the same circle of ample and respectable ladies who met to discuss whatever subjects the Chautauqua books encompassed, there came a time after the serious business was over when less elevated conversations were held. It might be getting close to the supper hour, and the tea-things would be back on the center table of the parlor, the cakes and cookies disposed of, with a short interlude of leisure to be enjoyed. Then husbands came in for mild rakings over, and the problems of children were explored. But occasionally the hearty laughter could be

heard that went with near-bawdy talk. There were being exchanged intimacies appropriate among married ladies. I recall
my mother telling her friends—I was reading in the sitting
room and my father was waiting for his supper; we were sitting
by the big base-burner stove—how when I was very small, she
had disposed of inquiries about my origin. Dr. Smith, she had
told me, had run across me lodged unaccountably in the hollow
of an overturned tree on Grandfather Smith's farm—which,
spread on the broad breast of a hill across the valley, could be
seen from our front porch. She had even pointed out the spot
to me, being carried away by her adeptness at narrative, and
going so far as not to be credible even to a seven year old. He
knew the Tugwells wanted a baby and so had brought him
around. It was not the first time I had heard the story; I had
been hearing it, in fact, for several years and had begun to
consider it an insult to my intelligence. As my mother's clear
voice reached us from the parlor, my father reached over and
cuffed me affectionately. We had a conspiracy, he seemed to
say. That was comfortable; it needed no elaboration. We
grinned at each other, and when my mother emerged to find
us innocently engaged in conversation and was inclined to be
suspicious, my father's indignant demand for food diverted her.

There was that about her—she was easily diverted. We often
used this tactic in self-defense. I must say, however, that it
failed in the worst crises. In these instances there was nothing
to be done but weather the blow as best we could. It never lasted
long, and she was never sullen afterward; in half an hour the
whole thing would be forgotten; but while it lasted it had the
force of a thunderstorm. We bent to the wind and waited for
the sun to reappear. In this particular case we averted the
potential danger.

The vulnerability of parents who have only one child must
be terrible. At the least, they have to guard against such an
outpouring of affection as will be too noticeable. But they are
more frightened in minor emergencies than the parents of
numerous children are; and, however hard they try to conceal

their special concern, it becomes obvious at times. We should have been a family of four; but after my brothers died, my sister did not appear for a couple of years, and these were ones when I was having measles, mumps, scarlet fever, and chicken pox, not to mention innumerable upper respiratory infections. There was special anxiety about a long siege of malaria too. Altogether, I must have kept the level of family anxiety pretty high and must have yielded a minimum of satisfaction. Another family story was often told which illustrates the heightened concern that centers in a single child.

When I was two or three I disappeared one afternoon. Search, at first casual, then worried, and finally frantic, failed to find me. My father was summoned from his business; after a while he enlisted his friends, and after about two hours the whole village had been turned out and was hunting in every likely place and some that were most unlikely. My mother was practically prostrated by her imagination, always lively enough, but in such cases monstrously inflamed, and was being comforted by hovering friends on the front porch. Suddenly the agitated women heard a small voice call from a nest of cushions in the nearby hammock under the trees in the front yard, and I turned out, rubbing my eyes as I emerged from the deep sleep of childhood, wondering what all the excitement could be about. It was a case in which no one could be blamed, certainly not me, and not even my mother for carelessness; yet the anticlimax of my appearance did make all the furor seem ridiculous and unnecessary. Some time was required to recall all the searchers and damp down the reaction. There was some muttered comment from the men, but the women found the occasion suitable for lemonade and cookies—which I shared. My mother was quickly restored, but she found it hard for some time after that to let me out of her sight. I was relieved when a baby sister appeared. She was eight years younger than I, and I could not very well express my real reason for approving her advent. There was no need. She was pretty and pink—a genuine English blonde—and even a small brother would be expected to find her acceptable. She performed her primary function very well, as I thought, by displacing me as the center of solicitude. I was coming to an age when freedom was essential to my dignity.

It had seemed to me more and more as I grew older that my freedom was unnecessarily restricted. I wanted to regulate my own activities, and these inevitably spread into new territory. I began to go afield on Saturdays with Jake Evans or with others; excursions into the woods or to the homes of boys who lived out in the country seemed more and more desirable. At Bemus Point my adventures on the lake or up and down its shores in the nearby creeks and swamps lengthened in both time and distance. I acquired a bicycle, and that gave me much greater range. My mother gave way with some petulance, but my father was on my side unless I caused what seemed to him undue worry. My point was gradually established, and as my sister increasingly occupied my mother's attention—my father was practically fatuous about her in a way that seemed to me extreme and in doubtful taste—I had less difficulty from restriction.

How much difference it made to me as an adult that I won a certain freedom of decision for myself as a boy can be expressed only in indefinite terms, but it was immense. As I look back from near life's end I am certain that no choice affecting my ways or my work was ever much entered into by anyone else. I made up my own mind out of my own experience and on my own responsibility and, furthermore, almost always without asking for advice. This may or may not have had uniformly good results, but that the choices were my own has a certain significance. My sons have been tested and advised from their first entry into the educational system, and it seems likely to continue indefinitely as they go on in their occupations. It was not so when I was young. From my first struggle for freedom as a young boy, duplicated, I am sure, by most of my contemporaries, I—and they—was granted the characteristic American right to make up my own mind and follow my own judgments. If we had some wisdom and if initiative came naturally to us, we made good use of this freedom. Not all of us were always wise, and some of us never were, and initiative had various degrees of intensity. But it planted in us, and allowed to grow, that independence and self-reliance a democracy must have, it seems to me, to *be* a democracy.

I seldom am heard to say that the good old days were really better than later ones, but in this matter of deciding I have no doubt that what we reached for and got was of the utmost importance. It is, after all, the individuals of this world who are its irreducible units. Everything that is sought or done is for them. If it is done by them or with their express consent, it will have the authentic title it must acquire to be accepted and permanent. Otherwise it will always be in jeopardy, subject to upheaval and revolt. This is the argument for democracy. It seems to me incontrovertible. People acquiring their own information, making their own decisions—even to delegate—and establishing their own institutions seem to me to have reached the ultimate relationship with each other. The problem of future generations will be to preserve this relationship in the difficult circumstances of an increasingly crowded and complex civilization.

I certainly had no such thoughts as these when I was a boy. But I did have the instinct to ask for my rights as an individual. That I was allowed to acquire them may have been more good luck than anything else; but most of that good luck was being born when I was and in the circumstances of village life with family connections of a fortunate sort. Does retrospective affection make mine seem to have been an unusually happy family to have been born into? I do not think so. I had a growing freedom, which gradually became very nearly absolute; but I also had some discipline. I had security and fondness that I could count on even when I was unwise or when I misbehaved. There were humor and worldliness, respect for achievement, tolerance and kindness as well as piety and a sense of tradition. I could be proud of my parents and inordinately proud of my country. I was part of them and would be a good and productive, an honorable, part. I seethed with ambitions that were nonetheless powerful for being still unfocused, and this came, at least partly, from the encouragement I was given to explore, to question, to think that everything about me could be improved. It was always taken for granted that I would do very remarkable things to help in this. I took it for granted myself.

Unfortunately, freedom, along with its advantages, has it drawbacks. People young and old are quite capable of making choices which have disastrous consequences both for themselves and for others. I should never have a moment when I doubted that democracy, resting on the free choices of individuals agreeing to act in concert, was the best, the only admissible, political system. But that its fortunes rested on the wisdom of majorities that might be mistaken was undeniable. The way to avoid this was not to give up democracy; it was to make decision-making a wiser process. To this conclusion about one fundamental I came thus early and never had reason to doubt.

Six

Democracy simply will not work without a certain machinery. If everyone is to participate in its decisions (and participation is the test of democracy), and if these decisions are to make it operate successfully, there must be information, available to everyone, and an educational system that will enable its citizens to use it. Arranging for full and unprejudiced information is not easy, and it is so expensive to build and maintain free schools that there are always bogglers to contend that the end is not worth the cost. Countries have seldom set out to attain really wide participation, and even the framers of our Constitution had no such intention. They meant to establish a republic, and they spoke of a people's government; but actually a democracy was the last thing Washington, Franklin, Madison, Morris, and Hamilton, for instance, wanted. It was not until the backwoodsmen from the frontier, the common folk of the farms and villages, and the city workers made themselves felt through new leaders that the electorate began to be widened.

There was a national expansion in the period between Jefferson and Jackson, but it became overwhelming and revolutionary in the 1830s. In their exuberance the common people during these years seized more power than they could use with even a minimum of wisdom. Their interpretation of the equality mentioned in the Declaration of Independence was a literal one. This resulted in some weird behavior; and governmental institutions, infiltrated by ignorant, and often

corrupt, spoilsmen, were nearly ruined. The fallacy of this sort
of equality was proved in this vast and costly experiment. It
was in the aftermath that education began to be put forward
as the means for creating a more reliable people's government.
Education would develop differences, allow some to go ahead
if they could, and place those who could not in useful situations, but its universality would be a guarantee that there would
be equal opportunity. And for those democrats who were
expected to vote, the resulting literacy would open out new
sources of civic information.

Nothing in America was so universally agreed, when I was
a boy, as that education was desirable. This was not always
because it was indispensable to democracy; indeed it was more
often because it was a way to get ahead. And it fitted not only
a social but an economic pattern. Free enterprise was competitive, and success in competition had begun to depend on
education—merely literacy at first, then the three R's, but, before
long, an acquaintance with more advanced subjects. It was
quite clear, when I came along, that education was desirable
and that everyone should have as much of it as he could
absorb and could contrive to get. The institutions for this purpose were still in a primitive stage, perhaps, but there was no
complacency about that, and the intention to improve was
being shown everywhere and all the time.

Like so much else, schooling was largely a local responsibility
and, consequently, far from uniform. Some communities were
ahead of others because they had more resources and some
because they had better leadership. These differences had become so deplorable that New York was setting state-wide
minimum standards and even giving financial aid to the more
backward districts. I myself was hardly conscious that there was
any authority higher than our own School Board, except that a
stranger occasionally appeared at Assembly and was introduced
by the principal as the superintendent. He never said anything
of interest. He must have been what I afterward learned to
call a presence. If he had any directions to give, they were given

to the Board or to the principal in private; but perhaps it did linger in all our minds that some higher ranges of Providence existed than those we saw every day. How far his commission reached, I am not clear, since our Board seemed always to be in lively charge, full of intrigue, and with a perennial quarrel going on between those who would enlarge and those who would contract expenditures. My parents were always on the side of expansion, and I grew up with a prejudice against skinflints and penny pinchers in all matters of public concern. My father had even more picturesque names for some of the individuals involved, and I used to watch them passing on the roads and streets with some wonder that such villains could appear so unconcerned about their sins. It never occurred to me that some of them may have felt it a virtue to check extravagances and may not have been exclusively intent on holding down their taxes.

One of these controversies occurred when Fred Hannum was replaced as principal of the school (about 1900). The whole village took sides, and my parents were pro-Hannum, almost savagely so. It may have been a good cause. They always told me that the issues had to do with innovations that Hannum insisted on. These were objected to by a minority; but villification eventually made the poor man's situation untenable. Anyway, he found himself a better job in Pittsburgh, as principal of a larger school, and left. My parents always felt that they had been defeated by his leaving, although the needed changes were successfully advocated by the next man. What infuriated my father most was that certain extraneous issues crept in. He said that there was really nothing against Hannum except that he smoked cigarettes and that this was no one's business except his own—which surprised me some, because my father never smoked and my mother was pretty well set against liquor, tobacco, and cardplaying during those years. So perhaps they were not so much tolerant as just Hannum's friends; I have no idea whether he was a competent principal, except that he had a long and honorable career in the profession of teaching, and I must suppose that he was.

There is a kind of addendum to be made to the Hannum episode. During the next year, when he was well settled in his new post, we went to visit the family in Pittsburgh. It was my first long trip by train and, I think, my first visit to a considerable city, although I also visited Buffalo during the exposition in 1901, just before President McKinley was assassinated. Threading through department stores with my mother and moving about the crowded streets was an exhilarating experience. But there was another which was not so happy. My mother, after my father had gone home and left us for an extra week, fell all the way down a flight of stairs and broke an ankle. I was not there at the time and so was spared the fright I might have experienced; she was comfortable, even if bitter against fate, when I came back to the house. It meant that we had to stay another two weeks, I believe, and in that time I got around Pittsburgh—including the steel mills—pretty thoroughly.

Everything in Pittsburgh was on a gigantic scale. The city was darkened by smoke in the daytime and lighted by flaring chimneys at night. It was grimy and gloomy and had some shocking slums. We rode on trolleys and walked—Hannum escorting me and another lad—through the workers' streets to the mills and were admitted through gates which might have been the entranceways to prisons. All within was a roaring inferno, the furnaces huge and menacing, the cranes monstrously revealed through clouds of smoke and steam, and tiny human creatures laboring within and around the vast erections which produced the metal. It was hard to conceive that iron could be molten and run redly through troughs as it poured out of retorts like so much glowing soup. I watched it all with open mouth and went away numbed by the overwhelming impact of the immense structures and their mysterious processes. Men, we heard, worked in that confusion twelve hours a day; and once a week there was a swing shift, when they worked straight through for twenty-four hours. Even at that time, when most laborers were used to working from dawn to dark, this was an incredible feat; I was told that those who were able to endure it were proud of their survival. But that there was another side to that story, I did not need to be told even then.

Pittsburgh, however, counted for education. This was another world for me. That I was thus early introduced to it gave me an inoculation against industrialism which was undoubtedly useful to a country boy. On a later visit to a distant relative in Dunkirk who worked at Brooks's, I was further indoctrinated. This cousin operated from a high cabin one of the mighty cranes that carried partly finished locomotives down a cavernous building. They swung in the air with no more appearance of weight than so many toys and eventually stood in the yards outside, crouched in their new paint, ready to haul the trains to which they would be appointed. He was proud of his machine and of his ability to manipulate it. This was something I readily understood. I thought it admirable, too; his was a responsible job. But he lived in a poor way, I thought, for so important a contributor to engine building—a tiny flat above a store, not at all comparable to the spaciousness, at least, if not the comfort, of Sinclairville houses, even those of workers.

But a boy's education includes other experiences than the pleasant ones of school, reading, travel, and games. It was when I came back from Pittsburgh, after my several weeks' stay, and was inclined to brag about my experiences, that another cousin, a boy who was a year older, suddenly conceived a distaste for my air of superiority and undertook to reduce my ego. He succeeded, too. I had always been competent enough in a scuffle and had no particular fear of taking a blow or two; but this was different. It became a campaign. Every time he met me he precipitated an attack, and he was enough older and stronger so that I could not devise any good defense. He beat me up badly several times and, what was worse, destroyed my morale. I had just been thinking well of myself as a sophisticated traveler. The comedown was anguishing. I felt the shame of cowardice, but I was quite unable to do anything about it. I took pains to keep out of my tormentor's way; once or twice I ran; and I began to be taunted by my friends who had never seen me in such a state before. This was an interlude, lasting several weeks, which I have never been able to forget. I dreamed of fights in which I trounced my tormentor; my mind was a seething chaos of fear; everything was tainted and distorted.

There had to be an end; and one day, cornered in the schoolyard, I really fought back. It surprised him so that it was he who this time broke off. I had not exactly won, but I felt a return of the courage that seemed to have deserted me. I persuaded my father to buy me a punching bag and presently I confided in him how craven I had been. I grew faster than that cousin, and what with my practicing and my returning confidence, I could soon meet him without the old impulse to run. When the inevitable happened, and others egged us on to have it out, I did not come out too badly and was at least rehabilitated in my esteem. This taught me to sympathize with the betraying cowardice that sometimes, in most peoples' lives, takes hold and deforms their behavior. What they do then, I had learned, is something they cannot help; they are living in an agony only they know of, that blinds them to ethical canons and undermines their resistance to indignity. It is at once the most pitiable of states and the one least likely to attract understanding and sympathy.

It can be seen that before I was very far along in my growing up I had begun to have some experience of the wider world, not very extensive and not very deep, yet serving to make me aware that our community was a small and unimportant part of a much larger and more consequential society. I was aware, also, very early that it would not be the scene of my future life. Wherever my ambitions might tend, they would run beyond the village and the valley. It may have been that my having my kind of mother and father produced this rather curious result, giving me a freedom only sons are not supposed to have. I had the best of village life, among friends and well-known families; but I was being led, through reading and some travel, to think of myself as a temporary resident, one destined at some time or other for different scenes. My mother was a romantic; I shared her moments of dreamy transport, but it was a kind of indulgence. My father was severely practical; I followed his dealings with sharp interest, but I myself expected to have larger ones some other place.

The importance of this was that I became independent. In spite of the security and fondness I could count on, I was conscious of having a separate existence even before my ambitions had any recognizable focus. Unfortunately, such a separateness, along with its advantages in helping an individual to become adult, has its drawbacks. People young and old are quite capable of making choices whose consequences are unfortunate not only for themselves but for others; and willful youngsters are very apt indeed to make them.

I do not see how anyone could have predicted whether I would turn out to make decent choices, except that I came from a respectable family, and that is only a partial guarantee. I do not know whether it is significant that no one of the boys I knew in Sinclairville became a delinquent as a youth or a criminal as an adult. Some of them had restricted lives; they became workers and small, rather indigent farmers and did not advance. But they occupied those stations with dignity; and although many of them fell into poverty as farming declined and the situation of workers failed to improve notably during their working lives, they remained respectable contributors and citizens.

This did not mean that their decisions would always be wise; they may have voted against needed public works, against those who would have improved county and state government, and against the challenging candidates on the national tickets of those years. What shall we say of this? There were some indefensible choices. Take Grant, for instance, long before my generation could vote; or McKinley, who was elected as a safe reactionary in 1896 and again in 1900; or Harding and Coolidge, who were candidates I later felt very strongly to be unworthy. During all that time the electorate was making gross mistakes, and no body of them was more determined in error than those of Chautauqua County.

But these political decisions were made by a democracy in full functioning, and it was customary to say that if there were mistakes those who made them were entitled to their views. The question would intrude itself, later in my lifetime whether, if the continued existence of the race was at issue, democracy's mistakes ought to be risked. This would pose an old question in excruciating form: the argument that people must be allowed their errors because, after all, it was they who had to suffer and they would not learn to be wiser in any other way became absurd. If extinction of mankind should result, what would become of the theory along with the practice? But that was still a long way in the future, and in the 1890s political choices, even national ones, involved no more than partiality in government, or at the worst corruption, and did not bear heavily on remote villages. That a weak President might soon allow a useless war to occur could not have been forecast when McKinley succeeded Cleveland; but the war, when it came, was one that was overwhelmingly approved, however foolish it may appear to later generations.

But I speak of the more distant consequences of the freedom and independence into which I was graduating as I grew up. Of more importance to me was its exercise in my own life and its consequences on my own career. When, for instance, I began to show resistance to progress in arithmetic and a corresponding facility with words, my neglect of the one and cultivation of the other was accepted as natural. No one told me that the remarkable achievements I hoped to accomplish might very well have been made impossible by my lack of appetite for the preparation required. I was not only not made to do anything I disliked, I was not warned that this might have unpleasant consequences.

In later years, after advances in transportation and communications had drawn the nations closer together and there was almost daily interchange of information, our democracy became self-conscious about its purposes; and there were many who wondered whether we could survive as a nation in the world if we failed to develop a defined aim and had no discipline for gaining it. There was preaching about it, and President Eisenhower appointed a Committee on National Goals. Eisenhower was not much of a thinker and he responded in this matter to a demand he obviously did not understand. Freedom, equality, universal participation—the conditions of democracy—were not ones a nation's regimented efforts could establish. No amount of exhortation would persuade people to be tolerant, to love justice, and to be charitable. Those are characteristics that must spread gradually and from other causes. True democracy results from mutual respect; and freedom, as Aristotle said, has its roots in courage. What I should have had, as all my generation should have had, was the assurance that the virtues we heard about on Sunday were valid for the rest of the week, and that courage was the support of conscience. Our nation was rooted in mutual aid, and we heard from the minister about good will; but at other times we were urged to forge ahead on our own. We went to school to acquire the means of competing with others. Our parents indoctrinated us in the shrewd practices of business. Thus the Protestant ethic was ruptured at its center. What would become of a people who professed one system of morals and practiced another?

The struggle between these systems would go on throughout my lifetime. Democracy would exist in perilous circumstances, threatened constantly by those who spoke of freedom but meant to have it only for themselves. Yet there was something in the American make-up which would not let it go. Men were always demanding to make their own decisions; they were always falling away from the canons of competition and self-interest to help each other; and they never seemed quite convinced that getting on in the world—making places and fortunes for themselves—

was enough. Even the most successful fortune makers usually gave away most of what they had so ruthlessly acquired.

Going to school day after day, playing games, going summers to Bemus Point, I gradually absorbed the idea that in getting on in the world I should also be making myself a good citizen. The Union that had been fought for so short a while ago, the nation that Washington had almost singlehandedly, it seemed, brought into existence—helped, of course, by John Jay, Ben Franklin and others—was part of me and I was part of it. When I sang its songs in school or on social occasions, when I read of its heroes, when I heard of all its distant wonders—the mountains, prairies, rivers, and bordering seas—the swelling pride in my heart was sometimes almost too much to conceal.

Seven

One of the sharpest distinctions in my mind between the conditions of my early boyhood and those which have gradually succeeded them is the conquest of anxiety and of the pain undergone by anyone who was injured or was seriously ill. How quickly we accept such advances! And how quickly we forget how such things used to be! In this connection I think of a terrible sickness known to us as lockjaw. Many persons in our valley died of it, and a more horrible death in a lonely farmhouse it would be impossible to imagine. But hardly less dreaded was rabies or, for that matter, blood poisoning, which followed so many of even the simplest injuries. These were practically uncontrollable, all involved excruciating pain, and once the disease had seized on its victim it progressed relentlessly to convulsive death.

Some of the lesser infections were almost as terrifying. We were vaccinated for smallpox, but diphtheria and scarlet fever had to be expected for nearly every child, and the lingering doom of consumption was known in many families. Ours was spared lockjaw and rabies; but we had to survive, if we could, many other diseases. It was not always possible. My mother's beautiful sister and my Grandmother Tugwell both died of consumption. One of my earliest recollections is of a frail old lady, cradled in a rocking chair and muffled in quilts, coughing her life away in our living room.

But awful as were the anxieties associated with diseases whose end was so certain, the reality of pain was even worse. It is quite impossible for later generations to conceive the courage required to endure the hurts of injury with any semblance of fortitude. And to face an operation, even a minor one, it was necessary to summon all the reserves an individual possessed— and a boy's reserves were, I am afraid, soon exhausted. For one thing, anesthetics were crudely administered. The fright from a nose cone held by force over a struggling youngster's face was justified by the postoperative sickness as well as the pain from the wound.

It was thought that my disposition to suffer from sore throats, bronchitis, and other heavy respiratory infections might be relieved if my swollen tonsils and stifling adenoids were removed. So one time I was taken to Jamestown, where a specialist operated on me in his office. There was slight pleasure in the unprecedented experience of staying overnight at the Jamestown House. I was too demoralized to enjoy any of it. There was a kind of dentist's chair in the doctor's office and an array of frightful-looking instruments in a glass cabinet. Also, there was a penetrating smell of antiseptics and, as I recognized, of the chloroform I was going to have to inhale. The doctor was businesslike, but there was a nurse who was sickeningly reassuring. I was not in the least fooled, and going under was just as bad as I remembered it to be from other experiences. When I woke up with blood welling in my throat and the back passages of my nose raw from scraping, I thought the hell I had heard a good deal about from my Baptist relatives could have been no worse. I had to go back to that office next day, after bleeding more or less all night in a hotel room, to be looked over and poked at again. It was all inexpressibly horrible.

I should be able to report that there was dramatic improvement in the condition it had been intended to cure. Unfortunately, there was no noticeable difference, and I had to conclude that my well-intentioned tormentors had been guessing. I indicated as much to Dr. Smith, but all he had to say was that he hoped I would not hold it against him. All the city doctors were recommending tonsillectomies, and it had certainly been a good thing to get rid of the adenoids. He seems to have had some idea that I would become a doctor, because he said, "When you have to do these things they will be done a lot better. There's a lot of progress going on." But I was unconvinced and resentful.

My affection for Dr. Smith was not diminished. I blamed the specialist in Jamestown. But that may have been because Burt Smith was my closest friend, whose house was almost as familiar to me as my own. And Dr. Smith at home was a wonderful companion for his boys and for me, although he had very little time to devote to us: he was always being called out on emergency cases just when we had begun a game or he had started on a tale. At such times we went out to the stable with him while the horses were hitched up and closed the doors when he was gone. But we knew he would not be back for hours. We might as well find something else to do. That game or that story would never be finished.

Our doctors often had to face the certain death of farmers who had wounded themselves with implements they used continually and had infections as a result. They carried their chloroform with them on their country rounds and operated as best they could when there were emergencies, but the percentage of success could not have been high. And such patients, dying in agony, tended by terrified relatives, was something frequently reported. This hazard was somewhat less in the village, because the doctor was nearer and more apt to be consulted early enough for cleansing or cautery in the case of wounds and early operation in appendicitis or other internal infections. But still disease and death were familiar and terrible to endure for everyone concerned. Almost no one was hospitalized; the nearest such institution was at Jamestown, and getting there was a different matter than it would have been in a modern ambulance. But I recall that Charlie Smith, the doctor's own son, did die after an operation in a Jamestown hospital. His appendix burst on the way, and peritonitis, then practically incurable, set in. Dr. Smith always blamed himself for not operating immediately in his own office.

My parents took all the precautions available to them. But all four of my mother's babies were born in our upstairs bedroom, and my father almost died there of what was probably a kidney infection. It was a room which had seen much suffering as well as the many delights of married life. I was allowed to spend some of my days of illness in the large bed, and almost every morning when I was very small I climbed in between my parents for such time as I could persuade them to delay getting up. I recall going off into the nightmare of delirium in that bed when my fever was high. I clung tightly to my mother's hand as I emerged momentarily and was terrified of going under again. But my worst experiences of almost unendurable pain are not associated with that room or that bed.

There was the time, for instance, when I jumped off the woodshed, which was being reroofed, onto a pile of old shingles and landed on a rusty nail that went all the way through my foot. My father was sent for and brought the doctor, who was fortunately in his office and not on his rounds. I was laid on the old couch in the living room—the one my grandfather had lain down on one day after his noon meal and had died on, in his sleep—and the doctor told me that what he had to do was going to hurt. I said something which was taken to be brave, but I soon dissolved in terror when I understood that he meant to burn out the wound. I fought the chloroform and through its fumes was conscious of the excruciating pain of the red-hot wire run all the way through the wound. For days I relived the experience over and over. The cautery worked; at least tetanus was avoided. But the awfulness of the descent into half-consciousness and suffering I still recall. How different it has been when my children have had accidents! They might not have liked the necessary injections or the cleansing of the wound, but they were never allowed to endure such pain.

Regular patients in those days had an intimacy with their physicians which went deeper than all the superficialities; their courage was cruelly tested and all their weaknesses were exposed. The doctor's compassion needed to be endless, his understanding complete. I still feel that Dr. Smith probably knew me better, seeing me in delirium, writhing in pain and weak from infection, with all my defenses breached, than anyone else can ever have known me. As I grew older, things improved. There were new ways of controlling fevers, of relieving pain, of avoiding infection. There could be more hope in formerly hopeless situations; and the suffering need not be so absolutely demoralizing. Even with his doctor, a patient could maintain some pretense of bravery. But it was not so when I was a boy. The best treatment had to be brutal and had to expect of the patient a stoicism almost no one possessed, and often the doctor had simply to sit by while death crept relentlessly into the chamber.

Another sharply recollected struggle with pain happened in the otherwise happy environs of Bemus Point. I jumped off the end of our dock one day onto the open shell of a fresh-water clam. The wound was a large one and the cut was deep. It had been in contaminated water, and the doctor did not see it for some time. It was not Dr. Smith this time but the Bemus Point physician, Dr. Schofield. He had to hurt me pretty badly, and I still recall my demoralization as the waves of pain involved in cleansing, cautery, and stitching had to be endured.

But there was a compensation for suffering. A boy got sympathy and attention he might not otherwise have had. If the hurt was hard to bear, the convalescence, if it did not last too long, was luxurious. And for others who went through the ordeals of accident or illness together, there was a knowledge of each other's compassion that people in other circumstances might never have learned. These days, people are whisked to hospitals and undergo their ordeals essentially alone; but also they are helped through their crises by healing and stupefying drugs. Many of the sharp and agonizing experiences of life that we knew have almost disappeared from human experience.

Something has been lost by the virtual passing from the scene of the family doctor. The species still exists, but he has undergone a considerable change. Dr. Smith carried in his head the life histories of many families; he helped bring their members into the world, tended all their illnesses, and eased their passage from life as best he could. He was a universal friend, always ready to listen when there were troubles to be aired, gentle with the frightened, jocose with boys and men, free with the kind of advice that strengthened us for our ordeals. He never lost his sageness, never became flustered, and always seemed to bring calm and confidence into the houses he visited. It cannot be that all doctors were so reliable and so wise. But the two that I knew best by early boyhood were examples to all their neighbors, and this in spite of their inability to do much that was remediable in many of the situations they were called on to meet.

Dr. Schofield in Bemus Point, as well as Dr. Smith in Sinclairville, was this kind of physician. While I was laid up with my wounded foot, he took me with him a number of times on his country rounds. He gave me what I am sure were much-modified accounts of his patients' illnesses. I usually waited outside for him, but sometimes I was asked in and given some sort of treat. Afterward the doctor would tell me about the patient, on the assumption—he too, for some reason—that I might grow up to be a physician. I seemed to be the sort, he said, and I couldn't begin too early. "You can't learn half of it in medical school," he told me, and he explained why. It was the understanding of the patient and the treatment of his anxiety as well as his disease, it seemed, that couldn't be learned in school. "But never be a country doctor," he advised me. "You are not likely to be called until it is almost too late, or else you can't do any good because the disease in incurable; and you have all those winter roads to drive over—hours and hours of stumbling through drifts in zero weather—and if it isn't snow it's mud. A city doctor can sit and wait for his patients to come to him, mostly, or get them into a hospital where he doesn't have to worry about simple diet and cleanliness as I do." But Dr. Schofield stayed there at Bemus Point until he died suddenly one day, still looking after the country people who needed him so badly.

It was a fine family. Mrs. Schofield was fussy, motherly, and kind all the way through. She had three daughters, a few years older than I, but her concern extended far beyond the girls of her household. Between them, the elder Schofields illustrated the finest of human traditions, a selfless love for others which seemed to have no limits. No physician in such circumstances could possibly accumulate much wealth—he was lucky if he could collect enough of his fees to feed and house his family— but somehow the Schofield girls managed to scrabble their way through enough education to open out careers for themselves— which they abandoned, all of them, for good marriages. As women, they carried on their parents' tradition of service; one married a minister, one a doctor, the other, I think, a teacher. But when I knew them, they were the kind of lively, vital, good-looking young women I saw so much of in my own home. Bessie, the oldest, was tall and a little grave; Bernice, the middle one, was inclined to be plump and was gay and out-going; Georgia, the youngest, who married the minister, was as lovely as a lily and as sweet as the larkspur her eyes might remind you of. The three of them grouped with their mother on the wide porch that looked out on the lake, chattering with innocent freedom, is a picture I shall always carry in my recollection. The Schofields were our only intimate family friends at Bemus Point. There were others—for instance, the Pickards, who were the proprietors of one of the summer hotels in the row along the lake front; but none were among the close circle my mother held together without apparent effort.

I am sure that the more severe risks of disease, pain, and early death in those days were one of the differences from later living that were significant, just as neighborly closeness was. The sharing of terrible experiences knitted neighbors together in a way not known to our suburban civilization. There were many expressions of this solidarity in loss and sickness. One I recall most clearly was the gift of funeral meats. When there was a death in the home, every neighbor prepared a dish of some sort and brought it with her on a visit of condolence. It might be a pan of baked beans, a ham or a roasted chicken, a cake, a pudding, a couple of pies—anything of the sort. The idea was, I suppose, that the housewife would be too distraught to cook for her family or too much involved in the funeral arrangements; at any rate, there might be enough offerings of this sort to last for a week. It may have been no more than a custom, grown mechanical, but surely it represented an original impulse to share another family's grief and to be helpful in emergency.

The Schofield family took me into their household when the doctor thought I ought to have more care than I could have in the cottage we shared with so many others. The girls treated me like a younger brother, or perhaps better than younger brothers are usually treated, and they let me go with what appeared to be the greatest reluctance. And at times when we had sickness in the house in Sinclairville, the neighbors came in and took over many duties; the women did the housework, and often the men sat up with patients who needed care during the night, allowing exhausted members of the family to have some rest. Such a thing as a professional nurse was not known among us; but there were many amateur ones who prided themselves on their handiness in the sickroom. And when a baby was due to be born, the event was participated in by most of the prospective mother's friends. In lesser emergencies, too, there was wide sharing. If for some reason an entertainment was to be staged—a birthday, an anniversary, a party for a visiting relative—there was a flutter of women in the house which made it an exciting place for those who lived there.

One important effect of all this togetherness was that everyone was intimately known to everyone else. The idiosyncrasies that might escape notice in another environment were commonly understood. This is why, I suppose, I still recall so well the three or four individuals who were alcoholics and were supposed to have sacrificed valuable careers to their weakness; it is why, also, the Landers twins, becoming elderly when

I was a boy, who worked as clerks in Crofoot's, were tolerantly ticketed as "ladylike." I could name perhaps fifty other individuals, without the least hesitation, who had some such identifying peculiarity. Knowledge of this sort made the whole village an extension of the family. Its people differed—some were queer, some were admirable, some we could have done without—but all belonged to us and we to them. Whatever the significance of this, it would be much modified by the changes of the next generation.

I conclude that latter-day folk have a less comprehensive knowledge of human nature at first hand and probably, for this reason, less tolerance. There is less sense of belonging, and those who differ from the norm in important respects are more apt to be regarded as subjects for coercion of some sort. We have lost the willingness to let them live along with us in their own way so long as they conform to a minimum of community requirements and be taken care of by their relatives. For our alcoholics and for the homosexual twins we had a kind of amused and kindly protectiveness. We did not expect them to change; but we did not expect to ostracize them.

If these characteristics of preponderant American life in the last decade of the nineteenth century are projected into a wider field, it can be understood why we had then less need of some elaborate and costly institutions we have since felt it necessary to establish and maintain. Hospitals, schools, recreation arrangements, highways, and many other such facilities can almost be said not to have existed then. Hospitals were for emergencies, and there were few of them; schools had no mission to prepare children for life; recreation was something people found for themselves; highways were locally built and maintained, mostly by shared labor. So it went. The vast organization of social life to which people would soon become accustomed was not yet in existence. One consequence of this was that there were hardly any taxes to be paid. If the cemetery, the library, the fire department, and the band were to be maintained, it was done by contributions or by non-govermental fees for service.

Even the government at larger centers, at Mayville (the county), Albany (the state), and Washington (the nation), was by later standards rudimentary. There were small budgets, few employees, and restricted duties. This did not mean that policies were not matters of controversy or that political campaigns did not generate heat. But it meant that what was argued over amounted to minimal proposals—in a later view. No matter what was decided about any of the issues, national survival was not in question—not even when other nations were boldly challenged, as Cleveland had challenged Germany over a South American issue involving the Monroe Doctrine. Nor was anyone's life or career likely to be jeopardized by one or another choice. Progress might be involved; but even about that, the choice was usually for somewhat more or somewhat less. There had been consequential issues in the past, many of them; there would be more in the future; but at the moment there were none of nation-shaking importance. Even the Spanish war, the first exciting issue I can at all recall, was not of the sort represented by the quarrel between North and South, for instance; it was a punitive expedition, undertaken indignantly, but without any genuine sense of risk. Partly for this reason, it was embarrassingly inefficient. More soldiers, by far, were stricken by sickness than by the enemy's weapons. And both leadership and organization were miserably ineffective. At home, we tried to keep our minds on our heroes; but they were not authentic ones, as we could not help but know. Still, the knowledge that it made but little difference, after all, reduced the demand for reform and tended to hide the national disgrace. Our interest was temporary in any case. We were immersed in our own affairs. These were to us the important matters, and we were only momentarily diverted to larger but distant concerns.

Eight

H. G. Wells would remark when he got to the sociological phase of his writing, that civilization was in a race between education and disaster. I should say that the determining stretch of the race was being run just before and just after the turn of the century. It was then that the scientists were opening out the approaches to nuclear theory, were realizing the implications of evolution, and were beginning to question the hard outlines of Newtonian physics. In America, Agassiz had been bested by Asa Gray, for instance, and Thorstein Veblen was upsetting the received doctrines of classical economics. Wells by then was already middle-aged and had written some entrancing fiction in the Jules Verne tradition, but none of it can have been in our library, and I did not discover it until I was well along in my teens.[1] Even if I had, it would not have led me before then to his wonderfully lucid expositions of liberal political philosophy. As a matter of fact, *Tono-Bungay,* the first sardonic account of business practice in England, was not published until 1909, and his *Research Magnificent,* which went straight to the heart of every young radical, was a good deal later.

There was a critical literature, of course, but I had as yet no use for it, being normally busy with a boy's affairs. But it was not any lack of this sort that kept education in its accustomed routines. It was mostly that our society had not yet got around

[1] *The Time Machine* was published in 1895, *The Invisible Man* in 1897, and *The War of the Worlds* in 1897, but these were English editions and would have circulated in America somewhat later.

to training its educators and building adequate schools. Both were improving, but neither had yet got far enough to be of much use in the future crises of democracy when the children of my generation would become the responsible statesmen of the Republic.

For instance, Harry S. Truman out in Missouri was already finished with all the schooling he would ever get. It was already too late for him to have been saved from becoming the kind of President who would make the decision to bomb Hiroshima. The education he got was the same sort I was getting a few years later in Sinclairville. There were private schools which had more depth and which accepted more responsibility for guidance; Franklin D. Roosevelt entered a new one at Groton in 1896; but that, like the English schools for the upper classes, was quite out of the reach of ordinary folk.[2] It would be easy to say that if Truman had gone to Groton and then to Harvard he might have met the fatal crisis differently. But any such generalization would be invalidated by knowing that he had advice from a panel of the most renowned scientists, who had helped to create the atomic weapon. They solemnly agreed to its use for the destruction of Japanese cities. It was, indeed, such scientists who had by then set the terms of the final dilemma— weaponry for total destruction long before there existed any means for its control.

No, something else was needed. There was more wrong than could have been cured by any conceivable concentration on scientific study. Not knowing how rapidly the crisis of civilization would develop, and having in mind other and generally humane objectives, William James and John Dewey offered another method. What was needed, Dewey said, was something

[2] In his *Autobiography* (1934), Wells would say of the 1890s, when he had been an irregular science teacher in London schools: "Now the urge to spread new knowledge of the modern type through the community was so imperative, and the resistance of the established respectable educational organizations . . . to any change and any adequate growth, was so tough, that a vast amount of educational jerry-building went on . . ." *American Ed.,* 279.

at once simpler and more difficult than the traditional schooling.
If children's minds were merely freed to explore all the realms
of knowledge suitable to their powers and interests, they would
grow to be the wise citizens needed for successful democracy.
They would turn quickly enough to such studies as the natural
and physical sciences once they were allowed to do so, and once
the significance of these studies had been explained. But both
these conditions had to be met. Children had to be free, and they
had to know why learning was important.

The Dewey conception was being embodied in the curriculum
of a practice school at the University of Chicago.[3] His *School
and Society* was published in 1899, too late to affect my education, and anyway, his influence, pervasive as it was, spread with
glacial deliberation. As Wells discovered in Britain, new ideas
met stubborn resistance in the bureaucracies of the established
school systems. There were practical reasons why the resistance
in America should be formidable. Teachers were ill prepared,
and the flood of youngsters inundating the schools was unremitting. Expansion could never be rapid enough, and improvement
often seemed an impossible objective. Textbooks and harsh discipline were props for harassed young women in the classroom.
Then too, there was the inevitable inertia.

The school at Chicago, and others at the more advanced institutions for teacher training, abandoned most of the old methods.
Instead of forcing children to acquire the precepts of a fixed program, Dewey would have children come into a widened environment year by year because they were encouraged to make discoveries rather than because they were pushed. But also, as Dewey
said so often, the aim ought not to be merely the making of adults,
even for the sake of a successful democracy. Children must be
looked at as people, too, ones with some rights. They ought to
enjoy their education.

The progressive methods would spread, but how slowly!

[3] This leaves out of account, of course, the long preliminary explorations
and experiments of Pestalozzi, Herbart, Froebel, Montessori, Mann, and
numerous others.

There were so many difficulties! The existing schools were quite inadequate even for the demands made on them by the old conception; their enlargement for the new one seemed impossible. If children were to be given more freedom, they had to have more room; if they were to be freed from texts and exercises, they had to have more apparatus. And, above all, their teachers had to be better trained and better paid. Changes so costly horrified school boards and caused taxpayers to shudder.

Opposition came from expected sources; but it came also from many who believed in strict discipline and who rejected the theory that children had personalities of their own to be respected. And many of the older teachers, and those who wanted licenses to teach without much training, ridiculed the new ideas. Also, the ingrown tory, the purveyor of precept, the anti-intellectual, stormily opposed the freedom proposed for children. Imagine a child being allowed to make choices! Religion was invoked, failure was pointed to by tests suited to conventional progress, and ridicule poured steadily from a conservative press. And yet change did come, for this new movement appealed to the other strain in Americans which was almost as characteristic as intellectual puritanism and which ran against and neutralized it—the belief in individual liberty and free development, the dislike of being pushed around or of seeing anyone else subjected to unreasonable authority—even children.

Those who saw what such a liberation of young minds might do to the Protestantism of hell-fire and damnation, to authoritarian business and machine-run politics, were not many and, naturally, they were divided, if they did see, between those who would be for or against. The cleavage was very deep, much deeper than anyone at first realized. It would in time polarize the world. The Roman Catholic Church could not accept freedom; neither could the authoritarians of Communism, of Nazism, or of Fascism. Among them, the protagonists of these dogmas would nearly tear the world apart before my generation passed from life. Meanwhile the ideas spreading out from the progressive movement would take hold on millions of minds, bringing a freedom never before known. Associated with the American belief in civil rights, it would create the first genuine democracy in history. The institutions of this democracy would be threatened constantly, and it had peculiarly weak defenses against subversion. Its opponents were always advancing democratic principles to gain advantages for themselves. The Catholics established a whole educational system to rival the public schools and claimed the right to do so by appealing to the religious liberties guaranteed by the Bill of Rights. Extremists too of left and right later would claim immunity from suppression, appealing to other freedoms—of speech, of the press, of assembly, and so on. It became a dilemma. The freedom appealed for was intended to be used to gain the power for suppressing freedom. The question was: should liberty be granted for attacking the very idea of liberty? This was like the dilemma of Lincoln in the early days of the Civil War. The Southerners—in the person of Chief Justice Taney—protested that the writ of habeas corpus, so central among the civil liberties of the Bill of Rights, ought not to be suspended even if it meant the freeing of openly rebellious citizens. Lincoln rather sadly asked whether all the laws should be put in jeopardy to preserve one of them. He had had to choose.

It would certainly have been better if all religious organizations had been refused the privilege of establishing their first private schools. And of course the totalitarians ought to have been suppressed from the first even at the cost of violating temporarily a principle. But democrats have this weakness—that even professed subversives must not be repressed lest the habit of suppression take hold and itself pass into totalitarian rigor. It was no easy matter to decide what was best as public policy, and for a loose and easy democracy it seemed impossible to reach any decision at all. In default of an agreed rule, enemies within grew very strong indeed. There was a dearth of Lincolns to take the responsibility.

The great wars of the first half of the twentieth century

would be fought in this context. When Wilson defined the American war aims as "making the world safe for democracy," he expressed the traditional ideal; but how well it was understood by those who were called on to fight for it, no one knew. And from corollary occurrences it would appear that there were not many who had much emotional commitment to the freedom he expounded so eloquently. The revolution of James and Dewey had not yet taken any great hold on the American mind. Even the later war with the totalitarians was approached by F. D. Roosevelt with cautious care for the opposition of those who thought democracy rotten and decadent and preferred the authoritarianism of the Germans and Italians.

No, democracy and its institutions were peculiarly vulnerable to undermining. And there was also another difficulty—that the subversives could be bested only by organizational methods which seemed to borrow from their own books. Democracy, to Americans, tended to linger in its backwoods stage. Its modernization seemed impossible without loss of its essential—the individual freedom of the frontier. And it was an extraordinarily difficult maneuver for such individualists to shape a more modern system of essential liberties, to learn the arts of delegation and of reasonable discipline.

As my twentieth anniversary came and went it would still not be certain that the evolution of democratic institutions would be allowed to run its course without violent interruption by fanatical dogmatists armed with the weapons of total destruction. We had to go slow; it was the nature of our progression; but the slowness might, as Wells had foreseen, end in a disaster. By then he would long have been gone, having done one man's best for liberty, a curious, unimpressive little man, armed only with a passion for freedom and a wonderful talent for communication.

There would never be many Wellses. There would be many others who, even if they lacked his talent, had the same sense of dedication, of responsibility to the future. But even during the years of my boyhood my fellows and I were being prepared to use the nuclear bomb. This was, for my generation, the dividing choice, as I see it. To have spoken for genocide was to go all the way over to those who are so certain of their own rightness that they will destroy whole populations, and risk the destruction of the race, to force conformance with their will.

The strange and tragic fact about this decision, the mark of moral exhaustion, is that it was made by a man who thought himself a liberal humanitarian, who was certainly a practicing democrat and no sort of religious or racial fanatic, and that it was participated in by some of the most honored intellectuals of my generation. It was the culmination of an inadequacy that must have had its origin in the old education. Deweyism had spread too slowly and was too little understood by those who profited most from its freedoms. Wells would have had to conclude that at Hiroshima education lost out to disaster.

But there were those scientists! And there were others in the deciding group around Truman—Stimson, Patterson, and others of their sort, high-minded men as well as highly educated ones. Even the best training evidently could make men no wiser than they were capable of being. And the reserves of wisdom in crisis were not sufficient to guide our leaders through the ordeal. But still, I must argue, no man is what he is without some educational cause. Somehow, what we learned or did not learn made my generation what it was. It was sometimes something ugly. There were successes, but there were also failures.

Of the failures, Hiroshima was the fatal one. I am tormented by the thought that those who did the deciding ought to have anticipated the consequences of their choice. We were not always reckless as this would make us appear. That is to say, we were capable of being better. Something prevented it in this crisis. Something was lacking in our conditioning. It was not that we were monsters. It was that we could not seem to prevent circumstances from making us behave monstrously.

Nine

As I progressed through the grades, certain differences between myself and others became more and more conspicuous. Some of my friends were mechanically inclined and some had a facility for mathematics. Just at what age I began to realize that I had a deficiency in this sort of ability I cannot recall, but long before I was willing to acknowledge it I began to take evasive action. There was not really very much to avoid at first, and I could usually go on pretending not to notice. There were books to be followed; the problems in them I could work out even if more slowly than some others, and anyway, the answers were in the back. But there were sessions of what was then called "mental arithmetic," and at these I was pretty much a failure. There were not so many of these or of that other popular drill, the spelling bee, as there had been in the earlier rural schools my mother told about—where such exhibitions were often neighborhood entertainments—but there were enough to embarrass me.

Oral countdowns in other subjects might have raised my estimate of myself, but there were none. At the spelling I was fair and sometimes advanced toward the head of the line by elimination, but I could never best a few of the girl pupils—destined to be teachers—who had the combination of industriousness and visual memory which leads to good marks in so many subjects—history (dates), geography (capitals, state boundaries, rivers, and so on), and even English (the ability to quote). Certainly I was not one of their respected rivals. My factual memory was almost as deficient as my ability to "figure." I had to be reconciled to something less than excellence.

Nevertheless, I did have one area of superiority; I had read far more widely than even the girls who knew all the dates of battles and great civic events. I might not be able to place them very accurately in time, but my understanding was considerably wider than theirs. They kept closely to the texts; I was apt to range outside. I am sometimes tempted to think that the class-rooms where I spent my days as a boy contributed less to my education than the marginal time I spent in reading. This was not always romance or adventure. I often followed up a theme I had picked up in Henty or some other storyteller. I could not go very far, usually, the library's resources being what they were (there was no school library and, for that matter, no laboratory, either, for the sciences); but I did begin quite early to have a researcher's interest in literature, in history, in biography, and, in an embryonic way, in ideas.

By the time I reached my teens I was, I must say, better read (an old-fashioned, but expressive, locution) than any teacher I had yet had, so that, in spite of my weaknesses, they respected me. Most of what I had acquired in the way of learning was the result of tangential explorations. And the respect I was con-ceded was due to the wisdom and warmth of most of my teachers, who, if they were not intellectuals, were indefatigable in bringing up the new generation to be literate. Their responsi-bilities were simple, but they were taken seriously. I was a little mysterious to them, having wider interests; but I was not sus-pect.

My mind was, in fact, like a warehouse full of goods with no orderly placing and little relatedness among the packages; there was no system of classification and no record-keeping. The accumulation was considerable, but whether what would be needed for any purpose had been acquired, there was no way of telling because there was no purpose. Still, the prestige of ownership did have one effect of some importance—it caused everyone to assume, from my earliest years, that I should go to

college when the time came. That did for definition. It was a
fairly unusual and a rather faraway goal, to be achieved only
by a few. None of my teachers had had such educations; like
my mother, they had gone to work after training courses, then
beginning to be given as a kind of extra high school year; but
this left them without the least familiarity with the regions of
learning they assumed would be open to me.

I have the pleasantest recollections of most of these teachers.
The education they provided was confined to the accepted
routines; but the demands were so slight, and the slow learners
so prevalent, that I could do almost as I liked. I do feel that I
ought to have been introduced more skillfully to the world of
numbers and somehow taught to acquire a familiarity with its
techniques; but otherwise the complaint I have, as I look so
far back, is more about the physical conditions than the intellectual atmosphere. Ours was no worse a school than most
others—much better in many ways—but it was still ugly, com-
fortless, bleak, and unhealthful. During our long winters a bank
of five-inch iron pipes carried steam from a basement boiler.
These rusty pipes ran around the outside walls of our rooms;
they gurgled, hissed, banged, and periodically seemed about to
explode. Those who sat in the outside rows might as well not
have been part of the class at all when the volleys were at their
heights; they heard very little of what was going on. And the
terrible blasts of heat from the pipes had to compete with zero
drafts from the ill-fitted windows just above. The icy chill ran
down a child's neck while his lower parts were cooked.

There was a smell, too, that was memorable. The splintery
floors were never quite clean, and every shuffle raised a small
cloud of pungent dust to mingle with that from the troughs
below the blackboards, where the erasers were tossed after
being impregnated with chalk. We were supposed to take in turn
the cleaning of the boards and the beating out of the erasers.
What use small boys made of these opportunities can be imagined.
The dust was simply transferred to all the other objects in the
room. Other perfumes mixed with the pervasive one of dust.

In a community which had not yet reached the bathroom stage of its progress, the Saturday-night cleansing in the copper boiler or the clothes tub, carried out in the kitchen with hot water from the range, was not always convenient in winter, and even at other times might be less than thorough. Also, it was obviously possible that some of the underwear in the room had been slept in. When well warmed, a neat and prissy little girl could be incredibly odorous. Ten of them and ten boys, together, could really create a miasmic atmosphere.

Only a belated examination indicates all this to me. It seemed at the time, as conditions of their lives do to all children, merely part of an inevitable arrangement. But I certainly had friends—because I remember it well—who reached a state which earned them the nickname of "Stinky," and one outstanding performer was simply but expressively known as "Phew!" These labels were not at all resented; they were distinctions to be proud of. A nickname signified affection or at least acceptance, and to be given one meant that intimacy with other fellows had been established. Nothing is more precious than this, no matter how achieved. If it was impossible to excel in running, jumping, baseball, or winter sports, or if there was some danger of being known as teacher's pet or a mama's boy, redemption could be attained by being known as the dirtiest, the smelliest, or the unruliest. Sometimes such a seeker for status would slyly rest his snow-wet feet on the steam pipes, thus setting up a competition which might last a week or more with others who also sought distinction. Little girls who sat nearby affected to be disgusted by this vulgar exhibition, but it drew appreciative guffaws from other boys and went toward the casual count of talents and achievements by which each of us was known.

We gradually outgrew these primitive habits. In fact, I seem to recall becoming interested in my appearance before adolescence, when such a concern, of course, becomes inevitable. I began to wet and comb my hair first, and this concession spread—but slowly—to the rest of my adornment. But before this there were some agonizing experiences as well as some triumphant ones. What must have been the most satisfying of these I do not remember; but like some other family recollections, I have heard about it so often that it has a specious reality. It seems that my grandmother was especially solicitous of the perennial flowers that flourished under her protection in a border around the house. These suffered from my infant invasions until my father one day took me up to the Sheldon emporium and had me fitted out with my first pair of pants. I must have been about four, and it was certainly time I escaped from skirts; but there was an explosion among the women just the same. My grandmother discovered, however, that the damage to her precious blooms was considerably reduced because I could now step over them instead of breaking them off with my skirts. So this offense was forgiven. What was not forgiven for a long time was that my father on the same excursion took me to the barber's—Cousin George—and had my curls cut off. They had been luxuriant and long; my mother thought them beautiful, and she was inclined to nurse the grievance caused by their loss. Afterward my father used to tell about the experience of bringing me home, shorn and in pants, quite as though he were recounting a major crisis in history; and I am sure my mother made it seem like one.

But she was incorrigible. She proceeded to deck me out in a Little Lord Fauntleroy suit which she made herself out of velvet. It had a big square collar trimmed with lace and was, I thought, the most degrading dress possible to imagine. I wore it to Sunday school once and thereafter staged such a scene when she brought it out that she finally gave up—but not until she had taken me to the photographer to have a picture made which would perpetuate my childish beauty. She has guarded that photograph all these years and still possesses it, one of the few relics that have remained to taunt me. She had no conception at all of the tortures to which a boy might be subjected by such a public offense. I did not propose to go on suffering them after one engagement with my unsympathetic friends, and my revolt was so savage that even she was intimidated.

I have a friend who contends that the happiest year of any male's life is that from about ten and a half to eleven and a half. There is then no bother about sex, and there is a distinct loosening of motherly ties. He looks old enough to take care of himself, but he does not yet have many serious responsibilities. While the girls of his own age are languishing over older boys, he can get on with his sports, his mechanical contrivances, his amateur zoo, and any other entertainments or projects he cares to invent.

This may have some claim to reality, but it seems to me somewhat idealized. The year was for me, at least, not nearly so well marked out as my friend indicates as average. Before I quite escaped from parental supervision I began to notice the girls—one in particular—and to turn weak at the slightest mark of favor. But the discipline of sentiment was not so unremitting that I could not develop other interests; and I did. I was fairly competent at games and fairly ingenious at contriving amusements. I lacked the ability to construct anything, but I often planned the jobs to be done by my gang. We had a creditable "shanty" at the top of our lot, some fifty yards from the house, and so situated as to be immune to surveillance from my mother. There, in spring, we boiled down the sap from a hundred sugar maples along the neighboring streets, sometimes actually producing a few gallons of smoky syrup and a few cakes of sugar. At other seasons it was a convenient hide-out for the mysterious conclaves boys find so satisfying. It was there that I learned to play poker, to cure corn silk and clovers for home-made cigarettes—and sometimes to talk more seriously about the possible future. But there was not much serious talk. Each day's own activities were too exciting.

Growing up in a democracy is so demanding a process and requires such constant revolutionary adjustments that its successful accomplishment by youngsters who never seem to give it the least consideration—who make their changes almost absent-mindedly—deserves to rate as one of nature's miracles. And the audacity of our forefathers in conceiving that a nation's most

serious decisions could be arrived at by universal participation
of adults raised in this way seems positively foolhardy. The
nation grew and spread far faster than its educational equipment. And as the growth went on, the problems became more
difficult, so that elementary education was no more of much use.
Yet few children survived the grades and went on to high school,
and even fewer went any farther. This was a matter of economics.
The facilities, of course, did not exist; but even if they had, most
boys would have preferred to stop school and go to work. Their
parents might not appreciate the advantages of schooling or
might need them on the farm, or they themselves might be tired
of discipline and poverty and anxious to be out and doing. The
general American devotion to education was real enough, but
there was a big minority of the skeptical, the selfish, and the
anti-intellectual. These all agreed in arguing that anything beyond the three R's was unnecessary or even dangerous and
unsettling. They might not really believe it, but it suited their
convenience.

The devotees of culture in Sinclairville were a rather small
group, consisting mostly of women. Its male counterpart was
by no means so well organized. No man would think of joining
a Reading Circle, for instance, even though he might have the
same interests as the ladies. So Chautauqua reached a largely
feminine audience. For this, as well as for other reasons, it
may have had less influence than I have represented it as having.
But then again it may have had results—as the small Dewey
school in Chicago did—far beyond the readily observable ones.
Its effect on the children of that generation was secondary, as
a rule; but for me it was somewhat more direct. I went there
fairly often in season—by steamer from Bemus Point, an hour
of travel which had in itself more interest than anything at its
end. While my mother was at lectures or concerts, I found
more exciting occupations. They had to be looked for, but they
could be found. There were other children around with no
more interest in adult concerns than I had, and friendships
were easily made in these circumstances. I may even have read

a few of the simpler Literary and Scientific Circle books; they were familiar from lying open on tables or being poked into bookshelves when finished with.

I do, therefore, count Chautauqua as an influence, especially in my later boyhood, if for no other reason than that it was there in our county and because my mother's pride in it was so constant. But besides that, I am sure that it did fertilize the cultural ground. It made all of us more respectful of learning, more disposed to serious study, less inclined to accept dogmas, and more aware of the wider world. None of these qualities was too prevalent in our country at that time. Chautauquans regarded themselves as inquirers; they were eager for knowledge. And this was good.

This may seem strange to those who know that the Assembly was begun as a training center intended to raise the standards of Sunday-school teaching. But the Vincents, father and son, who were most influential in its affairs during a generation, were remarkable individuals, determined to rescue church work from its preoccupation with old-fashioned hell and generally to liberalize religion. The evangelical tradition could have been reformed in no other way so well as by the enlightenment of its teachers. What the progressive movement did for the public schools, Chautauqua did—or began to do—for the Sunday schools.[1]

[1] The reader who may be interested in exploring further the influence of Chautauqua may refer to Bishop Vincent's own account, *The Chatauqua Movement* (The Chautauqua Press, 1885), or to *John Heyl Vincent,* by L. H. Vincent (New York: Macmillan, 1925). Going further, he may read *The Story of Chautauqua,* by J. L. Hurlbut (New York: Putnam, 1921), or *Chautauqua: An American Place,* by Rebecca Richmond (New York: Duell, Sloan & Pearce, 1943). There is also an interesting life of the co-founder, a businessman who ably complemented the old Bishop, *Lewis Miller,* by Elwood Hendrick, (New York: Putnam, 1925).

There is on the Assembly grounds a memorial library with a collection of early Chatauquana and a helpful staff. There anyone who is interested may read, as I have done (and, in my case, with recollections of my own serving to enlarge much of what I read), the files of *The Chautauqua Assembly Herald,* 1876–1905, and *The Chautauquan Daily,* from 1906. He may also find all the Annual Reports, a complete collection of the *Chautauqua Textbooks,* and the records of the Chautauqua Literary and

These movements supplemented each other. Many otherwise hostile school administrators and teachers were persuaded that progressive education was respectable because of its association with the religious institution at Chautauqua. There was also the direct connection with the University of Chicago, then so inspiringly new and ambitious, where the progressive ideas were generating and being tried out.

Chautauqua had gone a long way by 1898, say, from its start in 1871 as a kind of camp in the woods under ministerial auspices. It began as a hymn-singing, Bible-exploring enterprise; but very soon the Vincent intention became recognizable. He meant to raise the intellectual level of Methodism in particular and of Protestantism in general. That this endeavor was so successful was not surprising, looked at afterward. It was the kind of thing that happened more often in business than in cultural affairs. But given the demand that existed, and the abilities of gifted organizers, its mysteries vanish. What was surprising was the rapid spread of the Chautauqua mission to lay teachers. Twenty years after its beginning the sedate and industrious flocks of summer visitors, overrunning all the facilities that could be provided, were mostly the schoolma'ams of tradition, working earnestly to better themselves for their jobs. At Chautauqua they found respectable ways to break out of the old confines, to overcome the deficiencies of their training, and to renew their faith in the education to which they were dedicated.

It was, indeed, the conviction of deficiency, spreading out from Chicago and other centers and penetrating the teachers' consciences, that created the demand for Chautauqua's services. Here was culture, at once respectable and progressive. No revolution was ever furnished with such a remarkable cover.

The Assembly came conveniently in the summers, when teachers were on vacation; it held to the rituals and symbols of piety,

---

Scientific Circle, including lists of the books published for the home-study courses and others recommended for them. These amount to several hundred from 1878, for the Circle still flourishes in a modest way.

which meant much to a generation still centered in the rural churches; it furnished a certain recreation too; its participants could find amusement without shocking the most vigilant and suspicious of the orthodox. There were genteel social gatherings, improving lectures, and even mildly competitive games. It did, however, shut out the naughty world (with a high board fence) that used alcohol and tobacco and devoted itself to more worldly pleasures. Religion was conspicuous, but the old Bishop was a modern man. His determination to rescue the church from its camp-meeting degeneracies was inflexible, and many a self-advertising demogogue who began to exhort and work up a personal following found himself ruthlessly suppressed and even, when necessary, ejected. There finally was a rule against volunteer gatherings of any sort in the interest of planned and intensive work during the short weeks of summer. And his reaching out to the training of public school teachers was characteristic. The church he envisioned was not a Sunday affair. Religion was for weekdays as well as Sundays.

I have studied the program of lectures and readings for the year 1891, when I was born. By then the Assembly had emerged from its tent and muddy-lane period and was beginning to take on the physical respectability of permanent buildings, sidewalks and regular courses of study. These have, I think, a certain interest for anyone who is concerned with the failure of our culture to prepare itself for the maturity it would need when scientific achievements began to multiply so rapidly during and after the great wars of the twentieth century. The trouble with Chautauqua was that its influence did not spread with the rapidity required by the corollary disturbances demanding control. And it touched hardly at all the new immigrants or the Catholic congregations.

The program for 1891 was still somewhat makeshift. It had the mark on it of the lyceum, the popular lecture whose tone would have been set by the requirements of those audiences in high school auditoriums like our own in Sinclairville. It ventured into subjects that must have been thought daring by the current crop of ministers, yet it was calculated to be as little offensive as possible to the conservative mind. There was an early venture into anthropology which must have caused the fundamentalists to think. There was another series of lectures about psychology, and there was even some study of poverty and its causes. Most of the emphasis was still theological; the list of speakers and teachers was heavy with clergymen; but there also appeared G. Stanley Hall, Jeremiah W. Jenks, W. H. Mace, Melvil Dewey, and Frederick Starr. And anyone familiar with American academic history will recognize here educational theory, psychology, economics, history, sociology, and anthropology at its best university level. This was far indeed from the wild shouting sensationalism of the old Methodist camp meeting or the evangelism of the rural churches. It approached the level of organized education.

The most daring venture, so far as risking the displeasure of the orthodox middle-class Sunday-school teacher was concerned, would have been a lecture by Jacob A. Riis with the title *How the Other Half Lives*. This must have had the same theme as Riis's well-known book which would be one of my assigned readings in an economics course at the University of Pennsylvania twenty years later. It described the slums and the indignities of urban poverty. To Chautauquans, the slum dwellers were indeed the other half. Riis was, however, the most tolerant of critics; he loved his adopted land; but the newcomers he wrote about did live in almost intolerable squalor. To read about this among the quiet groves beside the cool lake, and to discuss its consequences between concerts and religious meetings, was to reorient the concern of a self-satisfied society. There was something insistent here which must be paid attention to. Bishop Vincent meant to see that that attention should be paid. Anyone not confused by the physical circumstances of Chautauqua must admit that the old Bishop was leading his Protestant brethren toward enlightenment about as rapidly as was possible.

By 1895 he had progressed considerably farther toward his

goal of standardized studies which would ready the stable folk of America for their coming responsibilities. In that year the records show that separate schools had been organized on the collegiate model: Arts and Sciences, Sacred Literature, Expression, Music, Pedagogy, and Physical Education. There was nothing frightening in these titles, except to the long-maned, ignorant, wild-and-woolly preacher of the backwoods parishes and the uneducated and traditional teacher. There were still many of these, but there were fewer in every passing year. Standards were taking shape and gaining recognition. At Chautauqua they were being enforced.[2]

I would discover decades later, exploring the history of social studies in America, that Chautauqua had been in those years a center for those studies, even if without much advertisement or recognition. There such pioneers as Simon Nelson Patten, Richard T. Ely, John R. Commons, Carroll D. Wright, C. R. Henderson, and others, including Lord Bryce, would lecture, teach, and sometimes meet to exchange ideas. This sort of thing happened nowhere else until many years later. As a young economist, I would like to think of those revered elders walking

[2] The schools at Chautauqua were first organized in 1887. I quote from an article, "The Chautauqua Institution," by Arthur E. Bestor, later president of the Institution, in *The Historic Annals of Southwestern New York,* edited by W. J. Doty (1940):

"Among Universities the movement for summer schools did not spread much beyond Harvard (where it was confined to field work in science) until Wisconsin took it up in 1887 and Cornell followed in 1892. The institutions laid stress upon courses offered to teachers, work which Chautauqua had specifically provided in the previous decade through its Teachers' Retreat.

"The Pioneer methods of Chautauqua had their greatest influence upon University practices through the work of William Rainey Harper. Dr. Harper joined the faculty of the Chautauqua School of Languages in 1883, and in 1887 he was made Principal of the College of Liberal Arts, a position he held until 1898. When in 1891 he assumed his duties as first President of the new University of Chicago, he carried into the plan of that institution three of the educational methods that Chautauqua had devised or had practiced: Summer Schools, correspondence study, and University Extension. By dividing the college year into four terms of three months each, and establishing a continuous session, President Harper permanently fitted Summer Schools into the University scheme."

and talking together earnestly in the shady paths of the Institution, learning from each other and discoursing to the gathered schoolteachers, perhaps also writing on tables in the boarding-houses where I too may have stayed, some of the pages we younger ones would still be studying. Perhaps as a boy, I thought, I may quite unknowingly have seen them passing on their thoughtful occasions. It was a pleasant notion.[3] Chautauqua—our Chautauqua—was a genuine influence in the freeing of the American mind. The influence did not spread rapidly enough to avert the tragedy of Hiroshima, but it did help to convict Americans of the sin that decision represented.

[3] It was natural that Richard T. Ely should be a Chautauqua author. He had been born in the village of Ripley. In 1890–91 his *Political Economy* was a C.L.S.C. book; in 1893–94 his *Evolution of Industrial Society* followed, and in 1903–4 his *Strength and Weakness of Socialism* was distributed to be read by all those circles of students. I do not know whether there were protests that this was going too far; there appear to be none in the record. But certainly the circulation of a book about Socialism, and a moderately sympathetic one at that, for such an audience, was courageously conceived in 1903. It will be of interest to the patient reader that, in 1891, 180,000 readers were enrolled in the C.L.S.C., and that by 1918 this number would have risen to 300,000, and that all this time 25 per cent of these would have been in villages of less than 500 and 50 per cent in villages of 500 to 3500—precisely where, it would be said, I think, the influence was most needed.

Ten

No one could have seen a more appropriate representative of the safety and satisfaction sought by common folk than the head of our nation in the late 'nineties. The McKinley I saw in the enlarged photographs put up in the post office was a soft, suety, jowly man in a choker collar, a white vest, and a Prince Albert coat who wore the sober expression statesmen felt compelled to display even if privately they were known to be lively cynics. Sobriety sat so well on McKinley that no one doubted its authenticity, and for once appearances did not falsify. He was one person who never in his life did an unorthodox thing or, apart from his Civil War service, an exciting one.[1]

Connection between such pompous remoteness and affairs in a hill village was not at all easy to make; and not many made it, I should think. But there was the embarrassing fact that my grandfather and my father were Democrats in a community where all respectable people were inevitably Republican. Only the riffraff, as a later President was to say, were Democrats.[2]

[1] Margaret Leech has presented the complete picture. *In the Days of McKinley* (New York: Harper, 1959) labors through the whole epoch. In spite of her best efforts, the President came out dull and turgid. Nothing could make him or anything he did seem interesting.

[2] Sometimes in later years I would cite this strange family political allegiance to show that the Tugwells were inclined to a praiseworthy nonconformism. I would make the claim once too often, however. In a conversation with President Roosevelt, the departure of whose father from Republican rectitude in Dutchess County would be even more unaccountable, I rather proudly referred to my inherited Democracy, and he said that I had better inquire whether it stemmed from anything more rational than Mug-

My father, as little political as anyone I have ever known, and having the deepest respect for all *his* father's convictions, accepted the paternal affiliation and would never even discuss its rationality. I can see now that it must sometimes have been an unhappy necessity for the completely conformist young business-man to have been, however quietly, on the side of Bryan and western radicalism and against that apotheosis of respectability, the guardian of gold and high tariffs, McKinley. But he did not waver. Never, in his long life, would he vote Republican.[3] If it made something of a problem for me that we should be Demo-crats, it may have been good conditioning for the later heavy disapproval with which I was often to be viewed as an adult. But I was distinctly resentful. There were not many boys with whom I could associate peacefully just before elections. And I recall some active—but unsuccessful—efforts to sabotage Republican torchlight parades which indicate a hopeless minority

wumpism. When I rejected this suggestion on the ground that this was a term applied to Republicans who in 1884 deserted Blaine to support Cleve-land and that my grandfather had been a Democrat since his first arrival in this country, he did not scruple to mention the nasty word "Copperhead." I said that my grandfather could not have been a Copperhead because this species was native to Indiana, Illinois, and Ohio. It was, however, true that he had only arrived as an immigrant in 1852. He had bought a sub-stitute in the war, and this was a subject my father had never cared to discuss. The President, never to be fooled about geography, was so un-kind as to remind me that Chautauqua County was very close indeed to Ohio. The discussion ended inconclusively; but I always felt that my political credentials had been unfairly doubted. They were as good as his. *His* father was an undoubted Mugwump and, I reminded him, he him-self had *once been a Republican*—as a Harvard senior he had enthusi-astically supported Uncle Ted in 1904 and only reverted to the Democracy, so far as the record went, when he wanted to run for office.

[3] How Republican we were in Chautauqua can be gathered from a few statistics. In the campaign of 1896, although Bryan spoke to an enormous crowd of some 12,000 at Celeron, and McKinley stayed at home on his front porch in Canton, the county gave Bryan only 6168 votes to McKinley's 14,335. The national count was: Bryan, 6,502,925; McKinley, 7,104,776. We might, on the figures, be called a stronghold. The same thing hap-pened in 1900, only it was a little worse. The national figures were about the same, but the Republican vote in our county rose to 15,320, and the Democratic count stayed at a little over 6000. This, it has to be admitted, was in spite of two Bryan speeches in his best vein—one at Dunkirk this time, as well as one at Celeron. In 1904—and afterward—things remained un-changed.

status. I simply did not have enough affiliates to make a showing. Democrats had either no parades or shamefully meager ones. I was never to be on the winning side in an election until Wilson won in 1912.

Between elections, however, there were certain public excitements in which I could join. Of these, the most inspiring was the Spanish war. My father had no impulse, so far as I know, to volunteer and was inclined to feel that it was a Republican mistake, likely to be bad for business. But he did not say much, and I joined heartily in all the victory celebrations. Without much discrimination, also, I was as eager as any of my friends to exalt the heroes of the bizarre campaign in Cuba, the victory of Manila Bay, and the bloodless capture of Puerto Rico. I had no more intimation then than any of my friends that there were jealousies among the military men, that some of them had hardly managed their part in the affair with good judgment, and that the Spanish were nothing to brag about as opponents. Dewey, Shafter, Miles, Sampson, Schley, Wood—all were splendid figures; and there was, besides, the glamorous Rough Rider. The Republicans did not get around at once to claiming Roosevelt as their exclusive property, so even a scion of Democrats could believe him to be as heroic as he believed himself to be. Since I kept up with events better than most of the boys, I had an advantage when it came to imitating the battles so luridly pictured in the press. I seem to have claimed a stellar role; at any rate, I recall repeatedly charging a line of yelling soldiers up the hill back of our house and deploying them in the field beyond. We had trouble finding any representatives for the enemy, their reputation for cruel treachery being what it was, but we managed by drawing lots, a process from which I somehow exempted myself. The San Juan battlefield became as familiar to me as it can have been to any of the generals; and if the family kitchen garden suffered, my father was so amused by our antics that he did not protest. And of course the whole thing was one my mother preferred to ignore. She did not picture me as a soldier and would not be seduced by my imaginings.

These excitements cannot have been very prolonged; yet there
were repeated victories and so frequent renewals, for several
years, of this military interest. The climax of the war was the
battle of Manila Bay, and this for me was notable as the first
occasion on which I was allowed the ineffable privilege of
setting off the village ordnance piece. This was a rare treat
more usually shared out among Allen Hinchliffe, Carl Rood,
Toots Anderson, and other older youths. The ceremony was
carried out under even more senior auspices. Jake Evans kept
the cannon in the back room of his store, and Juicy Harrison,
the livery stable proprietor and bus driver, was recognized as the
captain of the squad. On the Fourth of July and on other
extraordinary occasions the cannon was hauled out to the
center of the common, where it was stuffed with rags and
paper wadding and fired with universal satisfaction. How so
junior a participant as myself happened to be allowed to set the
match to the touch hole, I cannot imagine; but I was, and it so
elevated me in my own esteem that I kept a firmer hold than
ever on the general's job in the rear of our premises. On a later
occasion the old cannon burst, as was appropriate in an age
of declining appreciation of such intense joys as it represented;
but while it lasted its personality was unique and its contribution
to our social life indispensable. It was used many times in '98
and '99; and what a part it played on the day when our small
squad of blue-clad volunteers came home and was led up the street
with the band playing martial music! The cannon banged away
as fast as it could be rammed full, and was fired until its barrel
was so hot it set fire to the wadding. It was still firing as the procession disappeared down Main Street and the horns and drums
became faint.

We were isolated from many of the influences brought to
bear on city folk; but we were not immune—not altogether—
to the stimulating effects of change. When Major Samuel
Sinclear, in 1809, built his log camp for the winter at about the

location of our common, he had thought it would be a main
highway crossing, a four corners. In fact, the hills had made
impossible, or at least difficult, a highway to the west. But the
north-south road had attained a certain importance. It ran
from Dunkirk and Fredonia, out by Lake Erie, to Jamestown
and Falconer on the outlet of Chautauqua Lake; it even ran
on to Warren, in the Pennsylvania oil country, and then on
down to Pittsburgh. There was a railroad, too, which made the
same connection—the Dunkirk, Allegheny Valley, and Pittsburgh[4]—locally known as the Dolly Varden and regarded with
that mixture of affection and exasperation usually earned by such
institutions. No real catastrophe was required to stop its operations; heavy snows blocked its tracks in winter, floods washed out
the wooden trestles that carried its tracks across our ravines, and
its rather wheezy engines broke down in unlikely stretches where
repairs were difficult; but it carried a surprising traffic, and
most of us became as familiar with its red plush amenities, its
tobacco-kerosene-coal-smoke odors, and its flying cinders as with
the other phenomena of our village. It led to a larger world.
But it had made some effort to make contact with us, coming
around the foot of the hills to the west and bending northward
up the valley to our station before winding southward again
toward Gerry and Falconer; and the patience of its builders had
been exhausted about a mile and a half short of the village, thus
giving rise to an even more characteristic local institution. This
was Juicy Harrison's bus, a lumbering vehicle capable of carrying a load almost as voluminous as a railway car. It had a lug-
gage carrier on top and a driver's seat whose design was
borrowed, probably, from the stagecoaches of the West. Juicy
went back and forth to the station through the deep ruts of
winter—on sleighs then, the interior strewn with straw—and the
mud of spring and fall, with somewhat more regularity than
could be counted on for the train itself.

My own contacts with the outside world were mostly made

4 Whose first train had run the length of the line June 22, 1871.

in Jamestown, though sometimes with Fredonia and Dunkirk to the north. Since we had several pairs of horses in the barn, used by my father in his business, our journeys were usually behind a lively team—my father would have only spirited horses, the single exception being Dolly, my mother's mare, who was elderly and inclined to presume on her long relationship with the family. It was a memorable day when we set out early at a good pace down the valley road toward Gerry, cut across the flats to the foot of the hills, and climbed the long rise along their shoulder until the road turned downward and we scampered into Jamestown along its brick pavements. The journey home toward evening was always a sleepy one; and the cozy joggling in my mother's arms, or, when I was older, snuggled next to my father, was hardly separable next morning from its continuation between the sheets of my own small bed. When I awoke, I liked to crawl into the warm space between my parents and demand to have retold the story of the day before, together with any adventures I might have missed on the way home.

Although my father traveled on all the roads roundabout and saw, perhaps as often as anyone, the remote farmers in our hills, he was not of much use to them in the way of gossip, and he seems almost never to have talked with them about politics, which is so often a rural preoccupation. He was just not interested; and he was even less interested in what went on in centers farther away. I am quite certain that he never speculated about McKinley in his Prince Albert down in Washington, sitting at the end of his Cabinet table, bearded personalities on either side, all seriously considering problems of vast import. I suppose our several lawyers did. But how they considered that the stuffed Prince Albert comported with the semi-self-sufficient, half-isolated society which then existed over much of America, I do not know. They were not the special friends of my parents, and we had no political talk around our table or in our living room. That broadcloth uniform did somehow symbolize success to our felt-booted, butternut-jeaned farmers, I suppose. After all, Abe Lincoln, not to mention Grant, Hayes, Garfield, and Harrison, had appeared in that same getup whenever there were posed photographs to be taken. And they had had silk hats to finish the ensemble. These were not so tall any more as the one Lincoln had worn on the trip to headquarters at City Point or when he had spoken at Gettysburg—on these occasions he must have looked at least nine feet high. But they were still inevitable for public appearances. McKinley, when young, had run barefoot through the streets and fields of Niles, a small town in a country not very different—and not even so very far away—from Chautauqua County.[5] But when boys were told that they might, any of them, grow up to be President, it is certain that they pictured to themselves his adult frock-coated pomposity. They cannot have been much attracted to such an existence. Boys, however, take things of this sort easily and go on being, in their own minds, what they prefer—Rough Riders, cowboys, railway engineers, airplane pilots, space-ship navigators, and visitors to far planets. From all these adventures they can get home safely to supper. Statesmen have to endure banquets and make speeches. And these are not romantic attractions.

As to the farmer sloshing about his barnyard, the contrast between himself and the glossy, fat-handed President must have symbolized the remoteness of government from common con-

[5] James M. Cox, who had also been born and raised in Ohio, has told a story about McKinley which makes him seem at once more ordinary and more understanding. When he was a candidate for the Presidency, Cox said, McKinley was up early one morning and out on the back platform of his special train. Looking out across the tracks, he saw a small boy standing comfortably in fresh cow droppings steaming in the frosty morning. He called his entourage and, out of curiosity, asked each of them whether he had done this too in his boyhood. McKinley himself had, and he thought it an experience common to most rural Americans. This story was told in the first chapter of Cox's *Journey Through My Years*. That chapter in an otherwise rather dull book conveys some of the nostalgia for a country boyhood which so many of his generation felt as changes destroyed the older ways of living. He told of work on the farm, of popping corn and paring apples on winter evenings, of the fall butcherings, of country schooling, of election excitements, of sugarings-off, of Thanksgiving and Christmas with all their delights. These experiences were familiar at least to me. Ohio was very close to us in our corner of New York.

cerns. Neither could be pictured in the environment of the other, and it seems incredible that either can have understood the problems of the other. To our neighbors, real-life activities were carried on in overalls, or in business clothes not much less accustomed to the wear and tear of work. The activities in Albany and Washington were carried out in ceremonial dress, and the implication was that the activities were ceremonial too. The making of speeches, the signing of papers, the conferring around polished tables—all these went on at a different level from that which ordinary people were accustomed to. Government was a matter of dealing at arm's length with other governments or with disembodied entities such as corporations or institutions. It had nothing to do with caring for stock, harvesting hay, trading in the village, acquiring the ability to read, write, and cipher, raising a family, or running a business and getting ahead.

There was no connective tissue between government and people, at least none that was seen and felt in daily life. Taxes were for schools, roads, and the county poorhouse, and even these were partly supported otherwise—roads, for instance, were kept up by those who lived along them, working out their obligations in measured numbers of days under the town road supervisor. There was no organization for public health. We had Drs. Smith and Cleland to look after us. From them much was demanded. They drove their hard-worked teams days, nights, and Sundays—hitched to buggies, and, in winter, cutters —over the hills in every sort of weather, or they received their patients in their small offices at all hours. They may have protested health hazards and pressed for the building of sewers and protected water supplies, but that was not their duty. They were supposed to tend the sick for fees. When they did more it was beyond any obligation imposed on them by community or government.

So with school. When I was in the grades, there was certainly no consciousness among us that this was a function of government. It was a village affair, or so it seemed, organized by a group of neighbors for the benefit of their children.[6]

[6] The struggle for free, tax-supported, non-sectarian, state-supported schools had been a long one. It had begun by such indirect aids as that in Connecticut, where the proceeds of liquor licenses were turned over to the townships. New York, in 1799, set up lotteries for school moneys and repeated this procedure several times. National land grants to the states were dedicated to school purposes in Ohio by 1802. But by 1825 it had been realized that direct taxes would have to be levied. This system was a long time in becoming established everywhere. For one thing, the idea that *free* schools were pauper institutions had to be overcome, and this took some decades. In 1849, however, New York had reached a stage at which there could be a referendum. The result of voting in that year was (according to Cubberly's *History of Education,* 686) 249,872 for and 91,952 against. But the state's schools were not made wholly free until 1867. From then on there was a gradual development. But it had not yet produced anything like a modern system when I began my schooling in Sinclairville—and not even when I finished it in Wilson. In neither of these schools was there laboratory, library, gymnasium, or any attention to health.

Eleven

We were on the verge of change in many matters. Not only were we in the last decades of a period in which the reach of the Federal government was far short of the ordinary citizen except when it asked him to go to war or paid him a pension for having gone, we were also in the last decades of an older kind of industry, of self-sufficient farmers—of a simpler social organization in general. Social welfare was represented by the county poor farm; a national system for relieving or preventing distress was completely beyond the imagination.

The Pullman strike in 1894 had been the first shocking news of change that had come to many complacent persons. It broke in on their provincial lives with rude insistence. But because it was only an early incident, most of them were no more than momentarily horrified. They forgot it at once. What might have shocked them almost as much as the rioting would have been the disclosure that Robert Todd Lincoln, son of the Emancipator, had told his Pullman porters, when he had become president of the company, that they would be expected to extract tips from travelers in lieu of wages. Expect a man to live on gratuities instead of earnings for which a face-to-face bargain had been made? This went to a fundamental of the American philosophy.

The face-to-face bargain still prevailed in Sinclairville. But there were furniture factories and textile mills in Jamestown, and over in Dunkirk there was the Brooks Locomotive Works. These, especially the Brooks works, were large enough, even if small by later standards, so that there was a break in the nexus.[1]

Employer and employee no longer met and made a bargain in these factories. The employer was represented at second or third hand—usually by a foreman whose methods were his own and who was often capricious and irresponsible. But Sinclairville was not Jamestown or Dunkirk; it contrasted with these urban neighbors as much in spirit and custom as in physical organization; and there was no recognition that the future was represented rather by the cities than by the more solid and traditional rural communities.

We were not agitated in our valley. There had been no dramatic labor troubles very close to us. Of course no one could be ignorant of the hardships undergone during the years after 1893 when the depression so reluctantly gave way to the grinding cure of deflation. Once, even, we heard that the Fenton Guards from Dunkirk had been called to Buffalo to keep order among the unemployed and the strikers. But this had not had the impact of the Pullman strike, in which Federal troops had been used against subversive rioters. This was almost war. And there was no question of justification. Opinion unwaveringly supported the President. Sinclairville was for law and order in Chicago.

No one in our village worked for another if he chose not to, and it would have been an amazing idea that the government could have any interest in the arrangement.

It is easy to see now that the President's sending of Federal troops to Chicago was a warning that there existed social complexes in which strategic ganglions, if blocked, served to paralyze the whole. It was not so easily understood then. Still, when the President said that if it took the whole army to deliver a postcard in Chicago he would see that it was done, there was

[1] Brooks had the enormous number of 2600 employees in 1910. In that year 382 locomotives were turned out. For a brief account of industry in Jamestown, cf. Helen G. McMahon, *Chautauqua County: A History* (Buffalo, 1958).

universal approval. The public interest was extending to the ensuring of normal functions. It was not in accord with the principles by which we carried on business; but what were principles when business was interfered with? Besides, the inconsistency was not pointed out, and the capacity of our people for ignoring inconvenient deductions was infinite.

Governmental interference would soon enter, or already had entered (*vide* the Pullman matter) a phase in which there would be a struggle for control of its mechanisms. That was the meaning of the Cleveland-Olney controversy with Debs and Altgeld, aside from the gross injustices of this particular dispute.[2] For the nation this would be the most dangerous of any struggle in the new century until it was forced to turn confusedly to the challenge of totalitarianism abroad. The later struggles may not have been undertaken for sharply visualized reasons, but at least they did not take place within the vitals of the commonwealth itself. The internal convulsions were precipitated again and again by the unfair hardships of recurrent hard times; and such periods returned with frightening regularity. When starvation threatened and when employers denied any responsibility, the system seemed to have internal sicknesses. Why the businessmen were not the first to understand that their own security required insurance against the hazards of depression, it is hard now to explain.

Certain businesses were growing to monstrous size. Some of them spread far beyond the confines of any state. And these threatened to destroy the integrity of a Congressional system which had been shaped in pre-industrial days. Not only the states were subverted by the big businesses, a Congress elected by districts could be reached in the same way. It was a bad time for all governments—city, state, and national. The one solid resource in a sea of violently conflicting interests was the

[2] Cf. *Grover Cleveland: A Study in Courage,* by Allan Nevins (New York: Dodd Mead, 1932). At the distance of half a century, Mr. Nevins was able to make all this quite clear when he came to surveying Cleveland's behavior in this instance.

Federal Executive. And sometimes leadership came from the White House. Cleveland might be mistaken, but he did something; he did not hesitate. This was tremendous relief to a confused people. But he was the first President after the Civil War to show such strength and independence.

This internal struggle, which sometimes seemed to threaten the very life of the nation, just as the differences that led to the Civil War had threatened it, has about it now a quality of remoteness. Somehow during the days of the second Roosevelt's New Deal a new hold was taken on reality. The fighting was not stopped, not altogether; but as the issues became moot, there was less bitterness in it. And by the 'sixties it was hard to recall what it had all been about. The nation would no more consider going back to the conditions before social security than it would consider reinstating slavery. And collective bargaining by then was being questioned as a rather old-fashioned way of conducting industrial relations. To talk of a time before these arrangements were even thought of is to go so far back in history that only the grandfathers of present statesmen can recall what the quarrels could have been about.

The first intimations of the violent convulsions to come while the nation reached industrial institutions it could live with were very faint in our valley. And certainly they did not reach me. I was leading a boy's life in an age which, so far as I knew, was still free in the old individual sense. That there were forces working at the heart of things which, because of the backwardness of our village, of all the Sinclairvilles, would emerge half a century hence, there was certainly no hint in my education, either at school or outside.

If anything, I looked backward rather than forward, and so, I think, did my elders, in spite of rushing headlong into a revolutionized future. If it was a time of progress, it was not a planned—or even a wanted—progress. Changes were made as children improve their play—in order to make the game go faster—not with any sense of responsibility for remote results. So I would be glad to get a metal water wheel which could be set up in a nearby brook in place of my wooden one. That it was made for me from new materials and with new tools—including a lathe—was just a fortunate fact, nothing remarkable. But so similar developments seemed to the businessmen. My father, when I was about eleven, gave up the cattle and meat trade to become a manufacturer of food products—a canner of vegetables and fruits; and from my recollections of this industry I can see how fast we went from then on in a direction whose end no one considered.

About this experience I must tell a little more. Our region being so elevated, as indeed the whole southern tier of New York counties is, the growing season was not much over sixty days.[3] The last frost of spring or the first one of fall often intruded on what should have been summer. This sharply reduced the range of crops it was safe to plant. Just over the ridge separating our watershed from that to the north and west, the elevation was some hundreds of feet lower, and that was where the vast Lake Erie vineyards were. In our valley we could not grow grapes or even tomatoes; but something about the soil or climate—perhaps chilly nights and hot days had something to do with it—was favorable to the highest-quality green corn, peas, and beans.

For some time there had been established in Fredonia and Silver Creek a company for canning such products, along with the small fruits of the Erie shore. Because the company could use the upland products we could grow better, it was determined to locate a branch in Sinclairville. And my father became its manager and, presently, a part owner.

When it was built the factory was a frame affair of several large buildings and some smaller ones, which in a few years would become ramshackle and mercifully burn down; but by

[3] The floor of our valley, like the surface of Chautauqua Lake, was about 1200 feet in elevation. Some of the hills around rose 800 to 1000 feet higher. One hilltop in Arkwright was 2100 feet. Such height at 42° north latitude produced short summers, long winters, and extremes of heat and cold. It was up in Arkwright that it sometimes snowed in summer, or at least where the hail storms most nearly resembled snow.

that time my father would have moved on to larger interests. Just at first this new enterprise caused a real stir. Its season was short; its methods, by later criteria, were inefficient; but it provided employment and a market for farmers' produce, and its product was good.

The canning factory made a new center for our family life, and it began a new phase of my education. There was something more to do in summer now than amuse myself at home or vacation at Bemus Point; my recollection is that we seldom went to the lake again except for the briefest visits. The operations of the factory were endlessly interesting, and I asked nothing better than to be allowed the freedom of its premises. Educationally, it was my introduction to the machine process and to business. From this time until I finished my college years, every summer would be spent in or around this factory or the later one my father established in Wilson. I worked, as other boys did, at jobs which would now be considered unsuitable, beyond a boy's strength. Long before I was mature, I would be doing a man's work throughout my vacations. I did not suffer from it; I wanted to do it, and I am sure from my experience that in an ideal society boys' labor would not be prohibited but would be required—suitably adapted, of course, to their strength and capacities.

Until the last few years of this apprenticeship I had no responsibilities other than for the specific job I was doing. To have been more than a laborer I would have had to participate in the planning and fitting out that went on for months before the summer campaign (as it was always called) began. And during these months I was in school. But at one time or another I did hold every job in the factory while it was evolving from its beginnings to a relatively efficient operation. There came a time when the machines required more skill than I had, but by then I was being allowed to do more responsible work in the office or outside the factory itself.

This may be an important matter. Certainly one of the defects in the education of my generation was a kind of unrealism about practical affairs. The causes of this were doubt-less complex, but many of my contemporaries had a revulsion from business and especially from factory operations that I never felt. I speak now, of course, about my later university colleagues. Instead of experience, economists and sociologists had a weird set of assumptions. These were the materials for models of economic institutions which had no relation to the real ones. One thing I must say for myself: I never lent myself to the wide conspiracy among them to regulate a naughty economic system according to these assumptions.

To mention another benefit from the sort of experience I had, I never afterward approached the problems of labor—that is, human relationships in industry—as so many of my colleagues did, with the conviction that workers could do nothing but good or, conversely, nothing but bad, as the case might be.

My working experience also went some way toward correcting my revulsion from numbers. The machine processes in those early factories were not the precise and beautifully co-ordinated systems they later became. In our industry we were learning to become efficient in difficult circumstances. We were, for one thing, seasonal, and that hampered the building up of a perma-nent and experienced work force. We were also rural and lacked any community of mechanics to call on. Yet we did share in the growth of that intangible but effective quality which a later generation called know-how. When we were beginning, in the first years of the century, only one or two of the preparatory, sterilizing, packaging, and shipping processes were mechanized, and nearly everything had to be done by rule of thumb.

In my father's roll-top desk, guarded through successive seasons, there were small black notebooks filled with accumulated experience which he sometimes let me see but which only he really knew how to translate. In later years larger processing plants would maintain constant laboratory controls to guide each hour of operations. But my father changed his orders for the length and intensity of each process merely by using his judgment. He knew what the weather had been while the

ripening had been going on; he knew what his material felt
and looked like; and after a consultation with his notebooks he
acted accordingly.

I can see him now as he stood—a tallish, slim, serious young
man, hard straw hat pushed back, several workmen around
him—in the middle of an expanse of heaped-up pea vines,
piles of corn not yet husked, or string beans in bushels and
crates. It might be in one of the sheds or in the cannery yard.
He would take up a handful of beans, a few pods of peas, or
an ear or two of corn. His knowledgeable fingers would explore,
his eyes would search, and he would even taste. The others would
do the same. And out of this conferring process would come the
decision as to the blanch and cook for the day. They discussed
the grading and the need for cleaning and sorting and made up
their minds whether they were getting the produce at just the
right stage.

One of the judgments preceding this had been one about
delivery. Each farmer had signed a contract to harvest when
told, and a day or two either way could make a difference. If
the harvest was too early the farmer would be dissatisfied with
his yield; if it was too late the starches would be overdeveloped
and the quality would be inferior. During his first years as
factory manager my father was responsible for all this alone.
Later he trained me to be a field man and to recognize
instantly when the exact conjunction or climax was reached—
but that was when I was well into my teens and we had left
Sinclairville.

In this early period we did not have the capping machine
which really revolutionized the canning process. But we did
have the line, that precursor of the conveyor belt in more
publicized trades. Once our peas were shelled—and this, by
then, was already being done by immense rubber-flailed
threshers—they moved smoothly toward their fate. One process
fed another until they emerged in the warehouse ready to be
labeled and sold. Other vegetables and fruits were not so easily

processed mechanically; but the revolution was on the way, and year by year it made itself felt throughout the industry.

Progress consisted in reducing human intervention all along the route; and gradually, with the help of machinery makers, perfection would be achieved. All the early bustle and confusion, the escaping steam and vagrant jets of water, the piles of refuse, the juices underfoot, the continuous labor of cleaning up, the cries of instruction as something went wrong and foremen and mechanics ran to start things going again—all this would have disappeared. Everything in a canning plant now is neat, simple, noiseless, clean—and mechanical. But it was not so when I was young. Hundreds of us—I think about three or four hundred in that first small factory—assembled for the summer campaign, a considerable feat, since all were gathered in from the occupations they had been following since last September, and since our work would last only some three months. And they would have to be hammered into a going organization when the first peas were ripe in June, ready and willing to work night and day until the job was done.

That, then, was the school in which I was taught to appreciate the order and precision of doing things. I learned there, too, that progressive gains upon nature may be made by taking thought and by managing well. Never afterward would I be taken in by specious defenses of rule of thumb—that is to say, I would always recognize it as a makeshift, a preliminary to something better. And this was true both for industrial affairs and for social arrangements. That this was the way of human advance, I should never have the slightest doubt.

Twelve

In that school, too, I was taught that progress is always possible; and, perhaps because the older men around me were so endlessly ingenious and optimistic, I came to think of it as inevitable. The idea of progress was traditional in the Western world, but our American version was indigenous. We were part of the vast fluid movement of population toward the West, filling up all the millions and millions of empty acres and exploiting the riches of the new land. But it was certainly true, too, that Americans were inventive and energetic. In such industries as my father was helping to create, this characteristic was always conspicuous. A long prospect of improvement and enlargement was clearly to be seen. There would be more efficiency, more productivity, and more goods to share. That this forward and upward tide should not keep rolling would have been a strange notion, not that it should.

But there was in this another of those contradictions I must mention for the sake of wholeness. Abundance was taken for granted, but there was universal belief in scarcity. Nature was known to be generous, but she had to be regarded as niggardly. The benefits of consumption were obvious, but wise men were supposed to be thrifty and parsimonious. It is possible to explain this inconsistency as a legacy from pioneer life, which, as everyone knows who has studied or experienced it, was both rich and poor. An isolated family could be extravagant in some ways, but in others it must be restricted and even mean. A forest could be burned down, the lumber unused; milk could be given to the pigs because there were so few other consumers; a winter store of meat, eggs, root crops, and apples could fill a cellar to overflowing; but there might be only a few pounds of salt or sugar to last through a year. And clothing would be scarce because of the endless labor required to produce it; tools would be few and jealously cared for; and both house and furnishings would be crude and comforts scanty.

So, while progress went on and a new world was being built, those who participated were governed by reminiscent rules. We were, in Sinclairville, only a short generation, or perhaps a few miles, removed from actual pioneering; and the shape of our minds had a lingering antiquarian cast. The new attitudes, growing out of newer realities, were gradually becoming dominant; but nostalgia always modified their influence. Individuals adapted themselves to progress, especially in their working lives, but this did not reach their moral system or their social ideas.

I have thought since that this was important in my generation. Civilization moved forward, but men's minds lingered in the past. My later friend and colleague, William Fielding Ogburn, would give this a name—"cultural lag." And Simon Nelson Patten, who would be my most respected teacher, would agree to the importance of this dichotomy. He would say that our movement was forward into an economy of plenty, but that our philosophy was derived from the economy of scarcity from which we had emerged.[1]

No better illustration of this sociological generalization could be found than the Sinclairville of the 'nineties. But throughout

[1] Vice-President Marshall once explained how it was possible to believe something known to be untrue. For instance, he said, "I believe that the Democratic party is always right, but I know that it isn't so."

At this time, the Patten of whom I have spoken had already completed his formal education at the University of Halle and had come back home impressed with this contrast. He thought the Germans less controlled by the past, and in this respect more realistic than his own Illinois neighbors. Illinois, he said, was one of the richest areas of the earth, but its people clung to the moralities of their penurious ancestors who had come from the rocky farms of New England.

the hill country certain differences were about to become apparent. It was in the first phase of decline. This was not generally recognized; or perhaps it was, but unconsciously. No more of the southern English were coming to western New York, and there was a recognizable migration westward from our region. This was what the Patten family had done, but by now the promised land was Kansas or thereabouts rather than Indiana or Illinois. These were evidences of a certain recognition, and there were others. No more of the gracious white houses which distinguished our farms were built after the depression of '93, and every building on our Main Street had been built before I was born. In fact, I think the only buildings I saw going up, as long as we lived in Sinclairville, were my father's factory and a few barns.[2] Our village was like hundreds of others in the East; its general slow decay had already begun. With the wilderness not even yet quite subdued, the fight against it was already lost.

The decline of the hill country was partly the result of competition from more productive areas. Patten's Illinois fields were incomparably superior to any of those among the eastern hills, except perhaps a few in the wider valleys, and even these had the short growing season which nothing could be done to stretch. One of these valleys was No God Hollow.

No God Hollow was a place of no importance except to the dozen families living there. Why it had so picturesque a name, I never knew. That knowledge was lost among the records kept only in old folks' minds. It was merely a shallow depression in the hills a few miles northeast of Sinclairville, on the road to Ellington and Cherry Creek. But to me it was touched with magic. It was where I came closest to the exciting past which lived on diminished in that present.

The farms in the hollow were not very productive, and they had been cleared of timber so recently that many hardwood

2 This would have been true if I had lived there the rest of my life. Sixty years later some of the old buildings would have fallen down, and the rest would seem about to collapse.

stumps still had to be plowed around every spring. The crops were limited to silo corn, rye, buckwheat, beans, and clover; but most of the land had to be left in permanent pasture. This was true on the steepest slopes and where the outcrops of stones made cultivation impossible. Forests still covered the higher ground. They stood like a wall where the upland pastures ended. But they were farmed too. They furnished winter work for farmer-loggers, and some of them were cleared of all but maples to make sugarbushes.

One of these farms was in my mother's family. She and her younger brother had gone there to live with their Uncle Will Tyler when her father had died and her mother had married again. So Uncle Will was my only grandfather figure, my father's father having died when I was only four. He was gentle and affectionate, and I responded with a boy's fondness. Besides, he was well calculated to represent the pioneer attributes. He was long and lean and well bearded. When I knew him he was thinned and worn from a lifetime of toil on land he himself had cleared—and was still clearing after forty years of labor. He was twisted and racked with "rheumatics," so that every day's work was an ordeal. But for me he and the farm had values a boy rates very highly.

It would do the generation of my grandchildren, for whom I write, no harm to consider the cost of their heritage to those who preceded them. Uncle Will not only cut his farm out of the forest with ax, wedge, saw, and a team of horses; he went on to force from it the meager crops it was capable of yielding. It was done by what used to be called main strength. That effort, and the study, year after year, of every slope, meadow, grove, and brook, brought the family a living. But when, in those days, a living was spoken of, the word was literally meant. There was nothing left over—no margin, no luxuries. If there was a family crisis—an illness, an accident, the loss of a horse or a cow, the failure of a crop—it had to be borne somehow without paying for it in cash which could not be come by. And when the strength of youth and middle age began to fail, the chronic poverty simply got worse. In old age, unless there was a son to carry on, the weeds grew in the fields, the old horses died off, and food grew scarcer and scarcer.

Fortunately there was usually a new generation coming on, and when the old people wore out, the younger ones carried on. But for a half century or more of hard labor, a man and his wife could look forward only to sharing their home with children who themselves were none too well off. Sometimes the potentialities of tragedy in this situation were modified by affection and kindness, but it was not always so. Old age could be a realistic introduction to the hell of the Protestant pastors. In Uncle Will's case my mother's brother, Will Rexford, took the place of the boys he had lost. They were both at work trying to make the farm productive when I was a boy.

We lived in the village in a fine warm house. We had store-bought furniture, our rooms were wallpapered, we had carpets, base-burner stoves, running water, and china for the table. Uncle Will's house had the appearance of having been rubbed with stain; this was because there were no plastered walls, and the beams and boards had so long absorbed the smoke of temperamental open fires. The only light in the evening came from candles (or, later, kerosene lamps). Water came from a pump in the yard; there were homemade cord beds, split-hickory chairs, crockery and wooden bowls to eat from. There was a buttery, where pans of milk were ranged on shelves until they could be skimmed for the cream from which butter was churned once a week. When I knew it, carding and weaving were no longer done, but at the back of the capacious woodshed the carder and weaver still stood, along with a disused trundle bed, as though merely waiting to be brought out again. And perhaps they were, at least the bed, because my Uncle Will had a large family of children; but I am under the impression that my mother shared her good fortune with the Tylers, who had been so kind to her. Whenever we came to visit, I recall, we brought a good many packages—among them, I suppose, supplies of store-bought cloth.

But besides what we brought to our relatives, very little came into that household from the outside. It is easy to idealize it at this distance, I know, but it is true that I have a vivid and nostalgic recollection of everything about the place. We saw it, as we came down the slope from the west out of the woods, gray and inconspicuous down the valley. It was an unpainted one-story house that seemed to grow out of the ground. In winter it was surrounded and given a base by an insulation of leaves and manure contained in a boarded trench. This was to keep the floors warm, protected from drafts. In summer the old house was a sort of island—there was no lawn—in a sea of daisies, buttercups, Indian paintbrush, queen of the meadow, goldenrod, and purple asters. There were syringa, snowball, and lilac bushes, especially by the back door; but we seldom saw them flower—in spring, as in fall, the roads were practically impassable. It was mostly in summer or winter that we went there. In summer we jogged behind old Dolly, my mother and I, over the hills and through the ferny swamp, so surprisingly lit by scarlet bee balm and white elderberry flowers. In winter we traveled in fine style, bundled in a cutter, behind a lively team that made nothing of the ruts and drifts and thank-you-ma'ams along the way.

The lumps of packed snow from the horses' hoofs thumped on the dashboard as my mother and I went off to visit the No God Hollow family on winter Saturdays; and as we came back at night, the blue winter twilight filling our own valley as we came into it, I reluctantly emerged from the spell of the Hollow and became a town boy again.

The farm would be abandoned in another generation, its fields gone back to woods. Uncle Will Rexford found it impossible to raise a big family there. So would others of its farmers. And for a long time their houses and barns stood broken-backed from winter snows, the clapboards loosened by the storms, the shingles tearing loose and being blown away. Cattle continued to be pastured there, but they could not stop the forest from coming down the slopes again into the very farmyards. The woods absorbed the apple orchards already crippled by neglect, and their saplings grew vigorously where the manure piles used to be. The thorn trees, in sculptured shapes, clipped by the gentle mouths of cows, came down the hills ahead of the hardwoods, but little by little they too gave way before the returning forest. The immense labor that had gone into the clearing of that land and its breaking to the plow would all be lost, as from the beginning it had been bound to be.

The essence of the Hollow's appeal for me must have been that historic homesickness to which the very young and the very old are alike susceptible, the young because their lives are so complicated and require of them such strenuous efforts to get ahead, the old because departure from the familiar tends to strain old habits.

When Uncle Will took off his great overshoes and thrust his felt-booted feet gratefully into the oven, a small boy could crowd close to his chair and extract tales of an older day while he enjoyed a tumbler of cider from the barrel in the woodshed. The old man could point to the shotgun and the big-hammered rifle over the fireplace and tell of wolf packs running through the forest, of bear, foxes, bobcats, and deer, as well as smaller game—squirrel, partridge, and coons. He could tell, too, of the heroic labor involved in clearing land and building the first houses and barns, and then of turning trails into roads.

By the back door where firewood was chopped for the kitchen stove there always stood a fat, upended chunk where butternuts from the trees in the upper gulch were cracked. On many a summer day, as I grew a little older, the men came down from the barn at suppertime, the chores done, and after washing at the pump sat down and ate butternuts with me as I cracked them. Uncle Will would then begin a tale, perhaps to be finished at the table, of hunting, trapping, or other adventures in the woods. I heard in the same way about huskings, bees, raisings, and harvest celebrations. Of these last, I can recall a few, but mostly they belonged to an earlier time.

But in the village there were socials (more properly, I suppose,

sociables, although this never occurred to me before this writing),
sometimes in neighbors' homes, but often in the church or in
Grange Hall up over the Cummings general store. I am puzzled
by one contradiction in my recollections. These socials often
involved dancing, of the set variety, and when they did they
were wonderfully lively occasions. Charlie Dennison, one of my
father's best friends was a famous caller. He played an enormous
bull fiddle, and when he and the several other local players
really warmed up, the stomping, galloping dances and the
jigging music could have been heard a mile away. As a small
boy, I recall sitting late on the side chairs at innumerable such
occasions. Yet it is also true that dancing, along with cardplaying
—and, of course, smoking and drinking—were indulgences
forbidden to good church members. Perhaps it was only the
round dances that were forbidden. No one seems able to
straighten me out on this.

The era of the bee was not past, and country roads were kept
up by farmers who "worked out their taxes" by getting together and putting in a certain number of days at upkeep. I
noticed also that farmers did not work alone on their Hollow
farms, at least not always. They "changed work," a custom so
common as to need no explanation. Many jobs on a farm are
better done by several men working together, and when machines
are scarce, a mowing machine, a harvester, a fodder cutter, or
equipment for sawing wood or making maple sugar were often
shared. Whenever, in later life, I heard of the American farmer's
individualism, my memory of No God Hollow would cause a
small bell of skepticism to ring in my mind. I knew better.
Self-reliant our rural ancestors certainly were, and their co-
operation had to be volunteered; but they worked together
continually and shared the product of common effort.

I would not grow up to be a theoretical individualist. But I
have to recognize that practically all of my generation would.
Perhaps it had to do with the difference between life in the
villages and life on the farms, and that, although I was a
village boy, No God Hollow made such an impression on me.

More has to be said about these contrasting attitudes. Most of those who grew up sharing communal arrangements were dead set against their extension into other sorts of endeavor. Individualism was more pervasive, by far, than co-operation. This may have been because of teaching and preaching, but that is how it came out. It is difficult to sort out these influences and determine how some of them became dominant. But the end result would be a nation devoted to "free" enterprise (more properly called merely "private" as opposed to "public"). And when Hiroshima occurred, an enormous mechanism of justification would be in operation. Perhaps as much as a quarter of the national income would be devoted to this apologia. It might even be a greater percentage; no one could say, because most of it would issue from press, radio, and other media of communication at the instance of organizations, both public and private, whose budgets could not be added together. Practically the whole bill was met as "business expense" and was deducted from taxes. We thus elaborately reassured and persuaded ourselves.

That such a persistent and formidable campaign should be required to keep men separated, competitive, and self-centered could not have been deduced easily from anything to be seen in the simpler world of the 'nineties; but it does seem as though, looking back, I ought to be able to be more certain than I am about origins. I can only point to contradictory arrangements and inconsistent attitudes which, among them, must have been at work to produce this result. The impulse toward common endeavor, neighborly assistance, and community sharing must have been strong. It had at least part of the tradition of farm life for support—the part represented by "changing work," co-operative ownership, and the care of neighbors for each other in every emergency. But part of that tradition supported an opposite view—the part which grew out of the exclusive ownership of land and individual dealing with moneylenders and merchants. This last, I suspect, may have been determinative. When the village is looked at, as apart from the farmstead, and its prosperity and prestige at the expense of the farms is realized, possible explanations begin to appear.

The village swallowed up the farm, just as later the city swallowed up the village. And the rationalization in support of individualism is quite possibly reversed for this purpose—individualism may well be less a survival of farm habits into city life than the triumph of urbanization over rural ways.

At any rate, the dominant persons and interests fattened and grew more powerful on the productivity of a developing continent. And a good part of the product was spent on perpetuating the regime which was thus favorable. More and more would be spent in this way as the United States came to be a private-enterprise island in a socialized world and so more and more on the ideological defensive. The establishment of this dominance certainly began in the early interchanges between farm and village as well as between worker and employer in early manufacturing enterprises. I saw a good deal of both, but I must have lived with them too intimately to recognize in what was going on something significant for the future. Even yet it is not something I can feel any certainty about. I have to leave it as speculation.[3]

[3] The passing of the frontier is often given what seems to me a fictitious date somewhere between 1880 and 1890. Also, it is frequently spoken of as though it existed only in the West. What is lost sight of, perhaps because the western migrations were so massive and spectacular, is that there was a frontier wherever pioneers were establishing themselves in new country, clearing it, breaking it to the plow, setting up farmsteads and villages, and creating social institutions. That process went on, even in the eastern hills, until the time when neighboring farms, perhaps those over the next hill, had begun to be damaged by erosion and had already lost much of their productivity. Our community in the Chautauqua hills was one of those areas where pioneering went on until economic decline was setting in. No God Hollow, only a few miles from Mill Creek Valley, where Sinclairville was, still lingered in the pioneering stage well into the 'nineties.

Thirteen

It seems worth while, whatever influence is attributed to the surviving past in the present, to go farther back into the pioneering which lay so close to the surface of our village life. There may be differences about the extent of that influence; but no one, I think, will say that it did not exist at all. And I am fortunately able to look at that past not only through the eyes of Uncle Will and other oldsters who to some extent lived in it, but also through the more disciplined ones of that remarkable Sinclairville sage who was also its historian—Obed Edson.[1] It was fitting that he should become the recorder of our history, since he represented so much of it in his person.

An ancestor of his, another Obed Edson, had come to the site of our village with its founder, Samuel Sinclear, in 1809 and had been, in fact, Sinclear's stepson. The Edsons had been prominent citizens ever since. The Obed I recall was a spare, elderly gentleman given an antique aspect by his Prince Albert coat, his broad-brimmed black hat (a good deal like those I have seen worn by European priests), and half-length leather boots into which his trousers were tucked. He had a bald-eagle's head, a piercing way of looking at anyone he spoke to, and he moved so rapidly that if his coattails did not actually stand out they at least billowed in his wake. He was a lawyer with the kind of varied practice a village afforded, and his

[1] Whose *History of Chautauqua County and Its People* has been referred to before and will be again. My quotations from his writings are made with permission of the publishers.

office was a small separate building situated on the lawn of the house I was born in but where my parents lived for only a few years—until they moved in with my grandparents down the hill. In his solitary domain he made his own fires in a Franklin stove, shoveled his own snow, and, I suppose, did his own cleaning. This was a convenient arrangement for gathering an enormous litter of correspondence, legal papers, books, scientific papers, and pamphlets; also, there were stacked about many mementos of his archaeological work—odd bones, weapons, crockery, and other miscellaneous objects. For he was our local antiquarian and ethnologist as well as our leading lawyer. He was also an adviser and dispenser of wisdom for the whole community. At various times he was Master of the Masonic Lodge, active in all public improvements, prominent in the County Bar Association, and a trustee of the Chautauqua Institution itself.

This remarkable individual was a very proper object of respect, at least, and even of veneration for a bookish boy; and I have the sharpest picture of the old gentleman among his disorderly accumulations. I recall him best when his office was upstairs over Phillips' drugstore, where he had even more room for his litter. How it could have been moved from the one place to the other, I cannot imagine; but it had, and it was in the older quarters that my half cousin George had his barbershop. At the turn of the century our sage must have been putting together the materials for his *History*. And an orderly book emerged somehow from the disorder of his researches. I like to imagine that I may have visited and talked with him while he was in the very process—a boy of nine or ten who was curious but must have been a nuisance. At any rate, his work occupies a high place in my esteem, and to have been even remotely associated with it is a matter or pride—pride of the sort people apparently feel when they can say they have shaken hands with the President or some other notable figure.

The *History* has heroic qualities and an epic range. It is as much social and economic as political—when this sort of history was not being written by more celebrated scholars. It deals not only with the development of our land and our economy, our families and our government, our pioneering past, and even pre-history, but also with the world's cultural progress as it was being registered in our small area. It is divided, for convenience, into periods: the pre-discovery age, the coming of the white man, the achievements of the pioneers, and the early and later farming periods. And all are treated with equal facility.

It has to be admitted that historian Edson had a subject with many elements of dramatic interest; it was, however, a subject which had always been available, and no other writer had taken advantage of it. To have done so, and to have done it in the Edson way, any other would have had to have strong antiquarian interests and enormous local pride as well as a background of research and wide reading. And being a person of talent, he would yet have had to spend his whole life in our small upland valley among the Chautauqua hills, cultivating the arts and sciences pretty much alone and writing for an audience too limited to be very stimulating and almost too limited to support publication.

Obed Edson was thus unique. There were a few others in Sinclairville who were recognizably intellectuals, but I recall that three of them (two lawyers and the newspaper editor) took to drink and wasted their talents. American communities elsewhere did occasionally throw up such individuals, some of whom were respected leaders as well as men of learning, but not many of them were content to stay at home; most went off to the cities. The leadership allowed those who did stay was a kind of payment, I suppose; but usually it was not sufficient to keep them.

It would occur to me, not long after history split in two at Hiroshima, when I had occasion to visit Sinclairville after a long absence, that Obed Edson's reception of the news would very possibly have been more collected and orderly, and his a wiser orientation for his neighbors than was that of any public leader of the time. My own world seemed to have been broken irreparably into small pieces which I never hoped to put together again. He would have related the monstrous arrival, perhaps, to the ecological background, the historical succession, of which he was the complete master. He would have seen what the adjustment would have to be. I stood in the old street in 1946, looking up at the windows where his office once had been, and wished I could consult him as so many others had done in the crises of their affairs.[2]

Our history was peculiarly rooted in geography and in the plant and animal successions determined by it. But it would have been better if these natural determinants had been better understood. It is demonstrable at this remove that at least the magnificent stand of Weymouth pines on our higher hills, and perhaps even the hardwoods at the lower levels, ought never to have been cleared for farms. This could hardly have been anticipated in 1809–39, when the clearing process was going on. A vigorous race was pushing its way toward the subjection of a continent, and these uplands could not have been reserved and protected any more than could the short-grass country in the West which, it could be seen later, should never have been broken to the plow. The labors of pioneering in the East were far more prolonged and exhausting than those in the West because of the immense task of clearing and because of the mountains and hills in which it had to be done. But the West was not yet opened in the 1830s, and its competitive effects could not yet have been foreseen.

[2] The characteristics which make men thus trusted are unusual but not exactly random. The Edson family had produced such individuals at least ever since they had come to Chautauqua with Samuel Sinclear. Most had been merely what would be described as prominent citizens, but many had been professional men and leaders. I recently ran across a scientific paper produced by John M. Edson, who was Obed's father, in 1885, when he must have been a very old man. It concerned our local ornithology and was read before the Chautauqua Society of History and Natural Science at a meeting in Jamestown. Mr. Walter Edson, Obed's son, moved to Jamestown and was all his life prominent in public affairs as well as a respected member of the Bar. He too was a trustee of the Chautauqua Institution. He was succeeded in his practice by his son, back from the wars, named for his distant ancestor, Samuel Sinclear Edson, and recognizably of the admirable breed.

There is some sort of object lesson in the labors and sacrifices of several generations, with all the admirable virtues they generated, which were wasted because they should never have been undertaken. It would take a millennium or more of natural successions to re-establish the forests slaughtered to make Chautauqua farms. It required only a couple of generations to so exhaust these farms that they had to be abandoned.

If the Edson history could hardly have been expected to dwell on this tragedy, it could hardly have been expected to insist on portents only beginning to be apparent as the century opened, which, rightly read, indicated the decay of village life. When he was writing, the adventures, the victories, the successes of Chautauqua folk were the natural theme. The pioneer and his successor, the farmer, were the heroes. If Edson had been writing half a century later, there might have been no less antiquarian delight in the past, but there would have been melancholy too. He would have had to recognize man's inability to manage the expenditure of his effort so that it might be made to count for rather than against the struggle to progress.

Of this last there was nothing in the history; but the material for it was there, in the description of natural events, in the sense of geography, and in the understanding of ecology which so much history lacks. He began with an account of the region in pre-Columbian times and, coming down through a century of struggle, closed on a note of victorious prosperity: there were now fields and pastures where there had been only wilderness; the forests had shrunk pretty much to wood lots and sugarbush; villages had grown at nearly every crossroads; cities were developing; and the Chautauqua Institution, at the height of its fame, was lending a gloss of culture to our rural county. And, as I have tried to say, there was justification for a certain complacency. If ever there was a time and a place where everything seemed to be coming out right, when there existed peace, security, and permanence, it was in Sinclairville during the four or five decades preceding World War I. But it was true elsewhere as well.

It was then that the fruits of enterprise were richest. The resources of the continent were being mined, and taxes did not reduce incomes appreciably. The middle class grew by accretion from the lower-income workers and farmers until the distinctions among them seemed about to be obliterated. Small homes glowed with comfort; education was becoming freely available to all children. In short, the whole nation was beginning to swell with strength and assurance.

Why, in these circumstances, should a local historian in a settled community of excellent stock and apparently fortunate location have ended his account of the century just past with foreboding for the future? No one had begun to notice the swift erosion of the soil on slopes which alternately froze and thawed and where the rains came in summer deluges; no one considered the significance of those free lands in the West where food and fiber were beginning to be produced at costs ruinously lower than our own. We were lingering at a moment of climax, almost as classic as that of the great forest which had dominated our region a century ago. It was one, however, which, like that other, was vulnerable to approaching enemies. The forest went when the white man came; the farming economy of the hill country was to go when the soil had been exhausted and the West had begun to compete; the villages, which were adjuncts of the farms, would follow on into slow decay.

Fourteen

To the west of the ridge dividing our county, much of it elevated above 2000 feet, lay Lake Erie with its narrow shore plain; on all other sides there rose hills that were almost mountains; they petered out to the north, but on the east and south they became the foothills of the Alleghenies. Down the valleys to the south, creeks and rivers ran toward the eventual Mississippi basin; beyond the ridge to the north, shorter streams plunged down toward Lake Erie.

There were, besides, spring- and creek-fed lakes, of which Chautauqua was the largest; but others—no more than ponds, really—lay in many of the folds among the hills. Our own valley had almost held a lake, too, but its lower end had not been quite high enough to stop the drainage from the hills—almost, but not quite. Enough was contained to make an extensive swamp, where water stood most of the year in soggy pools, but not in any wide expanse. Mill Creek came down through Sinclairville on its way to this swamp from uplands to the north of us. In summer it ran ripplingly over clean gravel, clear and tame, or stopped on its way in deep, cool holes under shading willows. Many a long Saturday, Burt Smith, Earl Roberts, and I spent along its banks, making small dams, catching minnows and crayfish, hunting for frogs, and venturing into its pools.

But at times when the snows thawed rapidly up in Arkwright, or when there were summer deluges of rain, this same creek was capable of a horrible transformation. It could become overnight a raging, roaring torrent, yellow from the dirt it carried, sweeping before it uprooted trees, rolling great boulders for long distances, and threatening buildings that had seemed far removed from its bed. Then it filled small spectators with anxiety. They stood at its sucking margins, fearfully watching its rushing waves, and learned that nature could become quite suddenly awful, completely beyond control.

It was over the northwest-southeast ridge that the early French explorers found their way from the Great Lakes to the Mississippi—Sieur de Céleron, for instance. Later travelers, who had larger craft, preferred to go west by the Lakes at least as far as the present Detroit. But for the *voyageurs,* who had only canoes, this portage from Lake Erie to Chautauqua (from the present Westfield to Mayville), was more convenient than any other, especially if the objective was to reach navigable south-flowing waters. The portage was only a few miles. From Chautauqua Lake the Gulf of Mexico could be reached without another break.[1] These Frenchmen came from the St. Lawrence, the length of Lake Ontario to Fort Niagara (of which I shall have more to say). There they would have rested for the land journey (some twenty difficult miles) up over the escarpment to La Salle on the upper river above Niagara Falls. From there they could reach Lake Erie in their canoes by fighting the swift current. Once on the lake, they could coast safely along its southern shore to the Westfield landing.

Early travelers from other parts of the Northeast and from eastern New York found that the easiest route to the western country was through the Mohawk Valley and on over the

[1] "In the valley next west of Bear and Cassadaga valleys, and extending in the same direction from the northern face of the ridge, is that depression in which lies Chautauqua Lake, the largest body of water within the limits of the county . . . In this notch, cut so deeply across the hills, gleam its bright waters—a paradox among lakes. Poised in the crest of the highlands . . . it is so near Lake Erie that we expect to see its waters poured down the steep declivity to join and finally meet the sea upon the coast of Labrador. Instead of this we find it running southward, and after a long and sinuous journey of over twenty-five hundred miles, flowing consecutively through the Chadaquoin, Cassadaga, Conewango, Allegheny, Ohio, and Mississippi, to mingle at last with the waters of the Gulf of Mexico." *History,* I, 4.

levels to what is now Buffalo. But all used the road along the south shore of Lake Erie.

Extensive use of the Erie-Chautauqua portage stopped as soon as travel by wagon had begun. The main road emerged into the central plains—Ohio, Indiana, Illinois—without encountering more serious obstacles than the crossing of placid north-running streams. This travel had been enlarged with the opening of the Erie Canal in 1825. Indeed, it was by way of the canal, then by stage from Buffalo to Dunkirk, and over the hills to Sinclairville, that my paternal grandparents had come, as others from the southern shires of England were then coming.[2]

But in my boyhood even the Civil War was several decades past, and the pioneering phase of our life, except on hill farms not yet wholly cleared, had closed. It existed mostly in tales told to children, legends of braver days and hardier ways. My father's people, the Tugwells, the Truslers, and the Leaverses, came to a village already well established and livelier than it would ever be again. On the Rexford side it was different. They had been for generations part of the westward migration. Indeed, one of my near ancestors had been a Franklin, a descendant of one of Ben's numerous brothers, for whom one of the counties in eastern New York had been named; part of the family had stopped there and part had moved on westward. It was the history of these transported English families, settled in the Mill Creek Valley and in the hills and villages around, that Obed Edson wrote.

It is time, I think, because I have said so much about him, to present a more substantial sample of his *History*. The following quite typical passage is from his account of Chautauqua pioneering:

[2] Families with such names as Mathews, Franklin, Trusler, Smith, Putnam, Seaver, Reed, Wade, Mayborn, Appleyard, Leavers, Turner, Dennison, Dingley, Sylvester, Rood, Reynolds, Thorn, Brock, Tyler, Thorp, Coveney, Chambers, Whitney, Wright, Sheldon, Gage, Langworthy, Link, and Rexford —all familiar in Surrey, Dorset, Sussex, Kent, and Somerset. Merely repeating them conveys an idea of our founding stock. I was related to several of them.

Long years of financial depression and poverty followed the War of 1812, and the life of the settler in the backwoods of Chautauqua County was one of extreme hardship, and yet, stimulated by the prospect of the building of the Erie Canal to Buffalo, the population of the County rapidly increased. For many years the covered wagons of the emigrants were constantly moving from Eastern New York toward the Holland Purchase.

For years a continuous procession of white wagons came, each with a water-pail and tar-bucket dangling from the axletree, and perhaps an infant's cradle or basket swinging from the ash hoops over which its cover was stretched, displaying upon the canvas in large black letters the legend. "For the Holland Purchase" or "For the Connecticut Reserve!" They bore the family of the emigrant, his cooking utensils, his sleeping furniture, and sometimes all of his family effects. They were often followed by freight wagons, sometimes drawn by three, sometimes by five horses. On his arrival, the settler would go first to the land office at Mayville, and get a contract for his land, to be paid for at $2.50 per acre, ten or fifteen dollars down. He then, with the assistance of his neighbors, would put up a log house, after which he would make an arrangement with the merchant at the neighboring settlement for a credit of from twenty to fifty dollars to buy a pig or a cow or some necessary articles at his store, to be paid back in salts of lye made from the ashes when he should burn his first fallow . . .

These important preliminaries concluded, the settler commenced his principal work of clearing the land, a work which he knew it would take years to consummate. But he had a stout heart and was in the vigor of his life. Besides, he had what was even better, a brave and faithful wife, who had staked her life with his on the forest venture, and was there to encourage and bear with him the privations, hardships, and perils of frontier life . . .

We see him as he plants himself by some huge hemlock or maple, cast his eyes upwards to see that there is no peril from a broken limb or loose knot. Then he lightly strikes a blow with his axe into the body of the tree, as if to measure the distance; pausing for a moment to adjust his feet, the work begins. Blow follows blow, thick and fast, until the monarch of the forest comes crashing down. This process he repeats until tree after tree succumbs, and the great silent forest, which had so long sheltered wild man and wild beast, was at last laid low.

That more elaborate instrument, the plough, which has for centuries been the emblem of civilization, and that complex masterpiece of human ingenuity, the steam engine, until now the best symbol of modern advancement, have never been more effective or essential to progress than the woodsman's narrow axe. The most elaborate contrivances of human genius have contributed less to advance the human race than the humble implements of early days . . . A little piece of steel hung upon a handle of wood conquered the forest of America and carried civilization into the heart of the continent . . .

The woodsman was strong and sinewy and toughened by toil. Yet it was not his physical powers alone which enabled him to conquer the forest. Felling trees, cutting them into lengths suitable for logging, trimming their tops, cutting the underbrush, burning the fallow, he dispatched his work with consummate skill. So expertly he fastened the chain, and so skillfully he trained his obedient oxen that at a sign or by a word, with the aid of his ready handspike, they, with little effort, gathered the logs into heaps ready for burning. So neatly did he do his work that when the burning was over, not an unburned branch remained. He was in the true sense a skilled workman.

How lightly he handles the axe! How accurately he plants its blows! He cuts the gash which severs the trunk as smoothly as if it were chiselled by a carver's tools, not to display his skill, but because the lines of grace covered by his axe correspond with the lines of least resistance to his blows.

When large areas are to be cleared, to save labor, with a few strokes he cuts a notch in each of a long row of trees and fells one of the largest at the end of the line accurately against its neighbor, then they all come crashing down in succession. By carefully observing the direction of the cant and by placing his notch, he is able to fell them into windrows which often extend the whole length of the slashing. These great masses of timber are now ready for the conflagration.

For the first quarter of the century, fires were constantly burning in the fallen timber and fallows of Chautauqua. The light of their flames nightly illumined the sky. From hilltops along the ridge could be seen in all directions between Lake Erie and the Pennsylvania Line great volumes of smoke . . .

From the ashes of the burned timber, the settler received the first return for his labor. From the sale of the black salts of lye made from ashes he paid for his land. It was the chief staple. It was the only product which could be sold for cash and was sure to exchange for goods. It was made from the ashes of oak, maple, beech, and other hardwoods. The ashes were carried to rough leaches, usually made of bark, set conveniently to water. The lye obtained was boiled in a kettle until it became a semi-solid which was called black salts. Each merchant, besides his store, owned an ashery, where he received of his customers black salts and ashes which he paid for in money and in goods, at the rate of $2.50 or $3.00 per hundredweight. At the asheries the black salts were converted into potash by burning them in ovens. Later the potash was refined into pearl ash or saleratus. These were used to make soap, glass, for culinary purposes, and in many of the arts and medicines.[3]

The destruction of one of the world's greatest and finest forests for the residue of ashes after its burning can be regarded only with horror by a later generation. It would seem an intolerable outrage if the real objective had not been the establishment of farms. It becomes tragic when taken together with the virtual disappearance of those farms a few generations

[3] *Centennial History of Chautauqua County* (New York, 1904), 96ff. For other accounts of the county's development, see *The Historic Annals of Southwestern New York,* edited by W. J. Doty (1940), of which the relevant sections were also written by Obed Edson; and *History of Chautauqua County and Its People,* American Historical Society, 3 vols. (1921). This was "largely founded on the life work of the late lamented Obed Edson (d. 1919), without a peer as a local historian . . . whose very last contribution to the annals of the region he loved so well is contained in the political chapter." See also *The Conquest of Chautauqua,* by Arthur Wellington Anderson, one-time county historian, (The Jamestown Journal Press, 1932). This account is invaluable for the early period. All the quoted passages are authorized by the publishers.

later. How that magnificent stand of trees would be cherished now!

More than half of that forest went up in flames; most of the rest of it went down the streams to the south for sale as timber; the remainder, worked up into lumber in local sawmills, was used to build the clapboarded houses which dignified the farms and villages of my youth and to provide the raw materials for the Jamestown furniture industry. In my boyhood there were still two sawmills in Sinclairville and others in nearby Red Bird, Centralia, and Ellington. These mills worked up the logs cut by farmers during the long winters.

We used to hitch our sleds to the heavy sleighloads of snowy logs as they came through town on the way to the mill down by the railroad station. The handling of logs and their sawing into lumber was one of the familiar enterprises of the country-side. Many of my friends worked at it in one way or another at odd times or after leaving school. Timber was a by-product of farming. And most farmers had remaining wood lots into which they made inroads every winter. No connection was made between this tree-cutting and the increasingly destructive floods that swept through the valleys. The era of conservation had not yet arrived.[4]

We come, by 1850, to what the *History* called "The Agricultural Period." The first generation of pioneers was long since dead, buried in quiet hilltop cemeteries. Every native Chautauquan expected now that one of these burying grounds would be his ultimate destiny; he regarded it as a natural prospect

[4] F. J. Turner, in *The Frontier in American History*, (N.Y., 1920), said about this: "To the pioneer, the forest was no friendly resource for posterity, no object of careful economy. He waged a hand-to-hand war upon it, cutting and burning a little space to let in the light on a dozen acres of hard-won soil, and year after year expanding the clearing into new woodlands against the stubborn resistance of primeval trunks and matted roots. He made war against the rank fertility of the soil. While new worlds of virgin land lay just beyond, it was idle to expect the pioneer to stay his hand and turn to scientific farming. Indeed, as Secretary of Agriculture Wilson [Tama Jim] has said, the pioneer would have raised wheat that no one wanted to eat, corn to store on the farm, and cotton not worth picking."

that he should lie there with his predecessors. Obed Edson recalled their successes and failures in the light of that expectation. He had pride of place, and he boasted of his native county in the vital language of its people:

Chautauqua had now come to the front as one of the first agricultural counties in the state. Chautauqua County butter and cheese bore a reputation for excellence. The County had become famous for its horses and cattle and apples. Judge Zattu Cushing, when he came to the County in 1805, brought with him a half-bushel of apple seeds from which he started a nursery at Fredonia. Many other early settlers planted their first orchards with scions and with seeds brought with them into the County, selected from the favorite varieties of their old homes in the east. Among them were Spitzenburghs, Seek-no-furthers, Roxbury Russets, Rhode Island Greenings, and other excellent and now forgotten kinds. There were also many worthless kinds, useful only for cider . . . The apples of the hills were better in quality than those raised by Lake Erie, but the early frosts rendered the farmer a more uncertain crop. . . .[5]

But not only agriculture was the subject of his account; the cities and towns were celebrated too. The coming of the railroad was told about; and the struggle, before that, to open highways into all the difficult back country was recounted with something of the wondering interest contemporaries must have felt:

A principal route for stages (about 1860) from Buffalo, Dunkirk, and Fredonia, to Jamestown, Warren and the southeastern part of the County prior to the building of the Erie road, had been by the highway, one branch leading through the villages of Cassadaga and Sinclairville and the other through Stockton and Delanti to Jamestown. The ascent of the ridge by the Sinclairville branch from the north with heavily loaded wagons had always been a laborious task. Near Shimla was Scott's Hill, at the west border of the town of Arkwright. At the foot of this hill a team of oxen was in readiness

[5] *History*, I, 68.

to assist. At Walk-up Tavern, later known as the Kimball Stand, the passengers dismounted that the stages might the easier ascend . . . In 1852 the Fredonia and Sinclairville plank road was built from Fredonia through Cassadaga and Sinclairville to the Kimball Stand. It was twenty-two miles in length. North of Cassadaga it extended three miles through an unbroken forest . . . The hemlock plank for this road was manufactured and delivered along the line of the road for five dollars a thousand feet. There were now over one hundred miles of plank road in the County. These were excellent roads at first, smooth and firm. Heavy loads could be carried over them very rapidly. Such increased facilities for transportation and travel greatly promoted the prosperity of the County.[6]

Often, participating as small boys expected to be allowed to do in all sorts of jollifications, at socials, celebration dinners, squirrel-pie suppers, or sugarings-off, when the food had been disposed of and the tables had been cleared away, I watched the dancing begin. My companions and I were only spectators when it came to this stage, and we sat along the wall, listening and watching. Grouped with us, there were often oldsters whose dancing days were past, as ours had not yet begun, and they would be exchanging reminiscences. They deplored the modern changes, of course, and glorified the past—the days of their vigor. Sometimes we listened. The *History* tells something of what we heard:

During the early periods, churches and meetings were as well attended and the sober duties of life as well performed as at the present time, yet the people were not puritanical. They were social and fond of indulging in the few simple amusements that the time afforded. An old paper advertised that "a living African lion will be exhibited at the tavern of Judia Tracy in Mayville . . . No apprehension of danger need be entertained as he is secured in a substantial iron cage." Sometimes a single elephant was exhibited. It would be driven to the place of exhibition in the night, covered with canvas so as not to be seen by people on the way. These unpretentious

---

[6] Ibid., 63.

shows excited much interest; they were the forerunners of the car-
avan, a little later of the circus, and finally the mammoth hippo-
drome. Now and then a puppet-show, a performance of sleight-of-
hand tricks, or occasionally a public lecturer on some subject, would
visit the little settlements.

Dancing assemblages, or balls of the young people, were common
and were simple and hearty affairs. Contra dances, such as the
money-musk, Virginia and opera reels, and the French Four were
the usual dancing figures. Square dances were uncommon and
round dances were unknown. Sir Roger de Coverley, McDonald's
reel, the Arkansas Traveller, Resin the Bow, and other ancient and
lively tunes, played upon a single violin by a local fiddler, consti-
tuted the music.

The young men were an athletic, scuffling, wrestling race, who
delighted in nothing more than those ancient sports by which the
backs and limbs of all stout-hearted youths have been tested since
the days of Hercules. Wrestling was the popular outdoor amusement, practiced at every house- and barn-raising, town meeting, and
public gathering. During school days, a high school in athletics was
always established outside the schoolhouse, where, morning, noon,
and night, the boys quite as diligently plied and studied the wrestling
art as their books within doors.

When General Training Day would come at Westfield, Sinclairville, and Jamestown, strong and active young men would gather
from far and near. Where the crowd was the thickest, some athletic
young man of spirit, accomplished in the art, would mount a ped-
dler's cart, and announce by way of challenge, that "of all the men
he could see, there was not one he could not lay on his back; and
that he would be at the boat-landing at one o'clock." Promptly on
time the crowd would be there, and as promptly the dauntless young
man himself, and boldly he would walk into the ring. No sinecure it
was to hold one's own against all comers there, for ready for the
fray were the sons of the backwoods from the hills of Ellery and
Gerry, whose limbs had been toughened from swinging the axe in
slashings, and stalking through the woods for deer, with bodies in-
vigorated by feasting on cornbread and venison. There were also

rough rafting descendants of Anak from Carrol, Poland, and Kiantone, whose muscles had been hardened by hewing down pine trees and hauling them to the mills, pulling on oars, and roughing it on Allegheny flats. There too were tough, grog-drinking boatmen from down the river, equally ready for a wrestle or a fight . . .

But few holidays were recognized. Thanksgiving day was observed by only a few, and those the settlers from the New England states. Christmas was honored but little more. The young people often celebrated New Years with balls and sleigh rides; Washington's birthday was passed by; the Fourth of July was duly remembered. No day of the year, however, not excepting Independence Day, was so generally observed as General Training Day, often in other places called General Muster Day. The rough life of the backwoodsman, the familiarity of the people with the use of firearms, and the recent war in which the country had been engaged, were calculated to cultivate a martial taste and the military spirit ran high for many years. On General Training Days, the whole male population would turn out to witness the sham fights and military parade, and to take part in the festivities of the day. None lived long enough to efface from memory the fun and enjoyment. The apple carts and peddlers' wagons dispensing their stocks of cider, ginger-bread, and honey, and before all, the stirring music of the drum and fife were not soon forgotten. . . .[7]

The summer of 1896, when I was five, seems to have been a particularly pleasant one. Probably I spent a good deal of it at Bemus Point. Our historian recalls that

. . . it was remarkable for its mild and pleasant weather and its fruitfulness. Scarcely a frost occurred after the first of April. By the first of June field strawberries were ripe, roses in full bloom, the grass in the meadows thick and tall, the corn rank and vigorous. The summer was as beautiful as the spring. Thunderstorms purified the air, causing a dense growth of vegetation. August was a delightful month; the woods, meadows, and pastures were as green as in June but of a deeper shade. Never was there such a crop of

[7] Ibid., 48 ff.

apples. The orchards were so loaded with fruit that the limbs often broke and many apples were spoiled. . . .[8]

When he came to chronicling the century's end, the historian was overcome by nostalgia as he looked backward at what seemed to him the best times there had ever been or perhaps ever would be:

No century that comes after the present will be of equal interest. The tale of the pioneer, his free and easy life, his great expectations, the hardships he endured, the sacrifices he made, and the final success will always be of interest . . . If the pioneer were here now he would marvel at the changes: the railroads, the towns and cities, the green fields that spread everywhere among the hills. When the sound of his axe was first heard along the shore of Chautauqua Lake the Indians had not taken leave of Fair Point, the deer browsed in its groves and the wolf nightly howled here. Now all is changed; in the same groves thousands gather from all parts of the land . . . All this has occurred in the span of a single life. . . .

Chautauquans had emerged into a wonderful era; all was prosperity and progress; but still the old times had charm for an aging historian and his readers which the new ones could not match.

I may perhaps anticipate, for the sake of completing the Edson account, what would one day be said of the man who wrote most of the passages I have quoted:

During the night of 19 November 1919, Obed Edson, the grand old man of Chautauqua County, died at the home of his son Walter . . . aged eighty-seven years, nine months, four days . . . He was the best informed man of his day concerning early Chautauqua before the white man came. His research, early recollections, and wonderful memory, made him a veritable encyclopedia of local information, and he took perhaps a greater interest in history than he did in his profession. Living a life of activity and good works,

[8] Ibid., 77.

quietly pursuing the path that lay before him, shirking no responsibility, seeking no honors, he lived and labored long beyond man's allotted years and carried with him to the grave the love and respect of every Chautauquan . . .[9]

He did indeed.

[9] Ibid., 151.

Fifteen

Chautauquans were rustic in 1900 in spite of their cultural Institution. The countryside, only lately emerged from the forest in spite of the Dolly Varden Railway and a gradually extending system of roads, was isolated—or at least our valley was. The roads were not yet hard-surfaced; they were not so useful, in fact, as the plank roads had been. These were gone now, since the cost of lumber and labor had gone up; and the roads were no longer routes for carrying passengers and mail by coach. I can myself recall only one fragment of plank-road, pointed out to me by my father on one of our drives. It ran alongside the track then in use, rotted and torn to pieces. At that time, the roads were terrible. For several months of the year the mud was nearly bottomless, and during the rest the dust was at best a nuisance and at worst a real hindrance to travel. Only when winter froze the earth could we get around freely, and even then the snow often drifted over the fence tops and obliterated all traces of the way we were meant to follow.

Such roads were practically useless for the early automobiles. For years their range was strictly limited. But a change forced by the growing number of car owners began about 1900.[1]

I recall with complete clarity the first automobile I ever saw.

[1] By 1905 there would be 160,000 miles of hard-surfaced road. But more than half of that had been built since 1900. None of this reached Sinclairville and would not for several decades. But the good-roads movement was gradually gaining momentum and would come to a climax in 1916, when the Shackelford Act established a national highway system and began to extend Federal aid to the states.

It was driven to our house by John Light, who was working in North East, Pennsylvania, and who was courting my cousin, Celia Leavers. Celia was living with us, and John had borrowed the Oldsmobile from his employer for the formidable fifty-mile trip to Sinclairville and back. It probably helped John in his courtship; it certainly helped me to establish valuable prestige with the other boys. The year must have been 1899, and the time must have been summer. About these facts I am uncertain, but not about the vehicle itself. It was much like one of the rigs in our barn, the one we called a "trap," in which the riders, if there were more than two, sat back to back, and which had rubber-tired wheels.

This visiting automobile was cranked from the side and started with irregular popping noises—when it could be induced to start at all. Its convulsions could be heard throughout the neighborhood. When it settled down to steady running it was steered with a handle grasped by the driver's gauntleted hand. It had no windshield, and its lights were large brass kerosene lanterns beside the dashboard. I suppose its speed must have approached ten miles an hour, but that was quite enough on the roads it had to travel.

It arrived before our house late one afternoon, its adventurous driver and a friend protected by romantic linen coats and caps and large goggles. Almost before its dust had settled I was circling it raptly to absorb every detail. Before it left a day or two later, after stately parades about town, I had been allowed to steer it proudly through Main Street, huddled somewhat ignominiously between adult legs, but nevertheless, I imagine, assuming an intolerably self-satisfied air. I acquired a notable prestige with my contemporaries in that progress; jealous detractors were unable to think of any way to minimize my superiority.

This was a beginning. My generation, in its second decade, came to have a familiarity with motorcars which would be like our fathers' familiarity with horses and our sons' with airplanes. There would be overlapping. If my children knew both automobiles and airplanes, I knew both horses and motors. I was a little shocked late in life to have an almost-grown granddaughter say to me that she had never been on a train. I thought it was time and saw that she had a ride. It looked as though it might soon be too late.

The development of the internal combustion engine and other like evidences of practical progress were of infinitely more interest to me than public affairs. In 1901, when I was ten, I could certainly not have told a questioner that Theodore Roosevelt was Vice-President of the United States, that John Hay was Secretary of State, or that Benjamin B. Odell was Governor of my state. I might have known about McKinley, but I would have been exposed as wholly ignorant about any of the issues then shaping themselves as industrialism expanded and population grew. The midwestern resentment against the money power and the barons of Wall Street had, in fact, already passed its culmination. Bryan had not yet made his last bid for the Presidency. That would be in 1908 against William Howard Taft. But his magic was already diminished by two defeats. Theodore Roosevelt was making his way up the political ladder. The buccaneers of the Stock Exchange, Jim Fisk and Jay Gould, about whom Henry Adams had written so indignantly, had long since retired from the scene, to be succeeded by the less spectacular Morgan types. Even corruption in the big cities was past its most notorious phase but still, obviously enough, had not been conquered. The muckrakers were gathering their material and preparing the attacks on corruption which would seem to me a little later the crusade I would most like to join.

Of such matters in the crude, unprincipled area of business and politics, national or local, we school children heard practically nothing. We could, on the other hand, have described in detail every one of the early automobiles, and most of us could shortly have taken them apart and put them together again. I do not recall that I aspired to be a locomotive engineer—I was always supposed to be destined for a more learned career—but driving an engine was clearly the leading ambition among my friends. And several of them made it.

In 1902, when I was eleven, a tremendous event occurred. Because of it I graduated from being a village boy and became a sophisticated citizen of the nation. My father and mother and I made a six-month journey to Colorado. For me it was a tremendous experience. Every moment of it made its impact on my mind. Never afterward would I be quite the same. It is best described, perhaps, as enlargement or widening. It was very real, anyway, and I can recall it quite clearly.

We came back to Sinclairville in the spring—for what reason, I do not know, since most people, when they went West, stayed there. I was told afterward that we had gone partly because of my health; respiratory symptoms were then customarily confused with lung trouble. Anything so esoteric as allergy had not yet been suggested. Of course I was basically rugged, and there was nothing wrong with my lungs. This must soon have been obvious. At any rate, we did come back, and the western journey proved to be only an interlude. But I think it must have changed things for my parents as well as for myself; my father soon made a vital decision about his occupation, and if I am not mistaken it was about this time that my mother discovered how nonsensical were the sumptuary rules governing Congregational conduct. In my own life it ranked with the owning of an automobile. The journey made me restless; the automobile would eventually provide that restlessness with relief. We were a few years short of owning a motorcar, but the trip to Colorado was well calculated to prepare all of us for its advent.

We went tourist rather than first class—we were not so well off then as we later became—and the trip was probably beset with exhausting discomforts, although it did not seem so to me. On the contrary, the train had all the effect of flight on a magic carpet.

We necessarily started out on the Dolly Varden. That was

from Sinclairville to Dunkirk, where we connected with the main line of the New York Central,[2] changing at Chicago to the Burlington, which, with a good deal of switching, took us all the way to Denver. At Dunkirk, although we had a hamper of food, we had some sort of meal at the station hotel while we waited for the express train. It was there that I first saw one of the wonders of the journey. There were colored waiters. I found it incredible; and when we left and one of them shook hands with me, I looked to see whether any of the color had come off. He laughed. I have realized since what sort of laugh that must have been, but at the time I thought only of my own embarrassment.

The tourist cars were distinguished from others of better class by having hard seats of woven straw rather than plush-covered cushions, as well as not being made up into berths at night, by having dirtier aisles and washrooms, and by being more crowded. We were five days getting to Denver. That included an overnight stop in Chicago. My bewilderment in the busy city was less than it might have been had I not been taken the year before to see the Buffalo exposition. My father took us on a sight-seeing tour, ending up at a hotel near the station sometime after dark. I had seen the Loop at its busiest, the waterfront, and several famous buildings. These last were described with pride by the guide. I can recall him but not the buildings, except that they were of overpowering height.

Next morning we embarked on the Burlington's train for Denver. From here on I am not clear about the sequence. I recall arriving at another city which had immense railroad yards, where we stayed for hours. The windows were washed there—on the outside—and the aisles were swept. And presently we crossed the Mississippi, which proved disappointing. I considered that it should have had an appearance more appropriate to its name in my geography. There it had been called

[2] Advertised as the water-level route to distinguish it from the Erie, the Lackawanna, and the Lehigh Valley, which came across New York State through more southerly gaps in the Alleghenies.

"The Father of Waters," and this had evoked a vision of a sparkling stream flowing out from under the throne of the Hebraic Jehovah of my Sunday-school texts. The reality was quite different. The train merely crawled cautiously onto a wooden trestle, which began in the muck amid mud flats, and advanced across a sluggish expanse of yellowish water and ended in similar circumstances on the other side.

By the second morning the car was in a state that must have been equally offensive to the eyes and ears of adults. And my parents were understandably peevish after having slept uncomfortably leaning against each other. I had done better, having had a seat on which I could stretch out. Besides, I found my surroundings fascinating. I explored as far as I was allowed up and down the car among the discarded papers, banana peelings, satchels, baskets, and packages, was offered fruit from others' hampers, and made many friends.[3]

[3] I pause here to recall Robert Louis Stevenson's account of his crossing the continent some years earlier, when the amenities of travel had been even fewer. Yet trains had not changed much, and perhaps they never would until they disappeared for good. Air conditioning and diesel power would make them cleaner and somewhat faster; but as late as 1946 the president of the C.&O. spoke of them as "rolling tenements" and exposed the amazing percentage of equipment that was more than fifty years old.

Stevenson, too, met his first Negro on his transcontinental journey. This was in Pittsburgh, so he did not follow the water-level route; he crossed Pennsylvania and came up to Chicago across Ohio and Indiana. He noted, on coming to Chicago and taking a look around, that he had subscribed sixpence to Chicago's building after the great fire but thought now that he ought to have it back. By then he was already very tired from the train travel; and when it was time to leave the city he descended the platform like a man in a dream. "It was a long train, lighted from end to end; and car after car, as I came up with it, was not only filled but overflowing. My valise, my knapsack, my rug, with . . . six ponderous tomes of Bancroft, weighed me double; I was hot, feverish, painfully athirst; and there was a great darkness over me, an internal darkness, not to be dispelled by gas. When at last I found an empty bench, I sank into it like a bundle of rags, the world seemed to swim away into the distance and my consciousness dwindled within me to a mere pin's head, like a taper on a foggy night."

The journey for Stevenson became worse and worse. He had to change at Burlington after two miserable days and nights as he went on toward the West. He was sick and he had little appreciation for the beauty of the plains and mountains. He hated the dirt and litter; he hated even more the promiscuousness of coach travel. Still, far out on the plains, he noted once how much it was like the sea. There was "an empty earth; front and back the

My disappointment with the Mississippi was compensated
for next day when we came to the short-grass country and natives of the region on the train began to be distinguished from
Easterners by their clothes, their conversation, and their behavior. There were even cowboys returning from having val-
eted cattle from the plains to the Chicago stockyards or to midwestern feed lots. During one long afternoon they stood on the
open platforms between cars and shot with rifles and revolvers
at coyotes and prairie dogs. If they could see their quarry of-
tener than I, that detracted not at all from the fascination of
their salty talk, their picturesque dress, and the romantic associations called up by my discovery of their genuine existence.
The stolen hours with my dime novels gave me background.
Some of them had been westerns. I knew all about Buffalo
Bill.

This was the first in a succession of such marvelous experiences for me. When scenes read about are encountered in real
life, something incredibly rewarding occurs. The whole of a
background, a new world, comes alive, swelling and extending
the experience into an infinity of exquisite apprehensions. The
richest of all such experiences would happen to me years later
in successive stays in the England of literary tradition. To me,
as to many Americans, England would never be quite real and
matter-of-fact. I would keep seeing characters out of novels,
dwelling on eighteenth-century survivals, and being pleased with
antique remains. A small boy riding the cindery platforms of

---

line of the railway stretched from horizon to horizon . . . On either hand
the great plain ran until it touched the skirts of heaven . . . There was a
certain exhilaration in this spacious vacancy, this greatness of the air, this
discovery of the whole arch of heaven, this straight, unbroken prison-line
of the horizon . . ." But mostly he was preoccupied with his own discomforts,
the rude neighbors, the official boorishness, as well as his own worsening
sickness.

I am quite certain that my mother had not read this account of Stevenson's
to me, although she had read aloud *Treasure Island* and other stories, and,
on the whole, he was one of our most reliable household authors. *Virgini-
bus Puerisque* passed for a philosophical work with Chautauqua intellectuals.
But this story of travel would have been unpleasantly realistic, especially in
preparation for a similar journey.

a West-going train in 1902, in spite of his mother's anguish, had many such sensations.

On the last afternoon the Rockies, with the sun behind them, thrust themselves up from the plain. It was like the landfall of a ship, that train advancing toward the mountains over the billowy prairie, except for a clarity of atmosphere which would seldom be known at sea and which made the mountains visible hours before they were close. The peaks and ridges, seen suddenly and all at once, were pointed out by an excited homecomer, so that one moment I was among the rowdy cowboys riding an ocean of sparse brown grasses and sagebrush with treeless horizons, and the next I was anticipating something very different—for which I also had a literary preparation. Here there were rolling, empty spaces across which infrequent drooping horses and their riders made their way toward indistinguishable objects; there I should find mountains, forests, and lakes. It was only hours from the land of the covered wagon, the buffalo, Indians, and ranchers to that of the snowy peaks, the bear and mountain lion, rangers, prospectors, and miners. We sailed up and into the Denver station in a daze of tiredness mixed with excited anticipation. It was something of a letdown to find the hotel in Denver much like the one we had stayed at in Chicago.

We soon went on to Boulder, then a neat little city with an embryonic university and, what I found it difficult to understand, a Chautauqua, having its existence in tents at the edge of town.[4] The environment here was more dramatically satis-

[4] This was one of numerous spiritual extensions of the original Institution. It had no corporate connection but copied as far as it could the programs devised for the Chautauqua summers. Some of these organizations were itinerant; some had grounds—such as that at Boulder—to which they returned each season. Their purpose was uplift and edification, with some concessions to the human desire for genteel amusement. Cf. *Chautauqua: An American Place*, op. cit., II, and later. It should be noted that Chautauquas were related to the lyceum movement, spoken of earlier, which had been so important in small-town America during the nineteenth century. Cf. *Journal of Education*, March 1950, and *The American Lyceum, Its History and Development*, by Cecil B. Hayes, U. S. Dept. of Interior, Bull. No. 12, 1932.

fying. It was closer to the mountains, for one thing; they rose precipitately almost out of the city's streets. And to the east there stretched the familiar plains whose ranchers and cowboys frequently rode into town. We were not there long, but while we were, my father, on unforgettable weekends, took me on excursions, often complete with donkeys, up into the high country to the west. I made a friend or two, and there were sometimes parties for these hikes and campings-out. These experiences entered into and remained part of me from then on. Aside from the male companionship, I could hardly have helped being affected by the experience of looking away over the plains for scores of miles, of seeing ridge after ridge of the Rockies looming in the west, of visiting hidden lakes and camping beside torrents fresh from melting snows.

My past life in the snugness of the Chautauqua hills seemed tame by comparison, and I acquired a standard for the future. It is not too much to say, I think, that afterward I would tend to measure experiences on the scale of the plains and mountains. Much later in life it would occur to me that this was similar to the experience of learning some of the generalizations of science: the second law of thermodynamics (whose significance was indelibly impressed on me by Brooks Adams), the cooling off of the solar system as the sun's energy declined, the tendency of erosion to flatten the earth and hide it below the sea; and some not so pessimistic: the process of mountain-building in the geologic storms, the marvelous mechanism of the immortal germ plasm and the race-saving function of individual death. Later, at any rate, I related all these intellectual experiences to that first one of discovering the immensity of the wilderness and the insignificance of man. The mighty phenomena of nature were implacable, orderly, governed by principles (at which we mostly guessed); but anyway, the glory and mystery of the universe and our earth were there for a boy (or a man) to absorb.

We left Boulder after a few months and spent the rest of the winter in Canon City. This required a journey back through

Denver and southward through Colorado Springs. In that town, where we stayed over for a day or two, my father hired a carriage and took us for the regular tourist trip through the Garden of the Gods at the foot of Pikes Peak—an example, if there ever was one, of nature's offhand humor. It was a natural tourist trap. Everything in sight could be related to some picture in people's minds, an anthropomorphic exercise which gave them great satisfaction in the midst of the wayward results of an obvious irresponsibility at the heart of things. Thomas Hardy would have appreciated that trip among the eroded rocks under the looming mountain.

We settled into a small house in Canon City and enjoyed the much milder climate. I amused myself endlessly with boats and dams in the ditches filled with water—from the mountains —that ran foot-deep along each side of our street. And I was not made to go to school as I had been in Boulder, and so was spared the miseries of another accommodation to strange boys. But I did make some friends who showed me how to house and enjoy a flock of tumbler pigeons, and I recall taking chances with a burro and being tumbled end for end by a kick that landed squarely on my chest. That was humiliating for a boy who had known horses all his life, but I was not much hurt.

Not far from Canon City was the Royal Gorge, where, so deep and narrow was the defile of the Arkansas River, the Denver and Rio Grande Railroad had been forced to hang a bridge from each cliff for some distance to carry the tracks above the torrent. That was considered a marvel of engineering. But it was hardly less so than the right of way of the narrow-gauge railway that ran up into and through the mountain passes to Cripple Creek. Crawling on this chuffing miniature railway over flimsy wooden trestles and around hairpin curves cut into stupendous cliffs, we made excursions into the worked-out mining country. The train labored slowly in and out of cloud shadows, rising to new vistas with every turn, and ended up in the derelict town which had all the atmosphere the most romantic boy could have looked for. And besides, we could ride swift lifts down into the earth, where, as I recall, gold mining was still being carried on—or would it have been silver mining? At any rate, it was a reinforcing experience. Man's adventure on this earth was chancy and likely to come to nothing in the end, but it was glorious while it lasted.

I can recall almost nothing of the journey back home to Sinclairville late that spring. But one thing is certain; I carried with me recollections that would influence me all the rest of my life.

Sixteen

I came back to the Chautauqua hills with an effervescing experience thus at work within me. I did not resist, any more than any other boy would have, the temptation to make the most of my travels among my stay-at-home fellows. My sophistication, however, did not preclude the onset of a kind of pervasive sentimentality as I approached puberty. This was, with me, as I suppose it must have been with many others of my sort, a very marked phase and might very well have become permanent. It often did.[1]

It has seemed to me that in the complicated make-up of the young individual there can be distinguished two emotions, one or the other of which takes charge when circumstances are right but which lead to very different results. One is an intense appreciation of some art, the other a projection into the indifferent order of nature of an imagined guardianship. They occur so simultaneously that identification is difficult, and both may be competing for control of the individual. The one can lead to the beginnings of work in some medium that is at least honest and to a discipline that recognizes accepted standards. The other can lead to opposite results. These appear as the excusing of slackness on the ground that the difficulties are too hampering or that the art is not acceptable; hence our prevalent

---

[1] How else account for the existence and popularity of such individuals as Edgar A. Guest and his fellows? We had a local Guest in the Buffalo paper we had begun to read—a columnist named John D. Wells. He had a large and faithful following in western New York. But there were other betraying phenomena—Rotary and similar organizations, for instance.

anti-intellectualism. In the one case the young person falls into laziness and joins the chorus of depreciation. In the other he becomes a realist in judging the relation his work bears to the standards of his medium and everlastingly keeps at it. One young fellow says that he is not meant to be something; another says that he will be what he wants to be whatever the obstacles.

Laziness easily leads to self-pity and overattachment to all friendly objects and individuals. It argues against change and overdignifies all that enhances a meager talent. It puts emphasis on what is familiar, easily understood, and cheaply attained. Devotion to an art of some sort requires selectivity and concentration, industry and pitiless self-examination. The artist may have to settle for less, but he will always know what is best.

One of the most important objects of education and guidance ought to be the teaching of this distinction: how to encourage the one and avoid the other. And in those instances in which the talents are modest and the character mediocre, there ought to be allowed nothing for weakness—no babying, no pretending. The standards ought not to be adulterated. If the individual has to make a difficult accommodation to them, he ought to be helped to achieve it. There is plenty of use for secondary talents. But that they are secondary is simply a fact and has to be got used to.

In my generation there was no assistance at all in these matters. In fact, there was an agreement to bring about the wrong result. I can see now that I very nearly gave in to praise for the wrong qualities and accomplishments. This was largely due to the well-meant coddling of my mother and of others in the community—neighbors, ministers, teachers—who joined in the conspiracy to pass off guile and ease as learning and talent.

My mother read to me endlessly from sentimental literature produced to feed this strain in the American character, and I had none of the stiff demand at home that my progress in school should be creditable that I afterward learned was a regular feature of European home life. My deficiencies were excused; I was praised for meager accomplishments, and perhaps most of all for those I could fake without much trouble. I was even admired for the good looks and attractiveness which were more and more attributed to me as I grew—especially by relatives and friends who saw what they preferred to see.

I do not mean to suggest that a democracy should go much out of its way to favor its talented young people. I have always been suspicious of the apparatus for selection that has become so elaborate. I am not sure that the best can be selected, since so much depends on complicated emotional arrangements within the individual. Also, I suspect the whole selecting business because it postulates an elite which can by definition never be more than a small per cent of the whole. There are two observations I have to make about this. One is that the most effective—yes, I will say the greatest—people I have known could not have got themselves selected as first-quality people until they had matured. The other is that character—faithfulness, industry, loyalty, tolerance, kindness—seems to have little or no relation to tests for superior intelligence. And these are also qualities civilization needs.

I do not mean to suggest, either, that I ought not to have had encouragement when I needed it or praise when I merited it; or that the security of my environment led to weakening. The lack of these would perhaps be worse for a boy than overregard for his superficial accomplishments. What I insist is that someone should have distinguished for me what represented qualities on which I could build from ones that were not of my own making and represented no honest effort. I, like so many others, became, for lack of direction and critical appraisal, a kind of cheater. I did not mean to, I did not even need to, and I got no satisfaction from it, really; yet since it was easy, and almost required, I fell into the way of it.

I must say for myself, however, that I had one saving quality. I never fooled myself. I had a good deal of practical sense even as a youth, got, perhaps, from my businessman father, although I was always supposed to be so much my mother's boy. What saved me may have been the feeling from my first contact with writing materials that I had found something I liked to do that came naturally. The workmanship involved in expression took hold of me; it not only kept me at work, but it induced a critical self-examination such as every writer needs. I can see how others whose finding of a way of working is delayed and and who may perhaps never find an altogether satisfactory medium have a far more dangerous passage from childhood to maturity. In my own case, I did have an attack of sentimentality running even beyond puberty, but it never really took charge. I had a sort of secret life from about the age of eleven. I told no one about it, ever; and no one helped me, except my English teachers, who may have guessed but did not know what my ambitions were. I read and practiced secretly. I might not become really first-rate, but I would not become an Edgar Guest, either. It was something of a strain, living one life for others and another for myself. But that is what I did. And I imagine that many others have done it too.

I had what was probably as favorable a home environment as could have been expected short of growing up in a household where scholarship and skeptical criticism were matters of everyday concern. I was at least let alone. My mother may have had an outrageous prejudice which led her to exaggerate all my virtues and overlook all my vices, and she may have wanted me to admire the wrong things inside and outside of books, but she was a busy woman and could not insist on her point of view every hour of the day.

When I say she was busy it has to be understood that it is literally meant. Work went on from early morning until late at night. Ours was a large household. The house itself was of a size appropriate to it, and all the arrangements involved labor and inconvenience to a degree which would seem incredible to a modern housewife. This was in spite of my father's willingness to adopt every improvement that came along. For instance, we had the first bathroom in Sinclairville, installed in a special dormer addition, when I was five or six. But as long as we lived there the house was heated by stoves rather than a furnace. There were three of them, coal-burning monsters, very cheerful with their mica windows, but producing ashes that had to be coped with twice a day. Then there was the cookstove in the kitchen. This had an endless capacity for stovewood, it seemed to me. It was a traditional boy's chore to keep it supplied, and filling the wood box was a duty I graduated into as soon as I acquired pants in the place of pinafores. An extra supply was required on washdays, when the copper boiler on top of the stove had to be heated over and over again. The actual washing was done in the woodshed, in wooden tubs fitted out with washboard and wringer. And I can still recall how glad my mother was to have washing and ironing days behind her. Wednesdays she baked bread, perhaps a dozen loaves; but it seemed like a vacation after Monday over the tubs and Tuesday at the ironing board. Store bread was as yet unheard of; pies were on the table three meals a day, and elaborate cakes and puddings were expected regularly. When the season was right, the whole house was upset with the activities incidental to preserving, canning, pickling, salting, and otherwise filling the extensive cellar shelves against the winter. When I say my mother was busy, it is no exaggeration.

Besides the immediate family—my two brothers who died in infancy, my sister who arrived later, my father, and myself—there were always from three to six others. One or two of these were hired men, one or two were relatives who came to stay for months at a time, and two or three others were schoolgirls who were training to be teachers—that is, taking special courses a year or two beyond high school.

I have the happiest memories of the young women who lived with us in this way. There was a succession of them, and I recall every one with special fondness, although none stayed for more than the time of her training. They brought with them liveliness, helpfulness, and humor. They were always healthy and willing and, having grown up in farm families, were well accustomed to the household arts. They were not more concerned with education than was required for a teacher in a country grade school. And none of them intended to teach longer than it took to find a husband. They were glad to be in town at eighteen or nineteen, and a good deal of courtship went on while they were there. They helped with my mother's work in return for board and room; but they were members of the family from the day they came, and even after they were gone we regarded them as departed relatives. To this day, although such of them as are still left are long since grandmothers, our mutual affection is made known on all suitable occasions.[2]

Young men were, in fact, always hanging around, and even when there was no particular occasion for it, informal merry-making was always breaking out—parlor games, sugarings-off, corn poppings, taffy pulls, fudge makings, hay rides, or lawn parties. It was a household far too busy, too preoccupied with duties, too lacking in leisure or solitude, for coddling a boy unhealthily. The girls treated me casually, as they would a younger brother; the hired men tolerated me as the boss's son and contributed to my practical education; and the general busyness was such that I could be entertained by what was going on but could escape almost whenever I wanted to. I had a room of my own, too, south-looking, sunny, and bright with flowered wallpaper. And I had a desk where I kept all my precious things, fairly safe from inquisitive outsiders. It was homemade, with a drawer that could be locked, and there I stored my favorite clippings and my current literary endeavors.

It was something of a pleasure to be sick in that room, as I often was, and to stay in it all of a solitary day, reading and, if I was up to it, writing and fingering my precious possessions. I became healthier and stronger as I grew older, and naturally most of my interest was in the normal activities of a boy in

[2] As this is being written I have an affectionate letter from she who was Alta Alden from Dewittville. She says she and her husband are celebrating their forty-fifth wedding anniversary, surrounded by descendants; and she gives news of others of her contemporaries.

such an environment. I never lost my interest in my other life, but it was given fewer of my hours. Mine was, I should say, an extraordinarily ordinary life except for my secret activities. Looking back, it seems to have been a fortunate one.

Seventeen

It really is possible to accumulate possessions, as life progresses, of a sort impossible to inventory or to keep in a safe-deposit vault. For one grown old they possess a priceless pleasure-giving power. I had my share and, because I had them, have a certain respect for the environment that produced them.

It is nearly hopeless to try to describe, for those who have not lived in a country village, what ceremonies, holidays, socials, jollifications, visits, and family gatherings can mean in such a place. For those who have had these experiences, few words are necessary to suggest what a Sinclairville boyhood was like. For those who have not, they will probably seem to have been tiresome and provincial. But imagine the impression it must have made at the time for me to be able to recall now not only the names but the abilities and personalities of all the members of our village baseball team; or to recall the objects, almost all of them, displayed in the window of Sheldon's store when it was dressed for Christmas and I stood with my nose pressed against its frosted glass, snowflakes the size of feathers drifting down, and lights being lit up and down the street; or how the crisp, brown crystals made from maple syrup hardened on pans of hard-packed snow to be eaten with pickles on winter evenings.

A hundred pictures of things and events, most of them gay and pleasure-giving in the hearty way of small-town life, have for me almost as much vividness as they must have had when I was young. I suppose this is the betraying quality of memory; yet it does enrich the later years of those who have had hard, busy, or unhappy lives. The hurts and frustrations tend to dissolve in retrospect, and the moments of happiness, experiences of kindness, and disclosures of beauty tend to be enlarged. This undoubtedly causes the elderly to overpraise the past and to extend the mantle of serenity beyond the events it really covered. Yet the recompense is considerable, a kind of old-age pension which has no means test. Like the home in Robert Frost's poem, it hasn't to be deserved.

I have often thought that to grow old wisely means to separate recollection from contemporary action. The past can be enjoyed as something gone beyond recall, without assuming that anything different must necessarily be inferior. An old person ought not to expect that succeeding generations will want to re-establish a world which corresponds to his dream of a past purged of its inconveniences, maladjustments, and miseries. I have considered myself to be lucky in this respect. The past for me has become a box of jewels to be opened in moments of leisure; it has never been something I have been obsessed to re-create. This is possibly because I have been able to keep on trying to change things and so have always had work to do. But, even more, it has been because the avocation of writing is not dependent on being allowed to remain part of any organization. All that is really needed is paper and pencil—or typewriter. And even a pensioner can afford those.

As a matter of social defense, I feel that there ought to be some sort of test by which it could be told whether an individual is fixed in the past. He ought not to be allowed to vote, for instance, or to have a voice in any community enterprise after he has succumbed to his dream of the good old days. Of course it is not only old age which brings on this condition. It is more prevalent then because the store of recollections is greater and because time has worked its concealing effect. But this, like alcoholism, is really a symptom of a weakness which was always in the person's mind. He was probably never one to co-operate in changing the world for the better; he always thought it had better be left alone.

Why are some people always wanting to go forward, and why are some determined to use every means they can command (including the vote) to prevent it? There may be those who are born to be reactionaries; but there must be many others who have been made so by their education, their upbringing, or their occupations. When a majority is found to be determined on economic or moral suicide, I judge there are influences in the environment that made them so. Indeed, I still feel that there was something very wrong in the United States when I was growing up. It malshaped the larger number of my contemporaries, so that the institutions they have so doggedly maintained have become incompatible with going on at all with organized society.

Satisfying as our Sinclairville life was, it was no preparation for the future. Settled and relatively static communities, such as ours was, with traditional occupations and with accepted customs and attitudes, are apt to enforce conformance ruthlessly. We in rural America were opposing our views to an industrial and social revolution of irresistible power and vast dimensions. Sooner or later all the arrangements of living in a democracy are voted on and so are brought into conformity with majority conceptions. But what industrialists, engineers, and scientists do largely escapes any such control. And at some time there occurs an inevitable tragedy. Majorities are apt to go on approving old institutions through whose seams and cracks a flood of technical change is pouring. The vote is apt to go to the past, not the future.

When my boyhood friends and I were being subjected to the indoctrination process—learning, that is, that anyone who worked hard and cultivated the Protestant virtues could get along and perhaps become rich—the preliminaries leading to the nuclear bomb were being cleared away. While political platforms competed to reaffirm their devotion to the competitive system, the forces of the universe were being unlocked by the scientists and loosed into a world still holding to the principles appropriate in a village economy.

But I have to say that if we were not being prepared to be citizens of the world, our experiences—and mine particularly, because I had so understanding a father—were calculated to give us a robust attitude toward life. I might cite, for instance, two incidents I recall which introduced me to murder and to love.

Generally our lives in Sinclairville involved no violence of any sort. When savagery did occur, the impression it made was terrific.

So I recall with retrospective terror what happened to Axel Lawson one spring night. Axel was a hired man, one of a number of Swedish immigrants who owned farms or worked on them out east of Sinclairville. Once a week or thereabouts in season we used to see him drive down through Main Street in a one-horse wagon loaded with produce for the Jamestown market. At night he would come back, wagon empty, horse drooping, and would often stop at Anderson's saloon, if it was not too late, for a drink and a little talk. Then he would climb back on his wagon seat, chirrup to his horse, and start up over Cobb Hill for home. It was one of those familiar routines a village regards as part of its daily life.

On May 25 of the year I was ten he was seen going through town on his way to Jamestown, but he was not seen coming back; he was late. The next morning his horse, with an empty wagon, showed up in his home barnyard. Axel was not to be found. His employer knew his invariable route, of course, and before the dew was off he had retraced it until he found his hired man in a patch of trampled nettles and burdocks beside the road only a little way outside the village. It was a peculiarly secluded spot—ideal for a murderer's purpose.

It was easy to read the signs. An assailant had climbed into the back of Axel's wagon—probably while he was dozing—in his hand a heavy stone from a pile by the roadside, and had crushed his skull with brutal blows, so that the scene was bloodied and Axel a pitiful sight.

Investigation indicated robbery. There had been a few dollars somewhere about Axel's person, got from the sale of his produce. For that he had evidently been murdered. Our community was not prepared to investigate such a crime; and Axel lay by the roadside, his wounds exposed, his body sprawled in the frightening abandon of death, for the better part of a day. He was the center of a constantly growing circle of onlookers while the law organized itself, and for several days thereafter he lay stretched on a table in Taylor's undertaking establishment, well within sight of those who pressed against the windows. There was an inquest. Several witnesses recalled that late on the night of the murder a galloping team of horses had been driven down through Main Street and had been heard thundering across Mill Creek Bridge on its way south. Some said they had gone to their windows wondering at the runaway speed of the team, the racketing wheels, and the shouts of a driver. It had been a windless night, and the sounds could be heard; but it had also been dark as a pocket, and no one had really seen anything. There were no other revelations.

All this fumbling for the control of violence counted for education of a sort. The killing, the ineffective inquiry, the fact of the escape in the night, the inadequacy of the motive, the pitiful exposure of the victim to the indignity of excited comment, the complete success of the criminal—all these created a confusion which I was a long time sorting out and trying to understand. And there would always be the picture in my mind of the body in the weeds by the roadside, life suddenly gone for a reason out of all proportion to the preciousness of a life.

As it will in such a situation, tragedy developed several comic quirks. Footprints of entirely respectable citizens were found unaccountably in the vicinity, and one matron's backside was measured to determine if it fitted the impression on a mossy log near the scene of the crime where she admitted to having sat on the relevant day. Speculation concerning these incidental revelations, and the coarse comment they engendered, almost obscured the crime itself after a few days. The moral lesson, however, seemed quite clear to the preachers, even if it puzzled those in whom the skeptical sense was uppermost, and there were sermons of vehemence, if not practical sense, on the following Sunday. The incident faded, no solution was found, and the unsatisfied were simply left with an anticlimax for such lessons as it conveyed. The taking of a life had not been punished; the criminal had got away with his small loot and presumably had enjoyed it without penalty. It was all wrong, but there it was.

As for love, which one day made its way into my experience, it provided a much more agreeable introduction to an important phase of life. I suppose it could be said to have been both more and less satisfactory. Accompanying it were sweet torments that left their own sort of scar; but it was a necessary introduction to something that would always have to be dealt with. There was unmistakably about its incident the scent of blood-root, bluets, and hepaticas—Mayflowers, we called them. And its association in my mind with murder at this distance persists, I suppose, because its warmest demonstration occurred as May Phillips and I walked homeward from a visit to the fearsome scene.

There had been nothing new to see, but in the margin of the woods, just over the rail fence, there had been spread over the ground a wonderful showing of all the spring flowers, and we had filled my cap with the tiny blooms to carry home. As we had gone along the streets, I shy as usual—I had never even so much as touched her hand—and we came to her corner, she quite unexpectedly turned and, standing on her toes, deposited the most delicate of kisses on my cheek.

I can see now that this first feminine caress was bestowed in despair. I was awkward and reluctant, and something had to be done. She knew very well that for a long time I had been worshiping her intensely, but I seemed to be held in a vise of bashfulness. My small friend, I may say in excuse, was one of those delicate blondes whose taffy-tinted pigtails and rose-petal complexions persuade admirers that they are dealing with creatures so fragile as hardly to be human at all. The angelic appearance concealed a nature far more advanced than mine and one from which I might have profited much more than I did. It was impossible for me to conceive that our relationship could be brought to a level lower than the exchange of observations about devotion. And these cannot have had much substance in the eyes of a practical female. She was patient; she tried to instruct me. I failed, however, to overcome my awe, and my adoration was never translated into any kind of physical demonstration.

It was some two years after that lightly planted kiss before we moved away from Sinclairville and all that time I was her willing slave. Yet that was the only physical manifestation of our spiritual union. I imagine she must have been very annoyed by my reluctance to grow up.

Niagara

2   *1904–1909*

Eighteen

Migrating from Chautauqua to Niagara County made a change we had some trouble getting used to. Wilson was less than a hundred miles from Sinclairville, but in moving even so short a distance we came out of a high valley surrounded by eroding hills and onto a flat and fertile plain stretched along the south shore of Lake Ontario. Ontario is a sister lake to Erie, but deeper, colder, and more like a sea.[1]

The important thing for us as a family was that we left a declining agricultural region and came to an increasingly prosperous one. We were now to live in the productive Ontario fruit-raising country; we would be on the frontier with Canada, and we would be more within the influence of Buffalo, the metropolis of western New York, than we had been in Chautauqua. My father would become moderately wealthy, my schooling would broaden, and the place of our family in the community would gradually become more influential. The Tugwells in Sinclairville had been respected people of good but undistinguished stock, on a level with their fellows. My father in Wilson could be described, I think, as a leading citizen, and all of us would have the privileges and perquisites of that situation. But in the settled sense we would never be natives.

[1] Niagara County was organized in 1808, cut off from Genesee. Erie County was subsequently carved off the southern side of Niagara; this was in 1821, so that the present boundaries date from then. The town of Wilson was established by legislative act in 1818. The village of Wilson was incorporated in 1858. Luther Wilson, usually spoken of as its founder, was its first President.

The change meant, it will be seen, that we came out into a somewhat larger world and that, even in the larger world, we had a more responsible place. But it also meant that we severed some sustaining roots. For several years we visited Chautauqua County often, and we always had the feeling that we had come back where we belonged. We missed our old friends and our accustomed ways, and we did not like very much the rented houses we lived in until my father's growing prosperity enabled him to build us a new one.

We mourned the hills and at first found the flat country bleak. But we did immediately make new friends and very soon got used to the orchards and stretched-out fields. And we learned to like the lake and to accept its immense influence in the lives of everyone who lived along it. Besides, the better opportunities in a more prosperous country, and my father's growing income, enlarged the lives of all of us. Before long we were reasonably settled and familiar.

The Tugwells were what we have since learned to call extroverts. All of us were the sort who mix into everything going on and are likely to be chairmen of committees, delegates to conventions, masters of lodges, or entrepreneurs of enterprises. My father was, of course, manager—and by now part owner —of the largest business anywhere around and would soon find his way into many others, such as the local banks; my mother belonged to, and dominated, circles, clubs, and societies; even my sister was the active spirit among her girl friends and was always helping to manage their affairs. It can be seen that the only son in such a family would be in a fortunate position. For that reason, and perhaps for others, I always had plenty of friends and many activities. From morning until night there was much to do, and I tried to do it all as a matter of course. It was the way Tugwells behaved.

It is true that I still carried on secret work and that I had no one to share it with. But I had become used to that and accepted a separation between the one life and the other. I felt no strain about this. Writing was something I had to do, something I could always find time for. My family knew about it; but they respected my reticence, feeling, I suppose, that it was less deplorable than many of the things boys did. And my mother even took pride in it, although she was no more privy to my efforts than any one of the others. I always had a room or a retreat of my own, and it became a storehouse of precious possessions as well as a place where I could work without interference.

It was not yet the motor age. Our first automobile would not be bought until 1908, after a bad year for me during which Ronald Wright's family down the street would possess a Maxwell and we would still be horse-drawn. It is true that I had my own rig—a yellow-wheeled, rubber-tired runabout—and a horse to use for the many affairs that demanded journeys within a few miles' range—socials, parties, picnics, ball games, and calls on country girls. And this would have been considered a most fortunate situation for any young man until about then. But horses were becoming outmoded, and my longing for a motorcar was insistent. My father felt it about as badly, probably, as I. At any rate, in the spring of 1908, after much consultation, we acquired a Maxwell too—the first of a long line of such cars; after the first Maxwell, we owned successively Stoddard-Daytons, Roamers, Hudsons, Stearns-Knights, Buicks, Olds-mobiles, and many others. We had a new one every year or two from then on. They would not be very dependable for some time to come, and besides, the roads were such that the cars were put through terrible ordeals of rutty, frozen tracks, snow, sand, and mud wallows. Meanwhile, until 1908, I did have my horse, and it was more than most boys had.

A few years were required for my father to get his business to the state he wanted for it, but actually it went along well from the first. These were years of expansion. The depression of 1907 was terrible enough while it lasted, but recovery from it was rapid and, so far as my father's affairs were concerned, hardly noticed. The processing of food products for the growing population was bound to have a rapid expansion. It was less and less customary for housewives to prepare for winter by extensive home-canning operations, and anyway, more and more of them lived in cities away from the gardens and farms of the countryside. Some years were better than others, but there was never one in which my father had losses. Also, as his business grew, he became a more and more diversified entrepreneur. He took naturally to making deals, starting enterprises, helping to finance others; it was natural that he should be an organizer of the Wilson bank, become its president and eventually president of a group of similar small institutions. All of them would die in the cataclysm of 1929–32, but that was still a long way ahead.

Actually, living in Wilson was not very different from living in Sinclairville. Small towns in western New York are a good deal alike. The houses we lived in until our new one was built were not so large as the one we had left and they lacked conveniences, but we got along comfortably enough. There began, too, a new succession of training-class girls of the same sort as those who had lived with us before, and, as before, they became almost part of the family. They did not seem so much my senior now, and the sister attitude may have been just a little unnatural, but since all of them instantly acquired young men whose proprietary watchfulness precluded any unbrotherly thoughts on my part, our relationship was the same friendly one I was so well used to.

Besides, I had other sentimental interests, and they required all my attention. Also, I had an older friend. For Allen Hinchliffe, who had been a next-door neighbor in Sinclairville, came with us to be a kind of apprentice to my father. For years he worked in the cannery and lived with us. He and I had a room together most of the time until he was grown and married. I owed him the debt any young fellow owes an older one who will pass on to him the wisdom gained in the crises of growing up. He was not at all like me. He would have been an engineer if he had followed his bent; actually he became a businessman in the pattern of my father, built up a processing plant of his own, and branched out into other fields.

Winters in Wilson were severe enough. The northwest winds, blowing down from the Canadian wastes and across the lake, ensured that. But, although we were north of the Chautauqua country, we were at a lower altitude; and the big lake, although it seemed so cold—mostly, in winter, it was a bleak expanse of broken ice floes—actually served to moderate the temperature. This was, in fact, why the counties along the southern shore (Niagara, Orleans, Monroe, and Wayne) had become so famous a fruit-growing region. The lake might delay the spring as its ice melted, but that was good; it held back the bloom of trees until all danger of frosts was past. It also delayed the coming of winter. We had reluctant springs, but the falls were memorable.

During the long autumn, stretching out to Thanksgiving, the signs of summer faded so gradually that time seemed arrested. Those were the golden days of the Niagara year. The light nights of the full September moon merged into the chill ones of Indian summer. The small fruits had long since gone, but the red and yellow apples in the big orchards still hung on the trees as the picking and packing went on. The strange, long shadows of the north, together with the sharp etching of the horizon peculiar to the high latitudes, seemed to stretch space, as time was stretching, beyond all natural limits.

As the fall lingered, the apples were gradually gathered. Some were packed and shipped away in barrels; some were put into storage in the hope of higher prices later on; some were dried; some were made into cider and vinegar; and some were canned for winter pies. In all that country the apple was king, not quite as wheat was in Kansas or cotton in the South, for we had other products as well; but it was, nevertheless, of most importance among the others. And those of us who lived there knew about apples—how they grew and what to do with them —as naturally and intimately as a down-easter knew about ships and fish or a plainsman about grass and cattle.

In the first years of the century, however, the Ontario region was losing its monopoly. Other centers were developing—es-

pecially in irrigated western valleys and on the slopes of the
Blue Ridge. These produced new varieties, more attractive to
the untaught consumer, and they came to market ahead of our
more slowly ripened crop. Our farmers were reluctant to adopt
better grading and packaging, and Ontario apples were already
beginning to bring lower prices than those of competing regions.

Because of these changes there was a weakening confidence
in the mainstay of the Niagara economy. To add to other
difficulties, imported diseases were ravaging the orchards; and
before ways to combat them were discovered and generally
adopted, many old plantings, some of them nearly a hundred
years of age, had suffered damage that would in time so
reduce their vitality that many would have to be replanted.
Reluctance to undertake such an investment of land, labor,
and capital as this involved increased as competition became
more formidable. As a result, other fruits were now challenging
the apple—peaches, pears, plums, prunes, apricots, and cherries.
Taken together, these by now had an annual value nearly as
great as apples.[2] But still apples were the foundation of our
economy.

Fruit growing is very different from mixed farming, which
includes animal husbandry. On a well-run dairy farm almost
everything produced in the fields is consumed by the cattle, and
the only product sent to market is milk. Fruit farmers characteristically have no cows, or very few. Their orchards demand
much attention, but there is no such invariable daily routine
as the dairyman must keep to. There are two climactic seasons
in the fruitman's year. One comes in early spring, when the
opening buds must be sprayed with insect killer on a certain
day, almost a certain hour, to prevent invasion by the codling
moth. This day and hour does not fall on any fixed calendar
date. It depends on the weather, largely, which advances or

[2] And this is not to mention wheat; the old lake bed was streaked with
heavy clayish soils on which fruits did not do well but which were useful
for grain. Then too, nearness to Buffalo made ours an increasingly favorable
area for garden crops.

retards the budding. One of the valuable services of the County
Agricultural Agents is the organization of chain communications throughout the whole fruit belt to guide growers in beginning this spring attack on the insect pests. A complicated map
with accompanying charts is drawn from weather and other
data which places each orchard in a time sequence from the
county seat. Close watch is maintained, and at the right moment
the Agent phones the first farmer on his list. Then the rush is
on. But before going out to his waiting equipment, the first
farmer must notify the next man on the list; and so it goes
until the chain completes itself and the last man phones back
to the Agent.

All over the fruit belt that day there can be seen clouds of
greenish spray or dust. War against the invaders has begun or,
more accurately, has been resumed, for there is no armistice.
There has already been a dormant treatment or two during the
winter. As the crop progresses there will be at least a half dozen
more.

But insect control is by no means all that a well-run orchard
demands of a farmer, although by the time he has separately
treated several orchards of different fruits to their spring protection he may have had several strenuous weeks. His trees have
been years in coming to maturity after careful planting in
suitable locations on well-worked land. There has thus been
some specialized planning as well as tedious waiting through
the unproductive seasons before bearing begins. All the time
the trees have been growing they must have been fed, protected from pests, and cultivated. There are years of investment
in any orchard ready to bear its fruit. If a daily rhythm has
not been imposed on the farmer, a seasonal one has; and its
tolerances are very narrow.[3]

[3] The usual practice is to spray or dust seven or eight times during the
year. One of these is the important dormant treatment in dead of winter;
the others give protection during the growing season from various enemies.
Different formulas are used for various treatments. The old stand-by,
inherited from Europe, where the diseases and pests originated, was the
familiar Bordeaux mixture. Not until the 1940s did the new insecticides,
such as DDT, become available.

The second and more intense climax of the apple farmer's year is naturally the harvest in the fall. Then all the planning and waiting, all the expense, and all the labor are embodied in the fruits hanging among the fading leaves. They are ready to be gathered. To repay their generous keep, the yield must be bountiful. But also the crop must be wanted by consumers who will pay enough to sustain the enterprise. And this is a considerable gamble. The market price varies greatly with the size of the crop and with the size of other crops in other places. The return may be so small that the loss is disastrous. The winter, then, must be faced with discouragement, and it must be considered how the ever-continuing expense can be met.

We did not live on a farm either in Sinclairville or in Wilson, but we might almost as well have, for the village was a dependency of the farms around it, and my father's main business was directly auxiliary to agriculture. To the list of products processed in the old factory in Chautauqua County there were now added the fruits of our new country; and, of all these, the apple made the most striking change. For one thing, it prolonged the season for work until well after Thanksgiving and sometimes until almost Christmas.

By then, however, the immense bins holding many tons of fruit would have been emptied, the last steam blown from the retorts, and the last of the Sicilian families who worked in the factory would have gone back to the city. The vast rooms of the plant would be cold, silent, and empty except for machinery standing about packed in grease to protect it from rust. Only the warehouse would have a glowing center through the winter. But its location could be detected only by one familiar with the factory's geography. It was out back, an immense, plain building into which all during the season cans had been coming faster than they were shipped out. By now they were stacked to the ceiling in blocks only the warehouseman could tell apart. It was a wilderness of corridors only wide enough for the hand trucks used for transportation.

At the focal point there was a huge potbellied stove which

gave heat enough to keep the temperature from reaching the freezing point and around which the few off-season workers gathered in the intervals of sorting, labeling, boxing, and loading into freight cars the warehoused products as they were sold and ordered to be shipped. There they ate leisurely lunches out of their tin boxes, exchanged gossip, retailed jokes, and managed to hold out somehow until spring.

In May the first stirrings of the new season would begin. Sometime in June, the earlier the better for quality, the first peas would begin to come in, to be followed at once by cherries—and so it would go on into the fall again and the dormant winter months.

Nineteen

During my first years in Niagara County I was half a schoolboy finishing the grades and going on into high school and half a rather favored employee in my father's business. I was more familiar now with machinery and I understood the processing trade so well that I was something more than an apprentice. My father even began to think of me as his successor at the plant, although I feel sure he always had doubts about my liking for business. He knew I was really dedicated to some other craft; but, as good fathers do, he waited to see what would come of it. There was, anyway, a good occupation to fall back on.

School did take most of the days during ten months of the year, but the demands were mostly those of simple attendance; the work was gauged to the level of students so slow that I, and others like me, got through it without finding out what our capabilities really were. Except for reading, I had no homework of any importance. After school the hours were free for more exciting activities. As I grew out of the restrictions imposed on adolescents I grew busier and busier with teen-age affairs. I began to go to dances, and looking back, parties, socials, and various expeditions seem to have taken up most of my leisure time. But it was not so.

When we again possessed a house of our own I had, as usual, a room for my work. I was still experimenting, with as much determination as ever, in the various forms of the writing craft. If the thoughts I had were half formed, I was learning better how to express them. I could feel a certain competence beginning to materialize. A little later the third-floor attic was completely refinished for my use and I had what amounted to an apartment of my own. My ambitions were still unfocused. I knew no one who had made a career of writing, but I felt compelled to keep on working at it even if rather blindly; and I did, with amazing perseverance, as it seems to me now. It was unmotivated, unrewarded, and carried on outside the routine of other activities; but in a way I felt that all my other interests contributed to this one. That this was so, indeed, gave them their real meaning.[1]

My recurrent illnesses, the winter in Colorado, and perhaps concentration on my secret occupation had recently lost me a year of school. But I was about even with my friends. Anyway, it did not worry me, and I took no special pains to make up time. I did what I was supposed to do in school and was never noticed much except in English classes, and even in these my busy teachers merely gave me encouragement. There was not much else they could do. I never had more than mediocre marks because I never did more than the minimum required of me except in those subjects to which my wide reading brought incidental knowledge. One teacher told me that I usually passed because if I couldn't answer the question asked I could make up one of my own and do very well with it. Unfortunately, this did not work when it came to the Regents examinations set for New York State high school students. In these I often barely passed.

One of the fascinating elements in the background of life in Wilson was the great lake to the north of us. Later the similar pervasive influence for me would be the city—Buffalo —but that would be when we began to find the trip to the city easier than it was until the roads were improved. Until I

[1] Many years later, when Robert Frost was making one of his casual talks to a class at the University of Pennsylvania (taught by his friend Cornelius Weygandt), I was startled to hear him say that what was really important to a person was what he would neglect his studies for. I knew exactly what he meant. I had been doing it most of my life.

had finished high school, travel to and from Buffalo was by railroad. Automobiles stayed very close to home. The risk of a twenty- or thirty-mile journey was considerable, and the time involved, even at best, made it impracticable.

Just at first, and while I still went to school in Wilson, the lake and all its associations played a very important part in all our doings. If fruit, and especially the northern apple, was the dominant economic influence in the county, the lake was the dominant geographic influence. And even the apple, as I have explained, was due largely to the existence of the lake. It made our climate, determined our activities, and gave us pleasures.

Wilson had a harbor which was in a state of commercial decay. The accommodation for ships was really the dredged mouth of a shallow bay into which, a few miles inland, a sluggish stream made its way. It was called the Tuscarora River, a name borrowed from the Indians of our region,[2] who were now reduced to a few families on a reservation near Niagara Falls. The bay, which merged gradually into the river, stretched along behind a narrow peninsula parallel to the lake for about two miles. This was the island, so called, where summer people had their cottages. Together with a tributary or two, the river had formed a blocked-off delta on whose thousands of marshy

---

[2] The Tuscaroras were not natives; they had come north from the Virginia-Carolina border a good deal earlier in consequence of troubles there:

"The Tuscaroras, who now occupy a reservation in Niagara County, were located in southern Virginia and northern North Carolina before 1713 . . . They were hostile to most of the leading southern tribes but maintained a close friendship with the northern Iroquois, whom they knew as traditional kinsmen. In consequence of encroachment on their lands, they rose against the whites in 1711 . . . Finally defeated, the Tuscaroras abandoned their country and fled north to the Iroquois, who received them as the sixth tribe of their Confederacy, henceforth known as the Six Nations. A part of the tribe which had remained friendly during the struggle was settled upon a small reservation on the Lower Roanoke River in North Carolina. Here they lived for a time, until, weary of constant attacks and encroachments, they also gradually withdrew to the north. Like the other tribes of the Iroquois confederacy, they were divided in the Revolutionary War, a part joining the English, while the rest adhered to the American side, with the result that they are now about equally divided between New York and Canada . . ." *Niagara County,* by E. T. Williams (Chicago: Beers, 1921), 11.

acres tall rushes grew. Narrow waterways opened through the reeds, and they were mostly deep enough so that small boats could pass. They were margined with beds of white and yellow water lilies, the arrow-shaped leaves of pickerel weed, blue and yellow flag, and water arum. Their banks were covered with willows, osiers, witch hazel, shadbushes, swamp maples, alders, and dogwoods. In the meadows beyond there were wild columbine, golden rod, purple asters, queen of the meadow, and all the other seasonal weedy blooms.

The waterways and marshes stretching inland through the flat farming country made a strange and other-worldly region, lonely, mysterious, and, to exploring boys, enchanting. There were islands in them where enormous chestnuts, white and red oaks, and hemlocks furnished coverts for small animals. And there was a forested park of many hundreds of acres facing out upon the harbor mouth on somewhat higher land where there was an abandoned resort, popular half a century before but now decayed and falling to pieces.

The watery fields, where from a canoe or rowboat waving rushes seemed to extend endlessly in every direction, gave the illusion of being much more extensive than they were. And boys idling about among them could easily imagine themselves back in the wilderness of the ancestors they read about. We fished along the banks in earliest spring, sometimes through rainy Saturdays, tending smoky fires against the chill under the dripping trees as we watched our staked-out lines. We were able to catch big strings of bullheads that way; then, going upstream to where the freshets really ran full in the spring, we speared carp as they swam upward toward their spawning places. Later, as summer came, we haunted the beaches as well as the waterways. And we swam in the deep clear channel between the piers which had been extended many years before into the lake. These were twin constructions, built of thick planks, on driven piles and nailed with immense spikes. They were filled with boulders to give solidity. Strong as they seemed to be, they were, in my time, beginning to give way before the winter storms, and their stones were pouring out into the channel, so that ships could no longer come in.

Alongside these piers there were ruined warehouses, storage places for the apples and wheat which had gone out of the harbor to Europe before the railroads had been built. It was one of the dares among us to dive from the cornices into the channel thirty feet below. It was there that I really learned to be at home in the water.

We spent many Sundays in summer, or other days when work allowed, near or in the water, swimming, tramping the gravelly beaches, and rowing or paddling out into the lake or through the waterways of the marsh. Far into the fall, after the summer people were gone, we went in the evening to build driftwood fires, where we broiled steaks and roasted corn ears. We then sat talking and singing for hours. These feasts ended usually in a gorge of fruit—the last peaches from a nearby orchard, or gold-laced melons grown to such a size that five would more than fill a bushel basket. Because they were the latest, these were always the sweetest, the kind no city person ever tastes.

Gatherings and activities of this sort worked out into common attitudes, shared traditions, a body of knowledge. The songs we sang, the stories we repeated, the experiences we put into words became part of us; it was the way the countryside made its way into our thoughts and behavior. Perhaps a better way to put it would be to say that it gave us a foundation, what I later learned to call a culture. For some it was what would be built on; for others it was what they would cling to. But one thing was certain—we all had it.

Even in winter the lake and the harbor had their attractions. Once in a while the quiet backwaters, and even the wide expanse of the river bay, were frozen over. There came every winter long spells when the whole system had a glassy surface. This happened when quick freezing took place during a windless night. Then the word passed around, and every boy, certainly, and sometimes most of the village, it seemed, would move onto the ice. Lunches were taken, and up and down the shore fires blazed. Many of our elders retrieved skates from the upper shelves of closets and undertook to show us how sports on the ice had been managed in their day. But long after they had tired and gone home we younger ones kept at it, unwilling to let such opportunities pass without being exploited. When we tired of games played with homemade hockey sticks, we went on expeditions into the upper watercourses we otherwise never penetrated. The far fields and wood-lots never seen from the roads had the look of quite strange country. A few miles of skating became an authentic adventure.

Through the ice we could see waving waterweeds and swimming fish. It was remarkable how they could carry on down there in the frigid water. Swinging swiftly back down the streams between the brown fields of rushes, we would, after such journeys, come to shore in the harbor, tired out and with a mile or two to walk to our homes, feet numb from the long constriction of skate straps. Our mothers might meet us with reproaches; we might anticipate unpleasant interviews with authority tomorrow—if we had been playing hooky—but we had had a priceless day.

Late in winter, as the ice broke up and froze again and again, fierce March winds blew down from the north and piled mountains of battered ice along the shore. It was mercilessly beaten by the waves and ground itself fine with horrendous noises in the torment of the storms. Bundled to the ears and awed by the savagery of the spectacle, we walked by the shore and came home gratefully to civilized comforts. It used to be said that we had no springs in our country. April often reproduced February. It was the ice in the lake that did it.

We knew the lake in all its seasons and moods. Our elders might have grown away from it, snug in the village and busy with their occupations; but those of us who were boys felt its glamor. Its bays sheltered a prolific wildlife. There were muskrat, beaver, marten, mink, and otter. We seldom saw any of these in summer; but there were characters, who were our

friends, who still made winter's work of trapping them for
their fur. There were only a few trappers left—they were even
scarcer than the lake fishermen—but such of them as remained
we cultivated.

We never paid much attention to birds at the time, but I
later learned to appreciate how numerous they were around
the waterways. Gossipy red-winged blackbirds were everywhere, swinging on the reeds; and of water birds there were
ducks in season, coots, mud hens, long-legged cranes, and
schiedpokes. Kingfishers always lived in certain territories; and
hawks, hunting for small animals among the sedges, could
often be seen coming in from their lazy patrols in whistling
dives, then struggling into the air again with a helpless creature
dangling from their claws.

But perhaps the summer lake was best of all. Then, as it
finally warmed grudgingly into July and stopped smoking in
the sudden chills of the northern winds, it began to change
color. The turbulences of spring had stopped, the silt had
settled, and a hazy blue reflected the clearing skies. Thunder-
heads sometimes piled up almost as they do all year in the
Caribbean, and for a few weeks an idyllic season held on. This
was, of course, when we were busiest at the factory, and until
our summer home on the harbor was built years later, we saw
very little of the lake's best mood. But still there were intervals.
And to have a hammock on the shore, or just to lie in the grass
as the now gentled wind came in off the water, was often enough
even for a restless boy. If he had something to dream about, it
was ideal.

Sometimes we went out with the fishermen who lived and
worked around the harbor. Our industrious elders were apt
to regard those of them who remained as a worthless lot, and it
is true that they were reduced to a precarious state; but we
regarded them as familiars. Their broad boats, powered with
uncertain two-cylinder engines and filled with gear, and hope-
fully with fish as they came home from taking up their nets,
were well known to us. The sturgeon were so nearly gone that

I never saw more than a few, but whitefish were still plentiful, and there were pike, lake trout, and other less valuable varieties. The numerous Wilsons, Wheelers, and Pilkintons were usually tolerant of our company and managed at least to make us understand why they clung to their craft. They were losing out. But the lake was their homestead, and they had the same attachment to it that Chautauquans had to hill farms that could no longer furnish a living. The values were not commercial ones. It was something we could understand better than our elders.

To be strictly factual, the lake, much as it offered a boy, was no longer immediately important to the community. Its harbor had filled with silt, its fishing was not what it had been, and even as a resort it was nothing much. It had been very different a few decades earlier. It was when the railroad had come (the Rome, Watertown, and Ogdensburg), extending itself along the shore plain a few miles inland, that the focus of interest had changed. The rails came westward to us from farther down the lake, notably Rochester, and went on west to the foot of Lewiston Hill. There they bent southward and climbed the escarpment to Niagara Falls. From Niagara Falls they ran on to Buffalo. This took all the traffic away from the lake; the harbor was killed, and the inland sea was left to other uses than commerce.

After we came to Wilson, only an infrequent schooner visited the anchorage or tied up at the dock, remnant of a once-prosperous trade. And only a few times an old excursion boat, bringing crowds of trippers from Toronto across the lake, came in for a visit. On such days it was possible for boys to make a dollar or two working for Mr. Harris in the usually deserted amusement park which was opened for the occasion. We worked in the stands selling pop, candy, and sandwiches, or we helped to run the crazy old merry-go-round as it wheezed out the last few tunes of its existence. Those times became scarcer. Olcott Beach, six miles down the lake to the east, on the next little south-shore harbor, was the terminus of an interurban electric railway which had created business by establishing a full-scale amusement park and a quite pretentious hotel. Daily during the picnic season it brought swarms of city folk from Buffalo, Lockport, and the Tonawandas. Wilson was nowhere in this competition. We were not a tripper's resort, for which our elders may have been grateful but for which we were not. It made the place seem dull. And no doubt it was, if what was wanted was excitement.

Twenty

One of those who were of most use to me during my early years in Wilson was a man who would have been considered a very unlikely mentor, except maybe by Allen Hinchliffe, who must have learned almost as much from him as I did. This was Fred Loiacano, a Sicilian *patron,* who arranged for my father's several hundred immigrant workers. The recruiting and supervising of labor of this kind was an unwholesome business generally; but, like most indecent institutions, it had its advantages. For the employer, it furnished a whole season's workers without the bother of hiring and firing; for the employee, it made a seasonal outing during which all the members of the family could be earning something. Living conditions were execrable in the frame barracks customary then, and the *patron* usually exploited his people. Our living quarters may have been no more than a shade above the average, but Fred Loiacano was as far from being an exploiter as could be imagined. He was, in fact, a father and friend to his people, and his wife a mother to them.

Fred was saved from the pressures of his volatile flock by being patient and slow to anger; he was also conscientious and, not having children himself, very little interested in making money. He and his wife were fond of me, something which perhaps started because I was the boss's son but which went on because of genuine affection on both sides. For many years we had a common interest in improvements my father regarded as unbusinesslike and gave way to with reluctance.

This was only an extreme instance of a rule which made the village a different kind of place from the modern suburb which so much resembles it superficially. We lived in accepted intimacy together, all sorts of us. I knew and daily associated with individuals who were little better than idiots; also there were others who were tormented by various neuroses—the miser, the drunkard, the religious fanatic, and those who were cursed with various sexual aberrations. Then, of course, there were the decent and sensible people—the majority. All sorts had a place among us, and somehow we all got along.

I still think it was good for a boy to learn how to live even with the disturbed and defective. For they went to our school, we saw them at church and at our social events, and they worked alongside us. To us they were simply queer in certain ways, and unless their aberrations became intolerable they were treated matter-of-factly. But it was even more valuable to learn that normal, trustworthy, and kindly people could be found anywhere and that they did not need to be of my class or kind, or of face or ancestry like mine.

For this last lesson, I stood indebted to Fred Loiacano as much as to anyone. He spoke halting English, ate strange food, and drank sourish wine of his own making. Also, he was the first Roman Catholic I had ever known—not that his religious observances were very faithful. But he was a natural gentleman, humorous, wise, and with an infinite capacity for loyal friendship. During many an interlude when work was slack I sat on one upended tomato crate in the shade and Fred sat on another while he told me of the Sicily he had left as a young man, not because he had wanted to, but because it was a land without a future. Still, he recalled it with affection in such poetic terms as his English was capable of. He spoke of the lemon and orange groves, the purple sea below the mountains, the hot sun on the old stone houses, the roads and terraces—the whole panorama of the Mediterranean.

We were sitting, perhaps, in the cluttered cannery yard, machinery clanking and clattering, workers coming and going, and he was telling me of donkeys carrying crops to market or coming home again in the evening with a little salt or soap— all the produce had exchanged for. I saw why he and his contemporaries had left. I also saw why they could not rid themselves of a nostalgia which would take them back home in age if their earnings had been enough.

Fred protested that Sicilians had not lost their vitality; they had merely worn out their land. Or he suggested they may have had too many children—which was a new idea to me and one I put away for further consideration. But Fred thought that Sicilian customs were good, calculated to keep the breed strong. True, he was apprehensive about the second generation. They were escaping from parents who did not have the American ways youngsters got used to in school and on the streets; and because they lacked respect they did not get the discipline they needed. Through Fred I became friends with the volatile dark boys and girls. And it was true that a good many of them in the course of time did get into trouble. But there were others who began careers as doctors, lawyers, politicians, or business-men, and succeeded. If their parents went back to the old country in age, they themselves had no desire to do so. Many of the children of those boys and girls I knew would be in the invading army of General Patton which would cross the straits from Africa to Sicily. Some of them would recall a few words of their grandparents' language to use as they marched into the old towns. Some would recall the descriptions they had un-believingly listened to as children and discover that much of it had been true after all. This crusted antiquity was not for them, but it gave them status to have Sicilian blood. It was not some-thing to be ashamed of.

Even as I grew more useful to my father I developed certain differences from him which for years would trouble our relation-ship. I began to identify myself, for some reason, with those in the community who were less fortunately situated—for instance, the Sicilians, although they were not actually part of our village life. It may be paradoxical that I accepted readily enough all the prerogatives of my situation; but it never occurred to me that any sharing of vicissitudes was in order. It was quite typically American that my desire and intention were to better the lot of others, not to accept a less fortunate one for myself. I cannot tell why this happened, unless it was simply intrinsic in the democracy of the village and in that of our small industry where everyone knew everyone else. I even became resentful and, on occasion, acted as a callow advocate for those who were on the other side of the employment bargain. The fifteen cents an hour I earned during my teens was something I could spend for extras; but I had examples among those who worked alongside me of what that dollar and a half for a ten-hour day meant when it was the whole income of a family.

I was in and out of friends' houses continually, and I saw the leaky roofs, the shabby carpets, the mended furniture, the oil lamps, and the inadequate stoves which were all they could afford. And I knew that of all the boys who were my age I was almost the only one who could look forward with any certainty to education beyond the age when a man's pay could be earned. And when my father made his hard bargains with my friends' fathers, I resented it. This amazed him. He regarded it as a matter of principle. Even when the company was most profitable, he would have thought himself wrong to pay his workers more than the least he could hire them for.

The belief of businessmen like my father was that workers who were paid by the hour were fortunate to have employment and ought to thank their employers for providing it. They ought not to expect more than a rate determined by competition among them to get jobs. And there was no connection at all between the company's financial situation and the wages it paid. He grumbled about ungratefulness.

He also regarded, with a bitterness I heard a good deal about, the growing tendency of the state to interfere in such matters as sanitation and child labor. To have nosy inspectors invading his premises enraged him. Between him and Fred there was a conspiracy to keep the Sicilian children at work. They had a

way of disappearing completely, however, when strangers appeared, although they may have been doing piece work (pitting
cherries, peeling tomatoes, or snipping beans) alongside their
mothers minutes before. Fred was kindly enough, but he thought
children were better off helping their parents than playing in a
filthy compound, and perhaps he was right.

Mine was not a very positive objection to the attitude my
father held; it was, after all, that of businessmen generally,
and I naturally regarded them with respect. It was more at this
time a questioning, an unwillingness to accept the conditions
established for the lives of my friends. I had a sharp resentment
about some cases of hardship that I can recall, but this was to
an extent resolved because my father was also kind. He would
help out anyone who needed it. What he would not do was
go against the established business rules.

I can see now that I began to dissent from these rules even
before I began to think about them. I talked the problem over
in a fumbling sort of way with Allen, who was old enough to
have got some things in order which were still hazy in my
mind; but Allen saw nothing to get excited about. The rules
seemed all right to him. If anyone didn't like to work for wages,
let him work for himself. That was what he intended to do.
It was what he did do too. So, I must admit, did some of the
others I had sympathized with as wage workers. And none of
them turned out to be the sort of employers who believed that
wages were too low or conditions too harsh—ever, in any
circumstances.

I shouldn't make too much of this. For the most part, I took
as unquestioningly as anyone else whatever came along and
made of it what I could. I did have a tendency to inquire and
to generalize; but daily interests usually intervened before
these impulses got very far.

Just across the street, after we moved into our new house,
was Milburn Patterson, and only a few houses away was
Ronald Wright. We became intimates. Altogether in the village
or in the nearby country there were a dozen boys who were

friends and daily companions. We went to school together; we
worked together in the canning factory or in the orchards,
especially at harvest time; and sometimes we had winter jobs
on Saturdays in the storage houses where apples, pears, and
cabbages were kept in large quantities and had not only to be
put away in fall but sorted over and eventually shipped out in
winter and spring. Some of the boys were farmers' sons, and
they naturally never lacked for work, but they considered themselves aggrieved because they never got paid for it. We must
have been a busy crowd. I can recall no occasion when we
discussed matters beyond our borders; the rest of the world
might as well not have existed. It got no attention from us.

Our school was an ugly brick monolith, one of those buildings which seem dingy before they are finished. Its grades
occupied the ground floor, and the high school the floor above.
An afterthought addition in the rear served for teachers'
training classes.[1] When I reached the high school, after finishing
the grades and was a well-grown fourteen, our home seats were
in a great hall which held, at a guess, a hundred or more desks,
boys on one side and girls on the other. This barn of a room
doubled as an assembly theater and had sliding doors at the
rear which could shut off two good-sized classrooms to which
the more advanced students retired in groups of thirty or forty
with their English or Latin teachers. The rest of us gathered for
recitation in corners of the room.

There were large ill-fitted windows along each side; these, in

---

[1] "Another Niagara County Academy of the early days was called the Wilson
Collegiate Institute . . . This enterprise was started in 1845 and a two story
building was erected of Lake Ontario cobblestones in the same year." Williams, op. cit., 307. The site was donated by a Simon Sheldon; Luther
Wilson started the subscription list with a gift of five hundred dollars. By
1900 the Sheldons had disappeared, but the Wilsons were numerous.
The Institute was supported by fees until 1869, students coming from all
the nearby towns. But in that year four districts were consolidated and the
name was changed to the Wilson Union School. This was an evolution
normal to New York State—institute, union school, high school. In 1930
an entirely new institution would be built across the street, complete with
kindergarten, gymnasium, laboratories, cafeteria, library, and other novelties
of which we, as students, never dreamed.

spite of their size, still failed to light adequately the center of the room. But light was not my problem. My desk, because my name began with *T*, always seemed to be in a back corner just below one of those windows, and the drafts that blew through the rattling frames and down my shrinking neck were sharp as daggers. It was worse on the north side where the girls were, but for me it was serious enough where I was.

I still had respiratory troubles. My croup had been followed by a spasmodic form of asthma which seized me with frightening violence quite suddenly and wherever I happened to be. No one knew anything to be done about it, so that a good deal of the time I was a semi-invalid, one of those reluctantly careful young people who resent their handicap. I resented it the more because my growth was not interfered with and actually I was fairly rugged and athletic—except for the attacks, which came without apparent relationship to any cause. When I could, I ignored them. I was an enthusiastic player of games, but often I had to quit, disgusted, and go home gasping and wheezing.

Our athletics were not organized. We played baseball and other games with choose-up teams, and we had no coaching of any sort. But we did have some help in learning to box and wrestle. Dr. George Smith, our physician, and Orin Salisbury, our druggist, were village standbys. Dr. Smith would have a tragic end, going off into years of drug-taking and losing all his legitimate practice. At the end he would become completely derelict. But there was no sign of this in my school years. He was then almost a copybook family doctor, full of good advice, watchful and kindly. He felt the need of something more for the village boys than they were getting. In that climate there were weeks, even months, when outdoor games, except for occasional outings on the ice, were completely impossible. It was during these interludes that back-room poker games had a tendency to start and the poolroom became popular.

No crowd of boys ever grew up without getting into some trouble, I should think. And this was before there were Boy Scouts or any such organization. There was no gymnasium at our school, and our only playground was a rough, untended lot. This we used for baseball, but it was useless in winter. So when a sort of athletic club was organized under the older men's guidance, it met a genuine need. About twenty of us who were somewhere in the teens were got together, some money was raised, and a deserted loft behind the drugstore was equipped with wrestling mat, boxing equipment, exercisers, and such paraphernalia. It was not much. It was chilly and dusty in spite of our amateur housekeeping, but every boy will understand that it was precious because it was our very own. I recall it as the center of our interest through several winters—until, as often happens to co-operative ventures, it somehow fell into disuse.

Our school principal ought to have had something to do with the kind of leadership we got from Smith and Salisbury; but of any such enterprise he was wholly incapable. A. M. McIlroy had all the dourness of the lean Scot without the usual gleam of humor for leavening. He was a man of limited but genuine intellectual interests who had come to his schoolteaching by working his way through normal school and had got to be a principal somewhat late. He taught algebra, geometry, Latin, and what physics and chemistry could be managed in a laboratory which was little more than a bare room with a sink. He was terribly overworked, and I have thought since that he must always have been tired. But we made no allowances, and we never developed any affection for him. He was completely incapable of becoming confidential with a boy, much less a girl. So in school we had lessons but no guidance and certainly no friendliness from him. It was only when some teacher saw in a student—as teachers are always doing, bless their hearts— something to make grow that school became for us what it ought to be.

It seems to me that I always had at least one teacher of that sort. And I even had reason to be grateful to Old Mac, even if others did not. He softened when I had need of it most. For when I wanted to go on to another school and thought definitely about college, he undertook to tutor me in subjects not taught in Wilson. Many an hour he worked with me over textbooks he knew no better than I. But even if both of us were amateurs, our efforts allowed me to pass several Regents examinations necessary to further progress. I even think he had an affection for me; it was a wintry and reserved sentiment, certainly, but it must have been real. Why else would he have taken such pains to help me along?

I recall with some resentment the sorts of texts we had in those days. They were spare and forbidding or soft and repugnant—sometimes it seemed that they were both—and at the best they offered a minimum of education in their subjects. It was certainly made difficult for us to emerge into an understanding of the world's affairs. For a generation destined to live through the transformation involved in the coming of the automobile and the airplane, the invention of anesthetics and antibiotics, the familiar use of electricity, the adoption of new means of communication, and the development of new scientific perspectives—for all this we were grossly unprepared when we got through our high schools.

History was supposed to impress us with our ancestors' virtues and to show that our side had always been right in every contest, especially our wars; English literature began with Beowulf and ended with Wordsworth, Tennyson, and Scott, centering in a denatured Shakespeare; and American literature featured the New Englanders. My recollection is that Whitman and Poe were not mentioned but that Longfellow and Bryant were regarded as classic. If there was a way of concealing Shakespeare's bawdiness, his high, gusty humor, the texts sought it. Only an occasional teacher showed us how he caught the essentials of human nature in the net of his words, how rich his language was, how close he must have been to the people of Stratford and London. It was only because of one teacher that I discovered the relation of Milton to the King James Bible. And of the Bible itself, I learned from her that it was not only what our Sunday-school teachers said it was—a source of moral texts.

All this the generation of those who had the duty of bringing us down to Hiroshima failed to do. Worse, they swept our minds bare, so far as they could, of tentacles which might reach out for genuine learning. They taught us that all problems were simple—most of them matters of right and wrong, long settled and not to be questioned. If we escaped from their teaching, it was not in large numbers and it was not to considerable effect. They managed the thing effectively and economically, and most of us subsided into adulthood quite satisfied with our equipment for it.

I recall—how well!—the Doré edition of *Paradise Lost,* which for many years, along with a clasped Bible, a volume of Jean Ingelow, and others of Tennyson, Longfellow, and Riley, lay on our parlor table.[1] That it was on the table, not on the bookshelf, indicates its place in the scheme of my mother's regard. It was somewhat incongruous that Doré's Milton should be so highly thought of. Those landscapes, desolate and debris-strewn, peopled with naked and writhing creatures, were not the sort of thing my mother cared to dwell on. Of course there was hell and there was a devil, but this was not of interest to our family. There were other homes where this was not so, where Milton's Satan was an immanent presence, especially to guilt-ridden adolescents. The war between his hosts and those of heaven was a spectacle more credible in our northern land than the desert scenes and the semi-tropical atmosphere of the Old Testament. The parents of some of my friends made use of Satan very effectively.

Anyway, we were all schooled Protestants; and Milton, together with the King James Bible, as interpreted by our Sunday-school teachers, furnished our theological equipment. At our

[1] Actually certain other honored volumes were often there as well: Scott's *Marmion,* Will Carleton's *Farm Ballads,* William Morris' *Earthly Paradise,* Emerson's *Essays,* and a volume called *The Living Poets.* This contained both *The Wreck of the Hesperus* and *High Tide on the Coast of Lincolnshire,* which were favorite recitation pieces.

distance from New England, our puritan rule must have come to us more from Milton than from the early preachers, although the ministers gave us definite enough directions, learned by them, I suppose, from professors in divinity schools.

In Wilson there was not even a Congregational church, and we more or less threw in with the Presbyterians. In Sinclairville my mother's church had represented religion to me. The Congregationalists had a rather severe and somewhat spare tradition of conduct. Baptists were regarded as rather uncultured people, having relations not with New England but with backwoods evangelism. And Chautauqua had not yet done much to modify camp-meeting Methodism. Bishop Vincent's expulsion of volunteer exhorters from the Assembly Grounds and the prohibition of all unscheduled meetings, had some effect. But it was still sinful to smoke or drink or, very nearly, to do anything pleasurable. That this presented young people with a dilemma out of which the inevitable way was found goes without saying, but often there were guilty feelings involved.

But change was coming. Even my parents were disregarding the old standards, not forthrightly, but little by little without acknowledging it. Mine was a reasonable and tolerant home; I had no cause for complaint.

Twenty-one

My high school years were divided between Wilson and Buffalo. They seem to me to have fallen, as I passed from fifteen to eighteen, at a dividing time, not only for me, but for the nation. Nineteen-seven, 1908, and 1909 are not usually regarded as notable, but I fit into them events and decisions which would have long and serious consequences. Perhaps I should note that some of the decisions were simply refusals to decide; but these avoidances may have been the most important of all.

It is of course easy for an individual to interpret the formative periods of his own life as equally important for others and for society, and I have no desire to compress causes and consequences for the sake of dramatic effect; but those years, outwardly of little significance as they unrolled, do seem to me now to have been ones when fateful choices were made. To support this contention, I would recall that 1907 was a year of misery during which the first of the severe technological depressions occurred, and that several following were ones of slow and agonizing recovery. It was also the end of the Theodore Roosevelt regime and the beginning of the Taft reaction.

Taft's defeat of Bryan in 1908 was final for that generation's revolutionary impulse. Involved in it were not only the disaffected farmers who had been led by Ignatius Donnelly and others of his sort, but those radical reformers who had been attacking the system of industrial monopolies since the first Standard Oil investigation in 1872. Ida M. Tarbell's summary

of Standard's means of maintaining dominance[1] had had an
enormous effect. And a whole era of muckraking had followed.
Bryan had ridden the wave, but three times it had failed to wash
away the defenses of business.[2]

But muckraking had gone out of fashion very quickly, and
Populism had been smothered in the election of 1908. The
rejection of the agrarian grievances and the decision to accept
the business system made inevitable many of the tragedies of
later years. And the failure to do anything about the depression
of 1907—except to let nature take its course—set a precedent
for allowing others to happen successively until they ran on
into the holocaust of 1929.

About this time the population of the cities was passing in
numbers that of the rural areas, and this undermined the
dominance of the culture in which a majority of my generation
had been raised. Also, the scientific discoveries that would
revolutionize the technical basis of civilization were beginning

[1] Which had appeared in *McClure's Magazine* in 1902-3 and had been published in book form in 1904.
[2] Perhaps because of the talent for organization of one man—Mark Hanna,
who, with McKinley as front, frightened the electorate into rejecting Bryan
and accepting the safe and sane candidate of the Republicans. Herbert
Croly told that story in his *Marcus Alonzo Hanna,* and Vachel Lindsay celebrated the Bryan crusade in verse:

Where is McKinley, Mark Hanna's McKinley,
His slave, his echo, his suit of clothes?
Gone to join the shadows, with the pomps of that time,
And the flame of that summer's prairie rose.

Where is Cleveland whom the Democratic platform
Read from the party in a glorious hour?
Gone to join the shadows with pitchfork Tillman
And sledgehammer Altgeld who wrecked his power.

Where is Hanna, bull dog Hanna,
Low-browed Hanna, who said "Stand pat"?
Gone to his place with old Pierpont Morgan
Gone somewhere with lean rat Platt.

Where is Roosevelt, the young dude cowboy,
Who hated Bryan, then aped his way?
Gone to join the shadows with mighty Cromwell
And tall King Saul, till the judgment day.

to come, one after another, in close succession. These events, in turn, would make obsolete the whole body of received economics and political theory. There were already at work philosophers who would reconstruct social thought: Dewey, James, Veblen, Patten, Cooley, Wallas, and a few others. But orthodoxy had formidable defenses, and during my schooling years there would be little change.

The truth was that the education of the texts no longer explained the world we would find when we graduated. They did little more than elaborate and defend the myths which were growing farther and farther away from reality. Patten, Veblen, and their small company of colleagues already had their formative conclusions behind them. The same was true of James and Dewey; pragmatism was already well shaped. In fact, Dewey had made drastic applications to educational practice— the experimental progressive school at the University of Chicago had been started in 1902 and Dewey himself had moved on to Columbia, leaving the tree he had planted to grow.

Yet so slow would the changes be in coming that in 1945 Hiroshima would represent a collision between myth and reality. Most people would still not be prepared to understand its significance; if they had, the bomb would never have been used. Harry S. Truman was the product of a common-sense education, and he had been chosen by an electorate similarly educated. It seemed to him, and to them, eminently sensible to use the newly unleashed powers of the universe to settle, no more than a little before it would have been settled anyway, a struggle between two nations. That they committed mankind to possible extinction and to certain terror, they did not comprehend and would not afterward admit. But it was an event which brought intellectuals up short. Suddenly, after having been blind so long, they could see the abyss before them. And they asked themselves why they had not seen it before.

Decisions made during my high school years had concealed the end of the road we were taking. This does not imply that the great teachers then at work, and the scientists who were changing the world, would have no effect between then and the event at Hiroshima. Not at all. It does mean, however, that there were only a few of their students who recognized the significance of what they were being taught and who became concerned with the measures that must be taken to contain and to utilize the energies of the newly opened universe. The new learning spread very slowly against the opposition of the ortho- dox. And even those who understood the significance of what they were seeing went no farther than mere recognition; they could hardly have been expected to produce the plans for a new society at the first try. And especially they could not have persuaded others to accept their interpretations.

Considering the centuries required for the penetration of the Newtonian world by the Einsteinian theories, it might be predicted that social science would not begin to accept the new imperatives in less than a century—and a century of intense, generally supported application. But it was characteristic of our society that social invention was not supported but was suspect, not only by vested property interests, but also by vested intellectual ones. In such circumstances only the lonely worker could be a social creator. And lonely thinking could have only slow and remote results.

These were not matters I was aware of at the time, of course; yet I speak of them because they were so important for my generation. They had an effect on me even if I had no intimation of their existence. They were destined to cause maladjustments as theories were separated from their foundations, as beliefs and facts drew farther apart.

I might recall also that the political geography of the nation had been established before I was born; 1880 might be taken as a dividing date. By then the Civil War and the Reconstruc- tion, between them, had determined that there should be a solidly Democratic South and an equally solid Republican New England. The northern middle states were usually Repub- lican too, and this was enough to offset the doubtfulness of New York. The challenge of Bryan, three times repeated by

1908, had come from the Midwest, caught in the squeeze
between eastern creditors and falling prices for crops. But the
revolt had failed, and first McKinley, and then Roosevelt, had
won the Presidency. Cleveland in 1884 had capitalized on
Republican corruption and in 1892 on Harrison's ineptitudes;
but he had not at all represented the same forces as Bryan.
He had, in fact, been a Gold Democrat who was always more
sympathetic with eastern conservatives than with western radicals, with employers rather than workers.[3]

Bryan may have been confused and may after all have been
only the spokesman for farmers who wanted to get out of debt
by using cheap money; but still the unrest of those who had
suffered most from recurring hard times and who had managed
to share very little even in good ones was gathered behind him.
And in 1896 these almost made a majority; there were fewer
of them in 1900,[4] by which time the Republican monopoly of
respectability and Bryan's reputation for radicalism had become
fixed in the American mind. The Republicans could count on
most of the middle-income people and even on those among the
working class who were persuaded that their employers did in
fact provide the full dinner pail that was so much talked about.
But Bryan's farmers soon went back to Republicanism. Because
of this defection, a small clique of businessmen, organized by
Mark Hanna, could control the elections of those years. Money
did it somehow. And the political machines in the states and
cities, run by effective bosses, continuously conspired to deliver
votes for the national candidates they could get most out of in
the way of patronage and protection.

[3] As was shown so clearly in the Pullman strike of 1894, this incident had
its importance in American history because of its relation to the struggle of
the workers for recognition. The contest was lost; but that it so much
resembled civil war in the long run served as an example of what could
happen when a people allowed itself to be so divided. It was not enough
that the President, using the army, restored order. That order would break
down again and again until decency and justice were recognized. More
and more people were convinced that this was so as the years passed.

[4] A campaign in which Bryan turned to imperialism as his most important
issue, making much of the absurdities of manifest destiny. Even though he
lost, imperialism was never again an accepted policy.

This alliance, it was true, was vulnerable to the exposures of the muckrakers. And the muckrakers to expose, together with Bryan to lead, made a formidable combination throughout the first decade of the century. At the least, it ought to have resulted in the turning out of the Republicans and the coming in of the Democrats. That it did not was because the electorate was more oriented to old issues than to new ones. The South ought to have been Republican by now. In most respects its Democrats were indistinguishable in their ideas from the Republicans of the North.[5] But the legacy of Reconstruction prevented that. And many northern Republicans ought to have been Democrats but were kept from joining them by the faint tinge of traitorousness clinging still to the Democracy—which Bryan's radicalism, under Hanna's nursing, tended to reawaken.

Bryan's best possibility was to have joined western disaffection with a South which had a grievance. His failure to create such a coalition left the Democrats divided. The leaders tried to purge the party of radicalism by nominating Alton B. Parker in 1904. But he failed more abysmally than had Bryan. If the American people were going to have a conservative President, it was going to be a Republican one; the Democrats could not escape from Bryanism so easily. Seeing that this was their fate, they renominated Bryan in 1908. But the result was the same.

In 1912 things would be different. What would be most different, of course, was that now the Republicans were split. The Democrats almost threw away their opportunity for victory by getting into a savage fight over the nomination. It was not until Bryan threw his weight to the Wilson side that the convention in Baltimore came to a belated decision. But there

[5] Except about the tariff. But American farmers never seemed to consult their own interests about tariff policy. Even though they were exporters, most of them were convinced that high duties were favorable to their pocketbooks. Only in the cotton South was free trade understood to be necessary to a one-crop economy with markets abroad. It will be recalled that this was an issue as far back as Jackson's time, when a revolt over the Tariff of Abominations would have led to secession except for his stern insistence on the integrity of the Union.

was left an unresolved quarrel almost as dangerous to them as that which separated T. Roosevelt from his party. Still, Wilson did win the election, even if with a minority of the votes cast, and the Democrats were at last able to escape from both Copperhead and radical taints.

Wilson, as President, accepted only a moderate part of Bryan's program. Its passage still left so many issues still to be settled that the second Roosevelt, in 1933 had to begin his work where Wilson had left off. Even he never really got beyond elementary Bryanism.

This later Roosevelt would be helped by the gross failure of the Republican policies exposed in the debacle of the depression; but he was also able to do what Bryan had not been able to do —unite temporarily the West and the South. This served to elect him, but it also made practically impossible an advance into new ground; the Southerners would not go along. What did get done was old-fashioned, pre-technical, progressive—but not Einsteinian. The New Deal was not a program that the creative social thinkers, now mostly dead, would have approved. Dewey, still alive, looked on somewhat sardonically; but the others were gone, and in truth its measures were no more than palliatives, calculated to calm the symptoms of social diseases that would break out again and again.

These comments have run far beyond my high school days. But what would happen during the next fifty years seems to me to have been decided then. The issues Democrats and Republicans fought about settled nothing. They were irrelevant to the forces at work in the background. Still, a victory for Bryan might have opened the way for progress; one for McKinley shut all the gates to the future. I think this was realized by many of the Bryan supporters, even those who would not have gone beyond his program at the moment.

It may even be that my father saw this or felt it. He certainly had more interest in this campaign than any other before or after. He took me with him in 1908 to hear the Great Commoner speak when he came to Buffalo. And it may have been something more than his traditional adherence to the party that made him so ardent a Bryanite in that year. It was a most unlikely affiliation for a western New York businessman; it always had been; it was still more unlikely that he should have worked actively for a cause that could not possibly win. He was no crusader.

The Elmwood Music Hall, where Bryan spoke, must have held several thousand people; at any rate, it was crowded. We were well to the rear on a rather rickety erection of plank seats. We could hardly hear what the preliminary politicians had to say. But when Bryan spoke, his words came to us clearly and intimately without the loss of the least nuance. This was the famous trumpet voice. He began with a pleasantry which delivered the crowd into his power: "When I first began to run for President" he said with a grin, and paused. A ripple of amusement began and spread until it became a shout of approving laughter. And after that he could play at will with all the accustomed issues. His main argument was that the policies he had been advocating for years had been stolen by the opposition; they didn't intend to do anything about them, but it did make it hard for him to keep ahead of them when it came to campaigning. It was an ingratiating and wonderfully persuasive performance.

His portly figure and soft fat face, emphasized by the long hair which flowed down over his collar, his Prince Albert coat waving about his knees as he gestured—but, above all, his clarion voice, which seemed to have endless reaching power—all combined to make his listeners believe that he said more than he actually did. His issues in that year were well worn; 1908 was a watered-down 1896 so far as he was concerned. But a youth of seventeen was not likely to know that. I was glad I was a Democrat. I resolved always to be one. I hoped to help in some way to make the party what Bryan said it was—the hope of the common man, the enemy of privilege.

That there would not be much of a future for a Democrat in Western New York was completely overlooked in the enthusiasm of the moment, and that my father's Democracy was inconsistent with everything else he seemed to believe was also overlooked. Bryan had somehow made him feel that he was one of the little men whose rights had been invaded by the tricksters of Wall Street.

But Bryan lost again. At the time our disappointment was severe; the clock seemed to have been turned back, and perhaps it had been. Bryan might have been that bridge to the future needed so badly by the nation just then.

Twenty-two

Democracy's effectiveness is bound to be determined by the realism of its majorities—either that or the admission by the majorities that certain areas beyond their understanding will be consigned to those who do. When a majority in a nation, one of whose cherished principles is that all men must have an equal voice, fails completely to recognize the forces that are actually shaping its civilization, it cannot be hoped that penalties will be escaped. Such an expectation would have to rely on sheer chance. It seems to me that the years I speak of now were ones when majorities were most blind.

It was important that economic theory became irrelevant to the problems then becoming so insistent, because economists would be expected to furnish solutions in coming crises. It was equally important that political theory should have been irrelevant. Government was not readied for its coming responsibilities. There were not two crises coming, one affecting business and the other affecting public affairs. There was one crisis developing out of rapid technological change. Industry was most affected by this revolution; but that this was not recognized by economists or political scientists made adaptation to it impossible. Stubborn clinging to Smithian economics and to simple policeman government, while technology evolved, left the nation drifting when it most needed direction.

Progressivism, developing out of Populism, was the garden path down which democracy would be led by Bryan, by the first

Roosevelt, by La Follette, by Wilson, and then by the second Roosevelt. This sequence would be determined by the first rejection of Bryan. If in 1896 he had become the nation's accepted leader, the result might well have been the development of an Americanized socialism instead of the little-business progressivism which did develop. Bryan, as President, would have had technicians and co-workers, and they might have recognized the realities. In 1896 the disaffected farmers and workers were hostile to the institutions which had caused their miseries and were in a mood for public ownership of utilities and a general overhauling of the business structure. But once business had gained power through the Spanish war, it could never be dislodged. And its hold was immensely strengthened during the two world wars presided over by the Progressives Wilson and F. D. Roosevelt. Cashing in on war thus would happen three times. The cashing in would be massive; and the Federal government would emerge so entwined with big business as to have lost its freedom of action.

Theodore Roosevelt was far from being a profound student of the American culture; he was, however, conversant with political history, and he had seen enough of economic affairs to know that all the muckrakers said was true. He detested their sort—in fact, he attached to them the name that was to damn them—but he knew well enough that they had the facts. He himself did not go farther than the progressivism of La Follette—not so far when it came to action. There is a revealing statement of his in a letter to Lincoln Steffens. It shows how he shied away from the governmental interference he had seemed to approve in earlier correspondence between the two. To excuse himself, he fell back on condemnation of what he called, as scornfully as any businessman, "socialism." For a definition of what was really needed, he spoke of "the fundamental fight for morality." This he did not explain, perhaps because he could not. It was the weakness of all Progressives that they attempted to distinguish between what was good and what was bad in a system which, by the going standards, was wholly immoral.

Steffens had said in a letter to Roosevelt:

No, I don't think representative government will correct all evils. I do think, however, that fighting for it, consciously, will uncover not only the principal evils, but their common source, and that when we see that, we shall make such intelligent progress as they are making in England, France, and Germany toward the solution of the social and economic injustice which underlies most of our so-called political and moral evils.

And this, "the evil," which so irritates you, is something which is neither new nor unobserved. It is privilege. Trace every case of corruption you know to its source, and you will see, I believe, that somebody was trying to get out of government some special right; to keep a saloon open after hours; a protective tariff; a ship subsidy; a public service franchise. Europe is abolishing these privileges, and I am convinced that, to save our Republic, we also must follow that policy and stop absolutely the granting of special permissions. This means public ownership, and you don't believe we need to go so far as that. Neither does Mr. Taft. And I am willing to put the matter conditionally. Here is the plank I would like to see put into the Republican platform:

"We believe in the public ownership of any business that shall continue to find it necessary to corrupt politics, government, and the people of the United States."

You and Mr. Taft think you can regulate. But even if you succeed you will keep the government so busy fighting first one abuse, then another, that it will have to neglect, as it does now probably, those great fundamental social and economic reforms which are beginning to occupy other civilized governments.

To this Roosevelt had answered:

. . . come, come, friend Steffens, if your theory is correct the government has got to own every public service corporation, and own every possible thing there can possibly be bribery in; including the

Life Insurance Companies, by the way. When I was police commissioner I found that the drygoods merchants and the small Jew shopkeepers were blackmailed just as much as anyone else. They were given certain privileges designedly for the purpose of levying blackmail upon them. I think you are in error about Europe. The European governments do not as a rule own the saloons. They almost all have protective tariffs. They all without exception have ship subsidies. Many of them own the public service franchises; that is, for instance the railroads; but England does not own the railroads and her management of them is just as free from corruption as is the case in Germany and France where the government does own them. I do not believe that you have struck the right cause, nor come near striking the right cause, of our corruption, and I think you are trying to cure a symptom and not a cause. I am heartily with you in the campaign for the abolition of privilege. Curiously enough, events have forced me to make my chief fights in public life against privilege, but I know from actual experience —from experience of the most intimate kind in the little village of Oyster Bay and out in the West at Medora, when there was not a special privilege of any kind in either place—that what is needed is the *fundamental fight for morality*. However, I won't go into this until I see you personally . . .

For the government to own everything, from saloons and insurance companies to steamship lines and railroads, as to which there can ever be a question of privilege or blackmail, would, of course, mean socialism; incidentally, it wouldn't work; and would mean bankruptcy; but, aside from this, my knowledge of the postal service and of Tammany Hall, shows me that under government ownership corruption can flourish just as rankly as under private ownership.[1]

T.R. was a skilled political manipulator; but during his Presidency, when a farsighted leader might have defined the struggle going on between the two ideological nations created by the American people, he skated back and forth on the surface of contemporary controversy, keeping together a purely political

[1] *Letters of Lincoln Steffens* (N.Y., 1933), I, 197–98.

majority for which he had only party uses. At the end he left the Presidency to Taft and the party to the big businessmen he had castigated so violently.

Wilson and another Roosevelt were to come out of the same tradition. It is sad to say that Wilson's fine mind was almost closed to economic thought. It is even sadder to say that the second Roosevelt, although he would understand well enough what the issue before mankind was, would underrate the capacity of his fellow citizens to understand. He too would leave the crisis still mounting—how much more rapidly after Hiroshima! —and still unresolved.

So far as could be judged by those of us who passed out of adolescence on the way to adulthood in the second decade of the century, the progress of American business was steady. It went from level to level of productivity and profits. These were admirable achievements, the most admirable, in fact, of our time. We were ignorant, unless from accidental hearsay, of any dissent or protest beyond that in Democratic party literature. And even in civics classes this was not called to our attention. The controversy among the American people may at times have been violent, but it was about very narrow issues. It did not go to the questioning of the system itself. It mostly concerned who would have control and who would share most in the profits.

I doubt whether I knew then that in Germany there was a good deal of public ownership, even if under a Kaiser, or that in Britain, following a century of agitation by Christian Socialists, Cooperators, and Fabians, the preliminary battles had already been fought which would bring virtual state socialism into being within our lifetimes. And the revolution in Russia was so faintly reported that it might as well have happened on another planet.

Even the muckraking furor did not reach me or, if it did, was only another story of unseemly disturbance having no significance until I began to go to school in Buffalo. Then I began to hear and to think about such matters. How it came to me,

I do not clearly recall—probably from casual reading, perhaps in the newspapers, perhaps in the muckraking magazines. These had a few years of prosperity, supported by a temporary demand for truth-telling. It was almost over when I began to wake up; but still its echoes reverberated, and it must have been these of which I became aware. Upton Sinclair, Ida M. Tarbell, Ray Stannard Baker, and Lincoln Steffens were conspicuous characters in this strange episode. It was soon stifled, but while it went on it revealed some sickening facts. I should not know much about this in any organized way until my university years. But long before that I had at least heard of Tom Johnson, Peter Altgeld, Brand Whitlock, and some of the other state and municipal reformers.[2]

The reformers actually were not much more than critics; they had nothing beyond Progressivism to offer, unless it is considered that Steffens was really converted to Socialism. The items of their political program included the direct primary and a few other changes intended to make it more difficult for political machines, acting for business, to subvert those who made the laws and those who interpreted and executed them. What more there was could be classified as welfare measures. The economic program was limited to trust busting and to the regulating of competition among small businesses. Even a social security system was far beyond the reformers' horizon.

I do not forget that I was a high school boy with many interests, and that I was mostly busy and carefree. I should not like to imply that my own serious thoughts caused any persistent preoccupation with the country's ills. Such as they were, these thoughts were fugitive and unorganized. But I can see now

[2] The masterpiece of this era was Lincoln Steffens' *Shame of the Cities,* published in 1903. The first of his "city" series had been published in *McClure's Magazine* in January of that year. This issue also contained the third installment of Ida M. Tarbell's *History of Standard Oil,* as well as Ray Stannard Baker's *Right to Work.* The five years succeeding were the most productive ones for the muckrakers. By 1908 Steffens would have moved to Boston to try what he could do to influence government; and the advertisers would have smothered pretty completely the attacks of the other critical journalists.

that they were somewhat beyond what might have been expected. I have no idea why it was, but I was already a potential critic. My heart was not wrung by the unbearable sufferings of the working class or anything of the sort. And I myself was fortunately situated. Yet I was becoming aware of a division, and I knew which of two attitudes I must ultimately adopt.

I should learn in time, and from experience, that there was a kind of fraternity of those who dissented from orthodoxy. This would not necessarily be even an association. Dissenters were not easily classified or identified. We might be found in any occupation. Our lives were lived with those who believed differently; they were our friends, our family, our neighbors. We worked with them and we had our pleasures with them. But in about the most important commitment an individual makes in his life, we chose a different one from that chosen by those others. We were not many; whether we were increasing, who could say; there was never any count of heads. From looking at France or Germany it might be thought that our view was making progress, but it was not apparent here at home.

Numbers, however, did not matter so far as what each within himself believed and held to. It was a matter of inner conviction. If we had to be "in the right with two or three," then that was what we must accept.

What did this division among my contemporaries have to do with the developing dichotomy between science and society? It seems to me to have been this: that those who believed in free enterprise and atomized government must use as operative mechanisms deliberate divisiveness, competition, the pursuit of self-interest, the exploitation of other individuals, and the private appropriation of natural materials and forces. These were, of course, a majority and, being a majority, they prevented the politico-economic expression of the opposite—that is to say, co-operation, integration, loyalty to a whole, and guidance by a concept of public rather than private interest.

Let me say again that this conviction of mine developed very gradually. I could not possibly, at this distance, assess its influence on my behavior at any given time. And I may be inclined now to push its beginnings farther back than is warranted. Yet it was real, it did come upon me very early, and it did become so important that it would, a few years later, determine what my life's work would be.

But the way things were, there could be no doubt, was the way the American electorate wanted them to be. They might not like the results, but they would go on insisting that the production of these results—recurrent depressions, unemployment, starvation wages, indefensible working conditions, old age spent in the misery of grudging charity—had nothing to do with the system of production and distribution. Or perhaps I should say it this way: they refused to admit that the one caused the other. They wanted the one; they did not want the other; and so they were kept separate in their minds.

The Republican party of my youth—and my age as well, for that matter—stood squarely on the defense of business enterprise as the heart of the American system. Its fundamental tenet was that business was the first concern of the nation and that even government existed only to serve it. A good many years later, on a regular commuting trip between New York and Washington as the New Deal was about to become operative, I would pass several vast billboards carrying the legend: WHAT'S GOOD FOR BUSINESS IS GOOD FOR YOU. And this would be amidst the debris of the great depression. That is what the individualists— the majority—had believed all during my youth; and even the depression had not taught the lesson that free enterprise must come to the end that could be seen in 1933. Hardly a smoke-stack in the whole industrial complex between Wilmington and Jersey City showed any sign of life in the factory it served. But the cause was assigned to an unkind fate, not to the inner contradictions of the business system.

That system was conditioned by a corruption which existed at its very heart. What distinguished those of us who were on my side was that we believed men ought to be working not against each other but for each other, not subverting public institutions for their own benefit, but working in and with them for the general good. This I certainly did begin to believe when I was in high school and became more certain of as I went along. What was hard to accept was that others I respected and had fondness for held exactly the opposite belief.[8]

We were distinguished—those on my side—by not believing what the billboard instructed us to believe. I think some sort of test could have identified this conviction of mine when I was seventeen. The characteristics were there then, even in latent form. They were not subsequently implanted; they were from then on merely in process of development. But it was a deepening conviction, gradual and evolutionary, a going down one road instead of another, more and more recognizable as the one I belonged on. Men, I was convinced, should be working for the general good. It was as simple as that—and as difficult.

To travel this road, I did not need to be a Holy Joe; I did not have to become a minister or a missionary; I did not even have to love my neighbor as an individual. I could be quite realistic and quite cynical. It was the others who had continually

---

[8] In the year I have spoken of, 1933, Charles Edward Russell, a life-long observer of the American scene, who was then an old man, published a book called *Bare Hands and Stone Walls*. He had been, years before, one of the original muckrakers. Looking back, and considering the instances of corruption it had been his work as a reporter to expose, he had this to say (at p. 115):

"May I, with due humility, beg leave to offer the suggestion of a reporter of many of these incidents?

"Everywhere, in San Francisco as in New York, the prosecution of grafters failed. Well, why?

"Because, in each case, the public lost interest . . . It was not alone the evil influence of the utility companies . . . and it was not that the people in America were more knavish and less moral than people elsewhere. Beneath the seeming apathy, beneath the wide-spread appearance of a slovenly, neglectful attitude toward public probity, was a vague, unformulated, unexpressed, but persisting, intuition of a pivotal fact.

"Not the bribe-giver nor the bribe-taker was the real offender. It was useless to imprison men for doing under one guise what we were all engaged in doing under some other.

"For in the existing system of society what are we all but little crooks together? How is it possible for a man to be honest so long as for his daily bread he must strive to outwit or over-reach his fellows?

"Honest business? There is no such thing."

to live in a dream, to believe in myths, to develop a pervasive hypocrisy, to pretend, to fool themselves, and to risk exposure. If the disciplining of individuals was in the public interest, I felt compelled to accept it. That there were crimes and there must be punishment, I had no doubt; only they were, many of them, not the crimes people were usually punished for.

Another thing: I could and did dissimulate. I learned not to preach, not to insist, not to argue, even, when it could do no good. Also, I could compromise, agree to a little when I would like to have seen much gained.[4]

It is strange, even if an accepted fact these many decades, that there should be no outward sign apparent to me which would link those of every conceivable occupation, every contrasting temperament, every feeling about their fellow men as individuals or as classes or as races. But that is how it has been. For the most part, those of us who are holists know each other somehow and, moreover, we are recognized by those who are on the other side. But we bear no really distinguishing mark. One of us cannot be picked out on the street any more than a person of any other affiliation can—a Rotarian, a Mason, an Iowan or an Illinoisian, a Methodist, or, say, a merchant or a

[4] Of what I have been saying, I should, in later life, observe a conspicuous example. Franklin D. Roosevelt, in his public career, would exemplify the dichotomy. He would be hated because the "economic royalists" would understand quite clearly his affiliation; and he would be loved because, in spite of everything, we would know, on our side, that he belonged to us. The contrast between Roosevelt and Churchill during World War II would be a drama with this theme. The most conspicuous living members of the opposing forces in the world, who were temporarily and for limited purposes allies, would each be trying to use the other. The dissembling, the exhibitions, sometimes brilliant, of offensive and defensive tactics played out against a background of world conflict would be such a spectacle as had never before been seen. It reminded me of the vast scenes in *Paradise Lost*. Sometimes during the war years I would almost imagine I could see and hear the hosts of darkness and those of light deploying and maneuvering among the stars above the Potomac on nights when I knew that Roosevelt and Churchill were sparring and feinting, each at the head of his unseen armies. Strangely, it would turn out that Churchill's political constituency would be with Roosevelt, and Roosevelt's would be with Churchill. Of all the many momentous scenes the White House had known, this would be the grandest in scale, the most consequential in result.

salesman. But let one of us work for a week in any group, and, even if we have been most circumspect and completely unknown before, there will be an identification. It is hard for us to get along in most companies because of the majority that is against us. On the other hand, in special situations, where some members of our persuasion happen to have responsibility, we may be favored. It was often to be that way with me, and in the end I should have no complaint to make. But others of my contemporaries would have done better, and at the time of Hiroshima they would be—in the United States—in power. Roosevelt would have failed in everything except the suppression of the enemy in Germany and Japan. At home the enemy would be arrogantly successful.

Twenty-three

The theory of free enterprise rests on the absurdity that everyone can and should get the better of everyone else; and this, in turn, justifies the exploitation of the weak and inefficient by the strong and capable; going on to the logical conclusion, this, in turn, must end in economic suicide, since the weaker and more inefficient will become more so and finally will not be worth exploiting.

Our town, Wilson, if I may go on to talk about it some more, was still typical. The culture it represented might be one that would decline in the years ahead; but that had not happened yet. We had, in Wilson, not much more governmental apparatus than there had been in Sinclairville, and we lacked some of Sinclairville's amenities. There was, for instance, no water or sewer system; these utilities remained to be installed at about the same time as power lines after World War I.

Our water came from a well; a septic tank took care of sewage; and in our house we graduated from kerosene lamps to a carbide generator which it was one of my chores to keep in order. My struggles with that recalcitrant monster in the cellar were a matter of controversy for years in our otherwise peaceable household. I also had the daily task, when our new house was first occupied, of pumping water by hand from the well into an attic tank. It was natural that I should become a strong advocate of economy in its use; but this was futile, since we had a bathroom and since there was a hot-water heater attached to the kitchen range. In my view both of these conveniences were invitations to extravagant waste; bathing became a prodigal habit with the whole family, but especially with my sister. She liked nothing better than to lock herself in the bathroom, let the water run, and luxuriate in the tub.

My bitterness about this reached explosive proportions when on more than one occasion her fortifications were so efficient that she could not dismantle them and I was called on to rescue her by way of a ladder reaching to the window from the outside. This source of controversy was fortunately relieved when my father had a windmill installed in the back yard. This served to keep the tank full and, until electric power became available, was an accepted part of our domestic arrangements.

Cement sidewalks preceded cement roads by a decade or so. We had one of the first in the village, but they gradually extended through most of the streets and made walking, at least, less hazardous. Also, long before there were hard-surfaced roads there were graveled ones, and these went some way toward making it possible to use our automobiles in spring and fall. Not until I had gone to college, however, would Wilson be connected with the cities nearby. This kept us faithful to the railway. Meanwhile, however, our successive automobiles would thump and grind themselves to pieces in the mud, frozen ruts, or deep dust of the countryside. There were very few times even in summer when it was wise to undertake the thirty-two-mile journey to Buffalo. The twenty-five to Niagara Falls and the seventeen to Lockport were less forbidding, but they still required resignation to all sorts of possible mishaps.

People of a later generation, I am inclined to feel, do not properly appreciate some of the improvements they enjoy. Take tires, for instance. I can recall many a short trip being made an ordeal by punctures and blowouts. It was not at all unusual to have half a dozen in an afternoon. They had to be fixed on the spot, too. The wheels were not removable, and the tire had to be wrenched off and replaced or patched. Then it had to be inflated with a hand pump. A person could arrive home after such a trip wishing automobiles had never been invented.

But it was, of course, the indignation of tire-changers that finally impressed the manufacturers. It took a long time, but it finally happened. They improved.

It was about this time that a majority in our township exercised their local option and stopped the sale of spirits. There was not less drinking from then on; the trade merely became illegal and the product poisonous. Until then there had been two sizable hotels in the village and one for summer folk on the island. After the liquor trade was taken over by bootleggers, all three found it difficult to operate and, curiously enough, all were successively destroyed by fire. Thereafter travelers had no place to stay; there was not even an eating place. But there were other concurrent changes, and the lack of accommodation was no real hardship for anyone. Little towns near cities could not hold travelers overnight anyway. They had become suburbs. Besides, the traveling men, who had been the best customers of the hotels, were disappearing too. Chain stores had no use for them.

Wilsonians of my generation soon began to regard the city rather than their own village as the center of their activities. They began to live on a regional, a widened scale. In spite of all the examination the phenomena associated with this change have had, I am not certain whether gain or loss was involved. The hotels disappeared; the general merchandise and trading emporiums turned into branch stores such as could be found on any city corner; many villagers began to commute to work in city occupations; strangers came to live among us; the old school would be abandoned and a new one built. All these and many other alterations in the nineteenth-century way of life occurred in close succession.

Wilson lost its character. Its old families were thinned by migration. It acquired all the urban utilities—water and sewer system, electric power, and so on—and these, together with roads and automobiles, fixed the suburban character of the whole county. When the post-war additions of the 'twenties were completed, Sunday drivers would amble about our smooth, orchard-bordered highways in a perpetual holiday atmosphere. We were almost like a musical-comedy countryside.

We were not so securely Republican any more, something which in itself was a measure of change. We never went so far as to develop a Democratic majority, but in Buffalo a large immigrant population working in the mills, on the docks, and in the grain elevators found a means of protest in the Democratic party. The stiff governance of the old families whose mansions along elm-lined Delaware Avenue marked them as elite became harder and harder to accept. Some of that protest reached out to Wilson even then. The farmers stood on their Republicanism firmly enough, but there was a certain wavering in the village.

Our drawing in to the Buffalo center was gradual. But it was noticeable even before the roads were much improved. It was a natural market for the farmers' produce; and even if getting there involved expense and trouble, it was too good an outlet to be neglected. I recall, about 1906, going to market there with farmer boys who were glad of company for the trip. A team had to be young and strong to haul a load of fruit or vegetables through the night all the way to the wholesale center, and then, after a few hours' rest, haul the empty wagon back again in the warm afternoon.

The start out of the farmyard would be a kind of ship-sailing, after which the dispatchers might rest. But whoever was entrusted with the captaincy of the voyage had the fortunes of the farm in his care until he came back into port with the returns of his trading. We started out, up the town-line road, deep with the dust of late summer, the horses leaning honestly into their collars, the pulverized clay cleaving away from the iron-shod wheels. Even at a walk we left a small cloud in the air behind us. The seat, on springs and layered with feed bags, was not too uncomfortable, at least at first. We progressed slowly by the fields and orchards, green enough unless rain had recently been scarce, the roadsides showing the yellow of goldenrod, the blue of chicory, and the purple of wild asters. Each farmyard had a family group working to send off a wagon like ours or to clean up the litter left by one just gone. As we went along, more and more wagons turned onto the road before or behind us. We became a kind of procession.

After about eight miles we came to the North Ridge, a little later to the South Ridge, and then the horses were rested before they tackled the heavy grade of the high escarpment—called locally the Mountain. After the climb we could look back north-ward over almost the width of the county to the lake, dimly blue, back where we had started; and then we pushed off, as though on a passage through the open sea, across the flat plain toward Buffalo. There were twenty miles of this, and presently it would be full dark—nine o'clock, say—and time for feeding the horses out of nosebags in a convenient tavern yard. We ourselves had something too; and now came the long stretch. . . .

Sometime considerably after midnight we rolled down Dela-ware Avenue between the mansions, dark on their wide lawns under the tall elms. The era had not yet come when the avenue was closed to such traffic; and two boys from the country on a dusty, produce-laden wagon drawn by a drooping team could still drive into town between the palaces of the big businessmen. Not all of them were in use even then; their occupants were escaping to country estates; but their decline was not yet advertised to the world. They looked to us as haughty as ever, as unapproachable, as mysterious.

The produce market was much like that of any city of some half million people. It was only a few city squares away from the elegant repose of Delaware Avenue, but a greater contrast at five o'clock in the morning could hardly have been contrived. The avenue was resting in secure calm; the market was a turbulent swarm of traders. The market, of course, was on the other side of Main Street, the slum side, where the foreigners lived. They might not be poor, but they had not yet crossed over to the regions of social respectability. East Buffalo was mostly built up to two-story tenement flats, hard to tell apart because they not only were built on the same plan but were all the same dingy gray. The market was in the middle of this vast sprawl.

Markets are always one of the sights to be seen in any city—at least they used to be before the time of supermarkets and chain stores. In Buffalo this was peculiarly true. The German housewives, together with the gardening country out along Lake Erie to the south and out our way to the north, made the variety a rich one. It was less busy from Thanksgiving until spring, but in summer and especially in fall it had a really lavish display of fruits and vegetables. The canning factories had not yet made home-preserving obsolete among the German families, it seemed, and cellars were still filled with glass jars and crocks as ours used to be. Also, the individual grocer on the corner was expected to have a display of produce under his awning out in front of his store. He came down to the market before his store opened to get it.

The incoming wagons were assigned a place against the curbs all around the market square; the loads were uncovered; display was made of what was offered; and the buyers ranged up and down the sidewalks, elbowing each other to make close examination of what they might like to buy. The purchasers might be dealers at wholesale, retailers themselves, or even house-wives making their own choices among the baskets of fruit or bundles of vegetables. Mostly they were dealers or retailers, and they often bought whole loads at prices finally agreed on after a session of haggling. There were more or less regular relations among a good many farmers and dealers, ones who often met at the market. Each got to know the other, the farmer the dealer's reputation for fair dealing, the dealer the farmer's reputation for quality and honest packaging.

Loads were usually disposed of before breakfast time; then we were free to take it easy while we exchanged gossip with other visitors and had a big meal in the restaurant frequented by the white-coated traders and the blue-jeaned farmers. Then we began the long trip home. I would be well content with my experience; my friend might or might not be satisfied with the commercial results of the venture, and he might even be apprehensive concerning his father's judgment of the bargain he had made. But, at any rate, he had taken part in one of man's most satisfying experiences. Face-to-face bargaining involved real responsibility; it helped to change a boy into a man.

True enough, the important bargain-makings in our economy were no longer face-to-face ones. They were professionalized, formalized, and determined as matters of policy in exchanges between members of vast industrial bureaucracies. We might continue to send a few truckloads of tomatoes, cabbages, plums, cherries, beans, squash, peaches, and apples to market in Niagara Falls and Buffalo, but the bulk of these crops moved out into the channels of trade in car lots, either directly, in season, or out of the storages and canneries in winter. The farmer lost command of them at the storage or at the car door. Some far consumer received them from a dealer who had them from other dealers in a complicated chain. The same was more or less true of wheat raised in Kansas, cotton in Alabama, corn and hogs in Iowa, or beef from the western ranges. And these were simple transactions compared with those involving fuels, lumber, metals, and chemicals. When they came to the consumer it was out of a confusing process whose origin had been lost sight of altogether.

The near revolution in the western farm country headed by Bryan had really grown out of resentment that such a change had taken place at all. The producer still thought he ought to make his own bargains; he thought he was being done in by hidden enemies and he was certain that the whole marketing scheme was corrupt. Then too, he had had to borrow, first to buy land and then to finance his crops; and the lenders naturally wanted their money back. When the price of his crops fell he was simply unable to meet his obligations, and in any case he wanted to meet them with money worth no more than that he had borrowed. So the agrarians were money reformers; they wanted to monetize silver, issue greenbacks, or otherwise cheapen the medium of exchange. But they were never reformers in any other sense; especially, they were never collectivists. If they wanted government ownership of the railways or other utilities, it was because they resented the rates they had to pay, not because they believed in socialization. The progressives were self-interested. They wanted more, not less, competition, free enterprise, pursuit of profits. But, inconsistently, they wanted the process to favor them.

In view of the prevailing attitudes among both minority and majority groups in the United States during the first decade of the century, it is a strange and incongruous fact that during that same decade Albert Einstein, an obscure mathematical theorist living in Switzerland, published the paper in which the theory of relativity was suggested.

It would be on August 2, 1939, thirty-four years later, that Einstein himself, now exiled from Germany and an American citizen, would address a letter to President Roosevelt, saying that recent work led him to expect "that the element uranium may be turned into a new and important source of energy in the immediate future." This would be the actual transformation of mass into energy that he had forecast in the equation $E=MC_2$. He would go on to say that the new phenomenon "would lead to the construction of bombs," and it was conceivable "that a single bomb of this type, carried by a boat and exploded in a port, might very well destroy the whole port together with some of the surrounding territory."

For our purpose here it is relevant to emphasize the incident. Einstein's mind would have encompassed the mass-energy transformation, but not the probability that the bomb might be dropped from an airplane instead of being deposited by a ship. In somewhat the same fashion, one of the successful nuclear scientists in Chicago would say of the creation, just completed a few years later, that he hoped it wouldn't be *dynamite* in the hands of children. Thus clichés resist the erosions of change. So, sad to say, do ideas and attitudes.

Already Simon Nelson Patten, for instance, and John Dewey would have arrived at their relativity concepts in social theory.

For them Einstein's theorem, when they heard of it, would be no more than confirmation of what they had already concluded.

It would be some few years yet before I heard of either Patten or Dewey; and, even if I had, their theories would have made no difference in the experiences I continued to have. The economy and the society I lived in would go on as it had before. Economists and political scientists, too, would go on weaving their elaborate webs of reason while reality escaped and prepared horrible surprises for all of us.

Twenty-four

However people's mental habits clung to old conceptions, their environment was being enlarged and they had no difficulty about accepting their new freedom. The horse and buggy was rapidly being supplanted by the automobile, and the telephone was becoming an accustomed convenience. If the earlier roads in our region failed to reach Wilson, there was an important one several miles to the south of us. All we had to do was to reach it. The million-dollar highway, as it was called, ran along the North Ridge from Rochester to Lewiston, one of the state's oldest paths—used, for instance, by Washington when he made his grand tour. Its age and importance could be told just by seeing the vast spread of the white oaks along it. If we could get over the six miles to this main artery, we could go west to the Falls or east to Lockport and the other canal-side cities.

Another of the early roads, and one of the first to be improved, was that from Youngstown and Lewiston to Niagara Falls and on to Buffalo. I mentioned earlier the portage of Céleron and other French *voyageurs* from Lake Erie to Lake Chautauqua. Céleron, like all the others, had got to Lake Erie by coming up the whole length of Lake Ontario, landing below the Niagara rapids, at Fort Niagara, and making the difficult portage to La Salle above the upper rapids.[1]

[1] I quote again from *Niagara County,* by Edward T. Williams (p. 43):

"Within the walls of old Fort Niagara there are relics of two and a half centuries . . . In 1669 La Salle, the French explorer, who constructed at the village bearing his name, just above Niagara Falls, the *Griffon,* the first

Niagara Falls had once tumbled over the escarpment from one lake level to the other at Lewiston (long before it had a name, of course). But they had in time eaten their way backward more than twelve miles to their present site, where they have in recent ages been in the process of turning a corner. For the river comes down out of the east at the end of Lake Erie, rushing ever more rapidly until its upper reaches become an expanse of broken water, huge boulders, and vestigial islands; then it flows north to Ontario. The bass roar as the river leaps over the 165-foot precipice can be heard for miles around, and the white cloud of spray hanging over it can always be seen.[2]

The reason for agricultural prosperity in the county was that

---

vessel to sail the upper lakes, built the first structure . . . Again, in 1678, the year that Father Hennepin, La Salle's associate, saw Niagara Falls, the first white man to gaze on the mighty cataracts, La Salle built there Fort Conti . . . That fort was destroyed, and in 1687 de Nonville built another fort, called after himself. That fort was destroyed by the Seneca Indians the next year. The French, in 1725, erected a stone structure, the foundations of which remain . . . The French were supplanted by the British in 1759 . . ."

And so it went. Many of the battles and much of the maneuvering of the War of 1812 took place along the short Niagara frontier. Queenston Heights, Chippawa, and Lundy's Lane were famous, if inconclusive, battles. Buffalo was burned, but it was then only a village. The proceedings here, together with what is usually described as the "disgraceful surrender" of Hull and his army in the Detroit River country, determined that Canada would remain independent. Americans did capture York (now Toronto) in 1813, but the campaign of that year was a failure, and that of 1814 was no more successful. The peace, in 1815, left matters about where they had been at the beginning.

[2] Again from Williams (pp. 62–63): "What we call the Niagara Frontier, in a geographical sense, is called the Niagara Quadrangle in a geological sense, and lies between parallels 43° and 43° 30″ and meridians 78° 30″ and 79° . . .

"Another term, familiar to the Niagara locality, is the Portage Escarpment, which is so named because in Western New York it is formed by resistant beds of the Portage Formation. The average person recognizes the word portage as applying to an ancient roadway that ran from the top of the Lewiston escarpment to Schlosser Dock on the upper Niagara, through what is now the City of Niagara Falls . . . It was built, of course, to avoid the cataracts of Niagara, and it was related that in the early days the beautiful oak forest through which it ran was sufficiently open to permit a person to see six hundred paces . . . The first railroad in the United States was the tramway down the Niagara escarpment, at Lewiston, to the Niagara River boats . . ."

the land lay mostly in the old lake bed. The escarpment ran eastward some six or more miles from—and parallel to—the present shore of the lake and westward to the lake's end in Canada. It was the most striking physical phenomenon of the region. It was matched by two lesser ridges which had been later shores of a receding prehistoric sea. These tended to merge toward the east, but for a hundred miles from our end they were well separated and quite noticeable. Highways had run along them since before history had begun to be recorded, and especially the north one, nearest the lake, had become a regional artery. It was topped now with concrete, and automobiles, from their first coming into general use, had slipped along it in numbers. Its popularity was due not only to its convenience but also to its beauty. The ridge, being somewhat elevated above the countryside, allowed travelers on its road to view a panorama of rich farmland running into the distance on both sides.

A good deal of the county's heavy impacted soil was hard to work, but near the ridges the clay was lightened by the sand of the old shores and became almost ideally tillable. From the other side of Rochester all the way to Lewiston—and, for that matter, across the river into Canada—there stretched the richest fruit region of those decades. Besides a workable soil, it usually had rain enough, so that there was more a problem of drainage than of drought, and the modification of the temperatures in all seasons by the lake made farming less risky than in places where there were greater extremes.

Then too, there was less erosion in our flat country than in hilly ones like Chautauqua. The heavier soils, if well drained, were a solid foundation for the magnificent apple trees of the traditional breeds. Nowhere else—certainly not in New England, where most of them had originated—did they stand so long against weather and age, provided only that they were protected from imported pests. Characteristically they had been planted well apart; but, even so, their mature spread shaded the whole interval. In good years their yields would run to fifty or more barrels for each tree; but they were many years in growing, and since the more aged of them had been badly hurt during the uncontrolled pest years of the late century, they were losing out to the newer and quicker-growing varieties. So every year there were fewer orchards of the great tradition left; but when I was young there were still many. In their majestic age, and in the splendor of their blossoming and fruiting, they were a moving sight.[3]

The other fruits were less spectacular, just as foothills are less sightly than mountains; yet they lent the countryside their own kind of beauty. Even the humbler field crops, from squash to melons and from beans to peppers, made a handsome show. These were all to be seen sloping gently away from the roads along our ridges.[4] The farmers of our county knew their business, and as farming went, they were as free of hazards—weather, markets, pests—as could be expected. Their prosperity produced a reasonably advanced culture.

This could be seen, especially along the older roads, simply by taking note of the houses, the yards, and the complex of buildings around the barns. These barns were not the immense

[3] For years I made note of the planting practices followed by different orchardists in various places. In my own county I paced old orchards again and again. I never found a planting of the traditional apples less than thirty feet apart, and many were fifty feet or more. In my youth it was the custom—because of advice from the Agricultural College at Cornell— to *cultivate* orchards. The best orchard was one where no wisp of green was ever seen on the ground, except perhaps a spring crop of green manure to be turned under. When I had a farm I revolted against this practice. And now, for the reasons I then found so convincing, the general practice has changed. Greensward is now kept growing under the trees, and mulches of straw or other litter are sometimes added.

The difference in appearance of the orchards of then and now is immense. Clean cultivation permitted the development of a majestic tree; teams had to be driven under it, so the bearing branches were high up and required long ladders for the picking. Nowadays, with grass beneath, a good deal of the picking can be done from the ground. The trees are trimmed downward and kept shrubby all their lives. It must be said for the old way that it made the orchards more sightly. But the clean cultivation led to mineral wastes through leaching and, when there was any slope at all, to surface erosion. It was these obvious losses which led me to change. How the pundits at Cornell saved face when there came a turn away from the clean cultivation they had been so sure was necessary, I do not know. Probably the old professors sleep in retirement undisturbed by the revolution.

[4] Remember Montaigne? "Let me be taken in the midst of my cabbages . . ."

ones characteristic of a dairy region, which so often manage, in Iowa or Illinois, to make the houses seem by contrast to be pinched and mean. The older eastern homesteads had been models for the settlements in the West; but the pattern always seemed to have been skimped and the carpenters and masons seemed not to have known their jobs in the old sure way. Somehow, the proportions were wrong. The houses were dwarfed by the barns.

The farmers of our region, besides using the old commodious designs, had found materials at hand well suited to the purpose—matched stones from the lake shore laid up in stucco over brick. These were identified as Ontario cobbles; they had been worn smooth by the friction of the waves and gave the houses the finish of good workmanship, especially when they stood well back from the road and were amply planned. And when the yards were shaded by mature white oaks, chestnuts, or maples, backed by immense old apple trees, beginning just beyond the lawns, the whole seemed the very picture of the traditional prosperous farmstead—what in Chautauqua we had called a "stand" and had given a family name.

The older homesteads, established between 1830 and 1860, built from the profits of the earlier apple monopoly, were now, some fifty or seventy-five years later, well planted on their acres. Some, of course, had grown shabby as the families died out and strangers came in; but most had weathered the years well, gaining dignity as time passed. There were, however, beginning to be interspersed many less dignified places. These belonged mostly to German immigrants who had bought a piece off some old farm to be cultivated with an intensity their long-settled neighbors did not approve. Such industry required overwork, really, for the whole family; and the more prosperous Niagara farmers had got used to working more with their heads than with their hands. They were not driven, day in and day out, by the demands of stock. The new people among the old were not too many for assimilation, however, and there was no distinction made of which a boy would be aware. He would hear some disparaging talk, but not enough to seem an issue of importance.

From the village there was, well within a range that grew wider as roads were improved and automobiles became more reliable, many a farm home of the traditional sort where I was welcome. In the informal way of the country, those of us who were in our teens were quite free with each other's houses. I had, moreover, become my father's field man. This made it necessary for me to travel the neighborhood and brought me into contact with every grower of produce on his home place. First by horse and runabout, later by car, I got about the countryside from June until October. I learned the productive qualities of thousands of separate fields down hundreds of different lanes and became almost as well known as the rural mailman. I was reasonably faithful, I think, to my job. Still, I cannot deny that I knew very well in what houses were the prettiest girls and the best cooks. It was an occupation that lent itself to combining business with pleasure. I realize now that my father knew this quite as well as I. All these years later I give him marks for a tolerance I never thought of then.

The fall, as I have said, lingered late in our lake country, and I combined school with work for some time as the season advanced. But I do not recall that it made any difference. We never had any homework anyway. And it did leave me with some of my most pleasurable recollections. The tomatoes, red in the fields, and the yellow squashes and pumpkins scattered about kept ripening almost until the frost came; and long after that, on into October and even November, when freezes really began, the apples—Baldwins, Greenings, Northern Spies, Wagners, Russets—hung sweetening slowly in the sun as the pickers worked their way through the big orchards and the barrel-laden wagons creaked along the roads on the way to the storages or the railroad sidings.

It was then that the farmers and the local dealers, too, learned whether a year of work, as well as of borrowing or investing, had paid off. Profits, it must be said, did become leaner as time passed. Other regions were developing and, to tell the truth, were quicker to adopt improved methods both of cultivation and of marketing. But the adjustment was not altogether ruinous. The new canning factories helped, and good roads made more markets accessible. Also, turning to smaller fruits was easy for an apple grower. I saw the time when peaches became more important in the county's economy than apples. But it took some getting used to for the old-timers.

But the fruitgrowers, I always thought, had a pleasant life. Aside from the hustle of spraying days and the worry about the fall market, they were seldom rushed. They had all winter to trim their trees, and this was really a season of leisure for them. Later, a good many of them took to locking up and going South, but that was unheard of when I was young. Instead, more attention was given to social affairs, to the church, and, what is wonderful for any farmer, the enjoyment of leisure.

Spring was the same sort of awakening for the fruitgrowers that it was for their trees. Along the ridge roads and along the other roads parallel to the lake, the spring came slowly, but still it came; and its intimations were clear as the snow disappeared for good. The peach buds showed swelling first and were the first to burst into lavender flame. The old apple trees were more staid, as though their years had taught them to be discreet. The peaches, in fact, were sometimes caught by late frosts, since they were the first to brave the chill. Later, the apples, having lingered in red bud until the green of their leaves had become definite, would cover the whole county with a glory no Niagaran will ever forget or believe can be equaled by any show nature may make in other times and places.

Blossom time in the apple orchards brought the farmer fully awake. To miss the instant when spraying was indicated meant disaster, and he never did miss it. Still, he and his family had some spare time, and all the rest of us who were, at this stage, onlookers had more, for the enjoyment of the festival. We had none of those gala affairs with queens, parades, and all that sort of thing, which later became fashionable; but we did have blossom parties in our homes, there was acknowledgment in the churches, and we had an outburst of social affairs. In Niagara we had no sugarings-off such as there had been in Chautauqua to meet the spring halfway. The delay until the apples bloomed established the season more firmly. The pears, the cherries, the plums, and the quinces would burst out now, and the pear perfume would hardly be gone when the shrubs around our houses would flower—lilacs, snowballs, syringa, mock orange. Then, in May, when the peonies came out, we knew that summer was arriving. Soon there would be cherries and green peas for the factory, but for a month before this the factory had been busily preparing, everyone glad that winter was over.

Twenty-five

Something deplorable was happening all over the United States when I was growing up. The most convinced believers in free enterprise were finding it hard to defend the disorder, the downright ugliness of our unplanned towns and cities; and even the countryside was suffering the same sort of change. Take our county. There were really gracious homesteads surviving from a former generation. I doubt whether there was a single one established after the turn of the century. But there was a growing number of miserable places interspersed among the older ones. The houses were thrown together and surrounded by sheds and lean-tos; the yards were littered with rusting machinery and grown up to weeds. The whole effect on anyone driving along our roads was a ragged caricature of the traditional rural civilization.

And in the cities—Buffalo, for instance—there was Delaware Avenue, as there was Beacon Hill in Boston, Rittenhouse Square in Philadelphia, Euclid Avenue in Cleveland, and Nob Hill in San Francisco; but these neighborhoods were rapidly being inundated by speculative flats, rows of cheap and identical two-story houses, and shops and stores with loud competitive displays of all sorts. Any suggestion of order or plan was ignored. Even factories placed themselves at their owners' convenience and without regard to that of the community; warehouses, garages, gasoline stations, laundries, funeral parlors, and every other conceivable business lodged anywhere it seemed possible to do so profitably.

Americans, through the generations, had made a great point of men's rights to do what they liked with their own. They were now suffering the logical consequence of the rule's literal application. The popular philosophers who had used the slogan for revolutionary purposes had usually added—but, so to say, in small print—"so long as these rights do not interfere with those of others." The print had been so small that it could be ignored. And it was evident by the beginning of the century that the limitation had been altogether abandoned. It survived in law, but it had become lost in custom. Especially the rights of the community were ignored, and any attempt to define or defend them was met with the argument that business ought not to be interfered with. It was un-American.

The physical embodiments of this right of each individual to do as he wanted with his own were appearing in every remaining pleasant street or country road. And they were proving to be blatant, demanding, vulgar, and ugly. Their most characteristic representatives were the billboard, the gas station, the hot-dog stand, and the new so-called service trades—all of them appurtenances of the newer industries, especially the automobile. At any rate, the old America was being flooded out; and there would be question whether the debris would ever be cleared away and a disciplined reconstruction undertaken.[1]

The flood would not be very noticeable in Sinclairville, but only because Sinclairville was not growing. The countryside around it was beginning the long retreat from unprofitable husbandry to a forest economy. But little Wilson illustrated the process well enough; and the whole Niagara frontier had, in fact, become a commercial paradise, its natural beauties intruded on by individual enterprises of incredible ugliness. Easterners, at least, will know what is implied by saying that ours was a village without a common. It had simply grown up at a corner about two miles from the lake and had extended

[1] It was peculiarly sad that the fine old word "stand," with its connotation of homestead solidity, should have been appropriated by one of the shoddiest and most intrusive of all commercial uses.

itself backward along the crossing roads and out into several
nearby lanes. Two of these led to the lake, but the others ended
uncertainly in the fields. During the nineteenth century, Main
Street had already been vandalized by several builders of false-
front buildings. These were exactly like those of the frontier
towns in the West. But elms and maples did spread a summer
canopy over the excrescences underneath, and except for the
two elephantine frame hotels—which had the grace to burn
down—the summer appearance of the village was, if not distinguished, not altogether repulsive. There were even a few
cobbled houses. And before later comers began to buy intervening lots and run up 1910 model houses (of which ours was
one), the residential streets were quiet and dignified. If there
were no conspicuously fine establishments, there were no squalid
ones either.

When the warm sun of summer had shown that it meant
business and recurrent chills had stopped coming up from the
depths of the lake, pushing their fogs several miles inland, the
best months began. The big trees and the full green shrubs
would now hide the indecent exposures of the melting snows;
dust would follow each vehicle along the streets in a small lazy
cloud. Hammocks would be swung on porches or between
convenient trees on lawns. Small boys would be turned loose,
barefoot and carefree. Older ones would be starting their summer jobs.

What is recalled in age may very possibly not be what stood
out as important to a youth. I was as much caught up as any
of my friends in immediate affairs. I had my difficulties and I
overcame them as best I could. But many of them have become
dim. They cannot have been very important. Yet when a new
bicycle is wanted, it is badly wanted. When there is rivalry about
a girl, there are intrigues. When one job is wanted and another is
assigned, there is a grievance. I can only say that settlement of
such problems seems to erase the emotion involved in the
effort. I recall some things I am sure I scarcely noted at the

time, and I must have forgotten some that caused first-rate disturbances when they were going on.

The summer days and those of fall seem to me now to have been uniformly pleasant. I recall, for instance, that I did have pleasure then, as I still do, in the spread before me, as I drove about, of fields and orchards under cultivation. There are some people who have this sort of feeling only about the wilderness or, at least, about relatively raw natural scenes. For me there is nothing to match productive farmland, well taken care of, doing what good farmers expect it to do. If I could, I would always have a house looking over a spread of land in full production, being worked on and responding as it should.

I presume that if this was an original feeling it was an educated one after I had for years had a job requiring me to know exactly what was going on and whether it was being done well or badly. At any rate, it has stayed with me. And it has fixed some recollections that others of my contemporaries might not note at all as characteristic of our common experiences.

I recall how quickly the alfalfa and the canning peas matured as spring came on, how the sequence of blossoming passed from one orchard to another, how the haze of full summer and the strange clarity of fall changed familiar landscapes. Starting out on my bicycle to work in the morning before seven and, after a spell of office work, making my rounds in the company Ford, I must have taken a poet's pleasure in all I saw; I could not otherwise recall it so vividly now that I have forgotten so much else that occupied my days. I can still hear the rhythmic clank of empty cans coming down a chute and striking the steel conveyor as each was lined up to receive its contents. It was a sound that carried. It could be heard for a mile or more and was one of the characteristic ones I lived with. Less regular were other sounds—hammers on anvils in the blacksmith shops, the chirring of mowing machines or harvesters in the fields, the whistle of locomotives as the long freights pulled slowly through the grade crossings.

As for sights, the honey locusts and horse chestnuts bloomed spectacularly along the roads in June, but not before a succession of flowering weeds began to fill the ditches and fence rows. In summer the cicada whirred and the turtle dove struck its melancholy gong. In one of the lanes I had to travel or in one of the fields where I looked hard at the crop, I had only to stop for an instant for these sights and sounds to make themselves felt. They were the purest sort of pleasure, no inconvenience involved, nothing to be subtracted.

I have to insist, too, because I do recall it so distinctly, that some more serious and significant considerations were beginning to occur to me. Again, I could not recall my struggles with them if it were not so. I was a newspaper reader. I kept up. I had ideas about what ought to be done. These may not have been worth discussing, but I did discuss them. I recall remarking to Allen Hinchliffe that the old saying about people and their government could not be true. The saying would have it that people got the government they deserved. What, I asked, were leaders for, then? If government could not be better than the people it represented, what was T.R. talking about? Besides, government had been given the power to restrain offenders against its laws; this implied that it *must* be better than *they*, at least. It must be better even than average folk if our representatives were above the average—as they certainly were supposed to be. Allen had some ideas of a similar sort; he was even more skeptical. He thought the trouble was that such sayings protected time-servers. Leaders wanted excuses not to lead; either they were lazy or they didn't want to offend anyone. So there was a continuing conspiracy to cover up and maintain a pleasant inertia.

I went on from this to evolve a theory which was rather advanced, I still think, for my age. I maintained that there ought to be an effort to create institutions representing people's best intentions. Too much attention was given to simple restraint. That, and elaborate machinery for judging who was right in disputes, had become too important. No one was trying to find out what the future ought to be like for all of us and making an effort to bring it about.

I do not yet see that these were strange, or perhaps even unusual, thoughts for a boy of seventeen. Just because adults do not often catch them at it, the assumption cannot be made that attitudes which become prominent a few years later do not begin during the teens. Allen and I, and some others too, spent considerable time in the evenings or in interludes of work talking about such things. There was a lot of horseplay around the factory; the discipline was not severe; and the failings of each of us were rather mercilessly exposed and laughed at. So I recall episodes of this sort more clearly than ones with more serious intention. But still, I was beginning to be interested in public affairs, much, I suppose, as animals train for their adult responsibilities by playful simulation of the situations they will meet later on.

Somewhere in a civics text, one of the ones McIlroy, the principal in Wilson, helped me with, I ran across a reference to Bryce's *American Commonwealth*. I acquired its two big volumes and, taking it slowly, found that I could absorb what they had to say. This was the start of a long experience of reading the originals of what seemed to me important books. Most people merely read *about* them. It was a considerable event to discover that they themselves were not so formidable as they were made to appear.

At about the same period I also got hold of something easier, but still influential. This was Bellamy's *Looking Backward*. The interest I found in this sort of thing might have been a forewarning. I should have known that I was in touch with a future profession. Perhaps I did. I cannot be sure.

In mid-life I was forced to conclude that a person who moves about doing different jobs cannot have much of a library to call his own. It is just too great an extravagance. Besides, university or public libraries are never far away and never difficult to use. No less than half a dozen times I abandoned collections of precious books to friends or relatives before I gave up. The wrench was always painful. But there was no alternative.

There were, however, a few exceptions. So it always happened that, in spite of my resolve, some of my old favorites went with me. I was so fond of *Pickwick Papers* from the age of twelve that I wore out several volumes and could hardly have gone to sleep at night without knowing it was on my bedside table. It represented to me the irrepressibly hearty and free existence in the England I felt to be my own by inheritance. It was a critical, even an ironic, commentary on many phases of that life. Still, its humor and spirit were indomitable. I read and enjoyed it over and over. The more serious social commentaries, like the *Commonwealth,* I did not exactly enjoy; but I felt I had to know everything they had to say. There was satisfaction in accumulating the knowledge they represented, so much satisfaction that there could be no doubt about my bent. It was this kind of thing that I really wanted to know about.

I have already said that I had a weakness for anything literary, that I got pleasure out of reading fiction, that I pored over poems, and that history and biography were a kind of food, good food, filling and lasting. Aside from the snatches of the classics we were introduced to in our English courses, I accumulated a whole set of Shakespeare; but also there were Sir Walter Scott and F. Marion Crawford, who to this day are associated in my recollections—both romancers calculated to take readers completely away from everyday reality. It was perhaps a natural transition from Henty to Scott, the one right for a boy of ten or twelve and the other for one of sixteen. I devoured contemporary romances too, although I cannot place them in time. David Graham Phillips, Robert Chambers, and Booth Tarkington I consumed without much admiration. They did to read in bed. But Wells, Galsworthy, Joseph Conrad had put more in and I got more out. I began to distinguish between art and trash. It was probably not until several years later that the messages Wells and Galsworthy had for sensitive members of my generation began to come through their stories and appeal to me in other ways. These two would certainly have as much effect on me as a young man as any other single intellectual influence. Somehow I was susceptible to their message. This was no doubt partly because it came the way it did, through characters who acted as I hoped I might act or villains I could detest.

One exciting novel in an American setting, and one only, I think, had the same effect. That was *The Honorable Peter Stirling;* but this led me to others, not so exciting, so far as I was concerned, yet important as documents—*The Damnation of Theron Ware* and *The Jungle.* After *The Jungle* I was as indignant as its author could have wished. But it was not a story. It was propaganda. If I longed to emulate Peter Stirling, who went up against the forces of evil in their most modern and most confusing guise, that was only natural, I think, in a boy who was emerging from a literary world thick with senti-ment into one whose realities were often so different from the virtues I had been taught to respect. Sentimentality was loosing its hold on me. My mother was worried about it, but she had no idea how to turn me from the way I was going. She resorted to pretending that it was not so, and this, for her, was always a safe retreat.

Twenty-six

I was on easy terms with the wicked. This could only have happened in a village so nearly classless that all its members were in daily contact with each other. And it may be that it could only have happened to a boy who was friendly and who had no association with authority to frighten the sinful. Those I speak of did not come into my home, of course, although I sometimes went to theirs; and they were excluded from social occasions—those sponsored by the churches, for instance, or other respectable institutions. My mother preferred to ignore them, and my father regarded them with a sort of impatient humor. They were nuisances.

Most of these people were drunkards. Some of them were also morally loose. This word was usually applied to sexual misbehavior. But, as to that, exposures once in a while of informalities in the relationships of otherwise respectable folk showed that villagers were not so different from people elsewhere. I can recall at least half a dozen instances of really startling adventures among choir singers who practiced more than hymns, merchants who traveled for more reasons than business, and old gentlemen of substance who maintained establishments which were delightfully irregular. All this did not surprise those of us who were sixteen or thereabouts. We knew about it all along. But, with the tolerance of the young, who have their own affairs to attend to, we kept our knowledge from our elders. They probably knew as much as we did. But we never exchanged confidences.

Mere dabblers in forbidden pools of experience are not to be confused with the downright wicked. Transgressors were transients; there were others who were never to be included among the respectable. For these I had a certain fondness. In a way they were like boys. They simply could not take the rules seriously or, if they did, could not manage to live within them. They had some virtues of their own, or at least some attractive qualities. There were not more than a dozen of them in the community, although there were others who were doubtfully upright. Several were merely bar flies or livery-stable bums, sodden, derelict, and hopeless—rural variety of a species I was to become familiar with in cities where I later lived. These were tolerantly allowed winters in the county jail for offenses committed in a kind of conspiracy with the authorities, which was a decent arrangement. But there were others more rebellious and vigorous who had character and color. I sometimes thought there was something to be said for their attitude.

They were not, any of these last, really slaves to alcohol; their resort to it was, in some instances, a kind of protest against an existence they disapproved of so strongly as to be periodically able to tolerate it no longer; in other instances no protest was involved, but rather a passing in a drunken euphoria over into another world, where attractions were thus heightened and miseries were blotted out. They half lived in this world anyway; alcohol merely made it seem more real.

There were even a few of these wicked who were not devoted to the bottle; they were extreme examples of the Jake Evans type. I have described Jake as one who simply regarded the activities of civilized people as not worth much of a man's time. It could much better be spent in hunting, fishing, or merely loafing. Jake did not go in for misdemeanors; he was basically just a nonconformist. But some of my Wilson acquaintances made themselves actively dangerous. As for the shiftless, I was a boy, and it had to be recognized that the adult world had been arranged for adults.

I was becoming one of the sort who, if anything, was over-

conscious of rattles anywhere in the machinery. I mean to say
that I had a fair sense of order. But I never lost my sympathy
for those who refused to conform and preferred to live in
disorder. Mostly they ran small businesses, as Jake Evans had
done in Sinclairville. These could be closed when they felt
stifled or oppressed. No one would be hurt by their absence.
Two had barbershop poolrooms, one had a small grocery, one
was a shoemaker, another had an early gasoline service station.
But others were merely casual laborers who, because they just
worked around, could begin and finish when and where they
liked. Several had lived since boys as Civil War pensioners,
without having more than a tenuous claim to ever having been
soldiers. One old fellow used to make speeches in school on
patriotic occasions, although it was well known that he had
gone to war only in the last months of recruiting and had never
got farther south than Fort Niagara. He was merely a hypocrite.
He had always been a loafer, but he was head of the local post
of the G.A.R. and wore his blues, it was said, even when he
went to bed. Such matters were not ones to be indignant about;
they were amusing to a boy. But it would have been pretty
silly if he had taken them at their accepted valuation.

My more shiftless friends were good for me in another way.
They considered that my talents were very moderate. And, as
they measured talents, this was true. But also they let me know
that any objective that I had in mind was not worth the effort
anyway, so it was of no importance one way or the other.
Among those I knew less well, probably because they regarded
me as disapproving, were some older boys who would today be
called delinquents. Their outspoken criticisms of established
institutions went to the length of burning down hay and straw
stacks, sheds, and even barns and houses. Unfortunately, arson
proved to be habit-forming and they kept it up so long that
they were finally caught and brought to trial. It seemed to us
at first that they regarded their burnings as jokes on neighbors
who were so much against fire that they had organized a
volunteer fire department. There was a certain humor in calling

out a group of staid citizens night after night to put out fires in straw stacks. But when operations were extended to barns and houses, it finally became clear to the rest of us that the arsonists were destroying the representative symbols of organized society to show their rejection of providence and discipline. In the jail to which they were finally consigned with righteous to-do, I am sure no one bothered to wonder why they had so wantonly destroyed people's hard-earned properties. At any rate, they ended badly, like Billy the Kid. They were not shot at their nefarious business. But they did die of rotgut whisky and the diseases that malnutrition induces.

The particular fellows I have in mind were a few years my senior, but not so much older as to be unfamiliar. They had a way of going off by themselves on missions not known to the rest of us. We had an idea what they did, a suspicion that was confirmed one time in a way that I shall not forget.

On an early spring day one of my friends and I were exploring the lake shore. The ice had only lately melted, and there were piles of interesting debris left from the winter storms. But there was an offshore wind and it was unusually warm. We had our fishing-poles and some worms for bait, but we were not so much fishing as having a look along the banks and beaches we knew so well in summer. At any rate, before we came into a little cove we heard loud voices and what seemed to be shouts of laughter. This was strange, and we were cautious. We climbed to the top of the conveniently overhanging bank and had a look. The waves were not too loud, and the beach was a narrow one. There were two fellows just below us. We recognized them. They were the two we all suspected of being arsonists. They were sitting on the gravel, backs to driftwood logs, each with a whisky bottle. They drank and shuddered, drank and shuddered again. They hated the stuff, but they needed it too. That they were either celebrating a coup or working up to one, we could guess. They shouted and sang. What they shouted was a kind of saga—how smart they were and how stupid their victims were. They half shouted and half sang their last victory.

That old fool Meany with all his barns and cattle, going to church every Sunday and making everyone else stand around when he spoke—they'd fixed him. They had set his big straw stack afire and then joined the crowd standing around to watch. The firemen had raced out from the village dragging the pumper and then found the well too deep for their hose; the barn had been saved, but only just. It had been a marvelous exploit. The two of them had frightened the whole village and made the fireboys stay up most of the night.

We crept away after a fascinated half hour, and neither of us ever told. This in itself is interesting. We weren't so much frightened as wary of being involved. Besides, it was common knowledge that Foss and Jube were the probable fire-setters, and it was up to our elders to do something about it if the nuisance was intolerable. It was some time before my friend and I even discussed the occurrence. When we did, we agreed on one thing. Foss and Jube were getting mighty little satisfaction out of their revolt. They could only creep off into a chilly cove with cheap whisky and brag to each other. It was not much pay for all the risk and effort.

When I thought it over, the most obvious conclusion I could come to was that there was nothing really rewarding in such behavior. They could pretend to each other that they were smarter and stronger than anyone, but they could not spread the news and take a public posture. I could not think of anything that could be done with their sort except to lock them up. Such individuals break off everywhere, out of every group, and at every stage of the group's development. And Foss and Jube were only exaggerated examples of a very common thing. Most objectors and revolutionists were too timid for criminal activities, but they had the same impulses and were likely to be more dangerous because they were more cautious.

It was easy to see that there could be real danger in the generating of too much withdrawal. A later conclusion was that frustration and resentment could emerge in various degrees, often so managed as to be almost unrecognizable. Satisfactions of a sort were evidently to be had from hindrances. Even scrambled instructions, disordered files, invented gossip, misinterpreted policies, shirked responsibilities could be traced to this disorder of the mind. It was possible for this to happen without consciousness on the part of the saboteur that he was being governed by his compulsion. I must say that the study of organized treatises about human nature later in my life did little more than put into literary form much that I already knew from my village experience.

I could understand even from our factory organization that integration is dependent on the loyalty and co-operation of the whole group. A minor who feels that he ought to be a major, an employee who has reason to feel discriminated against, can cause trouble, and often trouble of a sort protected under the rules of a union. I very early concluded that an effort ought to be made to develop a consensus and to bind everyone to the policies it indicates.

The village was not an organization as a factory was, but it was a small and close society. Misfits were accepted as natural until they became dangerous. But there did seem to be a growing number of these. The more attractive ones had simply withdrawn from the competition to get on. They were apt to use all the spare time they could find for the cultivation of some activity they considered more important than those regarded as orthodox by others. These might appear only as amusing idiosyncrasies, such as becoming self-appointed guardians of others' conduct, the disparagement on principle of all community projects, or the excessive cultivation of a hobby. One of our old bachelors kept many dogs and cats in the hovel where he lived; another would expatiate by the hour on the evils of religion. Then there was the one who devised schemes for monetary reform, a vagary I would have cause to recall many years later when thousands of such cranks appeared from their formerly private retreats and were given serious attention. The Committee for the Nation, in New Deal days, seemed to be made up wholly of such fanatics.

Our atheist and our monetary reformer had such remote targets that they could be ignored. They were a constant source of amusement. Both happened to live on the charity of descendants who had been raised haphazardly and were not themselves leading citizens. The money man was, nevertheless, something of a dandy. He wore fawn-colored vests and a wing collar even when he had nothing in his pockets. The atheist was dirty and shiftless, and the fact that he was filthy as well as skeptical was often pointed out by those who were more orthodox. We were told that the conjunction was inevitable, but I do not know that the lesson made much impression.

These and other deviations from the norms of ambition in a competitive society were, as a matter of fact, taken by the young as the young take practically all behavior of their elders —without surprise and without much of any other reaction. That a dozen or so loafers and deviates of various sorts could somehow exist in a village as small as ours, mostly without any visible source of income, was simply one of those things we presumed to be inevitable. Without effort, and certainly not in the way our elders hoped we would, we learned a good deal from it. It was presumed that they would be supported by their families; but some of them were husbands and fathers, and these created a problem only charity of some sort could ease. There was no—or very little—feeling that any community obligation was involved. Only when poverty had gone to the absolute extreme did public assistance operate. This happened so infrequently that I am still not clear how it occurred. One thing was certain—there was no such governmental responsibility as, fifty years later, would be taken for granted. If there was a social worker in our whole county, I never heard of it. In fact, I never saw one until I had long since left Wilson.

I have already said something about my impulse to write. To one who does not feel that compulsion, it may seem strange that a boy should have the feeling that he *must* put words on paper. Writing is for saying something, for conveying information, for communicating. But to a writer it is that and a good deal more. It is something he would have difficulty in not doing. This does not always mean that he has talent, but it nearly always means that he will become a professional. He may, after experiment, discover that his range will always be limited and that, even in that range, he can become only passably acceptable. But that is hard luck. He has to write anyway.

But no writer ever lived, I suppose, who did not long to have readers. The art is one, after all, that requires others who will pay attention. A writer may know that his intention is known only to himself, that he has to practice, that he has to compromise, and that it is himself who in the end must be satisfied. Still, he does want readers. He wants to see his words in print. It is the natural end of his occupation.

It was this impulse which caused me to take measures. I secretly went to Niagara Falls one day, found the city room of the Niagara Falls *Gazette,* and spoke to the editor. I asked him if he would let me write his Wilson correspondence. After talking it over, he agreed. And for a year, then, I had an audience.

The Niagara Falls *Gazette* was the kind of newspaper to be expected in a city of twenty thousand people. Its advertisers hoped to draw country trade into their stores. So it made something of a specialty of columns written to interest people in the various localities. The big paper in western New York was the Buffalo *Evening News;* next, I suppose, would come the Buffalo *Express.* These were both fittingly Republican. The Buffalo *Courier* was Democratic, so it had only a small country circulation. But the *Gazette* was closer to us. And it did have— what the Buffalo papers did not have—columns of local news.

This was a very satisfactory experience. Whoever edited my copy was either generous or careless. Practically everything I wrote was printed. And after years of anonymous practice, to write things I knew would appear in print almost at once gave me as much satisfaction, I am sure, as reaching a wider audience gave to more experienced authors. I could not say that I was given any training. The only comments ever made were made with the scissors. But I did study the way others wrote and tried to adapt my style to what I could see was acceptable. I was paid space rates, which, as I recall, were two dollars a column. This was the most gratefully received pay I ever got. However little it was, it came from doing what I felt myself appointed to do.

We had no typewriter at home then, although I afterward acquired one, and all my columns were written on the old Oliver in the canning-factory office. In winter, when the factory was closed, the office was inhabited only by old Mr. Irwin, my father's bookkeeper. The typewriter stood by a window looking out over a coal yard and the railroad tracks. It would be hard to find a more dismal view. And a canning factory in winter has an air of abandonment that would be difficult to match. The office was warmed by a small potbellied stove; Mr. Irwin worked at his books at a stand-up desk, and I sat by the cobwebby window and composed with two fingers.

Everything about that scene and that job is as sharp in my memory as though it had happened the day before yesterday. Whoever was the editor of the Niagara Falls *Gazette,* he earned an apprentice's gratitude.

Twenty-seven

As I went along, fewer and fewer of my friends and acquaintances continued to be genuine familiars. Now that I was in mid-high school, it was clear that the graduating class would have no more than ten or twelve members of the fifty or more who had started. And most of those would be girls intending to be elementary-school teachers. Only a few looked forward to college; even the girls who wanted to teach would simply shift to training courses for a year or two. Those who dropped out altogether were not likely to become failures or to find their way into really dissatisfied minorities. Most would become good enough citizens, some of them substantial ones. But not many would develop philosophic attitudes beyond those of common-sense orthodoxy. They would be arrested at about where they left school. Partly this was because they would not have been taught any way of going on being educated; only a few ever came under the mildly corrective influence of the Chautauqua circles or other adult educational institutions.

Of course almost all of those who gave up school would almost at once have to accept such heavy obligations that all their efforts could easily go to keeping them up. They would find themselves, as family supporters, as merchants, farmers, or housewives, in a fierce competition too. They would work long hours and always be tired. They would have worries and obligations. They might get ahead, but it would be by acquiring goods or property, usually, and these acquisitions would usually be modest ones. Since there was no social security, a man had to provide for his own family, for his own old age, and for all the risks they or he would undergo until he did become old.

So, in an intellectual sense—and this was especially true of the boys—hardly any of them would go much farther. Chautauqua circles were largely women's organizations; and this was also true of the churches. This arrest meant that most men would become political reactionaries. That is to say, they would oppose civic improvements involving higher taxes, for instance, and would be suspicious of all changes they could not clearly understand and of leaders who seemed at all venturesome. Nationally, they would be withdrawing and suspicious—isolationist and xenophobic.

The few of us who would go on would be differentiated gradually from those who dropped out. Even the most naturally conservative among us would be introduced to the experimental philosophy in science laboratories, would begin to see how broad and deep the tide of evolution really is, and would learn that nothing is finished, because everything is bound to change. I omit here the problem of the reactionary educated intellectual. I shall necessarily come back to that. In my school days those who were stopping were not potentially intellectuals. They would be practical people, not creators.

They would make a practicing democracy difficult, because on the most important issues they would have no knowledge. Still, they would have votes; and these too often were at the disposal of demagogues or those who had something other than the public interest to forward. Of course those of us who did go on would change many things anyway. But it is forgotten in later generations how short a time ago intellectuals of all sorts were regarded with suspicion. The conflict between fundamentalism in religion and advances in science did not reach its real climax in this country until the new century was well begun. Universities dependent on funds provided by state legislatures were constantly on the defensive. Research and experiment were carried on almost clandestinely except when the results promised immediate profits. Pure research was pretty well confined to the private universities—a few of them.

The revolution in these matters, I am tempted to say, was the most significant occurrence of my lifetime. It is well enough understood that nuclear fission could not have been achieved by American scientists. Nearly all of those who made it possible were refugees from western Europe. But this has elements of contradiction too. To find freedom, Szilard, Fermi, and the others had come to the United States, where until lately there had been no welcome for revolutionary researchers. This has to be put down as one of those accidents of history with momentous consequences. The fact is that the atomic bomb did more than smash Hiroshima; it smashed American fundamentalism too. Thereafter respect for intellectuals would perceptibly increase.

Practical science did advance—that is, the search for answers to questions asked by businessmen, farmers, and merchants. But the social sciences were retarded because they were particularly controlled by common-sense concepts as well as by tradition. Government became obsolete in comparison with other social organizations. It became the creature of those who found use for it in their business. Legislators were often ignorant, sometimes irresponsible, and too frequently corrupt.

I must say again that the majorities in our democracy did not want progress to stop. They believed in it, almost fiercely. But their daily activities consisted in getting the better of each other, and when these activities touched government they contaminated it. How could it be expected that an economic and political society of this kind could have come to the crisis of Hiroshima prepared to accept its imperatives of integration and co-operation? Even if the penalty was extinction, acceptance still could not be managed, not right away.

But to a boy heading into an obviously prosperous future, there were no sinister signs. As he grew up he could expect to reach one level of achievement after another. Because this was so, he could enjoy what he did in the present—what he

did, what he learned, and what came to him. I was especially
fortunate. My father was making money; we were a family of
means. I had opportunities. And I had present excitements. I
recall some of them almost as vividly as when they were being
experienced.

The counterpart in Wilson of Obed Edson in Sinclairville
was an old gentleman—old in my time—named Hervey Sanford.
He may have been a lawyer; at least he was a Justice of the
Peace and dignified that office out of all proportion to its
usual significance. He was held in awe by all his juniors—which
included nearly everyone; and he was regarded as scholarly
and learned. He did not produce a local history, which may
have been because he was not really a native. He had come
from Maryland for some reason I never fathomed. In contrast
with Obed Edson, who had been an agnostic, he was a firm
supporter of the Presbyterian church. My attention was first
fixed on him during services soon after our coming to Wilson—
there was no Congregational church and my parents took
to Presbyterian attendance—because of his amazing basso-
profundo performances. At our first visit I happened to be seated
where I could see him, and watched with wonder as his
tangled white beard opened when the first hymn was to be sung
and there emerged the most amazing sound of its sort I had
ever heard. It thundered toward the high ceiling and echoed
among the beams; the windows trembled; and the puny sounds
made by all the other singers sank into and were smothered by
its profundities. A voice so majestic would command respect
for itself alone; but added to that were his patriarchal appearance, his learning, and his positions as Town Clerk, Notary
Public with seal, and Justice of the Peace. This was indeed
authority.

I used to go to his house occasionally when my father had
some business with him—papers to be attested and that sort
of thing. On one of these visits a subject somehow arose which
I went back several times to pursue. It seemed that I had
accidentally encountered what must have been one of the very

few people in our parts who had been an anti-Lincoln Republican in Civil War times. For my age, I had read a good deal of American history, and I have indicated how the boys-in-blue theme had moved me when I was much younger. Aside from the patriotic romances, I had had available only what was to be found in our meager school and village libraries, and all this was strictly Unionist in color. It had certainly never occurred to me that there might once have been differences in the North about the necessity for war or about the policies of Lincoln. Even his campaigns had been made to appear as contests between patriots and traitors in the South. I had acquired no conception of the turmoil and travail of those times, and especially of the bitternesses and divisions which had tormented even the loyal states while the war was going on. To be introduced to them by a respected elder was terribly disquieting in the way disillusionment usually is to idealistic young people.

It seemed that Hervey Sanford had been a newspaperman in Baltimore during the 'sixties and before; and, although he had been a Republican, he had, with many others, thought Seward ought to have been nominated. He had believed, too, that conciliation was possible, that the use of force was unnecessary, and that Lincoln was personally responsible for precipitating the conflict. He showed me some old clipping books filled with the most violent denunciations of Lincoln the candidate, some of them written by himself; and there were later ones attacking Lincoln as President in violent language. There were cartoons picturing the President as an uncouth frontiersman with an ape-like appearance. I read the articles and looked at the pictures with horrified fascination, resisting their argument, yet, I suppose, gradually becoming accommodated to the fact of their existence.

The old man was still savage when he discussed the issues of half a century before, and I got the impression that somehow the position he had taken had something to do with his having been displaced in Baltimore and having moved up our way—where at least he was unknown. When he sat back in his shabby armchair, his canaries singing over his head, and talked, I listened closely. He told me about the conspiracy to abduct and probably to assassinate Lincoln when he was traveling to his inauguration. It was a conspiracy that had centered in Baltimore and had been escaped by what seemed the merest chance. This had sobered the border press somewhat, he said; and those who, like himself, were still unreconciled had felt compelled thereafter to moderate their diatribes. But they had never been reconciled to the Illinois mountebank, and all that happened thereafter seemed to them justification of their attitude. He still resented, even these many years later, the growth of the Lincoln legend—the Father Abraham who had been martyred and was as nearly a saint to Americans as was allowable in their tradition of equality. The influence of the G.A.R., he said, had prevented his side of the story from reaching the public after the war, and all the histories had conformed to the legend. He still felt that the truth would in time make itself known; after all, the materials were too plentiful ever to be gathered up and completely suppressed.

The booming voice of the old man talking earnestly to a young man is something I can still hear, penetrating more than just my ears. It went to work on my whole conceptual structure, dissolving an important segment of my faith, and opening my mind to alternatives. The old desk behind him was surmounted by many crowded pigeonholes, and the sun came into windows well shelved with geraniums and begonias. It must have been somewhat like a girl's loss of her virginity in unlikely circumstances. That was a scene I shall never forget. It was for me a very important experience, a shadow falling on received dogma; but also an imperative for finding out what I must myself believe.

Experiences of this sort every boy must recall as stages in his deliverances from the supervision of his mind by the adults around him—at least every boy who has the makings of a skeptic, who has the impulse to think for himself, who has the capacity to emerge from sentimentality to realism. It usually comes at a time, too, when other important changes are taking place; and the most important of these have to do, undoubtedly, with his maturity as a male animal. But he knows, or he very quickly discovers, that he is not just an animal but a responsible potential mate for some girl.

My own feeling for girls was definite. I liked them. But I liked some more than others, and usually there was one who seemed to embody all the qualities I liked in all the others. It seems to me that I always had a more or less beloved object. She was not the same object from one year to the next, but she was no hazy ideal projection. There is no doubt, I suppose, that seventeen-year-old females are the most beautiful creatures on earth or in heaven. It is no wonder that seventeen-year-old boys find them irresistible. I was lucky. Almost always, the ones I found most attractive were persuaded to return my fondness; and I had an approach to maturity in this regard that was rich and rewarding.

I must admit that I was tortured by some of these associations. Unfulfilled sexual impulses, however well controlled they may be by respect, become difficult for all youths, and I was no exception. I hope that the successive adored ones to whom I paid ardent court regard our experiments together as I do now—as difficult, perhaps, but on the whole happy; beautiful and trying, but, in retrospect, more beautiful than trying. The girls I chose always seemed to know how to channel my ardors into transforming ambitions. At any rate, the tortures are now forgotten and the soaring sentiments are perfectly remembered.

Girls or no girls, friends or no friends, elders or no elders, my Wilson-based days were coming to an end. I should go on for a long time yet—the rest of my high school and all my college years, and even beyond these—coming back to the home place in the Niagara orchard country beside the great lake. All my ties would not be broken until my father died in his eighties and I approached sixty. But there would be a gradual loosening, and I should know less and less of all the detail of village and country life. I should always love the place unreasonably, even when I did not visit it for years at a stretch; and I should always recognize that I was part of it and it was part of me. We had knit together at one stage of our mutual histories, and what we had done to each other could not be undone. Still, now, I was for a wider world.

Buffalo

3

1909–1911

Twenty-eight

I lay awake for a long time one night early in January of 1909. A long campaign had been successful and I was to go away to school. I had chosen a military academy in Virginia for no better reason than that a fellow I knew in the neighboring town of Somerset was a student there. He had once commuted to Wilson, but he liked boarding school better. Also, he said, it was a much safer way to prepare for college. Graduation at Wilson was no guarantee of acceptance anywhere; but the academy made it a sure thing.

Anyway, it was an exciting prospect. So I lay awake as the wind blowing down from Canada whined in the chimneys of the good, plain house I was to leave tomorrow. For how many nights had I lain in this bed next door to my father and mother? It had been several years, at least, without much of any break. Often I had read secretly far into the night after folding a rug across the revealing crack under the door. Here I had suffered and struggled with asthma as it tore at my chest. Here I had thought out the things I wanted to write. Here I had laid out the campaigns incident to all my ambitions. Sometimes I had been troubled by the recollected beauty of a girl I had just come home from dancing with. It was a haven of a bed, in a nice east-looking room, and I was giving it up for a succession of strange ones.

I had no very clear notion of what the academy would be like, and no clearer one of the country where it was situated. I recognized just a slight reluctance to go such a distance southward. The United States was not yet quite united for me. If Virginia had produced numerous heroes, it had also been a battleground in the war my generation had not been allowed to forget. But, I had been told, the academy would have as many Northerners as Southerners; its location was of no significance. What I was not told was that the teachers would be southern, also military, and that this did make a difference.

I was not much traveled except for the journey to Colorado and some excursions on the Great Lakes. I could not imagine what the country below Washington could be like—or Washington either, for that matter. I lay and thought about it all. The bare branches of the maples creaked in the gale, and there was a whisper of snow at the window as I finally turned out the light for what I could expect to be my last night under the patchwork quilt I regarded as my own.

But I was back again in that same bed two weeks later and finding it difficult to explain exactly why. It had simply been apparent almost at once that the academy was not what I wanted. And I had acted. I had gone down to the railroad station, climbed aboard a train, and come on home. The necessity for explaining what must appear to be a silly and indecisive adventure was not pleasant. I had made something of going away. It had been, inferentially, a criticism of the Wilson school; and now I had abruptly returned. I was pursued, too, by messages from a puzzled headmaster; but these I did not worry about. I was more vulnerable to suggestions that I had been merely homesick. That made me seem infantile. But I had an alternative, and playing it up did something to rehabilitate me, at least in my own regard.

It will perhaps mean something if I say that I did not need—or, anyway, did not want—a corrective institution whose discipline was best suited to spoiled children whose parents were tired of them. I did not know what I was looking for, but it was not what the academy had to offer. If someone had given me the advice I should have had, I know now that I would have gone to some eastern school where boys are supposed to have latent intelligence as well as animal instincts. But as it was, I merely insisted that I had not liked it and that I would not go back. The whole combination of military school, of the South, of clownish student customs, of tobacco-chewing instructors, of winter bleakness in an ugly and unfamiliar town—the whole thing had just been too much. I turned aside painful explanations by putting forward the alternative I had conceived during my homeward flight. I would go to a Buffalo high school. I argued that I could board in the city and come home for weekends. That won my mother. My father, as usual, accepted my own choice. And I was allowed—after all, I insisted, I was almost eighteen—to make my own arrangements. I chose Masten Park for no particular reason except that it was an old and well-known school; and I went alone for an interview with the principal. Having been allowed to enroll, I found a respectable boardinghouse within walking distance—on Linwood Avenue—and at the beginning of the second term started in.

The principal was a distinguished man, noted as an educator then, more noted afterward as the father of two remarkable sons. He was Frank W. Fosdick.[1] There were more than a thousand students at Masten Park. This in itself was not unusual. Everyone who comes up through the public school system has to learn how to get along in crowds, which, in itself, is not so bad; crowds make a cheerful society when they have the common interests of teen-age students. But there is a drawback. The temptation is to skimp some relationships young people ought to develop—counselors in various crises, for instance. High schools in this respect are minor colleges, but without

[1] Principal from 1897 to 1926. He came, like myself, of a Chautauqua family, having been born in Westfield, on Lake Erie. I have already spoken of another member of the family, who wrote boys' books under the name of Harry Castlemon. The Fosdick sons who were to be so well known were, of course, Harry, the minister, and Raymond, the president for so long of the Rockefeller Foundation and, before that, during World War I, an Assistant Secretary in the Wilson Administration.

the dormitories and other arrangements for living which extend education beyond the classroom. At Masten Park there were no recreation facilities, no clubrooms, not even a cafeteria. It was, in fact, not much better equipped than the high school at Wilson, except for its greater variety of subjects and its well-prepared teachers.

There were indeed some notable instructors. If they had had easier schedules and consequent leisure for the cultivation of their subjects, they would have become scholars as useful as those I afterward met in universities. As it was, their energies had to be devoted to imparting such elementary knowledge as would meet the Regents requirements. Still, a few students, those who showed promise, were always given special attention.[2] The one who established between herself and me the traditional relationship of student and mentor was Marion Gemmel. I owed her the same debt I hope some students afterward owed me. Such debts are never paid. But at least I often thought of her at times when my own students seemed unreasonably demanding. When I did I was ashamed of flagging.

It was through Marion Gemmel[3] that I first began to understand some of the norms of life, to work backward and forward along the lines of evolution, to appreciate the mutual adjustments among living plants and animals and their environment. But these were a kind of dividend. Her first concern with her students was that they should see how marvelously animals and plants were made. From this they could understand why it had happened. And she was especially meticulous in demanding that they should discover how. She used to repeat over and

[2] When I think of the years during which classes came and went, all day, day after day, to be given such instruction as the texts provided and the teacher could add, I am appalled by the sheer numbers involved and the weight of routine my teachers carried. Frank H. Coffran in Latin and Greek, C. B. Hersey and George W. Turner in physics and chemistry, Alonzo J. Stagg in civics, Harriet Bull and Mrs. Ryerson in English, and Marion Gemmel in biology are the ones I recall best. Each of them had at least five class periods a day, each class having at least thirty students.

[3] A graduate of Smith in the class of 1897. She retired from teaching at Masten Park in 1927 and died in Buffalo a few years later.

over again that it was the how we must know. If we knew about that, everything else would come more easily.

The lesson in this was, of course, that observation of behavior was not enough. It was all very well to watch how living things behaved, to count and classify, and to build up statistics. But unless the mechanisms were analyzed, it was impossible to be certain that the data did not conceal more than they revealed. For a student who seemed to grasp the principles she hoped would be discovered by analysis, she would take pains and find time. She did for me. I had my own microscope and table in a corner. I often worked there when I should have been doing something else.

Since I was by habit a reader, it was not long until I discovered the classics of biological literature. Life was never quite the same after I read *The Voyage of the Beagle;* and I seriously considered whether I ought not to become a biologist. It is very likely that I would have, too, if I had not soon realized that more mathematics than I should ever be able to acquire would be necessary for work in the genetics of which I had a glimpse. So it was a transitory ambition. But my reading was useful enough later, when I came to the study of sociology at Pennsylvania. Plants, animals, men—how and why they behaved as they did—the methods of research were the same; and anyone who knew how complicated a small mouse was would not be much more impressed with the make-up of a man.

Except in biology, I was an indifferent student that first year. I passed exams, but not with much margin. And of course this was mostly because I did not do much work. I had no other experiences such as that with Miss Gemmel. Not even my English teachers discovered how much I would have liked to improve my writing. They were intent on an introduction to literature. We were supposed to have acquired a sampling acquaintance with a specified list of accepted classics. These disembodied pieces were attached to names with certain biographical data. But they were not very firmly attached, and we had no hint of the passion or labor that had gone into their creation. As for other subjects, the only one I found any genuine interest in was a course in elementary economics, which would lead to others with Jay Stagg. In these and in biology I was an interested student, at least; in English, in languages, in physics and chemistry, I could not have been distinguished from any of the others who got the lowest passing grades.

I do not blame myself too much for the way my time was spent. I cannot even regret that most of my energies went into activities other than intellectual ones—developing friends, learning about city life, doing something in sports, exploring further the enchantments offered by girls—all this sort of casual thing. If there came out of this, as I think, the conviction I seem to have had from about this time, that human beings were essentially unsuited to the kind of organization they were surrounding themselves with, it was worth while. The competition of economic and social life, carried on by individuals who were capricious and driven by hidden impulses, really made Buffalo life a disorganized but fascinating entertainment. But whatever generalizations I was coming to, they were slow in formulating themselves. I was mostly just having a good time. What I learned was not something I sought. It was a by-product of wasted time.

There was a residue of understanding, as I would later realize. It was precipitated out of careless and gay days and nights, and it left a more considerable impression than I would have thought possible at the time. I made many friends, some incredibly irresponsible, some staid and sober, many affectionate. I was with them from morning until late at night, not only in school, but in the streets, in beerhalls and saloons, in theaters, in amusement parks, in sports fields, and in their houses.

I already knew something of business and so understood what was going on around me. Buffalo, at the end of the century's first decade, was a small giant of a city, for the most part as ugly as the sin it sheltered. It flowered in the vast châteaux of Delaware Avenue and Chapin Parkway out of roots in east-side slums. The shops and stores of downtown—Main Street,

Court Street, and Lafayette Square—were nothing remarkable but still able to furnish all the appurtenances of civilization. The city illustrated the best and worst of industrial America. It was pushing, inventive, and vigorous; but it was also disordered, corrupt, and hideous. Like Cleveland, Detroit, and Chicago, farther west on the Lakes, it was run by its businessmen; and its businessmen had no ambitions other than making money and retreating to their palaces with it.

Cereals from the northern plains and iron ore from the Superior ranges came plowing down the Lakes in the huge bulk carriers—hogbacks—and the Buffalo mills turned the grain into flour and feedstuffs and the ore into pig iron. In its harbor, heavy midwestern cargoes were transshipped to the Erie Canal or the East-going railroads; and in the hundreds of grimy, greasy slips of South Buffalo, canalboats were emptied into ships for passage West. The frontier industries slaughtered cattle and hogs, made soap and breakfast foods (Shredded Wheat, Quaker Oats, Force), ran mail-order businesses (Larkin), manufactured machinery and automobiles (Thomas, Pierce-Arrow), turned out paper, wallboard, cement, and lumber products. It reduced metals, fabricated steel and wire, and produced chemicals by the trainload.

All down the Niagara to the Falls, through Black Rock, the Tonawandas, La Salle, and on into the Falls city itself, the mills and factories smoked, steamed, and fumed through the days and flamed through the nights. The heavy clouds from their chimneys lay on the windward countryside like a blight. And it was there that the workers' company towns were built —endless rows of frame structures, half hidden in fumes, without gardens, without decent sanitation—a browish swarming desert. But the industrial complex did turn out goods by the millions of tons, and they were shoveled or shoved into ships or freight trains and sent plowing or rolling away.

Around the Buffalo lake front and down toward Black Rock and the Tonawandas, the docks, piers, slips, and basins served vast warehouses, grain elevators, storage yards, and ore dumps.

Even in summer, when at least the lake in the background was clear and blue, the whole waterfront had the look of having been shaken out of a gigantic bag and left to smolder and rot in a swamp. In winter it was an arctic hell, half hidden in mist and smoke, the low clouds coming in on it from the west, everything crusted with dirty snow, dripping icicles, and sleet. Wandering through its mud flats, turning basins, and unloading slips was Buffalo Creek, most degraded of waterways, seeming to come from nowhere and ending in an obscene dispersal among rotting barges and rusting ships.

In those days this was the domain of W. J. Conners, universally known as Fingy, who was lord of the waterfront. The warehouses, mills, docks, and ships required a special breed of men, capable of enormous labors, indifferent to hardships, used to filth, and without thought for the future. Many of them were homeless; most of them illiterate, simple, savage, working hulks. It was to meet their requirements that the waterfront empire was maintained. The saloons, brothels, cheap eating places, pawnshops, flophouses—all the familiar businesses of such districts—functioned at the pleasure of the boss. Not too late in life he was a rich man; by then, too, he was a legend. More respectable citizens spoke of him in a shocked but half-humorous way, but they never gave him any real trouble. The empire lasted out his active years.

The waterfront blight crept up the streets into the city. Lower Main Street was becoming disreputable. This had been Grover Cleveland's favorite neighborhood, where for half a lifetime he had lived in furnished rooms and spent his leisure in saloons that now had degenerated into frowzy hangouts. What he had liked about them was the familiar company met in the elegance of mirrors, oil paintings, mahogany bars, and big armchairs around a card table where schooners of beer sat always at an elbow. In the noisy ease of saloons with sawdust on the floor Cleveland could really relax. They were elegant no longer. The mahogany was scarred, the chairs were rickety, and the company depressed. There were no more Clevelands.

A little farther east, Oak Street and its neighbors, as far north as Genesee, were given over to a red-light district where many of the establishments were generations old and maintained a kind of culture of their own. Their relationship with authority was an easy one. Corruption was an institution that no one expected to see disturbed. And Fingy Conners, piling up wealth, bought the Buffalo *Courier* and, when I was in high school, was building himself a green-tiled mansion at 1140 Delaware Avenue, spang in the middle of all the industrial aristocrats. He seemed not to know or not to care, having had the ambition so long, that the aristocrats were by then escaping into better-insulated suburban estates. They had limousines instead of coaches. They could travel farther from their homes to their Board rooms. And they could, they suddenly discovered, become country gentlemen. Delaware Avenue, at least its lower half, was already declining into a region of lesser uses—boardinghouses, professional offices, funeral parlors, shops, and clubs. The old mansions like that where Fillmore had lived, where McKinley had died in 1901, of which the merchants and factory owners had been so proud, were falling into strange ownerships and uses.[4]

When I knew it best Buffalo was certainly a city bursting with life and lusty growth, and its ugliness seemed no more than a natural accompaniment of this vigor. For the pushing and hauling was done by and for newly come immigrants from Ireland and Italy first, then from eastern Europe and the Near East. It was off the farms or out of the ghettos, translated without preparation to a completely strange environment. Many of its members did not even speak English, and they were well satis-

[4] The Conners family went on to become important in Buffalo's more exclusive commercial circles. A.W.J., Jr., was born in 1895 and went to Nichols preparatory school and Yale. He inherited the *Courier* and the *Enquirer* as well as other enterprises of his colorful father. He merged the Democratic *Courier* with the Republican *Express,* became vice-president of the Great Lakes Transit Corporation, a director of the Marine Trust, Sterling Engine, Maxson-Cadillac, and numerous other companies. He also became a member of the Saturn, The Buffalo, and the country clubs. W.J., III, served in World War II. Conners is a respected name in modern Buffalo.

fied if they found jobs and earned a bare living. Their humility
and disorganization would not last; but while it did, it was a
situation made to order for political bosses and businessmen.
These, like Fingy Conners, were Irish now, or German. The
old families had retreated to the banks and insurance companies. The Scatcherds, the Rumseys, the Hamlins, and the
Carys were no longer safely in control. The Germans owned the
breweries, the distilleries, the bakeries, the stores and saloons;
and soon they would be moving into the offices of company
directors and financial enterprises.

St. Joseph's, a German-Polish Catholic cathedral, was being
built—it was actually begun in 1910—in the old center of Protestant fashion, close to the new house Fingy was building. And
next door the Seymour H. Knox mansion was to be the home
of the presiding Bishop. Trinity Episcopal Church, once regarded
as the appointed home of cultured religion, was left stranded
downtown, its heavy Gothic rapidly being demeaned by surrounding taxpayers shops and boardinghouses, its parishioners separated from it in distance more and more every year. Even the
Germans were being visibly pushed by the Poles. The whole east
side seemed to have been taken over by them. Buffalo was said
to be the biggest Polish city in the world outside Poland, something the Germans, now in their third or fourth generation,
spoke of with evident disgust. For the Poles were regarded as a
raw and filthy people by the orderly Germans. And even the
more easygoing Irish felt the competition and deplored the
peasant manners of the newcomers.

All this was new to a village boy come to live in a Linwood
Avenue boardinghouse—one of those where some prosperous
family must recently have lived—new and fascinating. This was
a time when, for me, learning was much less a matter of school
and books and teachers than of companions, *Gemütlich,* and becoming a man of the world.

Twenty-nine

It would be wrong to suggest that my activities were monopolized by Masten Park; and, although their intentions, so far as they had definite ones, were different from mine, this was equally true of my fellow students. Later high schools would offer many social, athletic, and intellectual diversions not closely tied to classroom work. It was not so then. There was some of this, but not much, and what there was had little official support.

At first I went back and forth to Wilson by the train leaving from the Terrace station. On Monday mornings I traveled to the city by the early milk train; on Friday afternoon I returned countryward. We possessed an automobile now, but since there was no hard-surfaced road reaching Wilson, in the months when there was snow and mud we made little attempt to use the highway. Gradually we would work up to it, but before 1912, if a journey really had an objective, it was foolish to try to get there by car.

Travel on the milk train twice a week established a commuting rhythm, something of the sort that was submitted to by growing millions of city workers, except that mine was only a weekly, not a daily, journey. The trains I got to know so well were soon to be abandoned; the route was too roundabout. Mail and milk would be carried by motor trucks, and passengers by automobiles or buses. Buffalo was, after all, directly south of Wilson and much nearer by road than by rail. The railway, in fact, went first to Niagara Falls and then down the lake shore, following two lengthy sides of a triangle. Because of this, and because the train stopped at every crossroad, the trip took an hour and a half. Later we used to drive it in half the time.

The trains I got to know were obsolete even then. They had obviously been relegated to our branch road after long service on the main line. The cars had the familiar red plush seats of the 'seventies and 'eighties; they were lighted by gas; some had stoves in a corner; and their wheels turned with some reluctance on their axles. There was noise, dirt, smoke, cinders, escaping steam, and either frying heat or frigid cold. But the crew was as familiar as any other long-settled organization. Their lives were spent operating this train over the roundabout route from Rochester to Niagara Falls and on to Buffalo—then back again the same day.

The Buffalo Terrace station was really no more than a covered platform to which trains crawled from the central station through a tunnel under Main Street and from which they departed down along the back environs of the waterfront toward Black Rock on their way downriver to the Falls. Standing there waiting for the train in snow or slush, muffled against the killing wind from the lake, I was just between Italian slums and a decaying business district. I had plenty of opportunity, week after week, to learn such lessons as civic dishevelment could teach. What I was seeing should have been the fairest outlook in Buffalo. Actually, it was leprous. Not a single aspect of it relieved the offensiveness. This did not bother me at the time. I accepted this, as I accepted other aspects of the city, as connected somehow with a city's existence. Anyway, I was a transient here. It was not my responsibility.

I stood in the wind of winter or spring, after a short but miserable walk from the Main Street trolley, quite without feeling about my surroundings. But how could that have been? I recall this and other Buffalo scenes with the clarity of fine photography. They must have made impressions, even if I had no use for them as yet. I have more recollection of feeling about people. I was, for instance, learning about foreigners—anyone, that is, who was different from myself. There were in Buffalo more of these strangers than of my own people. Some of their customs were outlandish; some were strange but attractive. Anyway, here they were, and here was I moving among them.

I was accepting some of the responsibilities of being an adult before I really was one. I had money in my pockets, and if I chose to pursue a folly there was no one to say that I must not. There was not even anyone, in the anonymity of the city, to exercise the restraint of neighborly opinion. If I had chosen to experiment with some of the vices all around me, I could have done it without risk of meeting anyone I knew. No one could say back home that Charlie Tugwell's boy had been up to so-and-so. I certainly had not yet been taught that liberties are kept by using them moderately.

I will say this: I was learning that human beings have an engaging irresponsibility. This might be exasperating, but it was also the occasion for humor, and it gave them most of their interest. But I was learning some other less pleasant things about people. Because I got around the city a good deal and poked into its less respectable corners, I saw a lot of obsessed and driven individuals. Their resort to depravity and drunkenness sometimes seemed not to touch their inner selves, even if it gave them moments of forgetfulness. I was not the first to discover that even the worst people are not all bad, but it was a discovery I made for myself. No one told me.

Contact with the unfamiliar life of the city was not really intimate. I did not join it anywhere; I stood beside it, looking on. I did feel it was important to know what went on. But my instinct was not to let it touch me. If it did, I would lose my eye as an observer. If I was caught up in it, I would no longer be a student, an interpreter, trying to abstract its meaning. A trade had taken me as its devotee. It required that I should see all and know all. But it also required that I should not be all. So I could stand interested for an hour at half a dozen bars I knew, nursing the glass of beer that Buffalo bartenders would not think of refusing a well-grown youth, and smelling, looking, feeling the good fellowship there where some loud fellows were playing dominoes, stopping to devour portions of hassenfeffer and starting to play again. Didn't they have any jobs or businesses? But standing there by the bar, glowering into a glass, or at a table all alone, there would always be a man in torture, perhaps in terror, perhaps in a rage. The tortured ones drank whisky; the lighthearted ones drank beer. It was a sort of rule.

But the city was more than saloons. It had other attractions. There was, for instance, Shea's vaudeville theater. I managed a weekly matinee there nearly all the time I was in Buffalo. I liked the leisurely crowds going in to the entertainment and emerging into the cheerful twilight of Court Street. They would go home now to their dinners, and what they had seen and heard would be told over to others. So I liked my boardinghouse with its long table, its variety of people, friendly and glad to be together, singing around the piano in the evening, making foursomes to play card games, or retreating to do some reading. So I liked walking in Main, Pearl, and Court streets and in Lafayette Square, where the windows were full of merchandise and the passers-by were making up their minds what of it they could afford to buy. I was discovering that even a fellow who felt at home in the country and could look knowledgeably at every field he passed could also find warmth in the city and could understand why many people together were happy in a way that people never could be alone.

I asked myself sometimes—or rather something asked me, because it was never articulate or well focused—how to account for the orderliness of the world around me, such orderliness as it had. Those whose faces I looked into could not be the ones who had made a pattern of streets, arranged for municipal utilities, and caused government to be organized. How could people so obviously intent on individual objectives, so interested just in each other, so satisfied with an hour's pleasure, have created anything so organic as the city of Buffalo? It had officials; its police kept the peace; its hospitals took care of the sick; it had schools, libraries, parks. But when I looked at the men in the saloons, the ones slapping each other hilariously on the back, the others glowering into their glasses, I could not imagine them having contributed to the municipal arrangements. And the people on the streets, going in and out of stores, coming away from their offices at night and hurrying home—they seemed no more capable of the sustained effort that must have been made. There was leadership somewhere; there was forethought and creative planning. But I wondered that it had been encouraged and supported. I suspected that it had always made headway against opposition, in spite of inertia, and probably without approval.

I carried over from my biology one strongly felt analogy. There must be specialized connective and managerial tissue in the municipal organ. This was, for me, an important thought, one I came back to often in later years. That capricious and self-centered individuals are capable of producing something which would function with regularity in the general interest must be because there were those who specialized in planning, articulation, conjuncture, administration. These would be individuals too. But they would be different, much as the apparently similar cells of a body are different and, as they mature, develop into specialized members. I did not see how all this came about, but I knew it must be so. This was the *why* of my biology lesson. The *how* I had still to discover, but I knew that I wanted to discover it.

I even went farther—somewhat farther. I wondered whether I ought to have some part in arranging matters, whether I was one of the managing cells. This conflicted with my spectator-analyst role. But I had begun to have a strong motivation. I resented the cruelties of disorder. I could see dreadful things happening to people. Slums were not necessary; neither was the poverty of which they were the sign. I suspected that our organizing abilities had been concentrated too exclusively on producing goods and making money. And we had allowed cruelties to creep in and had become so familiar that we thought of them as somehow related to our productivity.

Industry and commerce were organized as autocracies. The aim of their owners and managers was the making of profits. In pursuing this aim they arranged people, materials, and even institutions so that they would contribute. They were single-minded about it. They even worked up the fiction that it was the duty of people and their society to contribute. But they acknowledged no debts or duties in return. Their existence in the community was all the pay they were required to give for the privileges they claimed.

But the fact was that they worked in luxurious offices, lived in elaborate homes, and generally enjoyed the amenities of civilization and managed to shut out of these enjoyments all those who worked for them. These last lived hard, took risks, saw their families suffer, and existed in slums. This had gone on for a long time, long enough to separate employer from employee and to set up a tradition of hostility. There was warping and frustration everywhere, and chronic rebellion was an accepted norm of industrial society. That was why men sat in saloons and tried to forget, why they glowered into their whisky glasses, why once in a while they broke into violent behavior.

I began to ask, as I am sure most young people with some sense of responsibility did, whether those who maintained this order of things ought not to be dispossessed. Would it be possible to replace them with others of equal ability who would have as their purpose to create goods cheaply and plentifully rather than just profitably? Thus all would be working harmoniously for ends that seemed intended by nature. The chief end of man could not be profits; it must be the dignification of man himself, the fulfilling of his dreams and the use of his capacities.

At that age I had the impulse to do whatever seemed possible to achieve a change. But as a schoolboy I had no opportunities, not even anyone to discuss such matters with. I was bothered. I could have become a radical. That was as fearsome a word then as later. And perhaps I would not have been willing, when it came right down to it, to turn against those who, from my father to all our family friends, were on the conservative side.

Anyway, the moments when I felt this way passed. I gradually acquired a circle of close and busy friends in the city. There was plenty to do besides think about the world's ills or about improving the lot of those who had been unlucky. And anyway, I often told myself, I was a writer, not a reformer.

The conceits young men have of themselves are important in ways we forget when youth has been left behind and more mature models of accomplishment have appeared. Many a young fellow has been sustained through the trials of growing up by picturing himself at the end, in full-blown success, arguing passionately in a courtroom, presiding brilliantly in an operating theater, making moving speeches in a legislature, touching people's emotions with a work of art, or simply sacrificing himself—with appropriate acclaim—for some cause. Many an artist, scientist, or statesman would have to admit to having had such a sustaining vision.

What such conceits owe to accidental contacts or to the influence of admired elders is certainly considerable, but I believe there is some shrewd selection among competing possibilities, so that usually an ambition emerges which is fairly suited to the individual's capabilities. This may be only latent, only felt somewhere below the level of consciousness. It seems to guide many of us, but it is an uncertain guide.

Young people are apt to be confused about this. They estimate too highly their ability to do things that have some appeal for them. But the attractiveness may be deceptive; may, in fact, arise from some romantic conception quite unrelated to any talent they may have. Many of them waste years and effort on some ambition which was always unattainable. And a more suitable aim for them may be discovered late, or even never discovered at all. In these mistakes there is tragedy. Wise guidance would be tender of precious dreams but would change ambitions so that the heart might be stirred by ends a boy or girl might succeed in reaching.

Such guidance is more important in a technical and specialized environment than in a simple one. The chance of disappointment is greater by the distance into areas of knowledge the young person must penetrate.

Those of us who were making the journey toward maturity during the century's teens had to meet all the disadvantages of increasing complexity, and we had no help or guidance of any organized or professional kind. A high school boy, a bundle of undeveloped talents, half-assimilated knowledge, and unfocused ambitions, was supposed to find his own way into the demanding civilization closing in around him. He was expected to do his own shopping among the courses offered in his schooling and to avoid those leading in the wrong direction. He had much advice. But it came from those who either did not know him very well—his teachers—or those who had plans for him— his parents. But no one really assessed his abilities and pointed out his opportunities.

I know that my friends and I not only had to make our own selections in school (within the limits of college entrance requirements), but we also had to make our way toward what we wanted through the mazes of city life. And the city was a serious risk. It offered amusements to waste our time and even depravities to harm us. But also it offered premature opportunities, and many of my friends were diverted to jobs when they should have gone on in school. Many of them had more advice than I, but I doubt whether it was any more useful.

Why was it that adults were so indifferent to the need for better guidance? Why was I—to be specific—wandering through an indifferent school and through the streets of an even more indifferent city, trying at odd moments to focus a comprehensible future and direct myself toward it? And meanwhile why was I spending my time in pleasant but mostly futile adventures and activities? It seems to me now a miracle that anything at all came of it.

An educational system directed to social ends, finding out and developing individual talents, setting young people on the way to making a contribution while they also express their own minds—this was something still known only to the philosophers. It was certainly not something consented to by actual educational authorities.

Thirty

Masten Park was a serious school. That is to say, its teachers and administrators meant to educate us. They were devoted and capable too. But some of them had carried their burdens too long and had become not indifferent but despairingly weary; and others, not so exhausted and still resilient, still had to struggle with a confusion that ought never to have confronted them. The nineteenth-century academies had been select. And they had had definite aims. They had at first been meant to educate intending clergymen; then their scope had widened to include preparation for other professions; but it had never been meant that they should meet the need of democracy for mass education. That was an aim which had grown gradually into the American tradition as the electorate had widened and as demands on its individuals had intensified. A man on his homestead or in his village who could read, write, and cipher was well enough prepared for the life he must lead and for the decisions he must help to make. It was no longer so. And the high schools were struggling to meet the new demands. The little red schoolhouse had had its day.

Democracy was already suffering from the ignorance of democrats. And up to a certain point this ignorance was being relieved in schools whose expectation was to prepare children for the competition they were entering. But teachers in most classes knew that they had before them no more than two or three out of thirty or forty who were going on to college. And many were merely marking time until they could go to work.

These last would have been better off in a vocational school, and those of us who were going on would have profited by more intensive preparation. There was some separation. The colleges specified that matriculates should meet certain requirements. So some classes were made up mostly of those who were preparing. In later years this separation would be more marked, but it was only beginning when I was in school. And teachers had to favor one or the other group.

The colleges still wanted those who entered to have had a beginning in Latin and Greek, or perhaps one of these and a modern language. So I began both Latin and Greek as well as German. My German teachers had to deal with many students whose families spoke the language at home. This was hard on the rest of us, and I never felt any sense of accomplishment. I passed examinations, but my reading competence was slight, and I never learned to speak more than a few elementary sentences. It is possible that this may have been congenital. I would have some use for other languages in later life and, struggle as I would, I should never master any of them.

It did not seem possible that I could be stupid in both mathematics and languages, but the fact is that I was. My experience in mathematics was even worse than in German. What I should have done, I can see now, was to go back and solidify my elementary knowledge. No one suggested this, however, and I resorted to memorizing to pass my examinations, a process so disagreeable that I failed to pass one of them, a humiliation I had never before experienced. This taught me a lesson that was unfortunate. This was that I had better not get involved in things I could not clearly see my way through. I afterward avoided mathematics on this principle and, after repeating the course I failed in, never went beyond the minimum requirements either in high school or college.

I ought to have been corrected about this. I still blame one of my mathematics teachers for my going wrong. He fancied himself as a humorist. It was said that he was a gifted mathematician, and he may have been. But he either valued his gift as a funny man above his duty as a teacher or he resented his immolation among ignoramuses. At any rate, he had a line of sarcastic comment on his slower students' mistakes which was trotted out daily for the edification of the brighter ones. The effect on me, at least, was to make me sullen. I figured to come as close to doing nothing as was compatible with getting by. But I cut it too fine and failed.

It was his report of my apparent mental weakness which brought me a still greater humiliation, one I still recall as one of the most devastating experiences I ever had to survive. Dr. Fosdick one day called me in to his office, put his fingers together in a gesture known to all of us, and told me he had written to my father that I wasting my time and his money. I ought to be taken out of school and put to work. This conclusion, he said, had been arrived at from consulting my mathematics and language teachers. And since these were subjects necessary to college entrance, I could hardly expect to get into any respectable place such as I had in mind. I seemed to have done well in English and in some other courses, but not well enough to compensate for my deficiencies.

I made no defense whatever. I was trying to master a constriction in my throat. He said a little more leniently that I might finish out the year if I wanted to, but it really didn't look as though I could improve enough to be allowed to go on. Naturally, this letter amazed my father, but I think he put it down to my having had too good a time in the city. And all he said was that I had better settle down and work harder. This I did. And there was enough improvement so that in a subsequent interview the principal thought I might after all get into college. But he was not enthusiastic. He noted again that I seemed to do well in certain courses, and he did take time to ask me what made the difference. All I could say was that I found some things hard to do and some others easy. Well, he said, there *were* requirements and, like everyone else, I would have to meet them. I escaped. And I never had another talk with him.

I had a pleasanter experience with my Latin and Greek teacher, even though I was no ornament to his class. I talked matters over with him to some profit. He knew I would never go far in the classics as languages, but he respected my interest in literature and made me grateful for extending that interest backward into the centuries when Latin and Greek had been used by writers who would have been surprised to hear of later generations struggling with their histories, their poems, and their plays just as languages. Frank Coffran was an elderly, fat little man with clayey jowls and eyes that watered uncontrollably. His ugly body held a genuine, if incongruous, love of ancient culture. He lacked the time to impart it to large classes who were facing Regents examinations in translation. Yet at odd moments, sometimes even after classes were over for the day and he must have been longing to get away, he talked to a few of us in ways that opened windows on an antiquity we had not guessed at. I was persuaded by him to add a course in ancient history, and this went some way toward establishing in my mind the picture of a rational, gracious civilization on the shores of that dark and wine-red sea which was so far from Buffalo in time and space as hardly to seem credible at all. Little Mr. Coffran had in his mind's eye an oversimple conception of Greek life, one that the dull texts of the ancient-history course did only a little to support. But I preferred to go on thinking with him that there had been once a miraculous flowering of art and reason in an ordered society. I had sense enough, however, not to think of this projected picture as having anything to do with prosaic reality.

What we were introduced to in our literature courses was not a philosophy and not even a systematized account of out-bursts of creativeness. But the classics, thanks to Coffran, were different. The literature might not be real, in the sense of con-necting up with present experience, but it had been whole and intelligible. Then too, it extended an interest I had had since I was a small boy reading mythologies. That the apparent se-renity of Greek life had been as hard come by as any civilization we later mortals might achieve, I did not then guess. In the interpretations I had of it, it seemed to have evolved naturally and to have been destroyed because its virtues were a challenge to barbarians.

This last I could understand. I recall wondering even then whether there was not some continuing compulsion which resulted in the destruction of order and reason wherever they were temporarily in use. The chief danger of democracy was that its majorities would be not only ignorant but envious, and that they would carry on a relentless war against their intellectuals. This would have the effect of stifling progress at its source and of placing power where its dangers would be maximized.

These generalizations when I was young were not much more than a nagging uneasiness. And they were not normal for me. I was an optimist. Why not? I could foresee a future for myself which was interesting and prosperous. I was well aware of the progress being made by the nation. And I was convinced that evolution was a process of improvement. Tennyson had spoken for me when he had said (in *Locksley Hall*) he "doubted not that through the ages one increasing purpose runs . . ." This seemed to me an expression of the conclusion to which any reasoning and informed person must come; it was not merely a poet's euphoria. As time went on I should become less optimistic and more impressed with the difficulties. In fact, Tennyson would before long begin to seem glib and superficial. If evolutionary progress was not to be blocked by the very people who would benefit from it, they would have to bring their social arrangements into the sort of order evolutionary forces could work through.

Thirty-one

American literature of the period before World War I is most often said to be either realistic or romantic; and this is a useful enough classification, although it does a disservice to some important writers who are not so easily labeled. By now I was aware of this distinction, and I was beginning to have a preference for the realistic, not too discriminating a one, I am sure, but still definite. I did not ask that what I read should be declared in advance to be suitable. But I did say to myself that some of what I had read was workmanlike and honest and that some was not.

Still, it has to be admitted that some flagrantly sentimental productions had by then become as familiar as my home or my friends. The rural versifiers who were mawkish sometimes and often recognizably phony had created, nevertheless, in their genuinely inspired moments, lines that were recognizable reflections of experience. Even balladry that seemed ephemeral was capable of evoking a genuine, sometimes an anguished, response. Few Americans born in the 'nineties were impervious to *Old Fashioned Roses*. And *Farm Ballads*, published in the 'seventies, had brought "Over the Hills to the Poorhouse" and "Gone with a Handsomer Man" into forty thousand homes in its first two years (so a reference book tells me), and no one knows how many in succeeding decades. Such books lay on innumerable parlor tables besides ours, and their verses were quoted on countless occasions. They were part of our inheritance, just as the Bible was. That all of us were familiar with them enabled us to communicate in a common vernacular.

A dozen or so of the more familiar lyrics were recited over and over at church or school affairs. They were expected and were always received with appreciation. My mother continued to read them to me whenever there was occasion—when I was sick, for instance. And I always expected that tears would be started by the lines of "Little Boy Blue." I knew that they called up the memory of her losses. And this must have been true of mothers all over the land.

I was not then, and am not now, so hardened as to contend that Carleton, Riley, Field, and the others did not have a gift for reaching people's hearts. To critics, their verses may have seemed meretricious, and many of them were; but in many of them, also, there was genuine solace. And that was more than the higher-browed, more meticulous poetry of those years achieved. Verses could be polished and elaborate and still lack the power to communicate emotion. There were some cheap magazines whose contents had more reach than most of the literary efforts to be found in *The Atlantic*.[1]

The same thing would have to be said about prose writers. My graduation from books written for boys had been early, not because I matured quickly, but because I ran out of reading matter and had to extend my range into adult fields. I had been able to collect on my own shelves not only the English stories with wide circulation—or many of them, such as Scott, Dickens, and Thackeray—but also I had sets, given to me on birthdays or at Christmas, of Aldrich, Stockton, Mark Twain, Cooper,

---

[1] Among the respectable but less moving books were Richard Watson Gilder's *The New Day* (1875), Sidney Lanier's *Poems* (1877), George Edward Woodberry's *North Shore Watch* (1883), Clinton Scollard's *With Reed and Lyre* (1886), Madison Cawein's *Blooms of the Berry* (1887), and Richard Hovey's *The Laurel* (1889). These were the models of polite verse for my following generation—along with the English and New England poets preceding them. If there is little to be said for any of these now, there is hardly more to be said for the Westerners—Joaquin Miller, for instance, whose *Songs of the Sierras* made a twin with Bret Harte's *Plain Language from Truthful James* to bring California into our poetic literature.

Hawthorne, and Irving. And besides, I had odd volumes of
Gertrude Atherton,[2] Frank Norris, Harold Frederick,[3] Paul
Leicester Ford,[4] Charles King, Lew Wallace, Francis Hopkin-
son Smith, Winston Churchill, Owen Wister, John Fox, Jr.,
Meredith Nicholson,[5] David Graham Phillips, Robert Herrick,
Booth Tarkington, and many others.[6]

A look at this list shows how little discrimination I had, although owning a book, or even being entertained by it, does
not imply real admiration for its author. I was faintly ashamed
to be so amused as I was by *D'ri and I,* and I knew well enough
that *Ben Hur* was trash. But I really liked the foreign flavor
of *Marietta, A Maid of Venice* and *Cecilia, a Story of Modern
Rome,* although their superficiality was obvious. My respect and
admiration, however, went to the honest workmanship of
Howells, Sarah Orne Jewett, and Garland. Curiously enough, I

[2] Whose *The Conqueror* made such an impression on me that when I visited
the island of Nevis for the first time half a century later the first thing I
noticed was a woman's-tongue tree such as had made such a clatter in the
rising hurricane described in the novel. Satisfied about this, I went on to
explore, without much satisfaction, the other scenes on that island and on
St. Croix, associated with Hamilton. My interest may even have showed in an
academic essay I had occasion to write in the 'thirties and which was repub-
lished in *Early American Policy; Six Columbia Contributors* in 1960.
[3] Whose *Damnation of Theron Ware* I read several times.
[4] Whose *Janice Meredith* and *Honorable Peter Stirling* I have already mentioned. Peter Stirling went a long way with me through life, perhaps farther
than I even yet realize. Such examples of the particular virtues an individual
most admires are apt to reach an inner source of inspiration and to go on
being an influence.
[5] The notice of whose death in Indianapolis, a survivor from the past, I read
of just as I was preparing to write this passage. He was one of President F. D.
Roosevelt's favorite authors. So was Winston Churchill, whose path had
crossed his as they both pursued naval affairs in 1918.
[6] To go on would be tedious; yet some of them meant so much to me that I
have a sense of guilt in not appending a note about them. I shall at least name
them: Mary Johnston, Edith Wharton, Stewart Edward White, Ellen Glas-
gow, Jack London, Robert W. Chambers, Lafcadio Hearn, F. Marion Crawford, W. D. Howells, James Lane Allen, Alice French (Octave Thanet),
Ambrose Bierce, Hamlin Garland, Edward Eggleston, Sarah Orne Jewett,
Albion Tourgée, Mary E. Wilkins Freeman, and Irving Bacheller.
This is so miscellaneous a list that I can hardly credit now the interest I had
in all of them. It shows at least a fascination for story writing. Some of these
authors would hardly have been prepared to admit that others of them existed,
or, if they did, were to be rated as serious writers. But I read them all and
found something I now recall in each.

have no recollection of reading William James at all. It may be that his prolixness put me off at the first try.

Like Theodore Dreiser's books, Hamlin Garland's, to which I should come perhaps a little later, were hardly to be called literature at all. They were lumps of earth and pools of water somehow translated into words. Their people were obviously puppets. Yet they were authors with a terrible need to penetrate the secrets of human nature. Their passion surmounted their ineptnesses as authors. Such writers might never deserve to be called artists, but they had the virtue of integrity.[7]

I have not said how much I respected some of the earlier American authors, perhaps because it was more respect I felt for them than affection. They were too much the same sort as Englishmen of their time. There is no sharp difference in mood or even workmanship between Tennyson and Longfellow. True, Longfellow used American settings for *Evangeline* and *Hiawatha;* but the scenes of which he wrote had hardly more reality than those of such European romanticists as Chateaubriand, who conjured forests and prairies wholly out of his imagination. There is not, actually, a pine tree within hundreds of miles of the country where Longfellow placed the murmuring pines and the hemlocks. And the lark often appeared in the New England of the versifiers in complete disregard of that bird's habitat. Thoreau and Emerson, sometimes Whittier, and of course Lowell were as American as Concord and Boston ever managed to be; but their transcendentalism, although it fitted the New England circumstances, had only a precarious hold on the

[7] Many years later I heard more about this as a literary virtue from Ernest Hemingway, who seemed to think it the first quality to be sought by a writer. When I had my discussions with him during a winter in Key West, he was working at *To Have and Have Not* and was preoccupied with the honesty of his presentation. He meant by this, he told me, that a writer must not try to gloss over reality, not to prettify emotion, not to interpret passion, but to let it come through hot and steaming or cold and bitter. In the course of our talks, he illustrated his meaning by lending me a book he described as one which had influenced him greatly; had, in fact persuaded him to explore the African scene. This was Sir Samuel Baker's book of exploration. But he also spoke of C. S. Forester's *African Queen* as an exquisite example of honest workmanship.

frontier. Still, I suppose my mother and others like her were generally in that tradition—New England moved a little west.[8]

My English classes were half reading and half a study of grammatical niceties. The lumpy reading was a poor introduction to literature. Anyone who read no Shakespeare but *Julius Caesar* and no Milton but *Lycidas* would certainly have a peculair view of the Elizabethan age and of Cromwell's time. And his understanding of these magnificent Englishmen would be even more peculiar.[9] Reading, however, was so much a habit that many of the cores of knowledge in the texts were in time surrounded by widening circles of a most irregular shape. I was inclined to follow leads that interested me most and not to take much trouble if material was not readily available. Also, this sort of entertainment made no deep grooves in my patterns of memory. But I still think it must have had the value of adding depth. Of course I was coming to a critical age when I ought to have felt more depth under my keel anyway; but even if I was not paying much attention to the set jobs of my education, the satisfaction I got from books kept me among the intellectuals—at least in my own mind. I was not the social tramp I might appear to be.

Also, the interstitial amusements which tended to become major diversions may have had their own uses. They may have prepared me for the social studies, which, when I had finally settled down, would turn out to be my life's work. I at least had a wide range of experience. And what I did not experience, I read about. It was some time before I was introduced to the formal study of social behavior; but even when I read the texts of the sociologists and discovered the fascinations of abnormal

[8] Lloyd Lewis' account of Hawthorne's struggle to maintain his hold on indigenous culture is a fascinating one; and of course Van Wyck Brooks had a somewhat similar theme in *The Ordeal of Mark Twain*.

[9] Much later in life I was excited to discover what I had missed in *Julius Caesar*. Listening to Sir John Gielgud as Cassius at Stratford, I suddenly realized that I was hearing a profound exposition of political principles. The resistance to meaning in everything they were required to read, so common to high school students, had made me quite immune until then to Shakespeare's wisdom.

psychology, there were not many surprises. What I had not learned in Buffalo barrooms and other such resorts, I had been told about by the novelists, the short-story writers, and the historians.

Anyone inclined to be literary must have owed much to the short story of this period. It went after its effect with scalpel strokes. This was its distinguishing characteristic, as a matter of fact; its practitioners were surgeons. They had no need to generalize or to underline morals. The vices and virtues came up into readers' minds with photographic clarity.

Poe and Irving had been earlier practitioners, and so had Dickens; but these I had known better in other guises—Poe as poet or mystery writer, and Irving as an essayist. The headless horseman and the ghostly bowlers of the Catskills were short-story characters; but actually the modern writers had not taken much from Irving. The dreamy leisure of his tales had long since vanished from our literature. It was possible to trace an evolution from Irving, Poe, and Hawthorne down through Edward Everett Hale, whose *Man without a Country* had been published in 1863, and Thomas Wentworth Higginson (*The Haunted Window*, 1870) to Bret Harte's *The Luck of Roaring Camp*, which was possibly the first of the economical swiftly told tales.

The Atlantic Monthly had begun to be published in 1897, when I was six, and now that I was in my teens was well established. Other magazines had followed. And the short story had been well suited to the demand for something terse, exciting, and decisive. By 1909 there were many such periodicals, some of them edited especially for boys. Since I had been able to read at all, I had been one of their readers. This had included *The Youth's Companion* until it had begun to seem juvenile, and my mother saw that we had subscriptions to *Lippincott's*, *Century*, and *Harper's*. Their stables of story writers were large, and many were admirable workmen.

It was inevitable that I should try too. It looks easy; actually, its form, as it had developed by then, was as stiff and demanding as that of the most disciplined verse. I soon found this out; but it did not prevent me from laboring at it. I worked nights, sometimes until almost morning. I tramped miles in the exaltation of composition. What I had written I worked over and over. Usually the rewriting ended in the conviction that what had resulted was not worth saving. But my energies rallied and I tried again. In the end, I gave it up as a major enterprise, but even in college I was still trying.

Later I turned to the less exciting work of academic writing. But even in that I could not escape the habit of meticulous composition. No one ever noticed this. The only reward for it was my own satisfaction in good workmanship. But I have never been able to feel that my labors of this sort were wasted. They may not have been wasted, but they were lonely. Scholars seldom have any literary sense, and literary folk seldom read scholarly productions. The attempt to join them is sure to be thankless.

Thirty-two

I went home in June of 1910, the last weekly trip of the year, with mixed feelings about my Buffalo experience. I had passed my examinations, but not with any considerable margin. I had, it is true, begun to find my way around in the city about as easily as though I had always lived there. The streets I most often used might almost have been the country roads I knew so well: Main, Masten, Utica, High, and the downtown streets, Delaware and Linwood avenues. And there were saloons, rathskellers, restaurants, and a few hotels, as well as the YMCA, which were as familiar as Salisbury's drugstore in Wilson. I had been amused at Shea's, at the Majestic —managed by Katharine Cornell's father—and at the old Star, where I had just seen Laurette Taylor in a play of her husband's, notorious because Laurette had appeared in a skimpy girdle of fig leaves. I was familiar, too, with the waterfront and the railway stations. But what did it count for? I could no longer be said to be a country boy; but, beyond that, there was nothing to brag about.

On this last day I was too late by a few minutes for the evening train, so I telephoned home that I would not show up until morning and went to stay at the ancient Arlington Hotel across the street from the Exchange Street station. The Arlington was really a station hotel, one of those places better known in earlier days, although they survive in Europe. They were then as much a part of travel as the trains themselves. Sometimes they were simply built over and around the station. Their res-

taurants were mostly for travelers, but not exclusively; before
dining cars were common, through trains stopped for half an
hour at mealtimes, and the passengers ate hastily but well. The
Arlington was not so closely tied to the railway schedules,
but its patrons were transients. I had stayed there a number of
times with my parents and thought of it as another familiar
place.

I had to be up early to catch the morning train. I had a
leisurely dinner in the quiet dining room, where the long-
accustomed colored waiters gave the considerate service natural
to a dignified institution. My room was large and comfortable.
I read awhile, then went for a walk. It took me through the
Italian slums beyond the foot of Main Street, where the streets
were crawling with children and the air was heavy with garlicky
smells. I stopped for a while and watched a passenger ship
loading for her nightly trip up the lake to Cleveland and Detroit.
I wandered eastward then along the waterfront and watched
the freighters maneuvering into and out of their basins or
loading and discharging at their piers. Afterward I turned north-
ward through a neighborhood of factories, warehouses, and
wholesale businesses, bare, grim, and deserted in the evening.
Finally I went back toward Main Street with its lights and
crowds and down toward the Arlington and bed.

For some reason it would be hard to explain, this evening,
like some others, has remained clear in my memory, unexpur-
gated by later experiences. I can even recall thinking, as I
undressed and as I lay awake awhile, that in my long walk I had
not seen one pleasing or really efficient and functional thing.
That was surely remarkable in an America which was supposed
to be the marvel of the world for productivity. The closest
approach to the image of progress had been a ship or two and
the train I had seen (a Lehigh Valley Railroad train) making
up in the yards for its night journey to New York and Philadelphia. But anyone could see that even these could be improved.
The ships, I thought, and certainly the train, must be older
than I, probably a good deal older. They must have seen thirty

years of service. Inside the factories I had passed there might be quite marvelous machines, but they were invisible. What was visible was a series of structures, dirty, nondescript, patched together, and carrying no sign of their purpose. They had not been designed to house any function. They sat there in the miasmic atmosphere of lakeside Buffalo, compromising with their cramped sites, patched and ugly.

The store windows I had passed on lower Main Street exhibited some advanced equipment; they were wholesale hardware and machinery businesses mostly, or ones selling automobile accessories or small power tools. These were fascinating evidence that some progress was being made. But, on the whole, in all this industrial part of Buffalo, there was very little reason to think we were so far advanced in efficiency as we liked to believe; in small things, yes; but not in large ones—the factories themselves, the railroads, or the shipping lines. Sheer manpower was still depended on to move and shape materials. Machines were not yet trusted to do what we knew they could do—not even the ones waiting to be put to work.

I could think only of one exception. Far across the stagnant harbor there loomed in the last light of the sun the cylindrical towers of the grain elevators beside the unloading basins, with the elephantine mills beside them. These were functional, mechanized, planned. There were very few men in and around them. The grain came out of the ships and, in time, out of the storage silos; then it was made into cereal products, and men did not have to lift, haul, or push it about. It was a nicely arranged operation.

Perhaps, farther out toward the south, under the smoke cloud at Lackawanna, the blast furnaces and steel mills were well adapted to their purpose. Some changes were going on. But they could not have been very revolutionary, judging from what labor people were saying. The way men worked in and around the furnaces was a national scandal—the twelve-hour day and the twenty-four-hour swing shift were still defended by spokesmen for the companies. No one credited the steel industry with intelligent management in those days, Carnegie and all his wealthy associates notwithstanding. Steel mills were like the slums, barbarous survivals of an earlier age, marked for abolition, but still not quite anachronistic enough to be completely indefensible. Stockholders made money out of them as they were; and, although workers periodically revolted, the revolts were not so costly as to force a wholly new plan.

This I had read about, perhaps heard about too. At any rate, even if I was a high school boy, I knew something about factories and how they should be built and run. Ours was no model, and our labor relations were not exemplary, not by a good deal; but I had thought this too bad and argued about it with my father. So I had thoughts about the way my elders and betters arranged and managed matters in the business world. They were skeptical, dissenting thoughts, but they were not ignorant and purely theoretical ones. It seemed to me that there was a lot to be done in American industry which required different methods than were being used.

I had been hearing recently of one institution where the study of these matters was a specialty. It was a place where several Buffalo boys I knew had gone to learn about the conduct of business and the management of industry. Instead of mathematics, students there studied accounting, insurance, and finance. They studied geography, economics, political science, and sociology too. And one boy I knew was already a graduate student who was intending to go into government service; he was taking a whole series of courses in constitutional law. This seemed to me an attractive alternative to a liberal-arts program consisting of the classics, mathematics, a little science, history, and literature. I was quite willing to forgo any more Latin and Greek, and I would rather study accounting than mathematics. History would be required anyway, but I liked that. The Wharton School at the University of Pennsylvania had prestige in Buffalo. I thought highly of the boys I knew who had gone there.

That entering the Wharton School was hardly consistent

with my other ambitions occurred to me only vaguely, if at all; certainly I had no inner struggle over it. I had always lived two lives. A Wharton education belonged to the first of them, the practical, working career that I assumed every one of my sort must pursue. Nothing could be farther from my expectation than being a poor poet in an attic. I hoped, on the contrary, to be independent, successful, well regarded, and perhaps even wealthy. I always assumed I could do that and live my own second life as well. I had so far, anyway, and why should I not go on? No one would want to write for more than a few hours a day. And that left a good many hours for being an executive. Also, I had noted that the Wharton course included as many cultural subjects—history, literature, languages, and the social studies—as a student might care to involve himself in; there was plenty of room for electives.

Nor did my aspiration to be a successful manager of some sort deny me the right to be a dissenter from much of the business practice I deplored. I wanted to change things, not to destroy them. I had not then, and never afterward developed, any nihilistic impulses such as revolutionaries so often have. Also, I was not inclined to blame individuals or wish to see them punished for their part in the arrangement of a chaotic system. They were caught in it.

The most violent changes in America during my lifetime would originate in scientific discoveries, not in ideological movements. This was something I began to realize very early; partly, I suppose, from my reading, but partly also from knowing something about industrial processes. This was deduction from firsthand knowledge, gained not as a worker but as an intimate of my father, who worked all the time at such contrivances as would improve the operations of his small concern. I assumed that bigger operations were similarly worked at. The people who did it might not be clever or broad—that was what Wharton was for—but the intention was to improve.

I have pointed out that Einstein had already published his Field Theory. Also, it is time to say that an obscure engineer had perfected the basic principles of what came to be called scientific management. The one was more spectacular in its consequences than the other; but I should contend that scientific management had more effect during my generation. It did in fact revolutionize industry and, in a sense, the social studies. I was never to meet Taylor, but he was one of four or five individuals who had the most effect on me in the long run.

At the moment, after walking through the factory and warehouse district of Buffalo, I thought only that there was enormous room for improvement. The fact was that as early as the 'eighties of the last century Frederick Winslow Taylor had been making the observations at the Midvale Steel Company which resulted in the development of his system. By the time of which I write he had arrived at most of his generalizations. They were waiting for me to discover in some of my classes at Pennsylvania. Not until 1911, when I became a freshman, were they widely publicized. Their first notice of this sort resulted from Brandeis' attack on railway inefficiencies, in which he used the Taylor principles to show how operations might be improved. From that time on scientific management would be cultivated, almost to a fanatic degree, by industrial engineers who afterward incorporated themselves as the Taylor Society[1] and would gradually spread to economics, sociology, and political science. Just now I had only a faint intimation that new discoveries waited for me. But that intimation was real enough. As I have said, my generation believed progress to be a regular characteristic of man's experience. This was the progress I was likely to have intimate contact with.

The morning, when it came, was a lovely one. Even in the degraded environs of the Exchange Street station, the June sun fell benignly on all-night saloons being hosed down for the new day and on pawnshops whose gilded balls had long since ceased to show their gilt. I had almost overslept, but there was

[1] About which I shall have more to say. Two of my early academic studies would derive directly from Taylor—*Industry's Coming of Age* in 1927 and *The Industrial Discipline and the Governmental Arts* in 1934.

time for a doughnut and coffee before I went out through the iron gates to the six-fifty. The familiar trainmen spoke to me with sleepy gruffness and, one of very few passengers, I settled into an empty seat with the *Courier*. When we had crawled out to the Terrace station and paused, then steamed out to Black Rock, we began to have glimpses of the Niagara as Lake Erie crowded itself into its swift-running channel. The river had lost the look of winter at last. The ice was gone and the muddiness of spring had cleared up. The water was blue-green now, and the Canadian shore was bright.

I opened the window and drew long breaths. It was a fine thing to be a young fellow with summer coming on. We had a new automobile—my father felt that he had to have a new one every spring; and the way he drove them, he was probably right. My closest Buffalo friends, Frank Forster and Leslie Hansen, would be down to visit. I had promised to show them the resources of the country as a kind of payment for their having initiated me into the city's mysteries. I exchanged quips with the trainmen and looked ahead with confidence to the adventures I could clearly anticipate.

The vast Wickwire steel plant came between us and the river, its chimneys billowing heavy streams of smoke, its furnaces ablaze. We ran intimately along behind a row of boathouses and river-front shacks which obviously had an interesting life all their own. That could be told from the glimpse I had of a red-haired girl emptying a pan of dishwater over a gallery rail and waving, as she leaned far over, at a man in a passing motorboat. There was something between them; I could guess what.

We rattled and banged into North Tonawanda as the conductor shouted into the rear door, "Change here for Grand Island"; he knew he had no passengers who would transfer, but he was feeling good, and on such a morning regulations were no burden even if they were ridiculous. Presently the no man's land of the chemical plants spread out on both sides of the tracks, hazed with choking fumes, the buildings smeared with poisonous colors, the dead land stretching out miles to windward.

We picked up a few passengers at the Falls station, crowded even that early with tourists who had come in on the night excursions and had not yet begun their day of sight-seeing. They sat around on the many cast-iron benches provided for them by a thoughtful railway, their bags and parcels around them; it was not hard to imagine how exhausted they would be when they came back to board their return train that night. Those benches had been put there before I was born; they would be there, probably, long after I was gone. Cast iron, I thought, was far too durable.

It was a short run through city streets to the Suspension Bridge station, where we lingered to take on additional empty milk cans going down to the country to be filled. When we pulled out, running noisily over the switches, the conductor, standing on the rear platform, sardonically saluted the enormous Spray Beer sign above the brewery across the way. This always got a laugh, and it pleased the conductor to get laughs. He sat down and picked up my neglected newspaper as we ran out along the brink of the gorge. I looked backward, and there, as always, hung the watery cloud for which the beer was named. The water in the gorge boiled and tumbled far below us and coiled out into the famous whirlpool. In five minutes we passed Niagara University; there some priests or some theological students were making hasty undignified progress along the campus paths—late, I imagined, to morning chapel or classes.

Then at last we came to the country. It first opened out to the view at Lewiston Heights; and I went out onto the platform, as I always did. This was the favorite scene, for me, of all I knew of; it had everything I most cared about—the distance, ending in the blue climax of the lake, and, in between, the orchards, the fields, and the vineyards, but also the grace notes of two old villages, Lewiston on this side of the river and Queenston on the other. Their big houses with the wineglass elms drooping above them were the very picture, seen from above, of American village culture. It was what, after all, I belonged to. It gave me a sense of identity, as I came back to it, that no city ever could.

From the little station at Lewiston Heights we went angling down the escarpment to Model City, where the first milk cans were noisily unloaded.[2]

From there the train chuffed cheerfully through the country, stopping first at Ransomville and then at Elberta with a clatter of milk cans. This was not a dairy country; but there did seem to be a good many farmers who kept cows and shipped milk. They were lined up to carry their cans home. They would be back that night to load the full ones on the train that got to the city that night. These dairymen were like the cherry orchards. There were only a few of them; but when you knew about them, their business was as interesting as any other, however big.

Presently, before many large thoughts could chase themselves through a mind, the train pulled into the Wilson siding, where it would rest while a fast freight passed, going toward Niagara Falls. I dropped off with some pleasantries following me, joined in by the engineer as well as the brakeman, and crossed the tracks to the canning factory just beyond the coal yard, dormant now until fall. My summer had begun.

June lay upon the fields and orchards of home. The bloom had gone from the bushes and trees and they had almost their full green, but a sharper, clearer green than they would have again. The roadsides were enflowered. In the yards of the

---

[2] "Model" because in 1893 a promoter—William T. Love—who was far ahead of his time, had projected an industrial center to use the power he expected to develop at the site. It was a good idea. The fall over the escarpment at this point would be higher by the height of the rapids than the actual height at the Falls. Half a century later the plan would be revived and carried out by the Power Authority of the State of New York under the chairmanship of Robert Moses. But Love had failed to raise the needed funds, depression had intervened, the buyers of lots had been left with worthless investments, and Love himself had disappeared. The "City" was a small railroad stop among the orchards. I had always known of people who owned lots at Model City and who were still resentful at having been swindled. But I have often thought that Love belonged among the adventurers of American business. Others with worse schemes than his had made fortunes and become philanthropists.

houses there were peonies blooming wildly, like pretty, blowzy women just come out into a warming wind.

The factory was in the state at which it always arrived just before the beginning of the canning season. Steam was up in the boilers, and the machines were having trial runs. Everything was in disorder; nothing had found its proper place. It would during the next week; it always had, anyway. When I sent in the first loads of peas the place would look like a well-kept kitchen in a farmhouse, not fancy, but capable of turning out first-class food. And from then on the familiar rhythms would seize on men and machines alike. Until the last cans went to the warehouse in the fall, that rhythm would dominate everything. The campaign would be on.

Thirty-three

That summer was much like a succession of others. They were interludes, really, in city life and in my schooling, when for a while I was a worker and when also I went back to old neighbors and acquaintances. This renewal would inevitably be somewhat affected by the new friends from school and college who would begin now to make our house a second home and my mother a second mother.

For her, however, each of these accessions was a delight. Some of my fondest recollections are of those occasions when she and one or more of my friends were engaged in the deepest of exchanges about morals, public affairs, or the problems of our civilization. They might take place anywhere—in the kitchen, even—but most of them were rocker-chair conversations on the front porch. People sat on front porches in those days, and ours was a second living room all during the summer. Usually my mother, using tricks I knew too well for them to be used on me, got the better of the arguments. It amused me to find my friends reading up surreptitiously with the purpose of flooring her in a next encounter; and sometimes they seemed on the way to doing it. But when her position was threatened, she had a way of seeing that the argument escaped from objectivity or changed its course so that no conclusive end could possibly be reached. She was accomplished at this sort of thing and got genuine satisfaction from it.

One of her aversions was Theodore Roosevelt, and for those who did not admire him that statesman furnished plenty of material for annoyance. He was not President any more, but he was often in the news, hunting in Africa, visiting European royalty, issuing pronouncements on any subject at all. He regarded himself as a universal guide to conduct, and my mother did not like it. My visitors usually, it seemed, came from Republican families. They had not thought much about public affairs, being normally busy with athletics, girls, and school; but they did regard T.R. as an acknowledged hero, and my mother's irreverence they found shocking. This made them easy marks.

One of the closest of my new friends, however, was too much for her. He refused to be concerned about T.R. or any other of the fallible statesmen my mother liked to pillory. He was of a scientific turn of mind. He was, in fact, intending to be a chemical engineer, an ambition that seemed to me amazingly difficult, and to my mother strange and remote. This was Leslie Hansen—familiarly known as the Swede, some of us having discovered that the way to annoy any Scandinavian was to confuse him with one of the others; and he was a second-generation Dane. He had the slow and sleepy appearance of his racial strain, but he was facile in mathematics and proficient in all scientific matters. This baffled my mother. He infuriated her by leading her into traps and then bringing out the reference works he always seemed to have handy. Her arguments with him were likely to end in indignant head-tossing. For she was a poor loser and used to marking up victories.

I have to say about her that she kept her place in young men's affections even if she did take delight in humiliating them and would never admit to being in the wrong. For one thing, she looked so maternal. Her hair had long since turned white. It was still luxuriant, however, and the aureole it made atop her now matronly figure was irresistible. They tried to be tender with her, but this never went very well. She preferred to be treated as an equal—but a sort of superior one, with certain privileges.

Then too, she had another advantage: she was a superb

cook. It cannot be merely the contrast between the appetite of youth and that of age which compels me to make the claim for her that she turned out better pies than were ever baked in New England, better puddings than were ever steamed in old England, and better meats than ever originated anywhere. And this was in spite of a reluctance to exercise the art. She would always rather do something else, even if that something else was only a conversation. And she had a way of going on strike when it was most inconvenient and leaving us to make our own meals. But when she was in the mood and really got down to it there was no one like her. It was partly, no doubt, because she liked good food herself. She followed closely the advice to housewives in the women's magazines. Under their influence and much to my father's disgust, she introduced salads as an everyday part of our diet. He was a meat, potatoes, and pie man; and Sunday without roast beef and pudding was an affront to his ancestors. Salads he could do without.

She was sensitive to the suggestion that her study of cooking was pursued in her own interest. She maintained that it was a menial activity that she sought to ennoble in the interest of others. But, I told her, there was the fact that between twenty and forty she had gained about a hundred pounds, which worked out at five pounds a year; and such an increase could have happened only to a hearty eater. This did not accord with the picture of herself she preferred to project, and eventually she did become a dieter. She never really slimmed down to her girlish weight, but the effort steadily diminished her usefulness as a cook. After a while we none of us could shame or wheedle her into really enthusiastic and sustained performance in the kitchen. Holidays with turkey and pudding as the *pièce de résistance* remained a challenge; and Sunday dinner could be remarkable, especially when there were visitors or when I came home on vacation. But at the time I write of now there was none of that lackadaisical spirit. We lived high— though, as is usual, we undervalued our luck until it was too late.

So our summers were pleasant. The clattering factory was mostly background for the work I was given to do out in the field. I had no responsibility for maintaining machinery or for keeping anything in order. I had to see that each farmer's crops arrived at the factory exactly at their prime. This involved closer attention and more meticulous arranging than might be imagined. But it was not really an exacting duty or one I could feel resentful about. I could often linger, and I often did.

One of my lingering places was at old Tom Stanley's out on the Randall road. There was a satellite pea-threshing station on Tom's place, and for several summers Leslie Hansen and Frank Forster worked there. It was a good place for city boys, both of whom were mechanically inclined and both of whom knew how to appreciate the entertaining environment of a farm in summer. The neighborhood was rich in novelty, and neither of them minded a hard day's work.

All three of us had an acute appreciation of all that was foreign to our usual experience. It was something to be savored. And old Tom was the embodiment of deep rural tradition besides being a pawky and wise individual. What he took pleasure in conveying to us, as outsiders, was the antic side of life as he knew it. We were such young fellows, and we were so green; it was like breaking up and cultivating a new field. The tales he had to tell us were not morality ones—quite the contrary —but they were well calculated to hold listeners. Tom was an earthy man with several grown boys. After his wife's death a few years before, he had married the hired girl and now had not only a capable and attractive housekeeper but a new crop of youngsters tumbling about the yard. He was mostly retired to a seat under a big mulberry tree—and, according to his claims, to the bedroom. The older boys, with some restlessness, did most of the work on the large farm. It was one of those Niagara farms which, besides orchards, maintained a dairy; and this made up an operation with ceaseless daily demands. Those grown sons of his were kept busy.

As an executive, directing young men who felt they ought to be establishing their own operations, and keeping track of several hired men as well, he had to be resourceful and tough. But with us he relaxed. We were not working for him, and if we wasted time it was not his responsibility. Our hilarity as he entertained us was ample pay for his efforts. And his busy wife added a few more to her boarders with no resentment. She was used to such demands.

Leslie and Frank enjoyed the country fare as well as the company. Three times a day the women loaded a long table for eight or ten men and waited on them as the victuals disappeared as if by magic. My friends had never before seen such performances and were awed by the gargantuan appetites of the men who worked ten or twelve hours in barns and fields. There were platters of meat, vegetables just out of the garden, pitchers of milk and cream, sweets and sours from the cellar, and never less than three kinds of dessert—puddings, pies, and cakes. It would be called plain, I suppose, but it was satisfying; and for a man who was hungry, it was exactly right.

Very little conversation went on at table. The men, hair wet from splashing in the tin basin out by the well, faces pink under an outer layer of tan, and smelling richly of stables and sweat, got down close to their plates and used their implements to good effect. Leslie and Frank soon learned not to hold back or try to talk; if they did' they were liable to lose out. Talk could begin when chairs were pushed back with sighs of repletion and polite belchings. The men went out then to loaf on the porch or in the yard, and the women sat down to what was left. The table by then was a scene of devastation, but they were used to it. In winter it was different, but when summer work was going on they never ate with the men.

Tom had no objection to an extra guest for dinner or supper, especially if he happened to be the sort who would listen. I was such a sort, and when I could I found it convenient to have business in the neighborhood at mealtime. Tom was a large-scale man, gone to fat in age, but it was not hard to credit the

stories he told of his own exploits. One interesting thing to me
was that his subject matter was so limited. He never spoke of
politics except to analyze the behavior of very local officials. His
circle was about five miles across; but within those limits he
had a restless curiosity about every individual and every occurrence. He had accumulated background for each of these,
and his erudition was worthy of a professional historian. He
knew what husbands were wanderers, what workers were worthless, what deals had resulted badly for neighbors, and what
every field and orchard was capable of producing.

During the hours after lunch, when the boys and men had
been sent back to the fields and Frank and Leslie could steal
time from their viners, and during other hours at twilight,
with the grinding of our machinery stilled, the cows milked
and turned back into the pastures, and the children skylarking
on the lawn, Tom sat in the swing with the three of us and
expanded. The fascinating thing about his performance was
his assumption that we were at the same time strangers and
familiars. He talked about the relation between individuals my
friends, at least, had never heard of before and would never
hear of again, and made it seem as important and vivid as
though the people he talked about were intimates. This, of
course, is the storytelling art. I suppose Tom had been doing
this sort of thing all his life; but his long and lonely days on the
farm in years past must have served to perfect his technique
through meditation. I could imagine him following a plow,
riding a cultivator, trimming apple trees in the snowy winter
when the winds off the lake nearly paralyzed a man who did
not work vigorously, and through the hours considering the
complexities of local life and getting amusement out of the
tangles people were always getting themselves into. None of
these ever seemed to him serious; they were mostly amusing,
and at the worst fascinating. Even the scrapes his sons were
involved in were material for his store of histories. They did not
touch him deeply, although he was always free with informed
advice.

Our sessions with Tom were made more memorable by the hard cider that always appeared. Tom valued his cider-making skill. By summer his last fall's barrels, six or eight of them lined up in the fruit cellar half under and half back of the house, had all been liberally sampled and graded. There were even a few barrels, back in the darkness, saved from other years, which by then were of such strength as would, he said, separate the men from the boys. No glassware was available other than the water pitchers from the table and the tumblers of daily use, and these were the measure of his expectation. Two or three helpings from one of those pitchers, filled from the vintage casks and drunk from capacious tumblers, made no discernible impression on Tom, except perhaps to increase his volubility, nor, I must say, did they have much more effect on his boys or the hired men; but the three of us, unaccustomed as we were to carrying such a load, often had some difficulty in keeping up without betraying an unmanly weakness. We did our best. And, on the whole, we earned at least the approval necessary for acceptance. Anyway, we were expected only to be listeners. If our raptness became a little hazy, Tom ignored it. It was his purpose to maintain an audience.

Leslie passed this test with higher marks than Frank and I could hope to attain. Being of Scandinavian extraction, he had a real appreciation of schnapps and failed to understand our complaints about its roughness. He did, however, admit to a preference for lager beer. It made a better beverage. This preference of his led to one incident that summer which was amusing to us but which would always be recalled by my mother with some indignation.

When the season for gathering and processing the green pea crop was over and the viners at Tom's farm were dismantled and put in maintenance status until another June came around, the boys came back from the farm to our house in the village for the rest of the summer. From about the first of August until school began again in September—Leslie was now going to

Pennsylvania, while Frank and I went back to Masten Park—they shared my quarters and worked in the factory while I went on with my field work, concerned now with beans, tomatoes, and the later fruits. There were days when they were not needed and when I too was not pressed, and we spent a good deal of time around the harbor or simply finding something to do at home. Boys on such occasions do an unusual amount of eating and drinking. And Leslie preferred beer. Soft drinks he found repugnant.

Knowing my mother's innocence in such matters, he came back from Buffalo one time with a case of the excellent brew made by the Kirchners at the German-American brewery (the two Kirchner sons were friends of ours). We put it on the back porch under some other boxes and kept several bottles in the icebox. Our deception was successful, and for several weeks we kept the supply going. My father was so busy during the summer that he paid little attention to anything around the house; and we simply told my mother, what she could read on the tops, that it was Pilsener—Pilsener pop! This tour de force required that we remove the labels, and it was inevitable that one of us would become careless about this. But it did not happen until my mother on numerous occasions had joined us in a sociable glass. If the customary arguments on these occasions were made more enthusiastic and less logical by the Pilsener, it was not enough to be noticeable. As time passed, my father came to an interlude and one evening he investigated a refrigerator leak that he had been trying to get us to fix. He discovered the beer, of course, and gave us a fairly dramatic going-over. My mother was outraged and retired to her bedroom in injured dignity.

We had no more beer at home that summer. But I must say for my father that it was not long until the absurdity of prohibition overcame his early training, and he began to accept the amenities of imbibing in a gingerly way. But my mother would never consent to do this unless she was given an out by some subterfuge. She would, however, allow herself to be deceived. And on many a picnic or other excursion she accepted assurance of the innocent contents of glasses she must have known were guiltily loaded. She did not ask for proof.

Thirty-four

During this summer, for some reason I cannot now recall but probably as a kind of pleasant reversion to the past, Leslie, Frank, and I cleaned up and put into service the rubber-tired runabout I had not used for some time. To draw it, I commandeered for the evenings a mare used during the day for handy hauling about the factory yard. She was a nice mare and we became fond of her, but it may have been a little hard on her to have a night shift added to her daytime duties. These were not tiring; also, she was handled by an elderly workman who had got to thinking of her as his own, and he was protective about her. Mason was as nearly empty-headed as a human being could become, but he bore a striking resemblance to McKinley. It pleased the boys to watch this statesman type loading and unloading his wagon and addressing the mare with affectionate obscenities. But Mason resented our using her, and we went to some trouble about abstracting her from the factory stable after he had left for the night.

Her duties on our excursions were no more demanding than her somnolent daytime ones. We usually drove out to some girl's house not too many miles away in the country, and the mare could doze at a hitching post until we got ready to go home. We never pushed her, and she had no real cause for resentment. But still she may have agreed with Mason that it was outrageous to take her out of the stable at all and expect her to haul the three of us around the country. At any rate, one night, when she may have been chilly and perhaps annoyed by the merriment she could see and hear through the windows and on the porch where the three Weekley girls lived, she simply yanked at her hitching strap until it broke and went on home. Our six-mile walk when we discovered the defection did us no harm, but it took an hour and a half and got us home very late—in fact, about dawn. And it furnished a saga at our expense which was quick to spread and was nauseatingly repeated in our vicinity, especially by Mason, who thought we had been served right. For of course the night watchman at the factory saw the mare come in and plant herself before the stable door, waiting patiently to be unharnessed and allowed to retire.

When he had taken care of the mare the watchman thought it best to call my father to see if there had been an accident. When we arrived several hours later the house was in an uproar, and we did not quiet it quickly. No one had known where we were, and my mother had insisted on phoning all the probable places without success. Altogether, she was worked up to a pitch of indignation which intimidated us. My father probably said to himself that boys would be boys and, after saying succinctly what he thought of us, went to bed again. But my mother was not sleepy. She wanted to know particularly why it was that we had not *started* home until nearly two o'clock. Had there been a dance? A social? Nothing? Then what *had* we been doing until two o'clock? This oldest of questions between generations got no more satisfactory answers from us than it ever gets from those who are questioned. And she worried the grievance until all our feelings were properly rasped, and then retired with such a monumental sense of wrong that even I was impressed, and my friends were completely subdued. She did not forgive us for days, and the house was funereal until she was distracted by some other interest.[1]

[1] One of the things we had been doing that evening was singing to the organ on which Evie Weekley performed. We went through the whole repertoire of popular songs—now that I think of it, without objection by her father, who was indeed a tolerant man but must have been tried by such performances after hard days of work on the farm.

I think it was during the same summer that Leslie and I got into another scrape, Frank having gone home for a weekend and not being with us. It was one this time from which we learned a good deal in a way hard to explain to others. My mother found a number of texts in what she heard of it, but our own deductions were not the ones she dwelt on at some length. My father listened to our account of it interestedly but without comment. I am sure he realized that our experience counted for growing up and needed no elaboration.

First, I ought to say something of the relations between myself and the men responsible for the operations at the factory. Since I had gone away to school, I was no longer so much one of the village crowd; and the appearance of my city friends, although they certainly passed every test and on the whole were tough enough, if not so knowledgeable as the village boys in country matters, had made some difference. I had real friends among the regular factory people. But such resentment or wish to show me up as pretentious—in whatever way so slight and indefinite an attitude may be described—was most openly shown by one of the foremen, John Dupre. John was a big man, strong, assertive, energetic, who had got to be foreman by en-

---

I was not then, and never became, adept at music. I had struggled for a few years with piano lessons at my mother's insistence, but the truth was that I was an impossible student. I could not carry a tune, and the piano pieces I learned were played, I am sure, with complete lack of expression. Still, no one could grow up in our environment without joining in group singing very often; and my departures from tune would be concealed in the general uproar.

These songs were of the phony rural sort—Riley set to music, and so on. Our folk music was no more than an imitation of the real thing. I often think of Foster—a favorite in my generation—who never journeyed south of Pittsburgh but who made Florida's Suwanee River famous and set all of us to singing about Old Black Joe. No doubt Foster had a real lyrical gift, but it was not authentic in the folk-music sense. But then neither were all the songs about the Emerald Isle and the old South sung by us New Yorkers on picnics and hay rides. "Aunt Nellie's Quilting Party" and "Jingle Bells," yes; but not "Mother Machree." If we sang about a South we never knew, we also had mission furniture in our houses, imitation Gothic churches, and incredibly tinted photographs of our loved ones as an approach to what I should later learn to call easel art. We were children in all the arts and inclined to accept sentimental imitations.

forcing his rule-of-thumb decrees vigorously. In a running factory there were emergencies every hour. John rushed to the seat of the trouble and, with considerable skill and calling on long experience, got things moving again with a minimum of delay. But he was impatient and even bad-tempered, and the Sicilians were reported to have warned him against provocation of their own more volatile youngsters. The stiletto was known to be their favorite way of settling a dispute.

Leslie, Frank, and I had heard indirectly of some remarks he had made about city boys, college education, and such matters. We knew they were about us and that he might have intended us to hear of them. Consequently we had studied the man with some care. We decided that there were signs of weakness at the center of the bluster. He had a high, squeaky voice and, although he was huge and hairy, he had tiny hands and feet. But that these were reliable signs we could not be certain. Leslie, the stolid-seeming Scandinavian, waited with anticipation for some occasion to test our conclusions. But, as I pointed out, it was not likely that there would be any sort of physical climax to Dupre's campaign. I was the boss's son, and so immune to open attack, if not to innuendo. They, of course, were identified with me. But when the incident occurred that I am about to relate, there had been for some time an uneasy feeling among us that all was not quite well—that we were not on solid ground among those we worked with. It was not pleasant.

It happened late in summer, the season of organization picnics, this time the Niagara County Pioneers. It took place at Olcott Beach, six miles down the lake, where the amusement park and small harbor had ample facilities for large crowds and where there was a lakeside hotel which had once been a luxurious watering place but was now entering on the first stages of a decline that would be final when the automobile had become more common. Its dining room and dance pavilion still maintained the closest approach to genteel standards anywhere in our vicinity. They were safely separated from the picnic crowds in the park adjoining, yet they were near enough so that adventurers like ourselves could enjoy both sorts of crowd.[2]

There were two ways to get from Wilson to Olcott Beach. A dirt road paralleled the lake shore, negotiable, even if dusty or muddy as the weather determined, either by horse-drawn rigs or by automobiles. We sometimes went that way, but more often we went by way of the lake, coastwise, from harbor to harbor in one of the numerous launches used for that purpose. The fishermen were desperately searching for alternate sources of income—fishing was no longer to be relied on—so they ferried summer people to and from the island and made excursions down the lake to Olcott Beach or, less often, up to Youngstown or Niagara-on-the-Lake. They never ventured the thirty-mile crossing to Toronto or other north-shore ports, but they made a fair thing of their coastwise business.

The launches, most of them, were indisputably fishing craft. They were broad in the beam, quite seaworthy if handled reasonably, but powered with such uncertain old engines that breakdowns were frequent. These contraptions seemed to know their masters but not always to obey them, and they were sensitive to alien control. It was quite usual for crowds of thirty or forty trippers, seated side by side on narrow benches

[2] The Olcott Beach park was characteristic of that time. It was a subsidiary facility of the International Electric Railway, which ran from the cities of Buffalo, Niagara Falls, Lockport, the Tonawandas, through the intervening villages to the lake.

The park was a weekend traffic maker. The decades 1890–1920 were the prosperous ones for the interurban lines. Before 1890 their equipment was not such that they could be popular, and their lines were not extensive enough to attract much traffic. And after 1920 they began dying out all over the country, killed by competition from good roads and automobiles. But at the time I write of they ran through the countryside less formally than the railways and with more frequent stops at convenient way places.

The amusement park, with its ferris wheels, outdoor vaudeville, skating rinks, dancing pavilions, midways, picnic lawns, and beaches was largely the creation of the railway companies.

There were those in Wilson who envied Olcott Beach its summer excitements. It was pointed out that we had a better harbor, for instance; but the interurban never reached us. And this suited the quieter citizens very well.

around the thwarts of these craft, to sway and swing for an hour or two on the open lake while a seamy fisherman labored and swore at his cranky motor. The smell of gasoline and fish, together with the motion, especially on a warm and windless day, was apt to upset landlubbers.

I had spent a good deal of time about the harbor, in and out of boats, and I knew them almost as well as their owners did. I also knew the lake in all its moods. Consequently in any emergency I was one of the hands rather than just a passenger, a duality which might place me in the stern as a temporary steersman while Jim, Joe, Fred, or Orly struggled with the power plant. This familiarity impressed my city friends, but it also led them to suppose that I had more knowledge and skill than I actually possessed. This was a mistake I did nothing to correct, but on the night of this Pioneers' picnic my overconfidence led us into difficulties.

Leslie and I had got to Olcott Beach in one of the launches, without girls and unattached to any party, an independence we had enjoyed until well after midnight, when we began to consider getting home. By that time Joe Starch would have his load assembled and waiting, probably, for the last stragglers to show up. When we arrived thus tardily at the pier where the boat was tied up, I noticed for the first time that the north wind was becoming something more than a breeze. If it should increase it would make the trip uncomfortable, because it would mean about an hour and a half in the trough of seas rolling landward. And no one who knew the lake liked to be on it in an onshore wind.

There was no crowd in Joe's boat. As the members of his party had appeared, he had advised them to find other ways to get home, and apparently they had. He and the rest of the ferriers had decided against going out. His was the least seaworthy of the half dozen boats at the pier; it was, in fact, a converted launch formerly used for pleasure jaunts, not the usual fishing boat. His was a wise decision, but Leslie and I had let things go pretty late; we wondered how we were going to get home.

We were talking things over quietly with the fishermen and a few others who needed to find a way home, when John Dupre and two of his friends showed up. Perhaps John had had the drink or two necessary to lower the level of his inhibitions and to make him indiscreet; at any rate, he was nasty about fishermen who were afraid of a little wind. One thing led to another, until Joe Starch flared up and dared him to get into the boat and take the trip with him back to Wilson Harbor. He at once jumped in, followed by his friends. The other boatmen protested. The wind was still rising, they told Joe, and in his boat it was simply not safe. But Joe's annoyance overcame his discretion, and he refused to listen.

John went on talking. Looking at Leslie and myself, he said in one of those false-friendly voices that deceive no one, and are not actually intended to, that he supposed we were afraid of the water on a rough night too. My judgment was no further developed than would be expected at my age, and Leslie had Danish courage and little experience. So naturally we stepped in. Uncle Johnny Pilkinton, my best friend among the fishermen, spoke up and told us that we were being foolish. Uncle Johnny had a boat twice as big and much more seaworthy than Joe's, and yet he had, he said, decided that the trip would be just too risky. But the matter had got beyond reason, and after a little more argument we cast off, Uncle Johnny watching us go with obvious apprehension.

Joe asked me to take the tiller until he got the engine going, so I sat up on the rear combing with my feet swinging. As we left the shelter of the piers and headed out into the lake, the wind in my face was so strong that I had to turn my head to get a breath. I knew well enough then that we had made a mistake, but we were committed now. As we ran farther out I held the boat quartering into the seas; but it was a struggle, and almost at once we began to take water. It came in over the bow in such quantities that everything was soon aslop.

There was no escaping it; everyone was wet to the skin, and
the wind gave those who were not working the kind of shakes
familiar in zero weather to a man who has been sweating but
has suddenly been immobilized. Just the discomfort was enough
to produce the jitters.

There was no moon, and there was a scud of flying clouds
hiding the stars. The shore was invisible, and the only guide to
steering was the wind, which, when we had started, had been
in the northwest; we could only presume that it had not
changed. I found that running so nearly in the trough of the
waves actually threatened to capsize us every few minutes. It
worried Joe, who could not be sure that I would ease off enough
when the high ones came, and he came back to give me advice.
But the engine was giving trouble; all that vagrant water
bathing the carburetor and the electrical connections was something no arrangement had been made to circumvent. So presently he had to go back to his nursing job and leave me to the
navigation. Taking hold momentarily, he had tried to bring
the course nearer west than northwest, but he had not been
able to do it any better than I. Heading out this way was taking
us farther and farther offshore and lengthening the run to
Wilson Harbor, but there was nothing to be done about it.
Joe set the passengers to bailing with whatever receptacles he
could find, but we were taking more and more water, and
even the amateurs could see that we were in serious trouble.
All we could do was to fight it through as we were doing and
hope that our efforts would be enough.

This went on for about an hour. By then everyone was
exhausted but me, and I was nearly frozen. I was sitting up
in the wind, wet through, and worried not only about my own
efforts but about Joe's ability to keep the engine running. I was
not really frightened; I knew boats and the lake well enough to
think that we would get through; but, I thought, anyone but
Leslie in such a situation as his would be scared to death. He
had hardly ever been in a boat before, and most of his swimming had been in a YMCA pool. He must have wondered

whether, if we turned over, he could make it to shore—well over a mile—in the turbulence and dark.

But just as my cold and exhaustion reached the stage at which it seemed unbearable, and when the rolling and tumbling were at their most frightening, my Danish friend began to sing at the top of his voice. He was bailing away as though he had been used to such a rhythm all his life. "Onward, Christian Soldiers" was not especially appropriate—we were not doing battle for any cause more defensible than mere survival—but it was a swinging tune. I was so pleased by this exhibition of exhilaration in time of crisis that I at once joined in. So did Joe, sitting on his haunches and guarding his spark plugs. There we were, on the furious lake, dark night about us, the wind battering our insufficient craft, and we had started a shouting song.

It was too much for John. That streak of yellow we had speculated about showed itself. He had some time since stopped bailing. Now he broke down and crumpled into a heap, wet, miserable, and afraid. He begged Joe to turn around and go back, as though that would relieve us of all our dangers. He whined and he quavered. Joe told him that turning back would be more dangerous than going on. Our only chance, he said, was to keep going—and keep bailing. He said that we would be safe as long as we had power, and the engine had kept going so far; it might last out the trip if water could be kept out of the boat. So he—John—had better bail if he wanted to make it. His two friends joined in; they told him to shut up and get to work. But he was whimpering and nearly useless when real disaster overtook us. The engine stopped.

Now we were adrift in a sea that was getting worse. At once we were turned into the troughs and rolled unmercifully downwind. Still, it did seem that we would stay afloat. We rode high and turned far over as we went down the slopes, but we took no more water than we had when we had been heading into the rollers. We could see presently that our real danger, aside from the possibility of capsizing, which we thought we could prevent, was that of smashing on the rocks between us and the shore. We knew they were there if we were in the stretch we thought we were in; and after a while we knew this was so —we could see the white water boiling around them and hear the breakers as we drifted toward land.

This was some time after the motor had quit, and John's demoralization had got worse. He was now actually hysterical. He cried and beat his hands on the thwarts, hid his face, or tried to, and prayed incoherently. This was too much for Leslie. It offended every conception he held of man's estate. And he started in on an exposition, which was exhaustive and devastating, of the disgrace it was for the human race to tolerate an animal of John's degeneracy. This was from a lad of nineteen to a man of some forty years. But it was also from one male human being to another. I recalled it afterward with wonder and admiration. It had little effect on John, however; he went on cowering and emitting childish noises. But aside from being a weight in the boat, he was no problem. He braced himself in a corner and did not move.

When we could actually make out the cliffs through murk and had got past the rocks which just there made a kind of reef—this in itself was a miracle—we suddenly heard a hail, and Uncle Johnny's big, steady fishing boat loomed on our landward side. He had followed us out into the night, and somehow he had found us. Uncle Johnny knew the lake, he knew boats, and he knew the limitations of men. He had used his knowledge. That, together with a sense of responsibility for all humankind, which some men have and some do not, had brought him through the night to our rescue.

There followed one of those superb exhibitions of skill to be seen only when completely competent men are operating in emergencies they understand and have the courage to surmount. Maneuvering in the spume and chop and pushed by a fierce wind, Uncle Johnny, after several attempts, succeeded in throwing us a line. When it took the towing strain, it pulled out the cleat to which it was tied. He circled, came back, and threw it to us again. Leslie and I tied it around our waists this time and braced against the thwarts. For two hours we held it while Uncle Johnny towed us carefully through the storm.

There were no further incidents. Joe never got his engine started again; and when we were at last being hauled into the harbor between the piers and then around into the still water of the basin with the wind merely whining above our heads and the breakers roaring on the beach outside, John sat up, ran his hands through his hair, and looked around. When we tied up to the dock, he climbed out of the boat and went off alone without a word to anyone. Leslie and I were exhausted. While we were getting up energy for the mile-long walk to the village, we suddenly became aware of our fisherman friends' reaction to the adventure. Joe and Uncle Johnny were bending over Joe's motor and talking about its failure in the unmistakable language of workmen with a puzzling breakdown to repair.

They were still talking when we left them to it, our thanks having been brushed off, and undertook what seemed an endless journey home. Bed never looked so hospitable, and my mother's attempt to elicit the story of the night was interrupted by the sleep which overcame us both.

John's breakdown was something that could hardly be kept secret, although neither Leslie nor I mentioned it to anyone at the factory. But John, so far as could be told, had put the whole thing completely out of his mind. It was probably some time before anyone ventured to speak of it in his hearing; he was, after all, the same big bully he had been before. But he avoided us; and when a meeting was inevitable, the conversation concerned pretty strictly whatever matter was in hand. Still, there had been two witnesses. And, if nothing was said, there was something in the air that John must have found nearly unbearable.

Thirty-five

My friendship with Frank Forster was not made firm in any dramatic way; it simply grew and deepened and solidified until it was one of the most reliable bracings of my life. Leslie was a year older than I, Frank a year younger; so Leslie moved on to the University of Pennsylvania first. I followed the next year, and Frank came to join us in normal sequence. All of us made many new friends during these separations, but none of us made any so close; and whenever we were together there was a sense of completeness we never felt so strongly when we were apart.

There were two of the Forsters—Linn, the elder, and Frank, the younger. They were of Welsh extraction, small-made, wiry, curly-haired, and neat. But Linn was blond and Frank very dark. Linn, being a little older, was apt to patronize us; but we took instruction badly, and he was often discouraged with us—something which also operated to draw us together. As we gradually became friends, I fitted rather nicely between them; and in 1910, when Linn went off to the Rensselaer Polytechnic Institute, intent on becoming an engineer, their mother, who was a widow, suggested that since their quarters were fitted up for two I might as well move in. This may have been a despairing acceptance of the inevitable, for Frank and I were finding it necessary to see a good deal of each other every day; at any rate, the suggestion was made, and I accepted. It was like legitimizing a common-law marriage, being a recognition of fact already established. But actually her approval of me was always a qualified one.

The Forsters were completely and unalterably orthodox, and they were bound to regard me as somewhat exotic, if for no other reason than that my country background was different from theirs. My preferences in all the matters of daily life— food, dress, manners—were village ones. But, on the other hand, I had moved into an environment I wanted to succeed in, so I was teachable. The weight with which both the Forster boys bore down on a certain pin-striped suit I had felt was in good style cured me of what may have been a tendency to flamboyancy in that direction. I never again ventured even a noticeable necktie. Fifty years later I often found myself asking whether Frank would approve a suiting suggested by a tailor. They taught me that I had been wearing my hair too long and instructed a neighborhood barber in cropping it. That too became a persistent directive. The general effort was to shape me so that I too would sink into the background, possess decorous manners, curb any tendency to exhibitionism, and be acceptable by their standards.

This will be rocognized as the sort of influence exerted on newcomers in the best private schools. It was sheer luck that I ran into it in Buffalo. The Forster boys had gone to grade school and were now going to Masten Park. They had had to, since their father was gone and their mother was educating them on a slender income. But she had made them genteel, and it was no superficial gloss. They had accepted it as an iron code. They expected me to consent to its governance as the price of friendship. And I did.

Having this sort of influence on me, the Forsters might be supposed to have shaped more than my manners. They expected their views of the world to be accepted too. Those were conservative views, Republican and upper-class ones, as a matter of course. They were the sort who blandly and without question exclude from consideration any suggestion of departure. They knew well enough that I remained unconvinced, but among us my unorthodoxies were not discussed. Disapproval was made thoroughly manifest without any attempt at proselytizing. If I chose not to accept the better way, I would in time come around. If I did not, it would be too bad for me and perhaps it ought to be ignored.

By then, however, dissimulation was with me a fairly well-developed habit. Living, as the Tugwells always had, in a Republican environment, they ordinarily preferred to keep the peace by not being offensively different. My mother, of course, had outbreaks. She took pleasure of an intense sort in baiting a women's circle, for instance, during a political campaign; and she sometimes stirred up an indignation that was not quickly forgotten. But neither my father nor I took any pleasure in such ventures, he because he was not much interested in politics anyway, and I because my ideas were more unorthodox than I dared admit. I certainly never exposed them in the Forster circle. But all my new family required of me was outward conformance, which, I am sure, they believed would in time turn into an inner conviction. It could hardly be otherwise with any well-trained boy.

Intellectually, Frank was inquiring enough—within limits; but those limits were for him like those nearly invisible fences consisting of one strand of wire and so charged that the most immense and ferocious animals accept confinement without rebellion. He seemed to function only within a certain range. I was made to feel that if I wanted to crawl under or jump over he would always be there in the pasture, placidly expecting me to discover my error, then to become lonely, and finally to return. Whereupon we would pick up where we had left off. I must say that for some years it was effective.

Mostly because of physical separation, but partly because of differing interests, Frank and I afterward grew apart. This has always seemed too bad. Both of us had invested so much in what we jointly possessed that a lifetime would not have been too long for gathering the returns on it. When he came home from war in 1919 he became a businessman in Buffalo, among our old associates, and was soon as prosperous as he deserved. I broke out of one environment after another and acquired new friends—and, I am sorry to say, enemies. He would never say so, but the suggestion has always been clear that I ought to know better, but that anyway it was never too late; he and I could always take up where we had left off.

There were few of my friendships later on that could honestly be said to be independent of accidental association or ideological agreement. But these are the most precious sort, and such as I have had, I feel grateful for. Leslie and I, although he was an engineer and I a teacher of social subjects, always agreed in everything that mattered. There were always things Frank and I could not even discuss. There were also people we could not see together, and of course ideas repellent to him and attractive to me. He would have been horrified at the thought of my developing into something of a socialist. He was an individualist, and so far as he allowed himself an economic philosophy, competition was its theme. He went ahead with his preparations for life without doubt or hesitation. This required that he should finish high school and then spend four years at the Wharton School, learning the techniques of competitive success. For one of his intelligence there would be no difficulty in such a scheme. He was good in mathematics and accounting; he took to finance, insurance, and such subjects; and he could always pass his examinations in sociology, English, and history. He went through with his program successfully and quietly. I am certain that in all his life he never made a speech to more than half a dozen people or took up a cause that would be noticed by anyone but his friends. He has always been a good man. But I could not be good in that way.

There were other friends and other interests in my life while I was at Masten Park.[1] Some of the friends were literary; in

---

[1] It can be of no importance to anyone but ourselves that some of these associations were ones that would be remembered for a lifetime; but perhaps I may mention a few names of those who were then in school but afterward had interesting careers of various sorts: William Bryson, Norman Weigel, the

fact, the literary society almost at once took me in and encouraged me to work for the *Masten Park Chronicle*. Just preceding me by a class or two, there had been two members of this group who were already notable. These were David Lawrence and Hilmar Baukhage, both of whom had careers in journalism of such prominence that they were always spoken of, particularly by their teachers, with immense pride. How my teachers viewed my own public career in later years, I never found out. But I could infer what that view was. Whenever an anniversary of any sort was celebrated, Lawrence and Baukhage were on hand to grace it; I was never invited.

If my teachers even then had doubts about my respectability, they were probably justified. And for more reasons than they would have cited. Apart from developing unorthodox opinions, I was taking less and less trouble to establish the background for them. My neglect of this sort became indefensible. I read less widely and gave less time to it than I had ever done before. This, I suppose, was because reading had always been a recreation for me, and now my afternoons and evenings were taken up with desultory sociability and with sports of one sort or another. The studious bent which had been habitual before now lay fallow, and it stayed that way until I went on to Philadelphia.

The Forster home was a tiny house on Masten Street, just south of Utica. The second floor was mostly Frank's and mine. We had specially made single beds which became couches in the daytime, and altogether we had there a den-like retreat. If so disposed, we could study; but more often it was filled with friends of hilarious bent. And Frank and I, with the resistance to sleep characteristic of youth, could carry on long conversations far into the night.

We went together a good deal to the YMCA, for we both had some ambition to be athletic, or at least to keep in good

Schopf brothers, Ralph Brett, Nelson Hubbell, Porter Steel, Remington Bird, Albert Cutler, Eugene Summers, Harold Brookings, Charles Goldberg, Dalton Meeks, John Lansill, Rex Crandall, Walter Dieckman.

condition. Frank was too small for football, but he did have one of the finest physiques and most efficient co-ordinative systems I have ever seen. It got to be a regular source of amusement for me to watch bigger lads presume on his diminutive size and find themselves in trouble. He was a good swimmer too, and we often used the YMCA pool. Occasionally we went to classes in the gymnasium, but mostly we played such games as basketball and volleyball with pickup teams. As I have said, there was no gymnasium at Masten Park, and our excursions downtown in the afternoon were fairly regular.

In my first Masten Park autumn I thought I might try for the football team. It was the thing to do. I hardly had the weight for it, but enormous size was not the consideration then that it afterward became. I had never played before—we had not been numerous enough in Wilson—but I thought I might have some qualifications. I was fast on my feet and was used to baseball and hockey. I liked teamwork; it gave me real satisfaction to be merged in a group with a defined purpose working hard for the result it was intended to reach.

I was not able that season to attain more than second-string status, but I was allowed to play in a few games and so earned my letter. I was proud to be called up to the platform along with the worthier players in an assembly at the season's end and be awarded the insignia I had earned. This was the only time Dr. Fosdick had spoken to me since giving me the advice to leave school and go to work. It was the last time, too, that he noticed my existence—an arrangement that was all right with me. I was on shaky ground still, and I knew it very well.

But football, much as I liked it, was strenuous. Bob Summers, our coach, believed in hard practice, and we had plenty of it. Bob was a young lawyer then, and he was not paid for coaching; there was no provision at all for such official athletics. How he managed to spend so much time at an endeavor out of sheer love for his old school is not at all clear to me. For he was a struggling and ambitious attorney who afterward became a well-known member of the Buffalo Bar. He had almost nothing to work with. We had lockers and a couple of cold showers in the dismal basement alongside the heating plant and the coal-bins, but there was no practice field and of course no stadium. We made use of a vacant field behind the German-American brewery. It was littered with beer bottles, old cans, and cobbles; and to this day I associate football with the smell of fermenting grain. But we worked there faithfully in the autumn afternoons, sometimes until darkness made further practice impracticable.

Bob had a clever Irish boy named Sullivan for quarterback, and it was around him that the team was built. Quarterbacks were more depended on then than in later versions of the game; they had more freedom and fewer instructions from the bench. Like most high school teams, we had difficulty finding heavy linesmen, but Charles Goldberg had both the weight and the brains to be a stalwart. He rather adopted me as a protégé, and most of what I learned he taught me. I aspired to be a halfback, so that my position was just back of Charles, and he gave me directions and encouragement. To the extent that I was a member, I played opposite Nelson Hubbel, the handsome right half who was our flashiest player and the school hero. I tried my best to be worthy of the association.

Somehow we did become a real team. Among ourselves there were few rivalries and there was an earnest merging of effort. Our objective was quite clear. We were to win, if we could, a schedule of games with other high schools. To do it, we were to use every energy and all the cleverness we could command. We were to accept direction from Bob Summers unquestioningly. This we did, and we had at least moderate success. I say we, but actually I never became more than a substitute. It was a situation I felt quite justified, but I worked as hard as though I too might expect to become a Nelson Hubbel.

The members of that team became very special friends. I count it as one of the tragedies of life that after graduation I hardly ever saw one of them again. We were so close, and then suddenly we were so far apart, and not because any of us would have had it so. It was the unhappy way things were arranged. I was, after all, not a Buffalonian as most of the others were. And in after years I would never have occasion to visit the old neighborhood, and not very often even Buffalo. I am inclined to mourn a little about this. For it was neither the first nor the last time I should make friends and lose them.

We seldom linger over the balance to be struck between the gains of change and the losses of broken associations, perhaps because our choices are not really considered ones. We are apt to weigh lightly the less tangible losses—such as friendships. Yet the transition from village to urban life such as I made required the sacrifice of values I knew were precious. It was that way with many thousands of my contemporaries. Indeed there must have been many who, at one stage or another, refused to go on when the chance came and who simply dropped out, staying where they were. I should not be able to say certainly that they were mistaken. They kept family and friends, put down roots—to use a country locution—and escaped the agitations and anxieties of repeated reorientations. Yet there is this too: neither Sinclairville nor Wilson would continue to stand still. The one would decline, the other would change, and life in neither would be what might have been forecast from my time there.

As I recount in age the successive changes I undertook, they seem to have a reasonable enough sequence. And perhaps the rolling stone did gather some moss—to change the metaphor, some memories to be recounted. The footnote I must add to this, however, is that most of my endeavors were less successful than I should like them to have been, and this means that whenever I recount them I find myself actively wondering how they might have been better planned and executed. All too often I can see where mistakes were made. And in retrospect I worry almost as much as I did when the original decisions and actions were being taken.

At any rate, I would not soon regain the team élan I had at Masten Park out behind the steamy brewery and in the slate-walled locker room—not soon, but still not too long afterward.

Three times at the university I would find the same loyalties, the same friendships, and the same willingness to sink self in a larger whole—once in my fraternity, once in the group working for the *Daily Pennsylvanian,* and then in the Wharton faculty I joined even before I was graduated.

But it still remained to be seen what my Buffalo experiences were leading to. The strain of the football work had to be paid for. We had had no training supervision, and no one had ever paid any attention to our physical condition. A checkup after the season was over, and an honest admission of my occasional struggles for breath, resulted in a stern warning from Dr. Rochester that I must not play football again—and indeed that I must be careful indefinitely about extreme exertion of any sort. So my excursion into the athletic life was finished. I was in permanent pawn to asthma.

Thirty-six

The prohibition against football or other of the more strenuous sports did not affect me in any important way; it merely closed one kind of recreation. But my time was fully enough occupied. For one thing, I was going out nights now in a highly organized fashion. There were enough calls, parties, dances, theater-goings, and so on, in the Masten Park circle to furnish amusement for the most devoted follower of such pursuits. And presently I seemed to have created for myself quite a society life. The sums I spent for theater tickets, cab fares, flowers, candy, and the other incidentals of social activity must have raised some question in my father's mind. But I have thought since that he probably approved. It was simply another version of his own amusements when he had been a young man in the Sinclairville of the 'eighties. Besides, he had a knack, then at its height, for making money; and I heard amazingly little about bills that were really considerable. I had accounts with tailors, haberdashers, florists, and livery stables. But they were always paid without comment. If I sometimes found myself a little ridiculous, it is not strange. I might have been thought anxious to become a society boy; it was not really in character.

Especially during the winter there was a succession of subscription balls got up by various school and other organizations. These were very formal. The ritual required full dress, the presentation of flowers, and transport in a horse-drawn coach —for these had not yet been supplanted by taxicabs for such affairs. And my memory calls up—pleasantly, I must admit—

many a winter night, perhaps blizzardy and mean outside, when after dinner a most careful dressing began in our upstairs retreat. The aim was to be spotlessly turned out by about nine, when the coach was due. The flowers had been sent in the afternoon. The ride to the young lady's house took place in dignified stiffness—collars were high, clothes were tight, and the ensemble had at least to survive intact the entrance to the ballroom. The lady's house reached and the coachman told to wait, the pleasure of greeting her took place in the parlor. My standards were high; and my young women, descending the stairs in their evening gowns, corsage fresh, hair elaborately done, gold or silver slippers—and a bit of ankle—visible beneath the lifted flounces then so numerous, were really a delight, and I was often consciously glad that I could afford the paraphernalia required for such excursions.

The coach smelled a little of the livery stable, but for five dollars—as I recall—the Buffalo equipages were put at the disposal of customers until three or four in the morning, and if there was some smell, there was broadcloth and there were long springs to rock a couple of young lovers on their way home. The dancing or assembly halls were not too far, usually just over on the west side, and, arriving there, a pair of carefully got up newcomers became part of a rustling and glittering crowd. Evening clothes do wonders for women, and when they are young and happy women, with no more than the hazards of ordinary American life to look forward to, the beauty has a special quality. The girls I recall were rosy, full of grace, and warm; and young men are so constructed as to have no more than nominal resistance to such charms. At least I was.

Those were the days of waltzes and two-steps, with an occasional Virginia reel or Paul Jones. Cards, small folders with fancy cords, suitable to be kept as souvenirs, were made out for each dance, often sometime in advance. I should guess that many a grandmother's attic trunk still holds carefully tied bundles of these dance programs, evidence of conquests or disappointments, but anyway of excitements such as no one has in sober age.

The carefully arranged cards left little room for that sudden surge of mutual adoration which makes a boy and a girl find it urgently important to be together for more than one dance. But there were possibilities in a trading process that was a recognized procedure. So such emergencies could, within limits, be arranged for. There were one or two memorable occasions when I came back from such a party with a different partner from the one I had escorted so carefully there. My first had not been abandoned exactly, but an exchange had been arranged. This must have involved prodigies of bargaining effort, but the emotion inspiring it was an urgent one, and it overcame all difficulties. The sudden focusing of interest aroused by a hitherto unobserved grace of movement, a newly seen smile, or perhaps the glimpse of usually hidden charms revealed by a low-cut gown—something of the sort had been irresistible. Giving way to it and overcoming the obstacles to partnering was a satisfying activity. I never regretted the effort involved in such pursuits. As we creaked home in the big coach, kept from the freezing wind by robes and cushions, the world could seem centered in a moment and a place. A girl in his arms is heaven enough for any young man.

The girls of my youth seem to me to have been lovelier than those I see around me now. They have long since become grandmothers, as I have become a grandfather—one of those pursuits became that serious; but perhaps I am mistaken about this, merely aged. Still, I am under the impression that girls —ordinary girls, not athletes—got more exercise in those pedestrian times. And there was certainly less resort to beauty aids. They seem to me to have been healthier, to have had a higher bloom. They were plumper too, unless I am mistaken. For dieting was not yet fashionable, and curves were not regarded as deplorable. I expect my granddaughters will set me straight about this. But if they move through their world with half the grace their grandmother had, they too will be objects of delighted pursuit. What am I saying? Some of them already are.

I had no illusion about the quality of the society I moved in so pleasurably. It was not Buffalo's elite. There would have been, in fact, several grades between my circle and that of the Rumsey-Goodyear-Milburn-Schoellkopf-Knox-Cary-Bissell set —the real Four Hundred. The city's annals are crowded with the extravagances of that upper class—not so spectacular in the years I write about as in the genuine Gilded Age, but still entertaining to read about. They seem incredible to a later generation; they seemed almost incredible to my own; still, they were not so far past as to be quite forgotten.

The society pages of 1910 must have reported only faded imitations of the events of ten or twenty years earlier. Surviving matriarchs were doubtless saying even then to their descendants that theirs was a stale and cheerless existence; things had been livelier and more colorful when the elite had really ruled the scene. A few times I touched the fringes of the then surviving social circle, but only at the larger charity balls and other such events. Often my coach passed those of the aristocracy along Delaware Avenue, and occasionally I made acquaintances who might have become friends; but actually I was happy with those I already had. I never, so to speak, moved up in the scale.

In the John T. Horton account of the society I have been speaking of there is a suitably sardonic account of the counterpart in Buffalo of the McAllister-Astor regime in New York. The show put on in pre-income-tax times, even in our provincial metropolis, was worthy of American ingenuity. And its vulgarity was an adequate counterpart of the way the wealth thus squandered had been acquired.[1]

Buffalonian businessmen had no need to apologize to those in other parts. Their exploitation of their environment was total. They fought the workers with a vigor not equaled often

[1] See especially the chapter titled "The Gilded Age" in the Horton *History of Northwestern New York* (Lewis Historical Publishing Company, 1947).

in any other region, and they yielded to demands only at the end of riotous rebellions. They were the loudest of Americans in their appeals for tariff and other privileges; and the loudest, as well, in their support of the free competitive system. Their lawyers were among the nation's leaders in developing yellow-dog contracts, fellow-servant rules, evasions of the anti-trust acts, and blocks against welfare legislation. They were, to a later view, incredibly arrogant and selfish. And their society was no more than a fair representation of their view of their own importance. In my time the vulgarities were somewhat modified and the crudities damped down; there were boys in the family coming home from Yale and Princeton, where the elite was taught not to be ostentatious. But the attitudes were the same. A man's business was his own to run as he liked, workers were ungrateful when they made demands, and luxury was the necessary incentive to call out initiative. Also, the income tax was still nothing to worry about. There was plenty of money, and it was a public service to spend it.

If the Cary-Rumsey-Goodyear gilt was somewhat tarnished in the first decade of the century, it nevertheless had the authentic *nouveau riche* gloss. Some bloody battles had been fought, and some concessions had been made; there was no longer quite the same confidence in superiority. But if it had been ten or fifteen years earlier that things had been at their best, they were still not too bad. There was no suffering—except a certain mental anguish, often voiced—along the avenue. The Waverley Balls had been discontinued, although they were still recalled with nostalgia. The last of these particular galas had, in fact, taken place in the home of Bronson Case Rumsey as long ago as 1898; they had been succeeded by less elaborate charades in more recent years. But there were still splendid entertainments in the châteaux and manor houses; the Charity Ball and even the 74th Regiment Ball were glamorous and elaborate. But perhaps it indicates the dimming refulgence of the really glorious era that a country boy could have gone to

several of the more public entertainments for several years
during his stay in Buffalo.[2]

The season in Buffalo made the most of its wintry possibilities.
The use of sleighs, like that of coaches in summer, was giving
way to motorcars; but smart equipages, with peppery teams,
were still commonly seen on the avenues; and in Delaware
Park, just after the heavier snows, there was a show of jingling
sleighs filled with fur-clad riders, rosy-cheeked in the cold. As

[2] I find Horton's account of the Waverley Balls so fascinating that I must
quote from his account of them: "In approaching this display of metroplitan
splendor"—Mr. Horton had been speaking of the original New York show—
"Buffalo came closest in the winters of 1872, 1888, and in the spring of 1898,
when the Waverley Balls were given in the great French house of Bronson
Case Rumsey in Delaware Avenue. Typical of these was the Ball of '88, a
year that spent its course while yet the Gilded Age was in full glitter. The
Ball differed in several ways from those described by McAllister. For one
thing the ladies did not dance with electric lights on their heads. This probably would have been a technical possibility. Since 1886 the Thompson-
Houston Electric Light Company had been furnishing the new illumination on
a small scale in the city; and no doubt some of their experts could have wired
the ladies' heads as prettily as it was done in New York. At the Waverley
Balls, however, this would have been an anachronism. Sir Walter had known
nothing of electric lights; if possible, his characters had known less. The
Waverley Balls were pageants from the pages of Sir Walter. Thus, they had
a literary tinge that the New York spectacles lacked. The tinge was especially
notable at the Ball of '88, when William Howells, appearing in ordinary
evening attire, was announced by the flunkey on the stair as 'Gentle Reader.'
In this role Howells was unique at the Ball; perhaps almost unique, in comparison with smart society, even on less festive occasions; for, as *The Morning
Express* observed, there was much ignorance of Scott in Buffalo at the time.
Of this state of affairs Miss Grace Carew Sheldon shrewdly took note. In the
next summer she went to Scotland and thus prepared herself to give lectures
on the author of the Waverley novels over against another Waverley Ball."
Nevertheless, the ball of '88 was a great success. "As the guests descended
into the great hall they paid their respects to the hosts and their ladies whose
position was on a dais opposite the stairs. Laurence Dana Rumsey stood for
Waverley; Edward Mavius for Saladin; Dr. Charles Cary for Richard the
Lion Hearted; and Bronson Rumsey Jr. was his squire, Blondel. In a petty-
coat of white brocade with bunches of colored flowers, the rest of her gown a
gobelin blue, a close fitting coif of the same on her head, Mrs. Laurence Dana
Rumsey appeared as Queen Henrietta Maria. Mrs. Edward Mavius, arrayed
in a white satin gown embroidered in gold, a green velvet, fur-edged mantle
on her head, was the Princess Anna Comena . . .

"The gay company of more than a hundred couples being at last foregathered in the great hall, there drifted presently from behind a screen of
palms, the sound of minstrelsy a-tuning. Soon the music took shape and
precision and the Ball opened with the Earl of Leicester leading Queen
Elisabeth in the Grand March . . ."

a reminder of village childhood, I often saw boys running after these rigs with sleds to be hitched on behind. They shouted and tumbled under following horses' hoofs, but it was so much a custom that the danger was usually averted. It was not beyond the dignity of the drivers to accommodate themselves to small boys' demands. Those boys also had the park's hills for sledding and its lakes for skating. Winter at its best turned into something of a carnival. On certain evenings the city band established itself by the side of one of the lakes and played for the circling skaters. Those of us who were of a romantic age could use the ice as a ballroom floor; we danced on the glassy expanse, skates giving us a freedom mere feet could not match.

Winter, too, was a time for the theater. The Star and the Teck, as well as Shea's vaudeville, were then at their best. The Star was not new—it had been opened in 1888—but the gold paint had been freshened, and the plush draperies had been renewed; they were a deep rich red; and coming in from the wintry streets was agreeably warming. It was a small house, but it attracted week by week Broadway plays and musicals, very often with the original companies. How well I recall them! There was *The Merry Widow* with Fritzi Scheff, *The Red Mill* with Montgomery and Stone, and Raymond Hitchcock in successive comedies. The small theater was better suited to Wilde, Pinero, Shaw, and their contemporaries than to musicals, but we had both and liked them equally. Somehow, however, Strauss, Lehár, and Victor Herbert with their fragile and romantic gaiety seemed to have more appeal for me just then. I went nearly every week. Sometimes it was the larger Teck, instead of the Star. There, among others, I saw Clyde Fitch's *The City* and a beautiful performance of William Gillette in *Secret Service*.

The theaters were always full, as I recall. It was not yet fashionable to go South, away from the searching Canadian winds. And the castles on the upper west side were all open in the winter, their inhabitants home from Lakewood-on-Chautauqua, Niagara-on-the-Lake, or the hunting country in the Genesee

Valley, where the vast holdings of the Wadsworth family were still intact; or even from places farther away—Saratoga, Newport, Bar Harbor, or the watering places of Europe. The social hegira was a summer phenomenon. In winter the fashionable folk all came home. Then for a few months the big houses bustled with activity, balls and entertainments went on night after night, the stables produced horses and fine equipages, and all the arts were patronized.

From some of this, at least, lesser folk might benefit. They might not have the front-row seats at the theater or the boxes at the great balls, but they could, in their appropriate degree, be present. It was all a life that most people—workers, tradesmen, and their families—might read or hear about with the same sense of remoteness that they might read or hear about the doings of European royalty. But it was not yet a time of persistent restlessness. There were occasional outbursts, especially when times were bad, and there was actual hunger or cold, and society went on with its customary gay schedule; but the welfare state was still far over the reformers' horizon, not even a realizable dream, so far as anyone could see. And the beneficiaries of unregulated capitalism were as yet not too much worried by intimations of change.

Thirty-seven

Even if I was spending time on amusements which ought to have been spent in worthier ways, I recall that year as notable for one advance. I had a fair plunge into economic and political studies under the direction of Jay Stagg. He was not a particularly inspiring teacher, but his classes were smallish and we had opportunities for discussion. He was a serious man with a small goatee which, together with an aloof manner, made him seem a little pompous. But he gave me a real sight of an important intellectual country. It was that region where businessmen operated and politicians competed for position. His lessons had to do with the bread-and-butter matters all my other studies failed to touch; it attempted to explain what those people I saw on the streets, in the saloons, in the factories and stores were actually doing.

This feel of reality was stronger in our political discussions than in our more formal economic ones. For Stagg was interested in the conduct of government and had himself tried to make sense of what was going on. When we got beyond the civics texts, which were mere outlines of governmental anatomy, we were pretty much on our own. It could not be said that we arrived at any systematization of our subject matter, but we had some lively talk and reached for a few generalizations. Bagehot was mentioned; so was Woodrow Wilson, whose *Congressional Government* was so much a standard treatise that it was in our school library. And before we got through we reached back to the Constitution makers. But the main interest was in Buffalo's own situation. This could hardly have been worse. The form of the government was awkward, the politicians were corrupt, and the city was perennially in a state of scandal. So we had object lessons enough of that sort. But Stagg called our attention to the very different situation in the Ohio cities where Johnson, Whitlock, Jones, and Hunt had fought and won some furious battles. These were the subject matter of the muckrakers, who had already passed into history. It was at least interesting to Stagg that I had heard of them, and he treated me in consequence with respect that was entirely new in my educational experience. For the first time I was able to exchange opinions and observations with a teacher on a plane that approached equality.

It was different with economics. There we were stiffer and more formal, because for one thing we were on stranger ground and for another because we were tied to systematic explanations that pretended to the status of law—like those we had learned to accept in physics and chemistry. I cannot recall for certain what text it was we followed. It may have been one of several, but I believe it to have been an abbreviation of one by Richard T. Ely which was then so popular as a college text.[1] Whoever the author, however, I now know that the content would have been about the same. For economics made pretensions that politics did not aspire to; the one called itself a science; the other knew itself to be an art. If this posture of the economists was unjustified, it at least had wide acceptance then. There was, to begin with, a set of assumptions founded on common sense that were not questioned. And the deductions from these

[1] Richard T. Ely was then professor at Wisconsin. The text in question was a short version of his large book and was prepared by Professor Wicker. Ely was another Chautauquan, having been born in Ripley; and he was the author, as I have noted, of several books circulated through the Reading Circles. One of these, considered rather daring, was a discussion of socialism. The daring consisted in a reasoned criticism rather than the denunciation most writers resorted to. Ely had a long and useful life, much of it devoted to the specialized field of land economics. He was a president in its early years of the American Economic Association and a friend of Simon Nelson Patten of Pennsylvania.

had taken on so elaborate and technical a form that no text writer among the older generation of American economists had attempted to do more than refine conclusions. There were economists who had very different ideas—I have mentioned Patten and Veblen—but neither was a writer of elementary texts, and their influence on teachers was still to be felt. What I was introduced to was a set of rules or laws which purported to make rational the affairs of the economic world. It was a bold intellectual venture, and it would have taken much more learned students than would be found in high schools, or even in colleges then, to have offered reasonable criticisms. Most were like me, I am sure; they learned the laws and believed—until they were disillusioned—that they had explanations of diverse and puzzling phenomena which otherwise had no semblance of order.

Laissez-faire economics of the English school, which our own economists accepted, has all the beauties of geometrical simplicity. It seems to explain much in a few formulas and actually to become, as it elaborates, a complete system. Its acceptance, to one disturbed by the disorder and naughtiness of the real world, was a relief. At least it was that way with me, and I learned its theorems with an enthusiastic concentration I had never felt for mathematics. Like many others, I assumed that the supply-and-demand formula, for instance, was an active law operating in the market place. I was different only in not holding onto this belief for long.

That there could be a unifying set of principles in economic affairs was an idea that had congenial associations in my mind. My philosophical indoctrination, gentle as it had been, had run together with the general assumption that one increasing purpose—as Tennyson had suggested—was operating to create a better world. That there was a disturbing vagueness about direction, I was aware, and at times I speculated about it. I was beyond the literal acceptance of fundamentalism of any sort, including religion; not beyond belief in the Christian ideals of brotherhood, but unable any more to take literally the

demonology of the Old Testament or the mythology of the
New. But that there had been a beginning in the simplicity of
one-celled life and an evolution toward complex mammals
had become self-evident. There was a most marvelous and
evidently continuous development behind the organism which
was man. It had finally given him the power of thinking and
of self-direction. Thinking could even be about matters far
removed from his own interests, at least his daily ones. To
ascribe this sequence to chance was to rely on an incredible
concurrence of events. There must, it seemed to me, be a
guiding urge, a principle, a hidden hand. So also there must
be some end in view, some criterion, toward which the human
species moved. There was order in the universe, but it was an
order too complex and too magnificent to be accidental.

Still, I was troubled by certain questions. There were mistakes,
or what seemed like mistakes, along the way, if a presiding
intelligence was accepted; and this was true even if it was
said that immense leeway must be allowed for the operation of
evolution. Individual life and death went to make up the
continuous improvement of the species; social life and death
could be accepted too. But there had been crises in the history
of man when he seemed to have survived at all only by good
fortune, and this was not a principle to be relied on. It did seem
that the serious struggles for survival might have ended in failure
as well as in success. And then man would have become
extinct. Some large societies had thus come to a dead end.
There were the Scythians, the Syrians, the Mayans, the Aztecs,
the inhabitants of Mesa Verde and the Gila Valley. They had
disappeared into the nothingness of the past, some of them
without evident descendants or cultural contributions to the
race. Still, there was the fact that man had actually survived,
had multiplied, and on the whole had prospered. Perhaps it
ought to be said that the more dangerous his passage from the
past to the present, the more it must seem that some intelligence
outside himself had been at work.

For a clumsily inquiring youth, it was a dilemma. To ascribe survival to a series of accidents was to accept an explanation even more incredible than that which rested on a directing Providence. One thing I knew. My generation of intellectuals would be denied the simple but comforting faith of the churches. How the eighteenth-century enlightenment had transformed the gentle intercessions of the Virgin with the stern heavenly Father into a more sophisticated interpretation of unifying principles, I was yet to understand. I had no knowledge of any religion but the Protestant one in which I had been raised. Already I thought its theology demanded more surrender of thought than could be expected. I had discovered transcendentalism. There was a time when I carried around in my pocket a volume of Emerson, bound in limp leather, which I read whenever I had a few moments of leisure. There was a goodness, a rich belief in the worthwhileness of life in Emerson; it went a long way to dispel the dark suggestion that all of us were living only because of fortunate chances. The creative springs in man must be the agent of a purpose, and that purpose must be advancement toward perfection.

This was a boy's own reaching for something beyond the voids of vast evolving mechanisms. I gradually connected it with the social studies I found myself attracted to. Man did not live alone. The societies he formed were like organisms too, wonderfully shaped by evolution. Through them too a purpose ran, or at least a principle of improvement. The social studies would make a contribution.

I had had a glimpse, in Miss Gemmel's biology teaching, of something to hold to. The marvelous adaptations of organic life, showing themselves finally in structure, had their counterparts in social groups. I even saw that one old difficulty was becoming less a puzzle. Darwin had been unable to explain certain phenomena of evolution except by accepting the family as the evolutional unit. Natural selection must work through groups as well as individuals. In a way I had arrived at an idea which would for me be a lasting foundation for my own thinking. There was more that I did not know than I could guess at, many gaps, many unanswered questions; but the transfer of my interest from individuals to groups was satisfactorily accomplished. The social sciences were the area of inquiry for me.

One of the worrisome gaps was filled by that stripped-down economics I found in the high school text. For here events, certain of them, in society were conceived as interacting to produce one evaluating result—a price. It was not explained as good or fortunate, but it was presented as inevitable in a society that was virtuous—that is, one which was free, enlightened, and industrious. Social groups were formed also—and this was the connection with individual biology—through competition and natural selection, just as an individual reached a status in the survival struggle. And just as natural selection operated to select the fittest individual, so economic competition operated to select the best economic unit—the industry or business.

It was inevitable that in this there should be a passage to morals. Natural conditions—that is, freedom and competition—ought to be carefully maintained so that the best individuals and the best social groups, including businesses, should survive. To the economists it was self-evident that survival under these conditions was the mark of virtue. The survivor deserved his success. It was right that he should have rewards and honors. That there must be some flaw in this reasoning, I was wary enough to suspect even then. No one had to look far to see instances of reward for behavior it would be idiotic to classify as deserving. What, indeed, was the lesson of the muckrakers? It was that vice was generally rewarded rather than virtue, and that the way of the reformer was hard. And great fortunes were founded on exploitation of workers and consumers in obvious contradiction of the economists' syllogism.

But the answer, I learned, was that in such cases there had been a breakdown in proper public policy. Competition had not been kept free. There were monopolists who contradicted the rule. But it was the business of society to see that monopolies were broken up and freedom restored and protected. If the public suffered from exploitation, it was its own fault.

There was no businessman who did not profess to believe in competitive enterprise, even those who were actively engaged in suppressing it. But it was a Sunday religion. They expected others to believe it while they practiced its opposite. They expected others not only to believe in its virtues but also to assume that it was being practiced. This allowed them the freedom the wicked always have who accept rules in theory but operate without the slightest deference to their guidance.

But what I learned then, and went on learning long afterward, was a very strange lesson, one it was difficult to accept and, when accepted, to understand. The economists who wrote about free competition were regarded as orthodox. Their design for economic society was acceptable. But when they insisted that measures be taken to enforce compliance with the rules, they were marked as dangerous radicals. In fact, most of the economists of my early years in the profession were thus regarded by respectable folk, especially those in the business world. They were, and had to be, against the bigness which became monopoly and exploited other businesses, consumers, and workers. They opposed all the devices used by monopolists—restraint, holding companies, trusts, and so on. The Progressive movement, as I have noted, already past its first strong challenge to big business, was based on this radical acceptance of free competition and the inherent badness of bigness. There had been anti-trust laws since 1890 and two decades of agitation before the first of them were passed; so the controversy I now began to think about, under the first guidance of Jay Stagg, was older than I. It had been going on, in fact, when I had been born. I could hardly have foreseen that it would still be going on when I was an old man. In my seventieth year, responsible officials of great electric-supply corporations would be fined and sent to jail for behaving exactly as the first conspirators had done who had precipitated the anti-trust laws of the 1890s.

This clinging to one code as a standard of morality while

behaving according to another which contradicted it was, of course, inherent in the system of free competition—capitalism, it came to be called. Monopoly was the end to which competition came. That it could be prevented somehow was the official progressive belief. It was a complete paradox. I was from the first uneasy about it. But I was persuaded that the economist's radicalism was an activist answer to exploitation. I was at least in sympathy with—and would soon be a member of—a guild which did not accept big business at its own valuation and which had a program of reform.

With what I regarded as a new sophistication, I had a fresh look around, at Buffalo, at my nation, bulging with industrial giants. And I began to think of government not only as a caretaker and policeman but as somehow responsible for maintaining freedom. It was the expression of man becoming socialized but also trying to maintain his individuality and enhance his well-being. I had come a long way from the village view of government as small associations which grew into fire and police departments, provided for schools, water supplies, cemeteries, streets, and commons, and made regulations having to do with safety and health. I already saw it as an expression of man's effort to control his environment and shape it as a means to his ends. If at the moment I accepted the view that its most important national duty was that of suppressing unfair competition, that view soon ran into questions having to do with the ends implied even in this policy. And the ends were never so simple as the mere policing of an economic melee. There were positive responsibilities. Much of what men wanted could be got only through their own creation—government. A fire department, a water supply, a public park were not different in nature from food or housing or security from the risks of life. But I arrived at this a good deal later.

My thinking had followed an ordinary course. I had begun at first to differentiate between the various duties of government. Some were repressive and regulatory; some were the supplying of wanted services or even goods. Town, village, county, city, state, nation—all governments were alike in this. Studying all of them and their interrelations in our system, I came to understand that they differed only in scale. They had been created to keep order, to mediate, and to furnish services—including security. There were differences about how far these services should go and also how they should be paid for. But there was a discernible rule in this. Take roads, for instance. They had at first been the responsibility of neighborhoods, then townships, then counties, states, and finally the nation. Along the way there had been constant redefinitions of responsibility, but there had been a steady extension of national interest in the system of highways. So too keeping the peace was ordinarily a local job, but it soon and often became too much for town or city police.

There were arguments about these matters as civilization advanced, but not disruptive ones. Most of the bitter differences arose about economic matters. There were those who believed that all these were properly to be left to private enterprise; others believed them to be the responsibility of government. There were serious conflicts over these issues. It was important to discover that even in a high school class we could discuss them without heat or rancor.

Thirty-eight

I have already spoken of Buffalo's industry. All during the nineteenth century, manufacture, mostly of semi-finished products, had been developing: pig iron (out in Lackawanna), brass, copper, wire, timber products (Tonawanda by 1880 was the biggest lumber port in the world), ships, locomotives, threshing and other farm machinery, and paper products, especially wallboard. The Union Bridge Company, at the time when the railroads were being extended most rapidly, was the largest of all the nation's bridge builders. Then of course there were the grain terminals and their subsidiary flour and feed mills which turned the produce of the prairies into flour for Easterners and feed for their horses and cattle. Presently, also, there came electric power from Niagara Falls and, almost at once, the electrochemical and similar industries. And the railroads themselves, centering in Buffalo from the South, the West, and Canada in the North, brought industry in a swelling volume.

The geographic reason for Buffalo's expansion was a cause also of the corruption which, if possible, was more degraded than that of other cities in that notorious age. What Lincoln Steffens had said of Philadelphia—that she was corrupt and contented—was not quite true of Buffalo. Her corruption matched any other city's, but her contentment was confined to the governing elite. There were occasional outbreaks of violent discontent. But since they were vigorously suppressed, they did not hinder growth. The city lay at the lower end of navigation on the Great Lakes, and it was a transfer station on the broad highway from the northern plains to the East. Even when the railroads took much of the older water traffic, they still ran along the level shores and through Buffalo on their routes to the East. The city was neither midwestern nor eastern but belonged somehow to both regions and perhaps it took the worst of each. From the Midwest came its grossness and crudity, its satisfaction in hugeness and in being tough and lavish; from the East came its love of money and its weakness for ostentation. There was sharp division among its classes, a division continually perpetuated by the inrush of foreigners, who for a generation would hardly dare think of themselves as the equals of their prosperous predecessors. Because they had come from the slums and villages of eastern Europe, their standards were primitive. A city whose houses and streets were untended, whose police were corrupt, and whose underworld throve, was not objectionable to immigrants. Such conditions might offend the Germans, but they were swamped by Poles; and matters went from bad to worse.

Still, the vast energies and organizing abilities necessary to managing this monstrous torrent of materials and men were found. Buffalo had ironmasters, shipbuilders, railroad promoters, traders, manufacturers, millers, meat packers, and all the other kinds of businessmen of the time who were so typical as to seem almost caricatures. The grain trade was dominated by Charles W. Evans, George W. Tifft, the Richmonds and the Jewetts; meat packing by Christian Klinck, Richard Bullymore, and Jacob Dold; soapmaking by Frederick, Charles and J. Adam Lauck; tanning by Bronson Case and Dexter Phelps Rumsey; milling by George Urban and W. H. Gratwick; the manufacture of farm implements by J. B. Pitts; timber by Edward and Britain Holmes; iron and steelmaking by Pascal Paoli Pratt and Josiah Letchworth; and so it went through a list with not a Polish and hardly an Irish name on it. They were all British and German.

Along with the enormous expansion of industry, naturally, went the arrangements for its financing; and some of the fanciest work of that ingenious generation is to be found in the records of the Buffalo banks. Mr. Horton has looked into these:

If Pascal Pratt, by ceasing to be an ironmaster, parted company with European noblemen, who kept on being industrialists, by becoming a bank president (he was President of the Manufacturers and Traders, and a Director of the Bank of Buffalo, and the Third National), he ascended to the highest rank of those whom, many years before, the Weltberger had labelled the noblemen of America. This was but half truth since the bank presidents had the substance rather than the trappings of power. In Buffalo they formed a compact and distinguished little chapter; with Elbridge Gerry Spaulding as their aging Dean. How compact they were the connections of the new president of the M. & T. made apparent. On his board sat Francis H. Root, sometime of the Jewett and Root Stove Works, now of Keating and Root of the Leather business. With Root sat Bronson Case Rumsey, to name but the two most prominent industrialists whose counsels helped guide the institution . . .

Other captains of industry and of commerce had similar connections. Jewett M. Richmond, one of the proprietors of the Richmond Elevator Company, had Bronson Case Rumsey and Sherman S. Jewett as colleagues on the Board of the Marine Bank, where sat also Gibson T. Williams, President of the Erie County Savings Bank. Over these gentlemen and their brethren presided Stephen M. Clement, who looked like an Earl and gathered presidencies and directorships as a Grandee of Spain gathered Dukedoms. Around Thomas Thornton of Thornton and Chester, the milling firm, as President of the Bank of Commerce, sat N. C. Scoville of the Car Wheel Works, E. L. Hedstrom of the coal trade, Edmund Hayes, the bridge builder, and James R. Smith of the lumber trade, also President of the Crocker Fertilizer Company. The same magnifico was Vice President of the Merchant's Bank under W. H. Walker, a boot and shoe man, around whose Board gathered the grain merchant, A. P. Wright, the maltster J. B. Manning, the lumber king W. H. Gratwick, the miller George Urban, and that indefatigable promoter of all sorts of enterprises, Jacob F. Schoellkopf.[1]

[1] Op. cit., 231–32.

This was how control was centered and maintained among the industrial aristocrats. But it was supported and given direction by a corps of legal experts who also helped to give Buffalo a reputation for business resourcefulness. Indeed lawyers, industrialists, and financiers were often indistinguishable, as were also lawyers and politicians.[2] For the princes of industry required that government should serve their purposes, a requirement that reached not only into all the city's offices but into the courts and into the state and national legislatures.

Grover Cleveland had been the best known of all this group because he had been pushed onto the national stage, and his history offered a curious lesson. He had been a reform Mayor and Governor; and although he had become a candidate only at the urging of the businessmen when corruption had passed all allowable bounds, they were no more than lukewarm in his behalf until, as President, he demonstrated his essential conservatism. Their connections with grafters, racketeers, and all that underground web of interlaced business and politics, which was characteristic of so many cities, was altogether too close to stand investigation. But Cleveland was a curious reformer. He was impeccably honest, his administration of public affairs was efficient, and he was industrious; but he was not a demagogue, not interested in disclosing scandals, and was, in fact, quite safe and sound. The result was that, in critical times for businessmen he carried them over into a new age relatively unscathed by the ordeal of agrarian and laborite rebellion. He was for sound money as against the Bryanites; he believed that bankers and industrialists, because they had demonstrated ability in business,

2 Some of the more prominent members of the Bar were Eben Carleton Sprague, Daniel N. Lockwood, George W. Clinton, Adelbert Moot, John G. Milburn, and George S. Wardwell. Most of that generation were gone by my time; but the firm names remained proudly on the doors of the older buildings, and there were many sons and grandsons to carry on. The Bar Association of Erie County had been organized as long ago as 1878, and a law school first affiliated with Niagara University of Buffalo had graduated its first class in 1889. But most of the prominent lawyers were graduates of the schools further east, or, like Cleveland, had read in the offices of their elders.

must know what was best for the country; and it was their advice that he relied on. He himself had been a successful corporation lawyer, a self-made one, and others of his sort—such as Richard Olney—were the most trusted members of his official family.

Cleveland was, by my time, a conservative legend. He had not returned to Buffalo to live after having been President. He had furiously resented the clergymen of the city who had sought to disgrace and defeat him during his campaign against James G. Blaine by exposing the extra-marital relations of his bachelor existence and especially his fathering of a child. He had settled in Princeton and always avoided Buffalo. Nevertheless, he was claimed by his home city and rated as a local hero.

Buffalo also had a proprietary interest in another conservative statesman—McKinley—for a reason which must seem peculiar. He had been assassinated there. The John G. Milburn house, where he had died, and the Ansley Wilcox house, where his successor, Theodore Roosevelt, had taken the oath of office next day, were regarded as tourist attractions to be pointed out with some pride. But it was Cleveland, who even more than the earlier Millard Fillmore—whose old home on Niagara Circle had become a hotel—was Buffalo's special pride. And the Cleveland inner shrine, the gathering place of his most earnest admirers, was the Buffalo Club, of which he had been a prominent member.

The Buffalo Club deserves a word for itself. It was actually a regional center of American capitalism at its time of most unlimited power. The club had not always been in the same place; by the time I knew of it, however, it had acquired the mansion of Stephen Van Rensselaer Watson, who had been the principal pioneering entrepreneur in the city's traction consolidations and who had died in 1880, leaving behind a vast house which even the fortune he also left to his descendants could not support, or perhaps they were not interested in such an establishment. At any rate, it went to the Club, and because it was centrally located and had a traditional magnificence, it was added to and embellished. "Here," says Mr. Horton, "the magnificos foregathered in the complacent, jovial, sedate, and dignified manner of men who have immense reputations to sustain. Here they met to confer, consult, and converse on matters both grave and gay. Here they played at billiards or at sedentary games like poker, whist, and backgammon. Here they drank old wines, ancient brandies, and aged whiskies; and on great occasions they indulged a fancy for terrapin, lobster, venison, canvasbacks, and *pâté de foie gras*. The atmosphere of the place was tranquil; the décor rich, massive, and sombre, yet somehow contrived to heighten the *joie de vivre*. The place was one where Major Pendennis and Colonel Newcome would have been comfortable and at home . . ."[3]

In that mansion, with its spacious rooms, its deep, rich rugs, its solid silver, its perfect service, momentous decisions were made, and all Buffalo knew that this was so. Ordinary citizens passing on the avenue looked at its high wrought-iron fence, its plate-glass windows, its expanses of brick, with a kind of awe. Politicos regarded its power and wealth with respect; workers hated its symbolism. It needed the pens of the muckrakers to expose its skeletons; but that exposure was mercifully withheld, as it was not from some other institutions, and it survived sedately into my day, the home of wealth and power for all the region roundabout.

My father long aspired to membership, and presently he would be accepted. Then he too forgathered, perhaps a little timidly as a newcomer, with the others under the benign portrait of Cleveland or around the richly loaded tables. Other clubs—the Saturn, for instance, and the University—would drain off the socialite and typical collegiate product of the next generation. But the old Buffalo Club would remain what it had been from the first, the resort of the wealthy, powerful, uncontaminated conservatives of the business community.

Buffalo businessmen were remarkably successful in holding

[3] Op. cit., 296.

onto their positions and their perquisites. It was inevitable that
they should be challenged by rising individuals in the new
racial groups, but they took in enough of them to keep from
being unseated. They kept control of the Boards and Finance
Committees, and their sons came back from Yale and Princeton
to replace them as they retired. Labor revolted once in a while;
there was a permanent struggle for higher wages, shorter hours,
and better working conditions. During depressions, desperation
seized the unemployed; but the Buffalo Club conferees, meeting
under the Cleveland portrait, plotting strategy in the leather
armchairs and across the mahogany tables of the elite, always
had the National Guard at their disposal. It was officered,
usually, by their own sons, and when the police could not
maintain law and order, the Guard was called on. The gains
for labor in these years were so slow as to be almost invisible;
an onlooker could see that changes were coming, but he could
also see that none of them would come without strife.[4]

The Club was also a place where members of the Bar, those
at the very topmost levels, mingled in an easy atmosphere with
their principal clients. It was, consequently, the place where
policies were made on all the issues of importance to business.
These members of the Bar saw to it that the local law school
indoctrinated its students properly. Dean Daniels and his faculty
were on the side of property and taught that latitude in acquiring it was necessary to the freedom of enterprise. That monopoly
often resulted—paradoxically—was a point that was glossed

[4] There had been one famous early dispute, called the Tow Path Rebellion,
which had given the businessmen their worst fright in the period before
the Civil War and had set a number of precedents for such struggles—such
as the use of the militia. And in the railroad strike of 1877, both the 74th
and 65th regiments had been called out. Again in 1894, in the aftermath
of financial panic, there was such serious disturbance that both regiments
were again activated. "At this juncture," says Mr. Horton, "the seat of
government in city and county shifted to the Buffalo Club. There the railroad lawyers . . . met with Sheriff Beck and Mayor Bishop, and, after a
long consultation, succeeded in overcoming the Sheriff's reluctance to request
Governor Flower to send the entire National Guard of the State of New
York." And so it always went. The embattled industrialists, from their seat
of power, fought every battle violently and made no concessions.

over.[5] That the Interstate Commerce Act was signed by their own Cleveland must have been a matter of sorrow to Buffalo lawyers, and that state regulation of the grain elevators was held by the courts to be constitutional must have given them a set-back. But the Buffalo Bar was resourceful. It went on finding ways for its clients to do as they pleased in spite of legislatures and courts that sometimes acted perversely.

It is of some interest that the ancient fellow-servant doctrine had as persistent a life in the precincts of Buffalo as it can have had anywhere in its notorious history. Our historian tells at some length of the ways in which that doctrine was used to protect property interests against the attritions of workers who felt that their employers ought to be responsible for their agents. Not until the issue was settled in Federal courts did the Buffalonians give up. So also with the tariff. Throughout the old century, and on into the new, the industrialists had been importunate in their demands for protection. And attitudes on that issue often determined their generosity or lack of it in political campaigns; free enterprise, but not free trade!

Labor troubles; a latent class struggle; racial animosities—all these tended to merge. There were conservatives and there were radicals. No radical ever came through the doors of the Club. A man could retire there from the scenes of battle, confident that all those around him would be sympathizers. But if the elite clung together, so did certain other groups in Buffalo —the Germans, the Irish, the Poles, and the Italians had a natural tendency to hang together. Sometimes these national ties helped in the labor struggle, but more often it made animosities easily exploited by employers to their own advantage. The press and the pulpit were safely enough allied with the elite. If few of the clergy sat before the open fires in the old Watson mansion, their vestrymen and lay supporters did; and the newspaper proprietors, the Matthewses and the Butlers, could often be found there. And among them they served to keep opinion fairly well disciplined.

[5] Horton, op. cit., 284.

Only the Conners papers, the *Courier* and the *Enquirer* were unreliable. Fingy was a Democrat and even an influential one nationally; and if the papers could hardly be said to be radical, their yellowish tendencies often made them sympathetic to embarrassing exposures. There was more than a touch of Hearst in their attitudes. How capricious this could make them, there was reason to know; they took the lead in several unofficial investigations and on the whole were not trusted to be gentlemanly when good stories were scented.

This was Buffalo, which was now my second home. It was an ugly city, getting uglier every year. It was a polyglot city, with layers of new immigrants, each infiltrated with newer ones, until the last—the Poles—came in underneath to support the whole as common laborers in all the hard jobs of industry and transportation. But where could a boy have been in more intimate touch with the characteristic society of his turbulent nation? What I learned in Buffalo was certainly not mostly from the school I attended. It was from the friends I acquired, from the sights I saw, and from the deductions I could hardly help making.

Thirty-nine

In one way or another I learned about Buffalo's background. I learned it the easy way—by hearing it talked about, mostly by Frank's relatives. There were a number of these who were nearer than we to the elite circuit. But what I gathered from such conversations was not what the Forsters gathered. Because I was more an observer than a participant—not really being a Buffalonian—the behavior of the successful was material for speculation. In my own way I was beginning to generalize, to make some meaning of my knowledge and experience. It was not a serious effort. I anticipated becoming a social scientist only vaguely, if at all. I was firm in my intention to go to the Wharton School, and I looked forward to going on with the sort of study Jay Stagg had introduced me to.

On looking back, it seems to me that Frank and I spent a good deal of time in the ways I have spoken of, none of which had much to do with education or even with getting on in the world. We were up early—in winter well before it was light in the northern latitude—and plodding up the hill to Masten Park. Buffalo on a slushy or freezing morning any time between November and April offers a most discouraging landscape, especially if you have not gone to bed reasonably early the night before, and we seldom had. If we were sleepy through our classes in overheated rooms, it is no wonder. But the classes were routine, which was a good thing, for neither of us had made more than sketchy preparation for them. We seldom did any studying except in off hours in the senior study room presided over by the elderly and disillusioned Dr. Trent; but, as I have said, it was enough for passing examinations, and we had no higher aspirations. In those days the admissions officers of universities did not inquire into applicants' academic histories. If they had passed Regents examinations and graduated from high school, that was enough. We intended only to fill out a certification schedule. I suppose I did less reading during my high school years in Buffalo than in any similar period of my life. And it got worse as I went along. I was too busy with other activities.[1]

Once school was over, early in the afternoon, we looked for something amusing to do, or rather we chose among many alternatives. Since Frank and I were never in the same classes, we had not seen each other, usually, since morning, so we often met at a nearby corner where there were two competing establishments, each having a traditional claim to Masten Parkers' affections. One was Doc Blight's drugstore and soda fountain, where milk shakes, sundaes, and sodas were dispensed more regularly than prescriptions. Doc always treated students as though they were nuisances, taking him away from the serious functions of a pharmacist. Actually he was an incorrigible gossip, a more reliable school historian than any of the teachers.

[1] The teacher who presides over his senior study room is apt to fill a well-remembered place in a student's high school career. And it was so with us. Dr. Amelia Earle Trent, then grown undeniably fat and bulgy, nevertheless projected an air of authority and decorum which was very good for a crowd of boys. She doubled as a teacher of psychology; but since that was an elective, she had few classes. I have before me, as I write, the Buffalo *Evening News* of July 12, 1947, which notices her death and causes me to realize that I never saw her after I left Masten Park. She was ninety-four years old, and fifty-five of those years had been spent in teaching, twenty-eight of them at Masten Park. She was one of the first women to earn a medical degree at the University of Buffalo Medical School and actually, I see from the obituary, was given her bachelor's degree *honoris causae* only after she had retired from teaching. She was a woman of dignity and culture, which did not prevent her from having a thoroughly practical understanding of young men. I was sorry to be left out of the list of "her boys," published in the *News*. Those who were included were David Lawrence, Raymond Fosdick, George Grobe (who became a U. S. District Attorney), and Vincent. J. Loughlin (a prominent member of the Buffalo Bar). I can only hope that the list was not hers but the *New's*. I would have liked her respect even at such a distance in time. Besides, I was one of the few who did rather well, as I recall, in her psychology course.

His chronicles were of a somewhat different sort than theirs would have been, but the accumulation became enormous.[2]

In later years recollections of my generation were fainter in Doc's establishment than they might have been across the street at Guenther's saloon, if that business had not acquired a new proprietor. He had not made many alterations, however, and there seemed to be no more change than added patina and a heavier smell of the same sort I recalled so well. This was a blend of stale beer, tobacco smoke, and unwashed males. As before, the woodwork was darkened by smoke, the floor was sprinkled with sawdust, and there were poker tables with arm-chairs around them where customers carried their kummelweck-roll sandwiches and schooners of beer to be consumed at leisure. But the sandwiches were no longer a nickel, as they had been; and neither was the beer. There was, however, the same useful door at the back through which students could crowd as authority came in at the front. I suspect that back door was well enough known to Dr. Fosdick. If he had really wanted to trap us it would have been easy enough; he probably made his visits only when one of the elderly schoolma'ams prodded him. He could not have thought Guenther's really a place of sin. In the German neighborhoods of Buffalo it would have been hard to convince anyone that beer was bad for growing boys. And the real problem, as he knew well enough, was that there were no other recreation facilities of any sort.

It was at Guenther's that we planned and organized our fraternity, half because about a dozen of us wanted in this way to seal our friendship, and half to express a rather sardonic view of high school affairs. We invented a fraternity of our own, I believe, because some of us, but not all, had been asked to join

[2] Some thirty years later I dropped in and sat down at the same old marble-topped counter. Doc was grayer and somewhat bent, but otherwise he had not changed. He did not recognize me, but he recalled my generation and several of its more heroic individuals. This was during the summer vacation, and he was more or less at leisure. He brought me up to date on school affairs. Needless to say, they were not going so well as they had in the old days.

the local chapters of the two or three national high school fraternities then in existence. At any rate, we soon had an elaborate ritual, a pin, and clubrooms. For this last we rented a typical dentist's layout on the second floor of a taxpayer building at Main and Utica streets. In our rooms, furnished with secondhand chairs, tables, and a sofa or two, together with a gas heater, we loafed, had long conversations, and conspired against the adult world. Our retreat was uncomfortable, dirty, ugly—anything else of the sort—but it was our very own.

The energy, the sheer inventive output of that lively group, devoted entirely to the production of trivialities, would not be believed even if it could be described. Still, none of us ever regretted any of it. And actually I suppose much of it went to enlarge our interest in the world. For we often explored matters far beyond our competence or knowledge merely as an exercise in competitive cerebration. Some of us were thus familiarized with reaches of learning we had not heard of before, or at least had suggested to us much that we did not know. We had long sessions over politics and religion, for instance, subjects Frank and I never discussed when we were alone. In the Forster book they were faintly objectionable. How could there be any question about the virtues of Republicanism, and why would anyone look beyond a genteel Protestantism? What was the use of discussing something you knew you would never do anything about? But there were some shockingly unorthodox opinions among the dozen of us, and they were aired for hours on end. It was sometimes obvious that the beliefs expressed did not run very deep and that the questions were not seriously raised. But it made for interesting conversation.

Mostly, of course, we talked about courses of conduct. Sexual ethics came in for repeated overhaulings. There were those whose professed attitude was crudely predatory. But they did not have it all their own way. There was a surprising dissent. But this endlessly fascinating subject did not monopolize our interest quite in the way it is supposed to do among males gathered together. I think our most interesting ventures had to do with the possibility of afterlife and even communication with the spirit world. And those of us who were skeptical, or who preferred to leave such matters to the priests or preachers, were still fascinated by attempts to invoke influences from some other where. We made tables jump by concentrating, and got answers to questions from imagined controls. We were puzzled, and we discussed the meaning of such phenomena at length; but we were at that happy age when it is possible to leave some matters up in the air, unanswered. We were neophytes in a complex world and we neither thought we knew all about it nor aspired to do so until in due time further evidence should become available.

Actually this phase of our association did not last long. We recruited a new generation for the fraternity and allowed our own attendance at its sessions to lapse.

During the summer of 1910 my friends were with me again in Wilson. Leslie tutored me in chemistry, and I took the Regents examinations in fall. This cleared away one of my entrance deficiencies. I varied these sessions with others in advanced Latin, and that too I got out of the way. But these efforts did not take more than an hour or two a day. There was plenty of time for other pursuits, even for some work. I still made my rounds in the country on my father's business, easy for me now because I understood so well what I was doing. We had another and bigger automobile, and the mileage we ran up in it was considerable, nights as well as days.

The business was prosperous and expanding. There were several outlying stations now for partial processing and, for the first time, a huge truck for bringing this produce to the main plant. There was plenty of work for both Leslie and Frank, but afterward none of us recalled it as hard; there was a lot of fun mixed in. The factory was rapidly becoming more efficient. There were new closing machines to take the place of the old cappers; the line was smoothed out; there were an increasing number of small electric motors for power to replace the complicated overhead pulley system operated from big

steam engines—the place was hardly recognizable as the same
one we had begun to operate a few years before.

Canning was becoming, in fact, like a typical American industry rather than merely an enlargement of home-preserving
processes. It was in that year, I believe, that my father began to
produce tomato juice, something he was very proud of. It may
have been somewhat earlier that he began to send out a few
experimental batches to jobbers and wholesalers to be tried. He
claimed later to have been the first to do this. I do not know
whether he was, and I suppose no one ever will know. But certainly it was an invention with considerable consequences. For
the country took to it at once. Other canners were soon producing it, and within a few years millions of gallons were being consumed every year. None, of course, ever equaled that of our
northern fields. That the product of August heats in the Pied-
mont did not discredit it altogether is surprising. But there was
a concurrent spread of knowledge about vitamins and a search
for low-calorie foods, and consumers probably supposed that
sacrifice was required in the interest of health. At any rate,
tomato juice caught on and soon became one of those products
whose absence from the family shelf cannot be imagined.

Whether or not he was the originator of tomato juice, as he
always contended, these were my father's best years. They were
the ones he would look back on in age with unshakable pride.
When his memory became uncertain and he sat for long hours
meditating on the past these were the times he liked most to
tell about when anyone cared to listen. He was a true enterpriser.
Everything he conceived came to life and made money for him.
The money gave him power, and he used it to expand into new
fields. This was when he began to see that it was not the small
businessman who did best in our economy; it was the man who
controlled the funds. So he became a banker. By modern standards it was in a small way. His deals and his new businesses
would hardly be noticed among those of a later time. But in his
circle and during his time he was respected. When he became a
member of the Buffalo Club, instead of going to Puerto Rico

or to Florida for the winter, he took a flat in Buffalo. While he spent his days at the Club or in concocting new enterprises, my mother worked her way higher in the world of women's organizations. She was successful too. For the first time she found a company she had to respect for its interest in public affairs. So while my father progressed toward the top in business and in masonry, which meant much to him, my mother made friends with the prominent women of the club movement.

For all the women's interest in politics, school affairs, and other issues, including suffrage for women, then so much discussed; and for all my father's earnest consultations with his business friends, there was never any suggestion, any suspicion, that all was not well in their world. That a world war and later a desperate struggle for survival would before very long face the business community, there was not even a faint hint in all their discussions. Like my father, the businessmen could scheme and maneuver and something profitable would result. It might be a new product, a more efficient factory, an improved process, the extension of public ultilities, a campaign to sell more goods, a deal to limit competition so that the conspirators could profit. These things were what they knew how to do. What was out and beyond the fringe of these affairs was belittled. They had no time for theorists, still less for scientists or other researchers. Such activities were not practical; and if businessmen had one word they honored above all others it was "practical." The worm of uncertainty, anyway, never entered their perfect apple. They were successful—they were apt to become pompous as they grew older—and the community still accepted them at their own valuation. It accepted their standards too. It was an age of business.

They were somewhat annoyed, but not much disturbed, by the claims of women to equality. I never heard my father say one word on this subject in response to my mother's uncounted thousands of them. I am sure that his attitude was skeptical. What he would have said, if he had not been interested in household peace, was that we had at home the best possible example of what women's influence on affairs would be like if they really got to be equal. My mother could talk, all right; but she could not write a check. She could not keep anything in order. Moreover, she could never keep household help—except the training-class girls, who, I suppose, had a special position in her affections because she had been one herself. There was money enough, and she was full of complaints about her heavy duties; but there must literally have been hundreds of maids, cooks, and so on, who passed through our doors. They did not stay—and did not want to—more than a week or two. And during the last days or hours of their tenure there was an uproar throughout the whole establishment which the blessed succeeding peace served to underline.

In September I journeyed to Philadelphia with Leslie as my guide and mentor. He was entering his sophomore year. I had known that a few students from the Buffalo area went to the university, but when we boarded the night train it was full of them. It was, in fact, a kind of reunion and they sat up most of the night in hilarious renewal of campus fellowship. I was taken in at once, a freshman who could be patronized and made to respect his elders. I must say, it was an agreeable feeling to be treated thus as a member, even if an inferior one. I was being allowed to join, on traditional terms, the select company of college men. I was more than willing to undergo the ordeals of induction.

But when I visited the admissions office next day, it became clear at once that I was still short on requirements. I needed more language and more science. It would be best for me to go back to high school, I was told. I would have just too many deficiencies to make up if I entered that fall. It would jeopardize my whole college course. So I went back to Masten Park and began another year of German, Latin, chemistry, and physics.

Forty

I was ashamed to be lingering in high school at my age. My short week in Philadelphia had made me a frustrated freshman. I was determined that I would be a real one next year, and whatever care I took about my school work was because I wanted so much to become a member of the community at Pennsylvania. So I made a good start in the first weeks. But there was a good deal of time to dispose of, and the activities which had become customary were no longer very satisfying.

It was mostly because of this that, when I heard of a possible job on the *Courier,* I got there as sooon as I could to apply for it. Perhaps no one else wanted it, or perhaps I was simply the first candidate. Anyway, I was told, without any investigation, that I could have it. It was not much of a job, but it allowed me to work in the same big room with the regular reporters, to listen to their talk, to see how a newspaper managed to appear every day, and to become a good deal more familiar with the practical operations of certain public institutions. I liked it. And almost at once I could feel my ambitions changing. This was something I could work at with pleasure. I envied the older sophisticates and spent as much time listening to their familiar talk as could be managed. Also, I studied their writing and practiced it when I could.

The *Courier* was not a pretentious newspaper, and no one who worked on it was anywhere near the head of the journalistic profession. But the city room, where I had a typewriter, must have been like hundreds of others, and its reporters must have been like others, too, in city rooms across the country. They were given stories to look into; they reported back to the city desk, and then they sat down and wrote the number of words considered appropriate. They got through their assignments with the least possible fuss, taking pains not be caught out in any mistakes, and wrote smoothly and efficiently with no more than a moment of head-scratching to compose a lead sentence. There were others, of course, who wrote special articles, and some who wrote editorials. These I seldom had a chance to talk to. It was the reporter on the daily job that I watched and tried to imitate.

I worked on the *Courier* all that year and never once saw the owner, but I hardly saw more of the editor, C. B. Bennett. It seemed to me that he paid very little attention to the paper. He was seldom in his corner office, and so far as I could tell gave few instructions to the city editor. Of course he had no need to. That individual knew his business and got through it efficiently under any and all stresses. What I did not realize for some time was that there was an understanding amounting to rule between him and his reporters. They did not have to be managed; they knew what to do and did it. If there was dereliction, they were abruptly fired. The turnover was considerable, and there was seldom any griping about it. A reporter was not examined on his past history very closely when he was hired. He simply said he had worked on other papers and named them. Then he was given a chance. As long as he produced copy with reasonable efficiency, he was left alone. I never heard one given any instruction. This did not mean that copy was not edited. It was, and drastically. There were two old-timers on the copy desk with eyeshades and red pencils who operated on everything written, with a speed and certainty I found amazing, and theirs was the last word. I gathered that they had instructions from on high about the rules. These applied not only to style and length but to subject matter. What the reporters had not understood—and most of them were well briefed—about subjects that might not be mentioned or individuals who must be protected, the copyreaders knew. A reporter was never certain what his story would look like until he saw it in the paper next morning, but the best of them came closest to the economy of the trade. They wrote few words that were wasted.

The technique involved in this fascinated me, but it was some time before I was allowed to try my first story, and I never got beyond fairly simple ones. The editor I recall best had no affection for young men learning how to write. He was not a born teacher as some editors are. He was one of those characters so familiar in newspaper offices at an earlier time—a peripatetic editor. He knew his job and was respected for it. But he was a periodic drunk. Anyone who hired him had to anticipate that every so often he simply would not show up. For all he cared, the paper might simply have suspended. He would be gone for several days. Then one afternoon at assignment time he would come in, put on his alpaca sleeves, turn on the light over his papers, and begin to hand out assignments. He never asked who had taken his place while he had been away and never expected to be asked where he had been. There were many rumors about this; he had no home but a room in a boardinghouse, and it mattered little to him whether he was in Buffalo or a dozen other cities where he had held similar jobs. His only devotion, really, was to the profession he knew so well. But he had been at it a long time; he was as high as he would ever get; and his dedication did not require enthusiasm. He ultimately gave me some jobs that were not quite routine and even some rewriting to do from the wires or cables—which the regular reporters mostly disliked; they preferred to go out after stories which would take them into interesting places, including, I discovered, favorite saloons, where they spent all the time they could without getting into trouble.

Mostly what I had to do, especially at first, was checking the day's grist at the several courts. This I could do after school

and before the trials were ended. If there were any developments
worth more than a mere notice, a reporter was assigned, so
I had few opportunities at first to try my ability to cover them.
But this was gradually modified so that I had some of the simpler
writing jobs. My other duty had to do with the financial page.
Stories for this came over the wires, and all that had to be done
was to cut them down and write headlines. I felt that I put a
good deal of imagination into the thankless task, but it remained
thankless.

During my year on the *Courier* there was a City Court with
a Chief Judge and seven Associate Judges; there was also a
County Court; and, in the same building, there was the eighth
judicial district of the Supreme Court. The City Court seldom
provided any news; drunks, prostitutes, petty thieves, and similar
offenders were summarily disposed of; most of them were simply
put away out of sight for a while. But in Judge Harry L.
Taylor's County Court there were often cases with dramatic
interest. And it is a fact that Judge Taylor was an enlightened
jurist. He had already been instrumental in setting up a proba-
tion system for adult offenders, and he had a consulting
psychiatrist who examined all criminals brought to trial before
him—a bold innovation at that time.

So I learned something during my routine chores in City
Hall and the courthouse. It was possible there to feel very close
to government. At least the processes of justice were going on
day by day; and my older colleagues, with more important
assignments, were familiar, almost to boredom, with the doings
of the departments and the Mayor. But they were cynical
about them. They knew too much about patronage, corruption,
and lackadaisical administration ever to believe the motives of
any public official good. They did not write as they felt. They
were confined mostly to factual accounts, but among themselves
they told much more picturesque stories than newspaper readers
ever read. After a few months of following them around and
listening to their talk, I felt myself at least sophisticated if not
informed. But I was young enough not to feel that reform was

never to be looked for. Besides, as I sometimes argued with my elders, the city's business did somehow get done. Its utilities functioned, its courts were open daily, fires were put out, and order was kept. Surely it could be hoped that there would at times be honest administration. The institutions were appropriate; they needed only to be better run. In spite of disbelief in any such regime ever coming into being in Buffalo, I did not quite succumb to the prevailing cynicism. I kept quiet, naturally; but I still recalled the legend of Cleveland.

There was, as a matter of fact, a latent reform movement in the city. Once in a while corruption and inefficiency had in the past become so notorious that exposure became easy. When this occurred to some ambitious politician or to a newspaper proprietor, a furor of activity resulted. These movements were more or less supported by associations of better citizens, and a succession of these had resulted in a Municipal League. This organization was, in fact, set up in 1910, and I heard it talked about in the *Courier* office and in City Hall. However stolid public employees may appear to be, connection with the underworld, nepotism, and inefficiency makes them vulnerable, and during the beginning of an exposure campaign they become excited and defensive. This happened in that year, and many of them seemed to me to be begging for a chance to squeal. Reformers have no difficulty in gathering information. Also, there is usually a newspaper that will print it, and the *Courier* did. It was all known to reporters anyway. They had only to be told to write what they could verify of what they knew.

Cleveland had gone some way toward breaking up the system in his time—when for one term he had become Sheriff—simply by being rock-honest and refusing to condone either corruption or laziness. But it had needed only a complaisant administration to have all the familiar abuses creep back again. The movement begun by the Municipal League in 1910 would result in a new Charter for the city and so a better government; but it would not happen until 1916, after the collapse of the Ward pumping station in Porter Avenue, which would suddenly reveal such a morass of corruption that defense of the going system became impossible. When the League set out to write a new Charter and install a new set of officials, the politicians simply ran to cover.[1]

When I argued with my unbelieving elders that the reform movement to be seen shaping up in 1910 would result in better government, they were able to cite other similar waves of change; they had no faith in any permanent reform. I am afraid they were right. The nation as well as the city would have to demonstrate a far more persistent demand for a decent public service before government could be taken away from demagogues and corruptionists. The good citizens of Buffalo soon returned to their own private affairs, and the new Charter proved as amenable to manipulation—or nearly so—as had the old one.

Aside from this contribution to my education, there was another sensation during that year which I watched with a certain interest. Voluminously reported in the *Courier,* as in the other Buffalo papers, was the furor caused by a newcomer to the state legislature in Albany. Franklin D. Roosevelt had made himself the most noticed of a group of revolters against Tammany. The impression at the time was that he had organized the movement and was its leader. He was a Democrat from the twenty-sixth District in Dutchess County, where Democrats were supposed to be scarce. Arriving in Albany without benefit of Tammany assistance, he and a few others organized a protest against the intention of the regulars to send Blue-eyed Billy Sheehan (formerly of Buffalo, so that the local interest in the matter was heightened) to the United States Senate. It was a blatant payoff of a utilities lawyer for gathering campaign funds from his employers. Charles Murphy, Tammany boss—and such others as Al Smith and Robert Wagner, to be heard of later—felt that the Senatorship was owed to Sheehan

[1] The new Charter was signed into law by Governor Martin H. Glynn in 1914. In the succeeding referendum it was accepted, and it went into effect in 1916.

for his services.[2] But young Roosevelt, so surprisingly elected from a safe Republican district, thought otherwise. So did a number of others, most of whom represented rural constituencies. There were enough of them to prevent the Democrats from getting together a majority; and for several weeks they held out against the machine, thus preventing any legislative business from being done. They met daily in Roosevelt's house, and they resisted both blandishments and threats until a compromise was reached. To be sure, another Tammany man was then agreed on—James A. O'Gorman—and the compromise, looked at afterward, could hardly be interpreted as much of a victory for the insurgents. But Blue-eyed Billy had been ditched, and to the public the insurgents appeared heroic.

What the ordinary newspaper reader gathered from the affair, in fact, was mostly that another Roosevelt had appeared on the political scene, shooting sparks and trailing glory—a new St. George charging the old dragon of corruption and favoritism. That this was a grossly exaggerated interpretation would not be known for a long time except to close observers. It was certainly not known to me.

The young Senator was evidently altogether a Roosevelt. His was an old family solidly seated in the Hudson Valley and related to the other Roosevelts at Oyster Bay. He had been persuaded to leave his job with a respectable law firm in New York to run for the Senate—a daring enterprise. But 1910 was a year of Republican losses in preparation for greater ones in 1912, when Taft would lose the Presidency to Wilson. The voters may have been voting against Taft even then and were probably glad to support any Roosevelt. At any rate, he had won.

This turned out to be the first demonstration of that uncanny political sense Roosevelt was to go on displaying all the rest of his life. Progressivism was about to become a label any politician must wear to be successful. Even Wilson did not discover it as

[2] A chapter of Ernest K. Lindley's *Franklin D. Roosevelt* (New York: Blue Ribbon Books, 1931), is devoted to this episode; see also my own *Democratic Roosevelt* (New York: Doubleday & Co., 1957).

soon as he; in 1910 Wilson was still known as a conservative professor sponsored by New Jersey's professionals for the Governorship of that state. In 1911, as a consequence of his assault on Tammany, Roosevelt became temporarily at least, as well known as Wilson. In the end, his Progressivism and his flair for dramatizing his own personality would make him successively Governor and President. But no one knew that then—unless it was the young man himself.

I read the accounts of the affair merely because I had an interest in politics and because it was a good story. I may afterward have heard of Roosevelt as a conservationist, as a legislative sponsor for municipal reform—but if I did I do not recall it now. And certainly it would have seemed fantastic if anyone had suggested that I should in any way have become involved, two decades hence, with the politician about whom the accounts were so voluminous in 1910.

I left high school and my newspaper work at the same time in June, spent the summer in the accustomed ways, and in September got aboard the night train for Philadelphia again. Leslie was still my sponsor. There seemed to me about the same number of Buffalonians, and they seemed as elated as ever at the prospect of another college year. This time there was no question about my entrance. I felt that there would be no question about my work, either. I was determined to be a regular in the company of my choice. In the club car I joined in a chorus of "The Red and Blue" as though I already had the right. It was one of the few the upperclassmen conceded to freshmen. I made the most of it; indeed, I was almost intolerably happy to have the privilege.